THE ROMANS
WHO SHAPED BRITAIN

SAM MOORHEAD
AND DAVID STUTTARD

THE ROMANS
WHO SHAPED BRITAIN

73 illustrations, 42 in color

Thames & Hudson

To our parents

Half title: Bronze 'radiate' coin struck by Carausius,
showing him alongside Diocletian and Maximian. The inscription reads,
'Carausius and his brothers'. Struck at 'C' Mint, *c.* AD 290–92,
and now in the British Museum.

Title page: Onyx cameo showing the Roman eagle,
Kunsthistorisches Museum

First published in 2012 in hardcover in the United States of America by
Thames & Hudson Inc., 500 Fifth Avenue, New York, New York 10110

thamesandhudsonusa.com

Library of Congress Catalog Card Number 2011935839

ISBN 978-0-500-25189-8

Printed in China by Toppan Leefung

Contents

INTRODUCTION
RE-IMAGINING ROMAN BRITAIN 6

1 TO BOLDLY GO... 12

2 ELEPHANTS AND CASTLES 39

3 REVOLT 64

4 SHOCK AND AWE VERSUS HEARTS AND MINDS 88

5 THE LIMITS OF THE WORLD 120

6 BAND OF BROTHERS 135

7 THE SCOURGE OF SCOTLAND 144

8 THE BRITANNIC EMPIRE 168

9 BLESSED ISLE 182

10 TURMOIL 198

11 MELTDOWN 212

12 PRAYING FOR THE COMING
OF THE ONCE AND FUTURE KING 239

EPILOGUE 251

TIMELINE OF ROMAN BRITAIN 252

GLOSSARY OF ROMAN ADMINISTRATIVE TERMS AND TITLES 256

NOTES 258

FURTHER READING 275

ACKNOWLEDGMENTS 283

ILLUSTRATION SOURCES 284

INDEX 285

Introduction
Re-Imagining Roman Britain

From the subterranean vaults of the temple of Claudius in Colchester to a late mosaic showing the head of Christ dug from a Dorset village, and from wind-blown ditches in a Perthshire field to the foundations of the palace of a client king at Chichester, signs of centuries of Roman occupation pepper the British countryside.

The history of that occupation has been thoroughly explored. Long bookshelves are filled with compelling volumes detailing the archaeological evidence (some on specific sites),[1] or the different social and cultural aspects of the province, its art or the lives of its women.[2] Recent works have challenged much of the traditional view presented by scholars in previous generations, while others have assembled a general synthesis of the history of the province.[3]

Even more recently with the advent of the Portable Antiquities Scheme in England and Wales, which encourages thousands of amateur enthusiasts to report the discoveries they make,[4] the sheer scale and diversity of Roman Britain have become increasingly apparent. Thanks to the unprecedented level of the recording of finds – some seemingly mundane, but others, such as the Frome hoard of 52,000 coins, making international headlines (Plates 30, 32, 33)[5] – evidence for new settlements is appearing almost by the week. A fresh picture is forming of an ever-more complex network of villas, villages and towns across lowland Britain. Likewise, new sites are being identified in the more rugged upland regions where the Roman army was garrisoned.[6]

It is, however, with the lives of the emperors, governors and generals who commanded those legions and helped shape those landscapes, as well as the Britons who opposed them, that this book is largely concerned. We follow the story of Roman Britain from the very first Roman soldier, holding high the talismanic eagle-standard as he leapt from Caesar's warship into what were quite literally unknown waters off the coast at Walmer, to the last cavalry officers, 'encased in metal plate and mail', rallying their men beneath the hissing dragon pennants, as they prepared for their final evacuation.

For the premise of this book is that the unbroken narrative of Roman Britain is a story made by people.[7] That this needs to be stated is a reflection of our times, when many modern historians, lost in the fog of academic theory, tend to treat their chosen period as a laboratory in which empiricism will provide a 'true' and scientific picture of the past. But because the past was created by unpredictable and emotionally driven human beings, there is a danger that answers thrown up by such an approach are, in fact, delusions.

Instead, our intent has been to put people back at the heart of the story, and to acknowledge how their ambitions, aspirations and passions contributed to the development of Britannia (as the Romans called the province). Without these people, no battles would have been fought, no roads constructed, no villas farmed, no towns built, no walls painted, no mosaics laid, no gods worshipped.

In a modern age when mankind (at least in the West) increasingly believes that everything must have a simple solution, and there must be rational explanations of both the problems of the present and the problems of the past, it is more than ever important to realize that the condition of humanity is to make decisions which are often based as much on personality and emotion as on reason and logical deduction. Some of those decisions, which – with the lazy benefit of superficial hindsight – may seem bizarre, make grim sense when seen in the context of the time and of the options available.

Context, indeed, is everything, and much of the seemingly familiar history of Britannia shifts into sharper focus when seen within the setting of the wider empire. So do the lives of those who shaped the province. The time which many Romans spent in Britain was but a fraction of their overall careers, and consideration of the different possibilities the province held for each of them is in itself instructive: Julius Caesar desperately seeking a propaganda coup to boost his standing back in Rome; unwarlike crippled Claudius striving for military credibility; the historian Tacitus playing down the achievements of past governors to enhance the memory of Agricola, who pushed far into Scotland; Hadrian, whose empire-wide policy of containment led him to build his Wall, and whose Jewish war gave future British governors their training; the ruthless Libyan Severus, who crossed to Britain to campaign and die; Carausius, the charismatic corsair, 'Britain's forgotten emperor', styling himself the true heir of Augustus; Allectus, his disloyal chancellor and his assassin; Constantine

1 Map of the Roman empire at its greatest extent, during the reign of Trajan, showing the provinces, cities and towns mentioned in the book.

the Great, raised to the throne by troops at York, the first Christian emperor, who founded a new capital on the shores of the Black Sea; Magnentius, reputedly born of a British father, a rebel whose defeat unleashed a ghastly reign of terror, the beginning of the end for Roman Britain.

The Romans Who Shaped Britain sees the history of Britannia through the lives of characters such as these – or such as the pagan Julian, under

whose watchful eye convoys of grain ships plied the North Sea between
Britain and the Rhine; or Count Theodosius, who battled to keep the province secure despite a devastating rebellion and increasingly desperate
attacks by tribesmen from outside the empire; or Constantine III, who, in
a bid to become emperor, led what remained of Britain's Roman army
to the continent, never to return. It tells, too, of the aftermath, with much
of the Romano-British population clinging to their disappearing culture
while saints such as Patrick and Germanus sought to impose their newly
focused Christian authority on a fragmenting land.

Equally important in shaping the pattern of the occupation were the native Britons: client rulers such as Togidubnus, ally of Rome, with his swathes of lands in southern England; Cartimandua, the queen of the Brigantes, whose messy separation from her husband provoked a war; and Prasutagus, king of the Iceni, who failed to save his land from Roman greed. There were great warriors among the Britons, too: Caratacus, who fought against the legions for eight years before being captured and paraded through the streets of Rome in chains; Boudica, whose revolt probably caused the Roman high command to contemplate withdrawal; and Calgacus, leader of the Caledonians, who made his last defiant stand in the glens of Scotland at the long-lost battlefield of Mons Graupius.

By telling the story through the lives of men and women set in a single narrative, the book seeks to present the epic sweep that is the history of Britannia. For, in its years of occupation from the first arrival of the eagles to the departure of the dragons four centuries later, the province changed significantly, both in reality and in the perception of the Romans. In the hands of artists, poets and coin designers, Britannia herself, the province's personification, underwent a number of transformations – from downtrodden captive to fecund matriarch to fearsome barbarian queen.

These 'virtual' transformations mirrored reality. If, in the early phase of conquest, Britain was seen as a mine for minerals and precious stone, by the end it had become a breadbasket, critical to the survival of the western Roman empire, a land of prosperous villas and booming industries, a crucial bulwark in a world increasingly threatened by internal insurrection and the pressure of attack from beyond its borders.

Each chapter begins with an imaginative reconstruction. Its purpose is to set the scene, to try to re-connect as people to those whose histories we are recounting, to remember that Britannia was not shaped by statistics or by artefacts but by people. While the emotions felt by the characters in the reconstructions are imagined, the details of the settings are based on sound archaeological or literary evidence.

Contemporary literature plays its part in revealing the lives of those involved. Historians such as Caesar and Tacitus, Dio Cassius and Ammianus; biographers such as Suetonius or the anonymous authors of the *Lives of the Later Emperors*; geographers such as Strabo; poets such as Virgil, Horace and Claudian; they all lend their voices. Archaeology provides important evidence as well. Thousands of inscriptions from across Britain and the empire, as well as letters such as the Vindolanda Tablets, give tantalizing glimpses of the lives of officers and men who left their crowded barrack blocks to patrol and garrison the province; and of civilians, as well, friends and families of front-line troops, mothers sending parcels to their sons on tours of duty, women holding birthday parties, households celebrating festivals.

Of course, we have also drawn on the work of modern scholars, and two must be singled out. Peter Salway's *Roman Britain*, now thirty years old, remains the most magisterial book on the province. Much new material has been uncovered since it was first published, but it remains an excellent starting point for the discussion of historical events. In addition, Anthony Birley's *The Roman Government of Britain* provides marvellously detailed outlines of the careers of those men who served in Britain. *The Romans Who Shaped Britain* seeks to compete with neither of these works. Instead, it is intended as a general introduction, a basic narrative framework, which might perhaps inspire interested readers to explore the story of Roman Britain in greater depth (perhaps beginning with the bibliography and the listing of original sources on pages 275–82).

1

TO BOLDLY GO...

First reaction: numbness, and the shock of the ice-cold sea; the current dragging hard against already sodden clothing. The next: determination to stand firm and not to drop the sacred talisman; but rather to raise high the silver standard of the legion's eagle and to wade (against all intuition) away from the safety of the ships. Then everything floods into focus: the noise, the shouting, and the churning waves, the lethal missile fire, the enemy themselves, their lines stretched far along the shingle beach, the flash of long swords and the whinnying of horses, the splash of armed men as they leap into the sea.

For, now, the legionaries are in the water, too, pushing forward, struggling to keep their shields above their heads, obliquely angled to protect them from the hail of spears. Time has become elastic. All each man knows now is the tunnel of the sea ahead of him, the fierce pull of the undertow, the clatter of the arrows as they smack against his shield. Occasionally, he is aware of the new trumpet calls behind him from the flagship, of warships grouping to the left, of long-range missiles screaming through the sky, of the thump and spray of shingle as they find their target.

At last, the water lapping round their ankles, the legionaries lock shields and form their battle line to make their slow but menacing advance up the sloping pebbled beach. Rank upon rank they emerge from the blood-streaked sea, the weak sun gleaming on their dripping weaponry. Inexorably they hack and stab their way still further, on towards the scrubby grassland, on towards the fields... and then it's over.

Before anyone can take it in, the enemy are gone: turned tail and fled. The fighting's done. The beach-head has been won. Against all odds Rome's eagles have been planted in this strange new land. Their general has proved his brilliance once more. And there he is himself emerging from the surf as, with the pommels of their swords, his soldiers beat their shields in rhythmic acclamation as they cheer and shout his name. For Caesar is now striding up the beach towards them, and tonight his Romans will encamp on British soil.

G AIUS Julius Caesar's battle for a bridgehead in Britain has attained legendary status. In no small part, this is thanks to Caesar's own account, written shortly afterwards for the consumption of the Senate (and People) of Rome, and the basis for our own recreation. Like the rest of *De Bello Gallico* ('The Gallic War'), the work in which the account appears, it is deliberately slanted to portray its author in the best possible light. It is, therefore, one of the earliest examples of what today is called 'spin'. Yet, taken with what we know from other ancient sources as well as from modern archaeology, it reveals as much as it perhaps wishes to conceal about the first forays of the Romans onto British soil.[1]

From the start, the expedition was badly prepared. Attempts at gaining good intelligence about the theatre into which the Roman troops were about to be led had been singularly unsuccessful. Writing of himself in the third person, Caesar describes how efforts to find out information from those who might have known had met a wall of silence:

> He summoned to his presence traders from a wide area, but he was unable to gain any intelligence whatsoever from them: nothing about the size of the island; nor the nature or the numbers of the tribes who inhabited it; nor their tactics in battle; nor their customs; nor about such harbours as might be suitable for a sizeable fleet of large ships.[2]

The reason he gives for this, that 'no-one visits Britain except traders, and even they know nothing about the country, except for the coastline and those areas facing Gaul' is palpably untrue. There was, in fact, close contact between the tribes living on either side of the Channel, as elsewhere Caesar himself tells us:

> The Suessiones...possessed huge tracts of very fertile territory. Even within living memory their king had been the most powerful in the whole of Gaul, ruling not only much of the [Belgic] territory but of Britain as well.[3]

In reality, there seems to have been a concerted campaign by those Gauls and Britons whom he interviewed not only to give Caesar as little information as they could, but to ensure that what details he did learn were so false as to make the prospect of sailing to the island as unattractive as possible. The inaccurate picture he paints of the interior of the island is probably, therefore, the result of propagandist misinformation.

More reprehensible was the poor intelligence he received from his own officers. In the days before the invasion fleet set sail, Caesar sent a warship to glean information about good landing sites. It was under the command of one Volusenus, who was considered the best candidate for the job. Caesar, usually so clear-eyed, had misjudged his man. Four days of reconnaissance, during which he sailed along the coast 'as far as he could without disembarking and risking contact with the barbarians', were to result in Volusenus' identification of the most suitable landing place as the beach beneath the white cliffs of Dover.[4]

It is probable that Caesar had already made a more serious misjudgment. To try to win over as many of the British tribes as possible to his cause in advance of the expedition, Caesar had sent Commius, a Gaulish tribal chief, on a 'hearts and minds' mission across the Channel, to announce the forthcoming arrival of the Romans and to encourage the Britons to 'entrust themselves to the protection of Rome'. Commius owed his position as 'king' of the Atrebates to Caesar himself, who described him as 'a man of whose bravery, good sense and loyalty he had a high opinion and whose authority was well respected in Britain'.[5] The respect in which he was held by the Britons would later be confirmed; his loyalty to Rome would not.

These were uncharacteristic slips for the usually canny Caesar to make, and they demonstrate, perhaps, his impatience to get under way. It was

CAESAR ON BRITAIN

Caesar tells us that the Britons in Kent were similar to the Gauls and the most civilized. He correctly states that they used gold and bronze coins and iron ingots for currency. He is also aware of the presence of tin in Britain. He says that the island was heavily populated, a statement which archaeology confirms, and adds that observations made using a water-clock show that the days are longer at this latitude. He mentions the Britons' use of woad to paint their bodies and that men grew their hair long and had moustaches. However, he is incorrect in writing that inland tribes do not grow corn, but live on meat and milk, and wear skins. Other comments about British attitudes to various animals (that it was unlawful to eat hares, fowl and geese) and their marital systems (that wives were shared between groups of ten or twelve men) cannot be corroborated.[6]

going to be a momentous operation, unequalled in Rome's history, and it could not afford to fail, even though to sail so late in summer was a risk. There was so much riding on it, not least Caesar's own political career.

Caesar had been born in 100 BC into the ancient aristocratic family of the Julii at a time when Rome's traditional certainties were being severely challenged. Since her foundation (traditionally in 753 BC), Rome had seen her power spread gradually into neighbouring areas of Italy. As her wealth and dominance grew, she inevitably caught the notice of her new trading rivals, and (just as inevitably) this resulted in a succession of wars. In the third century BC, Rome's citizen militia managed to defeat invading armies from both Greece and Carthage, and just under half a century before Caesar's birth (146 BC), two major victories, one over Corinth, the other over Carthage itself, had resulted in Rome's annexing of these two cities and of their spheres of influence. Just thirteen years later (133 BC), she gained control of wealthy Pergamum (near the western shores of modern Turkey), and so saw her rule extend to Asia.

The need to govern and protect these newly acquired overseas territories put Rome under enormous pressure. For one thing, new systems of government had rapidly to be created and put into place; for another, the indigenous peoples of Rome and Italy, many of whom had fought in the wars which resulted in Rome's growth, felt that they should benefit from her increasing wealth. In the same year as she gained Pergamum, Rome witnessed violence and bloodshed on her own streets, when conservative Senators sanctioned the killing of the People's Tribune, who had been agitating for reforms. A major rift had appeared between the landed aristocrats and the common people, a rift that ambitious politicians could (and would) exploit to their own advantage.

Yet even on her nearest borders, all was not secure. Even as Rome's influence was spreading south and east, a new threat came from the north. Tribes of Gauls, migrating from across the Danube, pushed first into the south of what is now called France and then into the north of Italy. Centuries before (387 BC) another wave of Gauls had swept as far as Rome, where their brief occupation of the city had passed into Roman legend. It was not something that either the Senate or the People wished to see repeated.

As one of their generals to fight the Gauls, they chose Gaius Marius, who had already proved his mettle on campaign in Africa, and whose root-and-branch reorganization of the army would have a major impact on

Rome's future. Key among Marius' reforms was the institution of a stand-ing army formed from a new professional class of soldiery, contracted to serve for sixteen years, at the end of which each man had earned a pension settlement of land and money. For poorer citizens, the appeal of this was obvious. Those who enlisted in Marius' legions could turn their backs on the humiliating drudgery of civilian life, in which the poor relied on the largesse of wealthy patrons. However, they could not shake off that mind-set entirely. Instead, their general became their patron. It was to him they owed their loyalty, and in a short time the consequences of this would become all too obvious.

As the embodiment of every soldier's pride both in the army and in Rome, Marius gave each legion a totemic symbol behind which to march: a military standard topped by an eagle, the bird of Jupiter, the most pow-erful god of Rome. Such was the almost mystic reverence in which the legionaries held their eagle, that they would willingly sacrifice their lives to prevent it from falling into enemy hands.[7]

It was behind their new-forged 'eagles' that Marius' men fought off the Gauls, and in the summer of 101 BC, the last of the invaders were defeated. The next year, Marius was elected to the supreme political office of consul for the sixth time. In mid-July, he learned of the birth of his nephew: Gaius Julius Caesar.

Young Caesar was to see nothing of his uncle for some years. During his consulship (100 BC), Marius found his loyalty dangerously divided between the Senate, to which he belonged, and the People, whose support he had courted. He responded by going into self-imposed exile. During his absence, however, tensions grew, and by 91 BC frustration among Rome's allies in the rest of Italy at their lack of parity with the citizens of Rome herself erupted into all-out war. Marius returned, and the revolt was quashed, but immediately afterwards rivalries between Marius and his former colleague, Lucius Cornelius Sulla, over who should lead the army to address problems in the east, spilled over into civil war (88 BC). For years, as her eastern provinces were ransacked by a foreign king, Rome herself became a battleground, fought over by her own commanders. Marius died in 86 BC, but peace was not yet restored. Fresh rebellions by Marius' son saw Sulla fighting on two fronts: against the threat from the east and against his enemies in Rome. At last, with the help of the young, flamboyant general Pompey, Sulla's side won through, and by the end of 82 BC Sulla himself returned to Rome where he was given plenipotentiary powers and appointed *dictator*. Two years later he retired to write his memoirs. In 78 BC he died.

The 80s BC in Rome were a dangerous time to enter politics, and yet it was during this period, at the age of just sixteen years, that Caesar, now head of his household since his father's death the year before, was appointed Priest of Jupiter. This seemingly religious post was, in fact, the first rung on the ladder to high political achievement. Even at such an early age, the young nephew of Marius had powerful enemies. Sulla was compiling lists of adversaries to be hunted down and executed, and one of those he targeted was Caesar.

2 Stone bust of Julius Caesar, now in the Vatican Museum, Rome.

For some time the young man was forced into hiding. Eventually, thanks to friends in high places, his sentence was overturned (albeit reluctantly, for Sulla could, he said, see in him many Mariuses). As for Caesar, he thought it wise to absent himself from Rome, so he headed east and joined the army.

Here he was put to use both as a soldier and as a diplomat. Early in his career he was sent on a diplomatic mission to the court of King Nicomedes IV of Bithynia to ensure the continuing support of this vital ally on the eastern front. The Roman army loved scandal, and was always happy to invent material if need be. So it is not surprising that stories were soon circulating that the reason for Caesar's tarrying in the court of the eastern king was because he had become his lover. After all, Caesar's eccentric dress-sense – he liked to sport loosely tied tunics with long arms and louche fringes – could be seen to suggest decadence. It was a reputation that Caesar fought hard to counter, not least on his return to the troops, when he threw himself into the thick of battle at the siege of Mytilene. Here he saved a soldier's life, and in doing so won the coveted right to wear an oak wreath on his head in perpetuity. Military banter suggested that it came in useful, too, to hide his premature balding (Fig. 2).

With Sulla's death (78 BC), Caesar felt he could safely return to Rome. His interlude in the east had been useful. It had given him his first real taste not only of fighting and camp life, but also of politics and diplomacy. His genius in both these strands of public life would serve him well. For the next twenty years he doggedly pursued the traditional Roman political career path, demonstrating his abilities not only in elected office but in the law courts, too, honing his powers of persuasive oratory, which even the politician and orator Cicero said were the best of his generation. In time, his military reputation grew as well, and by 60 BC, during his governorship of Spain, he was winning victories against intransigent insurgents, adapting his tactics to devastating effect in his campaign against guerrilla fighters.

The next year Caesar became one of the two consuls. He used his time in office to enact a series of laws aimed, for the most part, at improving the condition of the poor and of war veterans, a populist programme that was resisted by many in the more patrician Senate. Like his uncle Marius, Caesar knew the value of mass support. At the same time, he took care to cement strong political alliances. He was already closely connected to the billionaire Marcus Licinius Crassus (considered by some to have been the richest man in history), but he now formed a strategic union with Pompey, too, giving him his daughter Julia in marriage. Pompey, who in his youth had burst onto the public scene by fighting brilliantly for Sulla, had continued to dazzle. Now he was the most powerful man in Rome – and he was Caesar's son-in-law.

At the end of Caesar's consulship, the People's Assembly voted that he should become governor of the provinces of Illyricum and Cisalpine Gaul for five years. Pompey persuaded the Senate to assign Transalpine Gaul to Caesar, too. This territory, originally known simply as Provincia ('The Province', modern Provence), was a narrow coastal strip, formed sixty or so years before (121 BC) to protect the ancient trading port of Marseilles. Beyond its borders were what to the Romans seemed the badlands, the tribal areas they knew as Gallia Comata, 'Long-Haired Gaul'. For Caesar, this was where the future lay. By annexing it to Roman rule, he would gain not only land and resources, but the gratitude of the Senate and the People, and with that he could gain still further power.

The tribes that populated Gaul were far from being the primitive barbarians of popular Roman imagination. Instead, they possessed an ancient and far-reaching culture, whose skills ranged from the production of ornate metalwork to the study of the stars. Their values, however, were not the values of Rome. Instead of possessing a strict discipline of political hierarchy bolstered by aggressive foreign policies and enforced by a ruthlessly efficient army, Gaulish society was more fluid. Although loosely connected by customs and ethnicity, the tribes which populated the land now known as France and Belgium were self-contained and prone to rivalry, with no tradition of cooperating against a major external threat like that of Rome. Instead, their default reaction in the face of outside aggression was generally to move out of the areas that were being threatened and migrate elsewhere.

Such was the situation that Caesar encountered as he took over his command. The Helvetii, a tribe which had for some time lived in what is now Switzerland, were on the move, forced from their own land by pressures from the east. The route of their migration took them close enough to the borders of his new province (Provincia) for Caesar to present them as a threat and use them as a pretext for a war. Moreover, the Helvetii had once defeated Roman troops. It was time to settle scores.

With devastating speed, Caesar led his newly acquired army north to Geneva. Attempts to block the tribesmen's passage led not to their turning back, but to their taking a different route. To counter this, Caesar needed more troops. His answer was to raise his own legions from Cisalpine Gaul, with tacit promises of future Roman citizenship designed to bind them even closer to him in their loyalty. With them, he responded to a timely plea for help from the tribes of central and western Gaul, through whose lands the Helvetii were now travelling. In the battle that followed, Caesar won his first great victory. He learned much, too, from the experience, not least because he saw at first hand that the leadership of even seemingly sympathetic tribes was split and that by favouring one powerful man he might antagonize another. Such antagonism could be nicely used as an excuse for war.

Careful always to appear to act with the utmost fairness, Caesar used every opportunity that he could engineer to extend the theatre of war until it encompassed the whole of Gaul. He constantly sent home reports of both his and his soldiers' bravery, always taking pains to increase the loyalty of his troops by showing their actions in the most heroic light. Being far removed from Rome, of course, could cause him problems if his enemies within the Senate used his absence to attack him. So, in 56 BC, he coordinated meetings with the two men who, besides him, were the most powerful of their day, Crassus and Pompey, arranging for them both to meet him at Lucca in his province of Cisalpine Gaul. Together the three came to an informal agreement to support each other in a loose political alliance, pushing through legislation on which all agreed, and deflecting any opposition which appeared to threaten any one of them. Effectively, they had staged a takeover of the Republic.[8]

With his political rearguard safe, Caesar could now concentrate his energies on consolidating Roman rule in Gaul and potentially expanding it yet further. For it is not unlikely that, even as he was conducting his delicate deal in Lucca, he was entertaining in his mind a military operation on the fringes of the known world, which would bring him even more renown in Rome: a voyage across the very bounds of Ocean itself and the annexation of a strange new land. The conquest of Britain.

As usual, Caesar could produce good military reasons why the reach of war should be extended. Contrary to his later claims that there was little contact between those who lived on either side of the Channel, he now asserted that Britain was providing a safe haven for fugitive Gaulish tribespeople. Moreover, fighters from the south of Britain were crossing over into Gaul and providing help to their cousins in their resistance against Rome.[9] Clearly, for the security of Gaul, this situation could not be allowed to continue. Britain – or at least its southern coastline – must be subdued.

Suspicions of Caesar's plans seem to have percolated through to the people of the Veneti, who lived in what is now Brittany, and who had initially made treaties with the Romans. For a long time, the Veneti, expert seamen as they were, had conducted a profitable trade with the tribes of southwest England, visiting their trading posts at Hengistbury Head, Poole and Mount Batten (on Plymouth Sound), importing valuable commodities (including tin), some of which would find their way to Rome itself.[10]

Realizing that they were likely to lose their monopoly of this lucrative trade route, and considering the potential long-term implications of a Roman presence, the Veneti decided to renege on their arrangement. So when, as had been previously agreed, Roman quartermasters arrived to collect supplies of corn for the army, the Veneti seized them and took them prisoner, demanding the return of the hostages whom they themselves had sent to Caesar as a sign of their good faith. They then set about forming an alliance with the neighbouring tribes – including men from southern Britain – aimed at presenting a united front against the Romans. Caesar's reaction was nothing if not predictable.

With characteristic energy and foresight, he rushed into the heart of the disputed territories, sending a detachment of cavalry galloping east towards the Rhine both to keep an eye on subject tribes there and to prevent any incursions from Germanic tribes who might have been summoned by the Veneti to help them. At the same time, he led his legions against the Veneti themselves, while a fleet made up of Roman and subject Gaulish ships sailed north in his support. It was this fleet which eventually won the day. Unable to flush out the tribesmen from their coastal defences, Caesar's admirals were initially uncertain how to deal with the Veneti's ships. With exceptionally high bows and sterns and with relatively flat bottoms, these oak-built ships were designed for the rigours of the Bay of Biscay and the Atlantic Ocean. Ramming them was impossible. Instead, the Romans managed first to immobilize them by tearing down their sails and rigging with grappling hooks and then to board them. A number tried to escape, but were becalmed and easily overcome.

The Veneti defeated, Caesar made an example of them, slaughtering their chief men and selling the rest of their people into slavery. However, Caesar did not leave the western coast of Gaul without first having made a thorough inspection of the captured ships. Their design, so different from the vessels which plied the Mediterranean, intrigued him, and two years later, having experienced problems with conventional Roman ships on his first foray across the Channel, he would commission a fleet of his own built to a similar design for his second voyage to Britain.

For the moment, though, there was much to be done. With Germanic tribes still crossing the Rhine, the Belgic territories west of the river were unstable. There was urgent need for order to be imposed, and Caesar spent the remainder of that year (56 BC) and much of the next (55 BC) in conducting a campaign of devastating ruthlessness in order to bring the region under secure Roman rule. In the end, Caesar became so exasperated at the slow pace of his progress and at what he saw as the Germanic tribes' duplicity that he ordered a massacre of men, women and children on the western banks of the Rhine. Then, to warn those living on the eastern side, he built a bridge across the river, marched his legions across it, burnt every building he could find and cut down all the crops. The people themselves he could not locate. They had already fled. But confident that he had, in his own words, 'overawed' them, Caesar re-crossed the Rhine, destroyed the bridge and turned his thoughts to Britain.

✧ ✧ ✧

Caesar's reasons for crossing the Channel were many and complex. From a purely military point of view, his experiences with both the Veneti and the Germanic tribes of the Rhine had shown him two things: the need to police the natural borders which enclosed what he was determined would be the new and much enlarged province of Transalpine Gaul; and the necessity of ensuring that the peoples who lived beyond those borders were so aware of the might of Rome that they would make no attempts to cross them. However, Caesar's military objective was secondary to his political goals. Indeed, it was his political ambition that was fuelling his campaigns in Gaul. For him to remain a presence in the life of Rome, he desperately needed his name to be constantly on the lips of the city's Senators and People. To ensure this, he must constantly send back reports of ever-more spectacular successes, achievements which no other general had contemplated, let alone accomplished. Moreover, it was crucial for his ambitions that he could justify the extension of his Gallic command – even if this meant entering into a war that was technically illegal (Britain fell outside his jurisdiction).

A further and not insignificant motive was booty. Caesar was constantly in need of money to fund his political ambitions, and it would have been a major bonus for him if Britain could provide a solid economic return, especially in precious metals, the 'wages of victory' as they would later be called. He was also 'drawn by the lure of fresh-water pearls' (Plate 6).[11]

Perhaps, too, his own native curiosity, his restlessly enquiring mind, his lust to create his own mythology and become a second Alexander were all driving him to push beyond the limits of the known world, to cross the stream of Ocean, to set foot on a shore which had been wreathed in mystery and claim it for his own.

Whatever his overriding motivation, he had reached his decision. He would boldly go where no Roman general had gone before, and he would do it this year (55 BC).

The problem was, he had left it until late in the summer (24 August) and time was running out. He realized that, because not only of the logistical problems involved in a cross-Channel invasion but also of the unpredictability of the weather and the seas of early autumn, this could be nothing more than a reconnaissance expedition. So he assembled a relatively small-scale rapid deployment force: two legions would sail in eighty transport ships, while a detachment of cavalry would cross in eighteen more; in addition, a small number of warships manned by auxiliaries would accompany the expedition. In the meantime, further troops were deployed in northern Gaul to guard the ports and ensure that, with Caesar overseas, there would be no insurrections.

The narrowing window of opportunity explains Caesar's somewhat hasty planning (see p. 13). Having set the expedition in motion and raised expectations of its success both among his troops and back in Rome, he could not now be seen to fail. With the help of the tribal leader Commius, whom he considered an important ally and ambassador and whom he sent on in advance in the hope of orchestrating the surrender of the southern tribes, he might have entertained expectations that a well-choreographed ritual submission would await him. This would have been the ideal (if unrealistic) scenario. The least he needed to achieve was a successful landing on British soil, a quick-fought victory and the sending back to Rome of a few British captives. In the first few hours as his ships lay off the coast of Kent it must have seemed increasingly unlikely that he would achieve even that.

The legions and auxiliaries had set sail at midnight, leaving the cavalry to embark further up the coast and follow them. But by the time they reached the English coast, two things had become clear: first, that the ships carrying the cavalry had been prevented by the tide from making the crossing, and second that the place chosen by Caesar's scout Volusenus as their landing site was completely inappropriate. Moreover, Commius' mission to inform the southern tribes of the planned invasion had produced an effect opposite to the hoped-for submission.[12] As Caesar himself recorded in his despatches:

> He saw the enemy forces lined up on the cliff-tops. The topography was such that the cliffs came straight down into the sea to the narrowest of beaches, which meant that missiles could easily be hurled down onto the shoreline from above.[13]

In a hurried council-of-war held on the fleet's flagship under the White Cliffs of Dover, Caesar spelled out the situation. They would sail north up the coast until they found a site suitable to make a landing;[14] then they would fight their way ashore. So they sailed about 6 or 7 miles until they found the sloping beach at Walmer. As the Roman fleet nosed its way through the late-August waves, on land the British tribes were shadowing them in their chariots, on horseback and on foot. Even at Walmer, Caesar found he had a problem:

The ships could not be brought into shallow water because of their size, so the soldiers, unfamiliar with the terrain, carrying their weapons and their shields and hampered by the heavy weight of their armour, had at one and the same time to jump down from the ships, get their footing in the swell and engage with an enemy which was either standing on dry land or advanced only a little way into the water, unencumbered, on familiar ground, and fearlessly hurling missiles or whipping on their horses, which were trained in this sort of fighting. All this struck terror into the hearts of our men, who were completely unfamiliar with this type of warfare, so that they did not demonstrate that alacrity and zeal that was usually their hallmark in infantry battles.[15]

Caesar is clearly massaging the truth. For one thing, it is unlikely that the Britons had experienced any previous need to train themselves to ride their horses into the sea to attack disembarking soldiers. For another, it needs little reading between the lines to realize that the legionaries were reluctant to the point of refusal to leave their ships. Who could blame them? After all, Britain was, in the minds of many, a place of mythological menace – and, even had it not been, this was a wretched place to land.

But land Caesar must. His reputation and his future depended on it. He could not afford to turn the ships around and sail for Gaul, his mission unfulfilled. To break the stand-off, Caesar sent his warships round to the port side, where they came as close to shore as possible. These ships were equipped with the latest in ballistic weaponry, including long-range artillery, which Caesar now put to devastating effect, strafing the beach from catapults and slings. The tactic had the desired result. The British troops withdrew from the edge of the beach. Now was the time to attack, and now it was that the standard-bearer of the Tenth Legion leapt into the sea. In his report, Caesar implies that the man took it into his own head to jump. The truth may be rather different. On another occasion, Caesar had not hesitated to turn round a fleeing standard-bearer and shove him unceremoniously back into the thick of the fighting.[16] It is not impossible that now, when all hung so precariously in the balance, he had equally to coerce the standard-bearer to jump. Of course, in his report to the Senate, it would be much more politic to suggest the man leapt of his own accord – and, after the victory, the gallant soldier would never contradict him.

Seeing the legion's eagle being carried through the waves towards the enemy, the soldiers hesitated no longer, but, still covered by the missiles ripping through the air above them, they waded in full armour for the shore.

> It was hard fought on both sides. Our men were unable either to hold their ranks or get a firm footing or follow their proper standards, so soldiers from different troop-ships fell in behind the first standard they could find, which caused a great deal of confusion. The enemy on the other hand was familiar with the beach and, when they spotted from the shoreline any of our men severally disembarking weighed down by their armour, they surrounded them on horseback in their greater numbers, while others hurled javelins indiscriminately into our men's unprotected right flank. When Caesar saw this, he ordered that the ships' small boats and scouting vessels be packed with troops, and time and again he sent these to the aid of any of his men he saw in difficulties. When our men reached dry land, and all of them were in place, they launched an attack on the enemy and put them to flight. They could not pursue them very far, however, as the [ships carrying the] cavalry had not been able to hold course and reach the island.[17]

This was to prove a major problem for Caesar, whose chosen tactic after a victory was to send his cavalry to pursue the fleeing enemy as mercilessly as they could and so prevent them from regrouping. Now, though, all the Romans could do was make camp, hunker down and wait for the morning.

With dawn came a delegation from the Britons. One of its number was Caesar's old friend Commius, who had been sent ahead to alert the southern tribes to the Romans' imminent arrival. For reasons on which it is difficult (with such a time gap) to comment, Caesar accepted Commius' story that no sooner had he arrived in Britain than he had been taken prisoner. Now, he claimed, the tribesmen had set him free so he could parley with the Romans. Oddly Caesar did not see in Commius the trait, which he had already observed in his Gaulish cousins, that 'they are quick enough to declare war, but once they suffer any setback they lack the strength of character to see it through'.[18] Soothed by Commius' assurances, Caesar accepted the delegation's apologies for attacking him, made a speech about how he would have expected better of them, demanded hostages, and allowed the British to disband and return to their fields. 'Peace,' he wrote, 'was thus concluded.'[19]

Peace was, in fact, very far from being concluded. Two days later disaster struck. There was a violent storm. The transport ships with all the cavalry and horses on board were within sight of Kent when the winds scattered them back into the Channel, from where they returned to Gaul only thanks to the skill of their captains. Worse, Caesar's own vessels were badly damaged. Those drawn up on Walmer beach were waterlogged, while others anchored just offshore were smashed against each other and some were completely shattered. The consequences were potentially dire. With autumn fast approaching, Caesar faced the real possibility of being cut off in a hostile land with relatively few troops, insufficient supplies and little hope of being relieved before the next spring. It was a nightmare scenario, and one whose implications were clear to every member of the army.

They were clear to the Britons, too. While Caesar set his men to work repairing the ships and foraging for food, the tribal elders met to discuss tactics. It was decided that they would lull the Romans into a false sense of security and then, quite suddenly, strike. This they did when the Seventh Legion had left the camp to collect corn:

> Until now, nothing had arisen to suggest any suspicion of attack. With some of the [British] people still working in the fields, and others coming back and forth to the camp, the soldiers detailed to guard the camp gates reported to Caesar that an unusually large amount of dust had been seen in the sector to which the legion had gone out. Caesar guessed what had happened.[20]

The British tribesmen had been lying in ambush in the forests. When they saw that the legionaries had laid down their arms and were engrossed in cutting corn, they had made their attack. Quickly Caesar led out the cohorts who happened to be on guard duty, ordering the rest of the troops to arm and follow him. Had it not been for his swift intervention the Seventh Legion might well have been massacred. In his report, he gives a vivid account of how his soldiers were harassed by chariots:

> This is how they fight from their chariots: to begin with, they drive their horses across the battlefield, hurling their javelins, and usually the sheer terror which the horses and the noise of the wheels inspires is enough to throw the enemy lines into confusion. When they have positioned themselves among their own cavalry, they

jump down from the chariots and fight on foot. Meanwhile, the chariot-drivers withdraw a little from the fighting and position the chariots in such a way that their warriors have an easy means of retreat to their own lines if they find themselves overwhelmed by enemy numbers. In this way they combine the swift manoeuvrability of cavalry with the solidity of infantry when fighting, and by daily practice and training they reach such a pitch of proficiency that they can control their horses even at a gallop down steep slopes, pull them up and change direction in short order; they can even run along the chariot pole, stand on the yoke and in no time be back inside the chariot.[21]

In the face of these attacks, a swift regrouping and an orderly retreat to camp was all that Caesar could achieve, and for several days afterwards, the Romans stayed where they were, repair work on their ships slowed down by driving rain, while the tribesmen mustered in ever greater strength. At last the weather cleared and Caesar led his troops out of the camp in battle formation. At their head he placed thirty horsemen. These, he tells us, had been brought across by Commius. Perhaps Commius was himself among them. Perhaps it was his presence that caused the British not to fight. There was, says Caesar, a half-hearted battle, after which the British fled while the Romans torched 'all the buildings over a wide area'. The same day, he continues, 'envoys came to Caesar from the enemy to sue for peace'.[22] That night, the Romans put to sea and their ships and men slipped quietly back to Gaul. Yet even here, all did not go smoothly. Two ships were blown off course, and as the troops they had been carrying marched overland to meet up with the rest of the army, they were surrounded and attacked by 6,000 (nominally friendly) Gaulish tribesmen. Only Caesar's rapid deployment of his cavalry saved them.

We will never know the truth of what really happened in the last days of Caesar's first British expedition, but the story of a final easy victory, the British peace envoys, the Romans setting sail for Gaul with their honour at the eleventh hour restored, all seems a little too neat, a little too much like whitewash. But it made a good story. For Caesar that was all that really mattered. He had done what he had set out to do. He had set foot on *terra incognita*, and what was more he had returned, his army more-or-less intact, his reputation magnified. And if he had massaged the facts to show himself (and his army) in a better light, he knew that not one of his men would contradict him. As he himself wrote: 'With the campaigning over and their receipt of Caesar's dispatches, the Senate decreed a public thanksgiving of twenty days.'[23]

✧   ✧   ✧

No sooner had he returned to Gaul than Caesar was planning his return to Britain the next year. It is unlikely that he had seen enough of the island to convince him that its resources warranted another visit, but his honour and sense of pride were such that he could not allow the situation to rest as it did. For strategic reasons, too, he needed to convince the British tribes that Rome was sufficiently a force to be reckoned with that they would think twice before interfering in Gaul. So, learning from his first expedition as if it had indeed been purely for reconnaissance, he now put plans in place for a much more ambitious invasion. The winter would be spent in constructing a new fleet of 600 ships built to Caesar's own specifications. They would be wide flat-bottomed boats, designed for easier disembarkation, and modelled no doubt on the captured ships of the Veneti, which Caesar had examined so closely the year before. Material to build them would be imported specially from Spain.

3 Maps showing Caesar's expeditions to Britain in 55 BC (this page) and 54 BC (opposite).

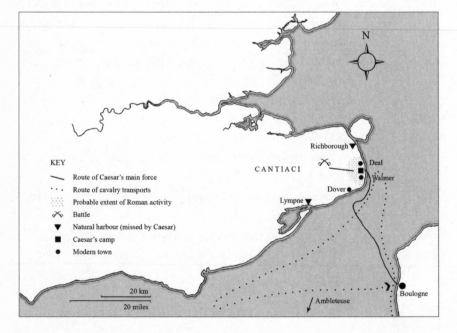

If Caesar hoped to set out again for Britain in the spring (54 BC), he was disappointed. First, trouble in Illyricum detained him, and then, just as he was about to put to sea, disturbing news came from the east, from the Moselle, where it seemed that the Germanic tribes were mustering again. Although he succeeded in quashing any potential rebellion both here and back in Gaul itself, it all took time, and it was not until the end of the first week of July that the invasion force could put to sea. This time, when he did sail, Caesar sailed in force. Five legions and 2,000 cavalry embarked onto the newly built transport ships. Accompanying them would be a further 200 vessels, commandeered from local tribesmen, as well as 28 Roman war galleys – and sailing in their wake were privately owned vessels, too, the ships of traders hoping to cash in, greedy for the promise of the riches they had heard of from the veterans of the voyage of the year before.[24] We do not know how many traders sailed. We do know, though, that no fewer than 30,000 troops were now heading for the shores of Kent.

The crossing took some sixteen hours. The current in the Channel sent the fleet off course, and it was not until midday on 7 July that the ships made land. Just as before, they beached at Walmer. However, unlike the previous occasion, they found the shoreline empty. The enemy was nowhere to be seen. The troops could land completely unopposed.

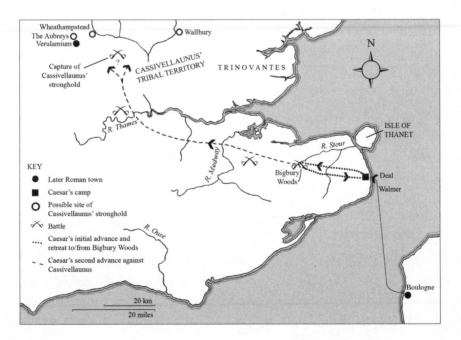

Caesar may have hoped this meant that the British intended to abide by such peace treaties as had been made the year before. If he did, he was mistaken. For Caesar was not the only one to have been busy in the months since he had sailed from Britain. Across the southeast of the island there had been frantic negotiations, with meetings held and treaties made, the result of which was a loose coalition of tribes under the leadership of Cassivellaunus, a powerful chief, possibly of the Catuvellauni tribe, whose capital was probably somewhere in Hertfordshire – and Cassivellaunus was determined to put up a fight.

No sooner had Caesar landed and chosen a site for his camp than prisoners were brought to him who claimed that the British had, in fact, intended to oppose his landing but, terrified at the number of his ships, they had withdrawn inland to their own encampment some 12 miles inland. This news galvanized Caesar into action. He knew from long experience the value of a surprise attack, so, rather than wait until the dawn, he led out his troops at midnight and struck out northwest. By dawn, he was looking down across the valley of the River Stour near modern Thanington. Already on the further bank, the British cavalry and chariots were gathering, the early sunlight catching on the highly polished ornaments hung round their horses' necks and glinting on the warriors' shields and spears. Less than a day after landing, Caesar had encountered the first signs of British aggression and he knew he needed to achieve a crushing victory.

Unfortunately he gives us little detail of how he achieved it. Perhaps this in itself speaks volumes – it may have been a very hard-fought struggle. All he records is that the British:

> ...attacked from higher ground in an attempt to bar his way. They were driven back by [the Roman] cavalry and took cover in the woods, where they occupied a position which was both naturally strong and well-fortified, preparations having been already put in place (or so it appeared) for some war among themselves: for all the entrances were blocked by trees which had been felled and densely packed together.[25]

In fact, the hillfort at Bigbury Wood had doubtless been prepared specifically to resist the Romans. However, the Britons had misjudged their enemy's capabilities, especially when it came to storming fortresses, and it was not long before the soldiers of the Seventh Legion had formed into a *testudo*, the tortoise formation, with their shields locked tight above their heads to protect themselves from missiles, and were building an earthen ramp. In no time, they had breached the walls and were inside, wreaking vengeance for the ambush they had suffered the summer before.

It had been a hard-fought day and there were only a few hours of daylight left. Rather than pursue the fugitives, Caesar pitched camp. In the morning, he was beginning to embark on a mopping up operation, when a horseman galloped into camp with news that was both devastating and yet all too familiar. A storm had blown up in the night. The fleet was wrecked. Caesar's sense of anger and frustration can only be imagined; more dangerous would be the reaction of his men, who were no doubt even now questioning their leader's competence in allowing the disaster of the year before to be repeated, or whispering their fears that this strange new country's gods of waves and weather were conspiring to destroy them. Still, there was nothing to be done but march back to the beach-head and repair the fleet.

It took the soldiers ten days, working solidly in shifts even throughout the nights, to repair the ships, and still forty of the vessels were total write-offs. When they had finished, the soldiers dragged them all onto the shingle as close to one another as they could, protected from attack by a huge stockade. At the same time, Caesar sent a swift galley back to Gaul to arrange for the building of new troop-ships. It returned with doleful news. Caesar's daughter Julia had died in childbirth. Not only was this a personal blow, it had political implications, too. Julia had been married to Caesar's chief rival, Pompey. A child, had he survived, would have bound the two men close together. Now that such ties had been so cruelly severed, the stability of their future partnership suddenly seemed less secure.

Caesar could not afford the luxury of grief. Instead he channelled such emotion as he felt into a renewed determination to destroy the resisting Britons. Leaving a detachment to guard the ships, he marched out with his legions, back along the way to Bigbury. The army had advanced only a few miles before the cavalry found themselves engaged in skirmishes with British war chariots and horsemen, whose tactics were to entice the Romans to pursue them into the more wooded areas, where they would be easier prey. Caesar claims victory, alleging that his men 'killed a good number, but lost not a few themselves through an over-eagerness to pursue'.[26] Given the nature of his reporting, this probably means that at best neither side got the upper hand.

Certainly Caesar seemed unprepared for what happened next. In the late afternoon, as his men were building their camp for the night, British warriors burst suddenly from the surrounding forests and fell on the duty sentries with yells and war cries. Two Roman cohorts rushed to their support, but even these were insufficient, and soon further reinforcements were sent in. The problem was that, to the Romans, the tactics of the Britons were so unfamiliar. As if to justify what must have been a close-fought battle, Caesar devotes a telling paragraph to the subject:

> The battle was fought in front of the camp in full view of everyone, and it was at all times apparent that, because of the weight of their armour, our men were not suited to confronting this type of enemy. They could not follow through when the enemy retreated; nor did they want to become separated from their standards. Likewise, it was dangerous for the cavalry to fight against the charioteers, whose tactics were deliberately to retreat, and when they had lured them some way from our legions, jump down from the chariots and fight on foot, with all the odds on their side. Against their cavalry, it was much the same: their tactics made it equally dangerous whether we fell back or pursued them. What made matters worse was that they never fought in close formation, but spread out with great distances between them, and there were reserves scattered about too, which meant that one group could cover another's retreat, while fresh troops took the place of those who were tired from fighting.[27]

Caesar's men won through, but at a cost. There was clearly some serious thinking to be done if the Romans were to have any hope of outright victory. Yet there was no time for a major revision of tactics. The British war leader, Cassivellaunus, was keen to press home his advantage, and the next day, as three legions were out foraging, the Britons 'suddenly swooped down on them from all sides, pressing their attack right up to the standards'.[28] By luck, the encounter turned into a pitched battle, as the tribesmen surged forwards against the Roman lines. It was the sort of fighting in which the Romans had been trained. The legionaries launched a counterattack. The cavalry charged into the melée. The Britons turned and fled, the Roman horsemen chasing them and cutting them down even as they ran. A rout became a bloodbath, as the Romans gave full vent to all the anger and frustration of the past few weeks. Cassivellaunus' grip on his new-forged alliance had been broken. The tide had turned in Caesar's favour. Now he would take the war into Cassivellaunus' own lands. He would cross the Thames.

It may have been at Brentford that he reached the river. Cassivellaunus' men had crossed already, perhaps by a bridge that they had subsequently destroyed. Now they were drawn up on the farther bank, the mudflats in front of them bristling with sharpened wooden stakes, while more stakes were concealed, deserters swore, beneath the water. It was a daunting sight, yet Caesar glosses over the encounter with a suspicious nonchalance in two sentences:

> He sent the cavalry on ahead and gave the order to the infantry to follow. But such was the speed and impetus of the infantry's advance, although only their heads were above water, that the infantry and cavalry attacked together. The enemy lines broke; they left the river bank and fled.[29]

Still Cassivellaunus would not give up easily. As Caesar's men made their inexorable march towards his tribal capital, Cassivellaunus constantly harassed them, using a network of roads and lanes as arteries along which to send his cavalry and chariots to launch attacks on any of the Roman cavalry who strayed too far. At the same time, he moved his people and their livestock, the prized cattle which represented so much of their wealth, out of the fields and into the forests for protection, perhaps installing them in such hillforts as happened to be near.

CASSIVELLAUNUS' STRONGHOLD

Caesar knew that Cassivellaunus' stronghold (*oppidum*) lay north of the Thames, but he had to learn the precise location by embassies from other tribes. Today the site is the subject of some debate. Some place Cassivellaunus' capital in the upper Lea valley at Wheathamstead, north of Verulamium (St Albans), a site surrounded by large ditches.[30] However, the archaeological evidence is sparse and other locations have been suggested, notably the hillforts at Gatesbury, Redbourn and Ravensburgh Castle, the large settlement at Baldock, and Wallbury Camp hillfort, near Hallingbury, in Essex.[31] As with so much of the history of Caesar's expeditions, it is virtually impossible to link his accounts directly with archaeological sites.

Though Caesar's progress was slowed down, it was far from being stopped, and by now the inevitable outcome was becoming clear. During his march north of the Thames, envoys came to Caesar from the Trinovantes tribe of Essex, asking for the return of Mandubracius. Mandubracius' father, the Trinovantian king, had been murdered by Cassivellaunus, and Mandubracius himself had fled to Caesar on the continent.[32] Now he had returned in Caesar's entourage. So, in return for hostages and grain, Caesar set Mandubracius on the Trinovantian throne to rule (in name at least) over his own grateful people. It was a clever move. One by one a trickle of tribal chiefs arrived in Caesar's camp to offer their surrender and their loyalty. Cassivellaunus' support was slowly haemorrhaging away. Moreover, from his newly declared allies, Caesar could learn much, not least the location of Cassivellaunus. Now nothing lay between him and the tribal capital, and learning that all Cassivellaunus' strength and wealth, his troops and cattle, had been gathered there, Caesar made one last push towards the final battle. His account is brief and to the point:

> He marched there with his legions; he found that the place was naturally strong and had been well fortified. Nonetheless, he attacked from two directions. Before long the enemy could not sustain the pressure of our troops' attack and hurriedly escaped through another part of the fort. A great number of cattle were found there, and many of the men who escaped were either captured or killed.[33]

Soon he received reports of two developments. The first was that the troops guarding the ships at Walmer had repulsed an attack by four kings of the Cantii tribe loyal to Cassivellaunus, and the last throes of resistance had been quashed; the second that Cassivellaunus himself, on hearing of this news, was offering surrender terms – and the man he had chosen to negotiate on his behalf was none other than Caesar's 'tame' Gaul, Commius. Swiftly terms were agreed and treaties made. The terms were not unusual. Caesar demanded hostages and tribute.[34] Moreover, Cassivellaunus was to leave Mandubracius and his tribe, the Trinovantes, in peace. Rome's writ was to hold sway in Britain.

The time had come for Caesar to sail home, so as the autumn equinox approached, in ships now laden down with hostages and booty, he put out late one evening from the shores of Kent and at dawn came safe to Gaul.

✧ ✧ ✧

In Rome, responses to this second expedition were curiously muted. Publicly, there was no thanksgiving from the Senate. In private, too, there was a sense of disappointment. Cicero, tirelessly dictating letters to his family and friends, commented to one, who was serving in Caesar's army:

> I hear that in Britain there is no gold or silver. If this is the case, I urge you to commandeer a war-chariot and get yourself back here to us as soon as you can.[35]

To another, he wrote a month later, with typical Ciceronian urbanity and condescension:

> We await the outcome of the British war: it is well known that the approach to the island is 'ringèd round with rigid ramparts'; it's already quite clear that there is not an ounce of silver on the island nor any hope of booty except slaves; and I imagine you're not expecting much in the way of literary or musical accomplishments from *them*![36]

In fact, like many in Rome, Cicero had a more than passing interest in the campaign. His brother was serving in Caesar's army, and it is perhaps not too fanciful to detect signs of relief when he learned that the expedition was at an end:

> On 24 October I received one letter from my brother Quintus and another from Caesar; both were dated 25 September and sent from the nearest part of the British coast. The campaign in Britain is over; hostages have been taken and (despite the fact that there's no booty) a tribute has been imposed. They're bringing the army back from Britain![37]

What Caesar's future plans for Britain were, we cannot tell. Perhaps he intended to return the next year to capitalize on his success and to consolidate, to organize the subject tribes, to push on further, deep into the heart of this now less secret land. This would indeed seem to have been his intention – the words he chose to describe the tribute (*vectigal*) and surrender of the Britons (*deditio*) are terms usually associated with the formation of a new province.

Certainly the tribes of southeast Britain must have spent the spring and early summer of 53 BC scouring the horizon in expectation of the fleet's return. But by now events in Gaul had taken on a momentum of their own. Caesar found himself tied down by insurrection, as the province he thought he had subdued flared into violence. Soon Gaulish tribes were rallying under a new charismatic leader, Vercingetorix, and when they heard that Caesar had pinned him down in a hillfort at Alesia (52 BC), reinforcements from across the Gaulish world struggled to get through to help him. Among these Gauls was Commius, who now turned against Caesar. At last he had shown his hand. Commius entertained no love for the Romans. Perhaps he had been what we would now call a double agent, working for the Gauls and Britons, all along. Perhaps, like Caesar, he was just an opportunist.

Alesia fell to Caesar and, in the fighting that followed, Commius led his guerrilla horsemen in sustained attacks against the Roman troops. At last, on the orders of the legionary legate Mark Antony, Volusenus, the man who had so disastrously scouted the British coast five years before, met Commius in battle and defeated him (51 BC). Commius escaped and made for the Channel, but the tide was against him. His boat was stuck fast on the mud flats, and the Roman cavalry was close. In desperation, Commius ordered sails to be raised. From the shore, Caesar's men saw them belly in the wind, and, thinking that Commius had got away, they called off their pursuit. As the sea lapped higher round its hull, the boat floated from the mud and, repeating his desire never in his life again to see a Roman, Commius sailed for Britain.[38]

By now such hopes as Rome or Caesar might have held of exercising control over Britain must, in reality, have dwindled. Along with them the tribute from across the Channel must have soon dwindled, too, before drying up completely. It was clear that Caesar would not be returning. By 41 BC, a mere thirteen years after the second of the two invasions, the island's isolation had been firmly re-established and the poet Virgil could describe its people as 'cut off from the whole world'.[39] In truth, as Tacitus much later wrote, Caesar had achieved little of any lasting worth:

> First of all Romans, the deified Julius [Caesar] set foot in Britain with an army; although he struck fear into its people by a successful battle and took possession of the coast, it can be seen that he merely introduced rather than bequeathed Britain to future generations.[40]

Back in Britain itself, the renegade Commius would rule, king of the Atrebates, from what seems to have been his capital at Silchester, issuing coins with his name emblazoned on them in fine Latin letters: COMMIOS

(Plate 3).⁴¹ No doubt from time to time news came to him from across the sea of his old adversary Caesar, how he had entered into civil war with his one-time ally Pompey, how he had won, how he was forming an alliance with a seductive queen in a far-off land, how he himself was striving to be king in Rome, how he was killed by treachery.

He would probably have heard, too, of the wars that followed between the man who once in Gaul had tried to have him killed, Mark Antony, and Caesar's heir Octavian. He would have learned how the war had ended, how Octavian himself was now the sole ruler of the Roman world, how he had taken on the title of Augustus (Plate 9). Throughout these later years, he would almost certainly have heard rumours of further Roman expeditions being planned to Britain, all of which failed to materialize.

How thwarted must have been the poets in Rome! Time and again from the comfort of their couches they had been scratching stirring verses on their waxen tablets:

Where Ocean embraces the world with its waters,
No kingdom will meet you with hostile weaponry.
Only the Briton remains, still undefeated by Rome's might...

wrote one⁴² in the build-up to the abortive campaign of 27 BC.

AUGUSTUS' ABORTIVE EXPEDITIONS TO BRITAIN

Twenty years after Caesar's second expedition to Britain, his adopted son, Octavian, considered another invasion (34 BC). Although he marched into Gaul, he was forced to call off the mission in order to quell a revolt among newly conquered tribes in Dalmatia, on the Balkans' Adriatic coast.⁴³ It was not for another seven years that Octavian, now known by the new title Augustus, again contemplated invading (27 BC). But still he did not cross the Channel.⁴⁴ Perhaps it was because Gaul was so unstable that it needed his full attention; perhaps he believed the Britons would make terms. With the next year came more plans for an invasion. Again they came to nothing, blown off course by rebellions in the Alps and northern Spain.⁴⁵ For a time, the military option was shelved. Diplomacy was tried instead, and in time two British kings, Tincomarus and Dubovellaunus, did come to Rome as suppliants.⁴⁶ For more than sixty years, however, no further invasions were contemplated – until Caligula made his doomed attempt in AD 40.

> Whether we chase the Parthians on foot or the Britons with our fleet,
> The dangers of both sea and land are blind,

trilled another,[47] while the mighty Horace went so far as to suggest that Augustus' very reputation might hang on a successful conquest:

> We believe that Jupiter the Thunderer holds sway
> In Heaven; on earth Augustus shall be held
> A god, when Britain and
> Oppressive Persia are added to our empire.[48]

It was, of course, a conquest that he hoped would be successful:

> May Fortune keep [Augustus] Caesar safe
> Who soon will sail against the Britons, the most distant race on earth.[49]

In the end it was all castles in the sky. Augustus never did set sail for Britain, and by the time that Commius' last hours came, perhaps around 25 BC, perhaps at Silchester, the wily old warrior could die content that he had indeed never set eyes upon another hostile Roman.[50]

How disappointed in his son he would have been. For the young man Tincomarus (c. 25 BC–AD 10), product of Commius' old age, was to make the long journey to Rome and kneel as suppliant before Augustus.[51] Already times were changing. Not for Tincomarus the isolationist position of his father. Rather, he would take care to straddle both the British and the Roman worlds, as the fine gold coins he struck would show. Some would bear the ancient British 'Celtic' horse design; but others, showing a classical-style horseman, may possibly have been engraved by a mint-worker lent to him by Augustus himself (Plates 4, 5).[52]

There are more ways to conquer than simply through war. Already the south of Britain was being sucked into the economic sphere of Rome. Roman luxury goods, silver, bronze and glass, began to find their way into the hands of powerful Britons; and with them, too, came wine (Plate 2).

Now that the Veneti's control of the western trade routes had been smashed (see p. 21), and Roman ties, both economic and diplomatic, with the southeast of Britain were strengthening, trading entrepôts sprang up in the Thames Estuary and Essex, and the Latin script began to snake its way round British coins.[53] A peaceful Britain proved herself to be a useful neighbour to the Roman world. It was only when the British tribes began to fight each other that Rome would be forced to act once more.

2
ELEPHANTS AND CASTLES

With its rings of earthwork ditches, its royal court and its shrines, Camulodunum, the stronghold of the British war-god Camulos, was used to power
and pageantry. Yet, familiar as its people were with ceremony, they could
never have imagined anything like this.

For, rank upon rank on the level ground before the royal enclosure, the
high summer sunlight glinting on their polished armour and shimmering
on their javelin tips, their tunics all a dazzling red, were ranged the legionaries of Rome. Joining them on the parade ground were the cavalry, their
horses' coats meticulously groomed, their lances raised straight in salute,
and near them the artillery: huge war-machines with which to strike cold
fear into their enemies.

But these were nothing to what now were coming into view. For joining
the parade were terrifying creatures, massive, tusked and towering high,
their flanks encased in armour, their backs supporting castles filled with
archers.[1] War-elephants had come to Camulodunum.

And then, when all were in their place, the trumpets blaring forth across
the settlement, the soldiers bellowing their greetings in this orchestrated show
of strength, there swept onto the field a golden chariot. Beside its driver stood
a tall and well-built man, his white hair circled with a golden laurel wreath,
his purple campaign cloak draping heavy from his shoulder as he held his
right hand high, acknowledging the adulation of his troops. This was a
moment he would savour, a moment that not one of his illustrious fore-
runners had enjoyed, a moment that would raise his kudos back in Rome
as high, no! higher than that of the great Gaius Julius Caesar himself.
The emperor Claudius was about to accept the surrender of the rulers of
Britannia.

✧ ✧ ✧

FOR almost a hundred years after Caesar, Britain and the Roman empire existed side by side without aggression. Merchants who did business with the newly-burgeoning settlements of Camulodunum (Colchester) and Verulamium (Verlamio; St Albans), and some of whom had possibly set up permanent offices there, brought back to Gaul and Rome enticing reports of Britain's potential as a source of mineral and agricultural wealth.[2] It was, they said, a land rich in silver, iron and gold, with fertile fields of corn, an ample and abundant source of hides and hunting dogs and slaves.[3] In making these claims, they were supported by the growing number of British exiles or hostages who were finding their way to Rome, all hoping somehow to curry the support of the ever-expanding empire for their own particular cause.

If, early in his reign, Augustus did toy with thoughts of bringing Britannia under Roman rule, in the end he made no moves to do so (see p. 37). Instead, he preferred to play a political game, supporting those kings whose policies were in line with those of Rome, allowing them to think that they were allies, and no doubt smiling when he heard that on their newly minted tribal coinage they were styling themselves with the Latin title *rex* (king).[4] So, throughout the latter part of Augustus' reign and that of Tiberius, his successor, there was no longer talk of sending the legions across the Channel. Why go to all the bother, danger and expense of launching an invasion, when the Britons were effectively submitting willingly to Rome? Such, it seems at any rate, was the official line:

> Now, though, some of their rulers have secured the friendship of Caesar Augustus by sending ambassadors and showing respect. Indeed, they have dedicated offerings on the Capitol and virtually brought the whole island under Roman control.[5] Also, they submit to reasonable duties on imports and exports to Gaul, including ivory bracelets and necklaces, amber and glassware and similar trinkets,[6] so there is no need to garrison the island. It would take at least one legion and a detachment of cavalry to collect tribute from them, and the total expenditure for such a force would be as much as the revenue collected. For, if tribute were levied, customs duties would inevitably decline and at the same time the use of force might lead to danger.[7]

However, by the time of the next emperor, Gaius (Caligula), all that had changed. The Roman empire had not been the only place that had endured upheavals. In Britannia, Cunobelin, the old king of the Catuvellauni, who had expanded his power bit by inexorable bit across his neighbours' territory, always careful to keep Rome on board, never rocking the boat too much, was dying (*c.* AD 39).

One of Cunobelin's last acts (and one which showed uncharacteristic lack of foresight) was to banish his son, Adminius, who in high dudgeon fled to Gaul.[8] Here, Adminius found the young, pallid, insomniac emperor Gaius, desperately trying to impose his somewhat eccentric will on the legions. For Gaius, Adminius' arrival seemed a godsend, enabling him, as it did, not only to write to the Senate declaring (with characteristic extravagance) that all Britannia had surrendered to him, but, more importantly, to prepare for a full-scale invasion of the island. It was the kind of flamboyant undertaking that appealed to Gaius. Besides, it would give him a much-needed propaganda victory back at Rome.

Immediately, arrangements for the invasion were set in train. Plans were made, ships built, supplies were sourced and requisitioned, weapons stockpiled, soldiers drilled. By the appointed date, all was in place (AD 40). And then disaster struck. The legionaries gathered on the sea front[9] refused to obey their orders. They would not embark. Not even the threats of the murderous Gaius would induce them to cross the Ocean for the nightmare land of Britannia.

Gaius, furious yet impotent, was humiliated. After all, he had long considered himself to be the darling of the army, creating titles for himself such as 'Son of the Camp' and 'Father of the Army'.[10] Even the name by which we know him best, Caligula (or 'Bootee'), had been given to him as

---

Cunobelin's Coinage

Something of Cunobelin's mastery of the political and diplomatic game both domestically and internationally might be gauged from his coinage. While he was probably one of the British kings careful to send offerings to the Roman Capitol, back home he stamped his coins with an ear of British grain. This is in marked contrast to his rival, King Verica, who was eager to demonstrate his allegiance to Rome by proudly showing the vine leaf on his coinage. The message to Cunobelin's people may have been that other kings might sell out to the wine-drinking Romans, but he, Cunobelin, was a beer-swilling Briton through and through (Plates 7, 8).[11]

a child by his father's soldiers, amused by his penchant for toddling about the camp dressed up in miniature armour.[12] Yet, Gaius had it in his power to humiliate his soldiers even more than they had humiliated him. Gathered as they were on the beach, he ordered them to collect sea shells and fill their helmets with them – booty, as he sneered, won from the Ocean. Then, to commemorate the event, he erected a great lighthouse, while, in a hasty attempt to buy their loyalty, he paid four gold pieces to each of his soldiers.[13] Back in Rome, on 31 August, his twenty-eighth birthday, Gaius was awarded an *ovatio*. Less than four months later he had been assassinated.[14]

As a precedent for a successful invasion of the island, this episode of AD 40 left much to be desired. Yet the necessity for an invasion, or at least the pretext for one, was becoming more and more apparent. By this time, Cunobelin, king of the Catuvellauni tribe, was dead. His two sons, Togodumnus and Caratacus, had inherited his kingdom – but not his diplomatic skill. Keen to assert their independence, they soon swept south and west into the lands of the Atrebates and Regini, tribes that had been well disposed to Rome. Verica, the elderly Atrebatic king,[15] took ship and fled to Rome (*c.* AD 41/2). The country was in turmoil. The political map of southeast Britannia had been redrawn.

By now, Britannia was already high on Rome's military agenda, not least because the Senate was in receipt of ultimata from Togodumnus and Caratacus, threatening vengeance if it failed to return political refugees.[16] So, perhaps fearing incursions into Gaul, or wishing to take advantage not only of the potential instability following the end of Cunobelin's forty-year reign but also, more astutely, of the inter-tribal rivalries which his death was bringing to the fore, the new Roman emperor, Claudius, uncle of Gaius Caligula, seized the initiative.

Notoriously absent-minded and short-sighted, the limping, drooling, bookish Claudius had come to the throne in circumstances which were unusual, to say the least. Kept from public gaze throughout his life by an embarrassed imperial family, he had been discovered in the palace cowering behind a curtain by one of Gaius' assassins and promptly proclaimed emperor. Still, if he was inexperienced in the arts of government, his antiquarian studies had taught him that there was nothing like a stunning and successful military campaign to bolster his reputation in the eyes of the people and the army alike.[17] The hand of history was on his shoulder, the pieces all in place for an offensive against Britannia.

Not least among these was the fact that there was already an invasion force ready and prepared: the army that Gaius had so notoriously been unable to persuade to sail. Furthermore, too many legions stationed on the Rhine would give a potential rival to the throne excessive power. Alongside the men, there were ships and warehouses still well-supplied with much

4 Map of Britain in the period AD 43–60, showing the areas directly occupied by Rome, her client kingdoms and unconquered territories.

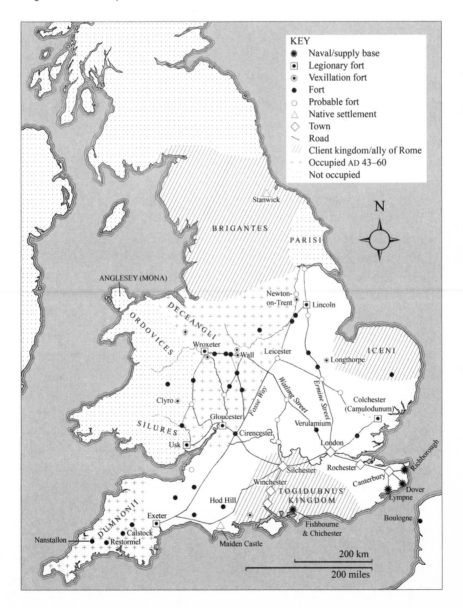

KEY
* ✳ Naval/supply base
* ⊡ Legionary fort
* ⊙ Vexillation fort
* ● Fort
* ○ Probable fort
* △ Native settlement
* ◇ Town
* ⌐ Road
* /// Client kingdom/ally of Rome
* ++ Occupied AD 43–60
* Not occupied

of the matériel required, including ordnance. In addition, exploratory negotiations suggested that many of the tribal leaders (both those in exile and those on the ground), who were opposed to Togodumnus and Caratacus, were likely to welcome Roman support. Rome, no doubt, already possessed good intelligence about the almost pathological rivalry between the British tribes, which prevented them from presenting a united front against a common enemy.[18]

To lead the invasion, Claudius appointed the seasoned general Aulus Plautius. He was a man the emperor knew he could trust. One reason was his pedigree.[19] His father had once been co-consul (2 BC) with the emperor Augustus; his sister had once been Claudius' wife; his own wife had connections with the family of Tiberius (and with the poet Ovid).[20] More importantly, the year before (AD 42), when in Dalmatia (Croatia) there had been a failed revolt against the emperor,[21] Aulus Plautius, senator, ex-consul and now governor of the neighbouring province of Pannonia, had not wavered. When the ringleaders were rounded up and executed, Plautius, loyal to the last to Claudius, played his part in restoring order.

Now, for the invasion force, Plautius was assigned four legions,[22] as well as the usual allotment of cavalry and auxiliaries. In all, some 40,000 men assembled, most probably at Boulogne,[23] in the shadow of Gaius' lighthouse (AD 43). But the Channel was wide, the cliffs on the horizon threatening, and the legionaries knew that last time they had refused to sail there had been no recriminations. So when the time came to embark, they disobeyed their orders. They stayed put.

For the second time in three years, there was stalemate on the Channel shore. Plautius sent an urgent message to Rome requesting guidance. In reply, and with some haste, there arrived in the camp the emperor's Chief Secretary,[24] the oleaginous Narcissus, a freed slave who had risen to become one of the most powerful and feared aides in Claudius' court. With the troops assembled on the parade ground, Narcissus mounted the tribunal to address them. The mood was ugly. There were angry cat-calls and abusive heckling. As the hostility mounted, one faction from the troops began to chant 'Io Saturnalia', the greeting used at the winter festival when slaves were allowed to lord it over their masters. The words were taken up by the rest of the men, but laughing now, the tension broken, ready now at last to do their duty. And in that moment, the fate of Britannia was sealed.

Or so the story went. In fact, it is quite likely that Narcissus had brought with him wagon-loads of freshly minted coin with which to bribe the troops. (A hoard of gold *aurei* from the period, found at Bredgar near Sittingbourne in Kent, might have been buried by a centurion or senior officer who took part in the invasion and either failed to return or to his frustration forgot where he had hidden them; Plate 10.)[25] It is no wonder, though, that such a bribe is passed over in official Roman accounts. On the eve of an heroic conquest, who wants to make their troops seem venal?

So, in late April, later in the year than had originally been intended, the Roman legions put to sea. According to the historian Dio, whose meagre narrative is the best we possess:

> They were sent across in three tranches, so that they might not be prevented from landing, which could be the case if they were a single body. Initially, they became discouraged in their crossing as they were driven back by the sea, but they took heart because a light from the east streaked westwards, in the direction they were sailing. They landed on the island unopposed.[26]

It is a notoriously vague and unsatisfactory account. Not the least perplexing element are the three divisions, which make no strategic sense, unless we are to imagine three successive waves of ships, each disembarking their men, before moving off to allow the next wave access to the beach-head. This, it has been argued, would have been a dangerous manoeuvre if the disembarking soldiers were under fire from the enemy.

However, Dio expressly tells us that the enemy was nowhere to be seen. His explanation is that the British had received intelligence of the Roman army's mutiny and believed, as a result, that this attempt at invasion would, like the last one, be abandoned. So they had made no provision to oppose it. It is not impossible that, on the Roman side, Plautius had himself been informed that the landing would be unopposed.

The precise site of the beach-head is unknown. Most likely it was at Rutupiae (Richborough) in the territory of the Cantii (who, having been annexed by Cunobelin, might have been relied upon for support against his sons). Here, a channel formed a natural harbour with safe anchorage, protected from the open sea by the Isle of Tanatus (Thanet). Having disembarked his men, Plautius made base camp, and, in the absence of an enemy to fight, he led out his legions to find them.

According to Dio, the forces of Togodumnus and Caratacus took refuge in swamps and forests (his notion of British topography relies perhaps more on his Mediterranean imagination than on conditions on the ground), hoping to use guerrilla tactics to wear out the Roman army. In doing this, Dio reasons, they were deliberately using a strategy that had been successful against Caesar a century earlier. The truth may be somewhat different. Caught on the wrong foot, the Catuvellaunian warlords may simply have been unable to gather their men in sufficient numbers to meet the Romans head-on.

It is possible that, capitalizing on the element of surprise, Plautius led his legions west from Richborough, without delay, along ancient trackways just north of the North Downs, taking care at all times to secure his supply line and the land around it with forts and outposts.[27] Past the ancient tribal capital (at modern Canterbury) with its roundhouses, stockade

---

THE LANDINGS IN 43

Richborough (Rutupiae) has generally been favoured as the site of Aulus Plautius' landings. It was certainly here that the later victory arch was erected to mark the successful conquest of the island (see p. 119). Juvenal (writing in about AD 100–110) jokes about Rutupine oysters, and Lucian writes of 'the wandering wave of Ocean and the storms of the Rutupine shore'. At Richborough, a double line of Claudian-period ditches nearly 2,500 ft (c. 760 m) long has been discovered. This may have been part of a large defended encampment that possibly enclosed 140 acres, enough land to house Plautius' invasion force.

In past centuries, historians have suggested other landings at Dover and Hythe/Lympne, and recently there have been strong arguments in favour of a major landing in the Chichester region of Sussex. An early legionary helmet was dredged from Bosham harbour; early military metalwork has been found at Chichester; and there was an early Roman supply depot at the later site of Fishbourne Palace. It has been argued that the Romans believed they would receive a friendly reception from the Atrebates, who lived in this area, because this was Verica's territory. However, since Verica had been expelled by the Catuvellauni/Trinovantes, this region could equally well have been hostile to them.

It is likely that Chichester was a convenient springboard to move westwards, but a Roman presence here could have been established subsequently, after Colchester was taken. Although the later road, Stane Street, ran from Chichester to London, it was not the most efficient route to get to Colchester at the time of the invasion.[28]

and sacred alder grove, and through the fecund countryside of early May, the trees in blossom and the first lush green of crops beginning to appear in patchwork fields, the army marched in search of battle. Dio tells us that two skirmishes saw off first Caratacus, then Togodumnus, as the men of the Catuvellauni struggled to come together in one united force.

Reports that the Romans had arrived were spreading rapidly throughout the island. To those tribes threatened by the expansionist ambitions of the Catuvellauni, this was welcome news indeed. Representatives began appearing in the Roman camp with offers of alliance. It might well have been at this time that the king of the Dobunni to the west threw in his lot with the Romans;[29] it was becoming apparent that the territory of the Catuvellauni was fast becoming surrounded. Although the ancient sources are silent on the subject, preferring to present events as military victories, it would appear that months (if not years) of steady diplomatic negotiations between Rome and key tribal leaders were paying off.

At last, at a river thought by many to be the Medway, the splintered forces of the Catuvellauni came together, and here they made their stand.[30] Dio's account, though in some places controversial, is vivid:

> The barbarians thought the Romans would be unable to cross the river without a bridge, so camped somewhat carelessly on the farther bank. But [Plautius] sent across his Germans [Keltoi], who could swim easily in armour even in the fastest flowing currents. They attacked the enemy without warning, but rather than firing at the men they inflicted injuries on the horses that drew their chariots; and in the confusion which followed not even the enemy horsemen managed to save themselves. Next, Plautius sent across Flavius Vespasian (who later became emperor) along with his second-in-command, his brother Sabinus. Somehow they crossed the river, too, and killed many of the barbarians, who were not expecting them. However, those who survived did not try to escape, but joined battle again the next day. The conflict was indecisive until Gnaeus Hosidius Geta, running the risk of being captured, defeated them so conclusively that he was awarded the *ornamenta triumphalia*, even though he had not been consul.[31]

This battle was clearly a major engagement, involving specialist troops and unconventional tactics, and (unusually for the period) stretching over more than one day. That the Romans' eventual victory hung in the balance, turning on the fierce and determined fighting of Geta's men, suggests a hard-contested bloody struggle.[32] We have no casualty figures for either side.

Beaten but unbowed, the Catuvellauni retreated north at low tide across the sand-bars of the Thames:

> ...at a point near where it empties into the ocean and at flood-tide forms a lake. This they easily crossed because they knew where the firm ground and the easy passages in this region were to be found; but the Romans in attempting to follow them were not so successful.

However, Plautius had intelligence of a bridge some miles upriver, perhaps close to modern Westminster.[33] Across this he led the bulk of his forces, leaving the same German troops, who had so surprised the Catuvellauni at the previous battle, to swim across the Thames and thus provide the basis of a pincer movement.

In the series of encounters that followed, the Romans were victorious, but, because of a lack of local knowledge (clearly they had been unable to recruit sufficient numbers of the Catuvellauni as informers), they invariably found themselves in difficulties when they tried to follow up their victories with pursuit. But just when momentum was in danger of being lost, the Roman high command received a piece of very welcome news. Togodumnus was dead.

Later official accounts told of how:

> The Britons, so far from yielding, united all the more firmly to avenge his death. Because of this fact and because of the difficulties he had encountered at the Thames, Plautius became afraid, and instead of advancing any farther, proceeded to guard what he had already won, and sent for Claudius. For he had been instructed to do this in case he met with any particularly stubborn resistance.[34]

This is the version of events repeated by Dio. Clearly, however, it masks the truth. For one of the original purposes of the British invasion had been to provide the stooped and scholarly emperor Claudius with a military victory that he could claim as his own. To enhance his standing at Rome, the presence of Claudius himself on the battlefield needed to be seen as indispensable to that victory. In fact the emperor, inexperienced in warfare, had nothing to contribute to the military strategy on the ground.

Plate 1 The emperor Claudius (AD 41–54) assaulting Britannia on a relief from the city of Aphrodisias in Turkey.

Plate 2 *below* The Iron Age chieftain's burial from Welwyn Garden City, *c.* 25 BC, with imported wine amphorae alongside British pottery.

Plate 3 *opposite top* Gold stater inscribed with the name of Commius (around the horse), *c.* 50–20 BC. This is the first British coin to be inscribed with a name. (Diam. 17 mm)

Plate 4 *opposite centre* Gold stater of Tincomarus, found on the Isle of Wight, showing a 'Celtic' horse, *c.* 20 BC–AD 10. (Diam. 20 mm)

Plate 5 *below right* Gold stater of
Tincomarus, showing a 'classical'
style horseman, *c.* 20 BC–AD 10.
(Diam. 17 mm)

Plate 6 Silver *denarius* of Julius Caesar, found in Kent. This is from a very large issue struck at Rome for Caesar in 49–48 BC. (Diam. 18 mm)

Plate 7 Gold stater of Cunobelin, *c.* AD 10–40, showing an ear of corn (emmer wheat or barley) and naming the mint as Camulodunum. (Diam. 18 mm)

Plate 8 Gold stater of Verica, *c.* AD 10–42, showing a vine leaf, found on the Isle of Wight. (Diam. 19 mm)

Plate 9 *opposite* Bronze head of Augustus (27 BC–AD 14) found buried outside a Kushite temple at Meroe in Sudan.

Plate 10 *top* The Bredgar hoard
of thirty-seven gold *aurei* buried
near Sittingbourne, Kent.
The latest coins date to AD 41–2.

Plate 11 *above* Gold *aureus*
of Claudius, showing the
triumphal arch celebrating the
conquest of Britain, struck in
Rome, AD 46–47. (Diam. 19 mm)

Claudius' journey to Britannia was pure propaganda. The biographer Suetonius had access to the imperial records. Tellingly and pithily he writes: 'Claudius undertook but one campaign, and it was of no great significance.'[35] The historian Josephus is more brutal still. The invasion, he tells us, was none of Claudius' work:

> It was Vespasian who acquired Britannia for the empire through armed struggle (until then it had been unknown); thus he enabled Nero's father, Claudius, to be awarded a triumph which had cost him no sweat of his own.[36]

Indeed, the real campaigning was being undertaken by Aulus Plautius and his generals. Following the death of Togodumnus, they must have been sufficiently confident of victory to authorize the imperial visit. Under no circumstances would they have sanctioned it if there had been any danger of its being anything but a success. True, there must have been pockets of resistance still to mop up, but they must have calculated that, in the time available and with the resources they had at hand, they could be certain of achieving sufficient security in the regions they had targeted to enable the visit to pass off without incident.

So, Claudius made his slow journey north, first by boat from Ostia to Massilia (Marseilles), then up the River Rhone and by land to Gesoriacum (Boulogne) for the Channel crossing. He was accompanied by his doctors, the future emperor Galba, and many potential rivals whom he dared not leave to meddle in Rome while he was absent. (Later all these rivals were removed by Claudius' regime. Behind his buffoonish façade, the emperor was ruthless.)[37]

Meanwhile, Plautius and his men were busy not only seeking out and destroying those Catuvellaunian tribesmen who were still offering resistance, but, just as importantly, receiving delegations and offers of friendship from more compliant factions of the Catuvellauni, as well as from other tribes in the south and east of Britain. One man, however, they could not find. As their grip on the region became tighter, they soon realized that Caratacus himself had eluded them. He had fled west to the hills of the Cornovii and the mountains of the Ordovices, where, for the next eight years, he would fight a rearguard action, until he too was taken (see below, pp. 62 and 66).[38]

Claudius' arrival on British soil in August AD 43 must have been choreographed with care to afford him the greatest honour. Whether he too landed at Rutupiae (Richborough) or sailed up the Thames to the cross-ing that Plautius had used some months before, we do not know. From the north bank of the Thames he possibly processed both with legionaries from the original invasion force and with others he had brought with him, including the Praetorian Guard, some 30 miles north to the future site of a fort and settlement which would be named in his honour, Caesaromagus (Chelmsford).[39]

However, this was not Claudius' ultimate goal. From Caesaromagus the great procession made its way along an ancient road that cut across the flat lands, golden now with ripening wheat, towards the settlement which, before it had become the seat of the all-powerful Cunobelin, had been the capital of the people of the Trinovantes: Camulodunum (Colchester). This great trading centre was the place now chosen to be the heart of Rome's government in Britannia.

It may be that Claudius' arrival was marked by a theatrical staging of the capture of the city. Certainly, such an event was later presented on the Campus Martius in Rome, when clad in his purple campaign cloak

5 A richly bedecked merchantman docked in Portus (the harbour of Rome), shown on a relief of the late first to early second centuries AD in the Museo Turlonia, Rome.

Claudius presided over 'the realistic storm and sack of a town with a tableau of the British kings' surrender'.[40] In the best tradition of Roman propaganda, this would certainly be enough to account for Dio's claim that he 'captured Camulodunum, the city of Cunobelin'.

It was in Camulodunum that the climax of Claudius' visit took place: the surrender of the British kings. Just who was present here we do not know. If Adminius and the aged Verica were still alive, they may have been included in the ceremony. Perhaps Togidubnus, king of the Regini, was present with the kings of the Dobunni, and the Iceni,[41] too. It is even possible that Cartimandua, queen of the Brigantes, was present. We do not know what each warrior king was thinking as he came before the squinting white-haired emperor with his running nose, his weak knees and his constant twitch. Perhaps they believed they were cementing an alliance; in reality they were surrendering their freedom.

It was the apogee of Claudius' military life, an event that he could never have imagined in his wildest dreams. As a child and a young adult he had been bullied by his tutor and disparaged by his family, the butt of constant jokes and insults,[42] but he had now surpassed even the great Gaius Julius Caesar. He had crossed the Ocean and conquered Britannia. In their zeal to gild the lily, the army had even hailed him more than once as *imperator*. (Curiously it was this that, for Dio, was a step too far. It was, he said, 'contrary to precedent; for no man may receive this title more than once for one and the same war'.)[43]

✧ ✧ ✧

Claudius did not stay long in the island. Sixteen days were all that were required. He had, after all, made his point, and now, leaving Plautius with instructions to 'subdue the rest' of Britannia,[44] he hurried back to Rome to ram it home. Dio records that the Senate, already apprised of his success, bestowed on him:

> ...the title of Britannicus and gave him permission to hold a triumph. They also voted the inauguration of an annual festival of celebration and two triumphal arches, one in Rome, the other in Gaul, from where he had set sail on his crossing to Britain. They awarded his son the same title – in fact, he was commonly referred to as Britannicus.[45]

Suetonius, drawing on the imperial archives and perhaps on distant memories of eye-witnesses, writes that Claudius' triumph:

> ...was an extravagant spectacle. He summoned not only his provincial governors but even some exiles to Rome to see it. Among the spoils of war was the naval crown (which he nailed onto the Palace gable next to the civic crown) to represent the crossing and purported dominion of Ocean. Messalina, his wife, followed the chariot in a state carriage; behind her marched those who had won triumphal regalia on the same campaign. All were on foot and wore purple-bordered togas except Marcus Crassus Frugi, who rode a richly bedecked horse and wore a palm-embroidered tunic, because this was the second time he had won this honour.[46]

Later, Suetonius tells us how among Claudius' favourite freedmen was:

> Posides the eunuch. At his British triumph he even awarded him the *hasta pura* [the headless spear], along with soldiers who had actually fought in battle.[47]

From other authors, stranger details of Claudius' British triumph leach through. One tells how 'he did everything according to tradition, even ascending the steps of the Capitol on his knees, supported by his sons-in-law on either side'.[48] Another describes how Claudius sailed from Ravenna 'into the Adriatic, in what was more like a floating palace than a ship, when he celebrated his triumph over Britain'.[49]

It all underlines what a hugely significant event the invasion had been (or was portrayed to have been) for the psyche of Rome. For years, it could be milked for all it was worth. After all, in Seneca's words:

> He gave the order for the Britons beyond the shores of
> The familiar sea
> And the Brigantes with their shields of blue
> To submit their necks to Roman chains
> And Ocean itself to tremble
> Under the new governance of Rome.[50]

Claudius was not alone in receiving honours. Back in Rome from his tour of duty (AD 47), Aulus Plautius was awarded an *ovatio*, high honour indeed, for his successful conduct of the campaign. And so he has passed into history. Of another general, who may have played an equally important role, we now know next to nothing. Indeed, we might never have even heard of him had it not been for a throwaway remark by a later historian. In the work of the fourth-century Eutropius we find that:

Claudius brought war to Britannia, where no Roman since C. Caesar had set foot, and after it had been defeated by Cn. Sentius and A. Plautius, distinguished and aristocratic men, he celebrated a magnificent triumph.[51]

Who this Cnaius Sentius was, we simply do not know. Perhaps he is the Cn Sentius Saturninus whose triumphal statue at Rome is mentioned in a wax tablet from Pompeii.[52] Perhaps he led the force that came with Claudius; perhaps he was responsible for helping to assimilate the client kingdoms under Roman rule.[53] Whatever his role, our very ignorance of him makes him important. He is a beacon highlighting for us how the memory of men important in their day for shaping Britain can so easily be lost to later generations.

In the years that followed the invasion, further signs of Claudius' victories in Britannia would appear across the empire. Far away to the east an arch was erected in thanksgiving by the citizens of Cyzicus (near Erdek in Turkey). In the elegant city of Aphrodisias (also in modern Turkey), a sculpture would be set up showing the emperor seizing by the hair a female figure, violently pulling back her head, grinding his knee against her thigh, as her tunic falls open to expose her bare right breast, and rides up to reveal her naked legs. She is the personification of Britannia, her first known representation anywhere in art (Plate i).[54]

In Rome itself, emperor Claudius kept the memory of the legacy of his Britannic adventure very much alive. In AD 46/7, he issued coins to celebrate the conquest (Plate ii), while around the same time the imperial mint at Caesarea in Cappadocia (central Turkey) struck a commemorative silver coin.[55] Meanwhile gold crowns poured into Rome, presents for the emperor from the grateful cities of Gaul and Spain, and Antioch.[56] And eight years after he had left the island, Claudius could admire the legend engraved on his new triumphal arch (Fig. 6), dedicated:

...by the Roman Senate and People because he had received the surrender of eleven British Kings, defeated without loss, and for the first time had brought barbarian peoples from beyond the Ocean under Roman rule.[57]

6 Part of the inscription from Claudius' triumphal arch in Rome (AD 51/2), which celebrated his conquest of Britain. The fragment is now in the Capitoline Museum, Rome.

It may be that among these surrendering eleven kings was a ruler from beyond the British mainland. For (writing 300 years after the event) Eutropius tells us that Claudius had 'added to the Roman empire certain islands located in Ocean, which are even more remote than Britannia and are called the Orkneys'.[58]

Given the timing of the inscription on the triumphal arch (AD 51/2), another of the kings may well have been Caratacus. For, having rallied the renegade tribesmen and harried the legions from his fastnesses deep within the mountains of the Ordovices in Wales, Caratacus had eventually met the Roman army in pitched battle, where he was defeated (see p. 66). Fleeing north to the lands of the Brigantes, he had thrown himself on the mercy of their queen, Cartimandua, who had become a client ruler of Rome. She had already nailed her colours to the mast of Rome, and she gave him up to the Romans, a prized prisoner. By now, the name of Caratacus was well known everywhere. He was, after all, at the top of Rome's 'most-wanted' list. So his arrival at Rome in chains was a great coup for Claudius. The historian Tacitus, with typically studied ingenuousness, takes up the story:

> The populace were summoned as if to a grand spectacle: on the parade ground in front of their camp, the Praetorian Guard were drawn up in full uniform. Then there was a procession of [Caratacus'] client kings; next his decorations and torcs and the spoils from his wars with other tribes were shown; soon after were displayed his brothers and his wife and daughter, and finally [Caratacus] himself. The others, in fear, debased themselves by pleading. Not Caratacus. He neither looked downcast nor made any appeal for mercy. Instead, when he came before the tribunal, he spoke as follows:

'If my noble birth and my good fortune had been matched by only moderate prosperity, I should have come to Rome a friend and not a prisoner, and you would have been all too willing to enter into an alliance with a man, whose ancestors were famous, who ruled so many peoples. But now my fate is as degrading to me as it is glorious to you. I had horses and men, weapons and wealth. Is it surprising if I gave them up unwillingly? For if your ambition is to rule the world, does it follow that everyone else should welcome slavery? If I had been captured at once without a fight, neither my fate nor your glory would be famous. Moreover, if you kill me, all will be forgotten. But if you let me live I shall be an everlasting reminder of your mercy!'

At this, the emperor pardoned him, together with his wife and brothers. ...The Senate was later assembled and many effusive speeches were made on the subject of Caratacus' capture, which was, they said, as wonderful as any previous display of captured kings before the Roman people.[59]

Now free, but in a foreign land, the British king is said by Dio to have:

...wandered about Rome after being freed; and when he had seen its size and splendour he exclaimed: 'You already have such countless treasures. How can you covet our meagre huts?'[60]

This scene of Claudius' clemency, the mirror of that great set piece in Camulodunum, is the last time we hear of the emperor's connection with Britannia. Less than three years later (AD 54) he had succumbed to a very messy death.

In Britain, however, his memory lived on. At Camulodunum, the first Roman colony in their new province, the site of the altar once consecrated to Claudius and Rome, a new temple rose tall. It was dedicated to the Divine Claudius. Its statue beamed down on the fast-forming city, where everything the emperor had hoped for seemed to be being fulfilled. For on this foreign soil (so much more satisfactory than crowded Italy) were settled veterans; and even in this distant land men wore the Roman toga.[61]

The smiling statue would not stand for long. Already resentment was brewing among the British tribes, and it would not be long before it erupted in rebellion.

3
REVOLT

It was a tough decision, one of the hardest calls that he had ever had to make. He was leaving London. And he knew the consequences. They had all heard what had happened up in Camulodunum. They had heard how the barbarians, with that woman at their head, had swept through the streets like a tidal wave of fury, torching buildings, smashing statues, slashing, hacking, stabbing all that they could find until the lanes and alleyways were splashed and syrupy with blood.

And then the atrocities. The playing with the captives as a cat plays with a bird. Taunting them and torturing. Young women, screaming, hunted down, stripped naked, hung from trees, their breasts lopped off and sewn into their mouths, the girls themselves skewered on sharp stakes and left to die an agonizing death. And meanwhile the barbarians were feasting in their blood-drenched groves, their shrines to Victory, glutting on the flesh of cattle seized in brutal raids as sparks danced and smoke billowed from the blackened carcasses and skeletons of temples and basilicas and homes.

The people of London, the traders and the bankers, all had begged him to protect them. And he would have done. If only he could have been sure of victory. But he and his generals had assessed the situation and in all honesty they did not see how London could be saved. So this morning Suetonius Paullinus had gathered up as many of the Londoners as were prepared to leave, turned round his troops and led them north. It would be a grim march, to be sure. There was not one man who would not be thinking of the fate of those they left behind. But it had been the right decision. Paullinus was sure of that. In war you sometimes had to make hard sacrifices, and he was determined that, when he did join battle with that woman, he would destroy her.

✧   ✧   ✧

I F anyone thought that Claudius' great tribal durbar at Camulodunum, with its elaborate submission of the now vassal kings, meant that Rome's military mission in Britain was accomplished, they were sadly mistaken. In only a few years' time, the stage-managed triumphalism of the event would ring very hollow indeed.

No sooner had Claudius left Britain than the work of conquest began in earnest. As the slow process of building the infrastructure of a province in the southeast carried on apace, the legions fanned out, establishing fortresses in key strategic sites.[1] To the southwest, as Vespasian led the Second Legion to Exeter, probably besieging hillforts such as Maiden Castle and Hod Hill, 'he fought the enemy thirty times. He conquered two very powerful tribes and captured over twenty towns as well as the Isle of Wight'.[2]

Meanwhile, the Fourteenth Legion marched up the track which would later become Watling Street to Leicester and the heart of the Midlands, while the Ninth moved north along the future course of Ermine Street to Lincolnshire. In time a new road was constructed linking Exeter and Lincoln, the Fosse Way, which would in turn form the backbone of the frontier zone of Britain in the late AD 40s and throughout the 50s.[3]

At the same time, under the governorship of Ostorius Scapula (who replaced Aulus Plautius in AD 47), the Twentieth Legion marched west from its old quarters at Camulodunum towards the modern site of Gloucester, where it planted a new fort at Kingsholm. Back in Camulodunum, a *colonia* was founded, a model city to house veterans, a beacon to the native Britons to show them how civilized people lived.[4] Administered by a

---

BESIEGING HILLFORTS

Iron Age hillforts are found across southern England. They were not all permanently occupied, but could provide defence for agricultural settlements and animals, as well as being storage areas. As a result of his famous excavation at Maiden Castle in Dorset, Sir Mortimer Wheeler claimed that the hillfort had been stormed by the Romans – one British skeleton was found with a catapult bolt embedded in its spine. At Hod Hill to the north a volley of catapult fire against the major round house seems to have led to a surrender of the hillfort without any further fighting. The Romans then built an auxiliary fort in the corner of the site. Both sites certainly show the efficacy of Roman artillery against British defences.[5]

hundred magistrates, from whose number two senior and two junior magistrates (*duoviri iuridicundo* and *aediles*) were elected annually, Camulodunum's model of government was to be that of Rome itself. Only Roman citizens could own property, while around the city the old tribal land of the Trinovantes was divided up and parcelled out to Roman veterans. Within the circuit of the now dismantled walls, the roads and many of the Roman military buildings were remodelled for civilian needs, and the old Principia, the headquarters complex of the Twentieth Legion, seems to have been converted into the new forum and basilica. To the east, in what had been the legionary annexe, a theatre, the first in Britain, was built. But it was another construction sited near here a few years later which would help to spark the tinder box of British revolt: the temple of the Divine Claudius. Renaming ancient Camulodunum Colonia Victricensis ('City of Victory') was one thing; getting the defeated inhabitants to pay for the worship of their conqueror would be quite another.[6]

If Camulodunum was the provincial capital, the base of the governor, Ostorius Scapula,[7] other towns built squarely on the Roman model were soon beginning to appear. London, for example, freshly founded on the Thames, was fast becoming the commercial centre of the province, the hub of financial life and trade.[8] Other towns took shape at Canterbury, and at Silchester and Winchester, both sited in the territory of a favoured client king, a British ruler with a very Roman name: Tiberius Claudius Togidubnus.

Togidubnus, it has been suggested, was a relative of Verica, king of the Atrebates, who years before had fled to Rome to seek the emperor's support. Now a trusted vassal and effective ruler over his compliant tribe, the Regini, Togidubnus was rewarded lavishly by his new Roman overlords. Tacitus tells us that certain other territories, probably those of the Belgae and the Atrebates, were added to Togidubnus' kingdom.[9] He would later be handsomely rewarded for his unswerving loyalty (see p. 101).

Togidubnus was not alone. Other client rulers enjoyed their own rewards. In the north, Cartimandua, queen of the Brigantes, would be well recompensed for her show of loyalty in betraying Caratacus, the freedom-fighter, to the Roman army, while in East Anglia, the king of the Iceni, true to the allegiance he had sworn to Claudius, ruled his people with devotion for the good of Rome.

Elsewhere, however, the situation was far less rosy. When Caratacus had fled to Wales he had chosen his territory well. Even when he had himself been taken, the tribes of the Welsh mountains, the Ordovices and Silures, still held out with stubborn spirited resistance against the Roman legions. Ever since he had inherited the governorship, Ostorius Scapula had been faced with what had seemed to be a chaotic situation. Now, fuelled by his success in capturing Caratacus, Scapula, an ex-consul and a mountain-man himself, turned his wrath against these rugged tribesmen and vowed to annihilate them.[10] It was a vow that did him no good. When they heard of it, the men of the Silures did not hold back. From their mountain fastnesses, these swarthy warriors with their curly hair launched wave upon wave of attacks against the Roman army. In one, a legionary commander died; with him eight centurions and a large number of men. Another raid launched by the Silures on a group of soldiers foraging would have seen a total massacre had not Scapula himself called out the legion to defend his harried men.

From the mountains and the marshes, the Silures kept up their resistance, stealing out on missions to conduct guerrilla war. Soon the other local tribes were joining them: news had quickly spread that two Roman auxiliary commanders had allowed their men to plunder indiscriminately, taking captives, seizing booty, behaving in an arrogant, high-handed way. For Scapula, it spelled the end. Campaigning in the wet and mountainous terrain of Wales had been dispiriting enough. Now that there was all-out war he could go on no longer. 'Worn out by the worry of his responsibilities, he died, and the enemy rejoiced.'[11]

However, the Silures did not rejoice for long. There were many more governors where Ostorius had come from, and among them men who would not be put off by the cold and rain of Wales. Like his two predecessors, the next governor to come to Britain had been a tough commander. Now in his late fifties, Aulus Didius Gallus had risen through the political ranks, gaining valuable experience of administration and diplomacy.[12] He also played an important role as curator of Rome's water supply (*curator aquarum*), when he supervised the construction of two major aqueducts.[13] By AD 45, Didius may already have commanded the campaign that annexed Thrace, and put a new pro-Roman ruler on the throne in the Crimea. In his early days of campaigning, before he had been consul and governor of Asia (*c.* AD 49–51), it may be that he had his eye on Britain.

However, by the time that Didius was appointed to the post of Britain's governor (AD 52), he had decided he no longer wanted it.[14] Why would he? He had enjoyed a glittering career, and by now the island's reputation was hardly alluring. The strain of the post had even killed his predecessor. Still, he was professional. He vowed to do what he could, and in the end, despite the fact that the Silures took advantage of his inexperience of his new province to overwhelm a Roman legion, Didius did manage to defeat them.

'Weighed down by old age and already rich in honours'[15] as he was, Didius must have longed for a life of peace in Rome or Ephesus, but it was not to be. Soon civil strife broke out within an allied tribe, the Brigantes, the dramatic result of the break-up of the marriage of Queen Cartimandua and Venutius, her husband. Resigned to having to intervene for the sake of stability, Didius came down on Cartimandua's side and sent in his auxiliaries. Peace and order were restored, but for many Romans this was not enough.[16] They wanted conquest, and Didius' successor seemed just the man to give it to them.

Quintus Veranius, forty-five years old, with his connections to the imperial family and a fine military pedigree,[17] was nothing if not confident. He had every reason to be. His career until now had been a triumph. After the usual training in junior office, Veranius had found himself Tribune of the Plebs in AD 37, and, as such, after the assassination of Caligula (AD 41), was sent by the Senate to request that the cowering Claudius should accept the role of emperor. Two years later, while Claudius and his elephants were lumbering north to Britain, to the cheers of the loyal assembly at Camulodunum, Veranius went east to take up his position as the governor of the new province of Lycia (southwestern Turkey). If this were not enough, while there he found time to annex another province, Pamphylia. For five years, he stayed in the east, quashing any opposition, laying down roads, initiating building programmes, consolidating his new territory, reforming the old constitution, working tirelessly to bring the area into the Roman sphere. His reward was not only the *ornamenta triumphalia*, and the dedication to him of a book on military strategy,[18] but the consulship of AD 49, and the honour of presiding over games given by Nero, the new emperor, in AD 57.

His was a rising star indeed, and when Veranius arrived in Britain the same year, there must have been many who had high hopes of him. What were the Welsh mountains, after all, compared to the wild peaks of Lycia? What were the shoals of British politics to a man who had so successfully navigated the hidden reefs of Nero's Rome? Veranius responded to his new task with energy and gusto. Before long he was in Wales, spiritedly ravaging the land of the Silures. But then he died (AD 58). How, we do not know. With his last words he expressed his frustration. If he had only lived for two more years, he gasped, he could have brought the whole of Britain under Rome's control.[19] Veranius had always been a confident man; in two years, had he lived, even he might have found his confidence somewhat shaken.

✧ ✧ ✧

Despite troubles in the west, in AD 58, Rome had good reason to be optimistic about her now fifteen-year-old province. For, while the army was conducting its funeral obsequies in honour of Veranius, much of the occupied territories of Britain were experiencing a fair degree of stability. The 'lowland zone', southeast of that line between Exeter and Lincoln which was traced by the Fosse Way, had been effectively subdued. From Exeter, the legionary fortress of the Second Legion, now fully furnished with a bath-house (the oldest on the island), Devon and Cornwall too were controlled by detachments, based in forts at Nanstallon, Restormel and Calstock.[20] North of these, the Twentieth Legion was pushing the frontier forward, moving into a new fort at Usk in South Wales. At the same time other forts at Clyro, Kinvaston and Wall, built during the Welsh campaigns, remained manned and vigilant. In the Midlands, the Fourteenth Legion may by now have relocated to Wroxeter from their previous base at Leicester,[21] while further north around the frontier country of the River Trent the Ninth kept a watchful eye on the now-pacified Brigantes (see p. 93) from their forts at Newton-on-Trent, Longthorpe and Great Casterton.

There was more going on than purely military activity. With the increasing Romanization of the island, a two-way trade was picking up. Already, only six years after the invasion (AD 49), Britain's mineral reserves, initially controlled by the army and subsequently farmed out to mining agents, were being exploited.[22] If exports of such commodities were rising, imports of goods such as olive oil and wine, essential for the well-being and contentment of both military and Romanized civilians, were increasing significantly.

Meanwhile, building work was going on apace in urban centres such as Canterbury, Verulamium and London. But it was at Camulodunum, the seat of the governor and the provincial capital, that the grandest scheme of all was hatched. For in AD 54, in the months after the emperor's death, planning got under way for the construction of a massive temple to the newly Divine Claudius. Standing close on 60 ft (20 m) high, its pediment supported on eight towering columns, this was the first truly monumental Roman building erected on British soil. Associated with it was another structure, a triumphal arch, which, like a glittering statue of Victory nearby, proudly proclaimed not only Rome's domination but the key role which Camulodunum had played in Britain's submission.[23]

Yet any victory comes at a price, and, for some of the defeated, that price was high. To the people of Camulodunum, somewhat more grue-some reminders of the might of Rome may well have been on display. It seems that people passing the triumphal arch were greeted by a row of severed heads skewered onto stakes, a brutal testament of Rome's domin-ion. These, we may assume, were the remains of Britons who had most flagrantly opposed their new masters. Even among some of those who seemed to submit to Roman rule, passions were beginning to run high.[24]

Rome's record when it came to dealing sensitively with peoples it had conquered was poor. In parts of Britain it was disastrous. At the new *colonia* of Camulodumum, tribal land, which had for generations belonged to the Trinovantes, was arbitrarily confiscated and divided up between the new settlers, veterans of the Roman army. To add insult to injury, it seems the ancient religious centre at Gosbecks was now closed off to worship-pers. The contemporary historian Tacitus, as ever so clear-sighted, paints a bleak picture:

> The Trinovantes felt a bitter hatred for the veterans, since the new colonists at Camulodunum had driven them out of their homes and thrown them off their land, calling them prisoners and slaves. The soldiers encouraged the veterans' illegal behaviour, since they shared their way of life and hoped for similar license themselves.[25]

Those who had been displaced seem to have been relocated at a new town, Caesaromagus (Chelmsford), an enigmatic site, scene of a desultory building programme, on the road from London to Camulodunum. It also housed a Roman garrison.

Even those tribal leaders who appeared to be thriving under Roman rule had reasons to fret. In an apparent attempt to integrate them into the wider fold of empire, many had been 'invited' to join a provincial council of British elders, one of whose duties was to oversee the imperial cult. With the inauguration of the building programme associated with the new temple of the Divine Claudius at Camulodunum, the elders got their first taste of exactly what membership of the council would involve. For the council was expected to meet all the costs. Tacitus is once more alive to the implications:

> The temple dedicated to the Divine Claudius was seen as a bastion of perpetual Roman rule, while those men chosen to be its priests saw their entire wealth disappear in the pretext of religion.[26]

Faced with growing debts, the Britons found that there was no shortage of rich Romans only too happy to offer them loans. Claudius himself had lent lavish sums of money; now, too, the fabulously wealthy philosopher and adviser to Nero, Seneca, was delighted for the Britons to borrow from him. It seems the Britons may not have been entirely familiar with the concepts of interest and repayment, and they may not have fully understood quite what they were agreeing to. Certainly, their reaction when the debts were called in was extreme.

Events conspired. One of the tribal chiefs who had taken out considerable loans appears to have been the king of the Iceni. Like Togidubnus and the leaders of the Trinovantes, the Iceni had been content to become a client people of Rome, one of those tribes perhaps who had offered their allegiance to Claudius at the great tribal durbar in Camulodunum in AD 43. Under the agreement that had been made then, the two sides would help one another: the Iceni would offer no resistance to Rome; Rome would support the Iceni.

Within five years, however, cracks had appeared. Undertaking a campaign towards the Rivers Trent and Severn (AD 47–48), and fearing insurrection in the territories to his rear, the then governor, Ostorius Scapula (see pp. 65–67), ordered many of the British tribes to surrender their weapons. Among them were the Iceni. Not unsurprisingly, since they had been conspicuous in forming an alliance with Rome, the Iceni were outraged. They rebelled. Despite performing what even the Roman Tacitus describes as 'many valiant deeds', the Iceni were defeated in fierce fighting, and for a while the region settled down.[27]

For the next twelve years, Prasutagus, perhaps put in place as king of the Iceni by the Romans after the revolt, seems to have ruled in relative peace. With his ever-growing loans, he could afford to buy the best. At what may be the royal enclosure at Gallow's Hill near Thetford, where three buildings are encircled by a ring of ditches and palisades, fine terra nigra ware from Italy and Gaulish Samian pottery have been discovered next to British brooches and Icenian coins, evidence perhaps of the new spending power of Prasutagus, or of his wife Boudica (whose name meant 'Victory'), or of their daughters.[28]

But then things changed dramatically. Prasutagus died (AD 60), and how the Romans then behaved almost lost them their province. Under the terms of Prasutagus' will, half of his kingdom was bequeathed to Nero, emperor of Rome. For Nero's finance officer in Britain, the procurator, Decianus Catus, this was not enough. He wanted all of it. Under pressure, perhaps, from above, Catus led those troops over whom he personally had control across the border into the land of the Iceni and there he began to strip the kingdom of its assets.

It was part of a pattern being seen across the empire. Nero needed money, and his biographer Suetonius tells us that one of his many sources were the newly dead:

> He seized the estates of those ingrates who had not made him a chief beneficiary; and fined the lawyers who had written or dictated the wills...He never appointed a magistrate without adding: 'You know my needs' and 'Let's make sure that that no one is left with anything'.[29]

In Prasutagus' case there may also have been the question of the unpaid loans he had received from Nero's predecessor, Claudius. This must have seemed as good a time as any to call them in. Nero's tutor Seneca agreed. At the same time that Catus was claiming Prasutagus' legacy and retrieving the money lent to the Iceni, Seneca's agents were touring Britain, calling in his loans. They totalled 40,000,000 sesterces[30] – on their own enough to bankrupt the whole island.

Nero's views on client kingdoms were, anyway, less than positive.[31] During his reign he got rid of two, in Pontus and in the Alps. Now, the financial crisis, which the calling in of British credit would undoubtedly precipitate, would furnish the ideal circumstances for winding up the system of client kingships and replacing them with tax-paying *civitates* (singular *civitas*) under Rome's direct command. If this was, indeed, Nero's plan, he had severely misjudged the Britons.

He was not alone. The Romans had long treated the British tribesfolk with arrogant disdain, but when Catus swaggered into the land of the Iceni with his soldiers and centurions, Tacitus records the staggering inhumanity that he unleashed on Rome's so-called allies:

Prasutagus' kingdom was looted by centurions, his palace by slaves, as if they had been captured in war. First his wife, Boudica, was whipped, and his daughters raped; all the leading men of the Iceni were stripped of their ancestral possessions, as if the whole kingdom had been bequeathed to Rome, and the king's family were treated like slaves.

For the Iceni, this was the end: 'incensed by this outrageous behaviour and their fear of even worse to come, when they became part of the province, they took up arms'.[32]

Years of simmering repression had exploded into rebellion. And from the lands of the Iceni the insurrection spread:

The Trinovantes, together with others who had not yet been crushed by servitude, made a pact with secret oaths to win back their liberty and also rose in rebellion.[33]

No other tribes are named, but it is possible that at least some of the Catuvellauni still harboured hatred of the Romans for the way in which Caratacus had been humiliated, and in the west, the Durotriges too may still have borne a grudge.[34] About this, the sources are silent, but they all agree on one thing: that the timing of the uprising could not have been better planned. For, even as the British tribes were setting out on their trail of terror against the towns of the southeast, the bulk of the Roman army was far off to the west, on the very coast of Wales. Under their new governor, Suetonius Paullinus, they were on campaign against the Druids.[35]

Paullinus had been in place as governor for less than two years. Born around AD 11, he was now around fifty years old, and had probably been chosen for the post because of his military experience in the African mountains of Mauretania. Here, he had enjoyed considerable success, quashing a revolt and 'overrunning the country as far as Mount Atlas'.[36] He was no mere brute, however. Some of his personal scientific observations found their way into Pliny the Elder's Natural History, where we find descriptions of forests filled with elephants and snakes:

...beyond to the River Ger, through deserts of black dust, with scattered rocks sticking up which looked as if they had been burnt – a place which was uninhabitable because of the heat, though [Paullinus] experienced it in winter.

We read, too, that Paullinus was:

> ...the first Roman commander to push across the Atlas Mountains and a little way beyond. He gives the same estimate of their height as others do, but he adds that the lower slopes are covered in dense forests of tall trees of an unknown species with tall trunks distinguished for their lustre and their lack of knots. The leaves resemble those of the cypress except for their heavy scent, and are covered with delicate down, from which, with skill, clothes can be woven like those made from the silkworm. The top of the mountains are covered with deep snow, even in summer.[37]

Clearly, he was the right man for Wales, where Veranius' untimely death had left unfinished business (see p. 69). Moreover, Tacitus notes, Paullinus was driven by ambition to emulate the recent glorious successes in Armenia of his colleague Gnaeus Domitius Corbulo, his:

> rival both in military expertise and in reputation among the people, which lets no one go unchallenged. His ambition was to defeat the enemy and so equal Corbulo's glory in recovering Armenia.[38]

He hoped the situation he would find in Britain would give him every opportunity to do so.

Immediately he made for Wales, and soon he was engaged in fierce fighting with the Silures and the Ordovices, battling his way past the Black Mountains and the Brecon Beacons through to Snowdonia until he reached the northwest coast and the Menai Straits, which separate the mainland from the island of Anglesey. This was the headquarters of the resistance movement.[39] Many of the Britons, fleeing before Paullinus' advance, had flocked here for safety in the grim knowledge that it was on these shores that they would have to make their final stand. Across the Menai Straits, Paullinus made his preparations.

> He built flat-bottomed boats to cope with the shallows and the shifting sands. In them crossed the infantry; the cavalry followed by wading the channel or swimming beside their horses where the water was deeper.

On the island, too, they had been getting ready, steeling themselves for the coming battle, readying themselves to engage in both actual and psychological warfare:

On the shore stood the enemy lines, bristling with weapons and with warriors, while women ran among them, dressed in black robes like Furies, hair uncombed and with torches in their hands; around them the Druids stretched up their hands to heaven and uttered terrible curses, a strange spectacle, which struck terror into our soldiers' hearts so that they stood, as if paralysed, an easy target; but then, roused by their general's orders, and by mutual encouragement not to cower before a regiment of frenzied women, they carried the standards forward, struck any whom they met and enveloped the enemy in the fire of their own torches.

In the eerie wake of battle, Paullinus and his men set up a garrison and then explored the island. What they found was, to their Roman minds, horrific. For they discovered the sacred groves of Anglesey:

...which had been devoted to their savage superstitious rites; for their religion dictated that they should drench their altars with the blood of prisoners and consult their gods through human entrails.[40]

The groves were now systematically destroyed. But it was now, in the dazed aftermath of victory, that grim news came from the east. In his rush to push back the boundaries of empire, Paullinus had committed a cardinal error. He had not taken sufficient care to secure his rear. What he had thought was a settled peaceful province had erupted into rebellion.[41] And what was more, the revolt was being led by a woman.

According to the ancient sources,[42] it was Prasutagus' widow, Boudica, still smarting from the treatment she had suffered at the Romans' hands (see above), who led her people in rebellion. The historian Dio (noting in passing that she was 'unusually intelligent for a woman') describes her in these terms:

She was very tall and stern; her look was penetrating; her voice harsh; a mass of auburn hair fell to her hips and around her neck was a heavy golden torc [Plate 12]; she wore a patterned cloak with a thick cape over it fastened with a brooch.[43]

He goes on to tell how, having collected an army about 120,000 strong (almost certainly an exaggeration), she mounted a high man-made earthen platform and, spear in hand, harangued her people.

If she did indeed make such a speech, there was no written record of it, but Dio imagines the sort of thing she might have said. He has her speak of freedom and of slavery, of how, seduced by Roman blandishments and tricked by empty promises, the Britons had allowed themselves to give up ancient rights and to submit themselves to taxes, willingly paying the price for their own slavery. 'How much better,' he has her say, 'to have died by the sword than live and be taxed for it! But why do I speak of death? Not even that is free with them; you know what we pay even for our dead.'[44]

With the widow's words still ringing in their ears, the Britons under Boudica swept south. Their mission: to eliminate the occupying Romans, both military and civilian, and to wipe out any trace of them from Britain. Their first target: the city which more than any symbolized Rome's rule, the provincial capital, Camulodunum.

At Camulodunum itself, as reports filtered through of the approaching British forces, panic soon set in. In the increasingly terrified city, says Tacitus, people began to see omens everywhere:

> For no apparent reason, the statue of Victory fell down and turned its back as if it were fleeing from the enemy. Frenzied women kept on chanting of coming disaster; strange groans were said to have been heard in the Senate-house; the theatre rang with wailing; while in the Thames estuary the ghostly spectre of a colony in ruins had been seen. Even Ocean took on the appearance of blood, and when the tide went out the shapes of human corpses were left on the shore, which filled the Britons with hope and the veterans with fear.[45]

They had every reason to be afraid. Camulodunum was unprotected. Its walls had been dismantled and, in the growing confusion, no one thought to dig the ditches or to build the ramparts that might protect them. In desperation, the veterans, knowing that Paullinus and his army were weeks away in Wales, despatched an urgent message to London begging for help from the procurator Decianus Catus. Catus replied by sending a mere 200 men, inadequately armed.

Almost before they knew it, Camulodunum was surrounded. Nothing had been done to evacuate the city. Along with the few fighting men, women, children and the elderly were trapped. Those who could do so fled for safety to the one building they might hope to secure: the temple of the Divine Claudius, the very symbol of Roman oppression that the Britons were intent on destroying. Here they held out for two days, listening no

KEY
◇ Town
▪ Legionary fortress
• Vexillation fortress
■ Auxiliary fort
⊚ Hillfort
⚔ Battle
O Native settlement

BRIGANTES

ANGLESEY (MONA)
(60)

DECEANGLI
ORDOVICES
Trent Vale? ■

Templeborough ■
Newton-on-Trent •

Legio IX in
this area

Lincoln ■

N

Wroxeter
Mancetter Great
? Casterton
(60)
The Lunt ■

R. Trent

ICENI

Caistor ◇
Longthorpe • (Venta)
Gallows Hill O
■ Ixworth
Coddenham ■
• Gt Chesterford

CATUVELLAUNI

R. Severn

Watling St.

Ermine Street

Gloucester
Usk •

Fosse Way

Towcester ⚔ ?
(60)
St Albans
(Verulamium) ◇
■
Dorchester-
on-Thames

Chelmsford ⚔

Colchester
(Camulodunum)

TRINOVANTES

London

R. Thames

DUMNONII

South Cadbury
⊚ ⚔ (60/1?)
Exeter •
■ Waddon Hill

Winchester
◇

TOGIDUBNUS'
KINGDOM

■ Nanstallon

Legio II
Augusta
in this area

DUROTRIGES

200 km

200 miles

GAUL

7 Map of Britain at the time of the Boudican revolt, showing the major towns,
forts and battlefields.

doubt to the hideous sounds outside as the *colonia*, its buildings and its
luckless people were ruthlessly destroyed. At last, even the temple fell,
taken by the Britons by storm. The fate of those inside is unimaginable.[46]

Now, too late for the unfortunate population of Camulodunum, the
Roman army was at last ready to respond. From their base, probably at
Longthorpe near Peterborough,[47] a detachment of perhaps 2,000 men
from the Ninth Legion, together with some auxiliary infantry and cavalry,
marched south under their commander Petilius Cerealis. It was too little
and too late. When they met the Britons in battle, it was a massacre. With
his men falling slaughtered around him, Cerealis and his retinue turned
their horses' heads and galloped back to the safety of the walls of his fort.

In London, the procurator Decianus Catus, 'frightened by this disaster and the hatred borne him by the provincials, whom he had driven to war through his greed', hastily packed his bags. He scuttled down to the docks, and from there set sail for Gaul.[48]

He was lucky. Not everyone had the luxury of flight and, now that Camulodunum had fallen, Boudica and her army had their sights trained on London. But even now, for a brief moment, hope glimmered for the Londoners. News came that Paullinus was on his way with the most rapid units in his army. When he arrived, however, his assessment of the situation was grim. In a few brief sentences, Tacitus describes both his decision and its consequences:

BOUDICAN DESTRUCTION AND LOOTING

Archaeology provides extensive evidence for the destruction of Colchester by Boudica's rebels: the burnt remains of walls, painted plaster and roof tiles, along with furniture and quantities of pottery and glassware. Because the buildings were torched, remains of carbonized organic material, such as wheat grains, dates and flax have been discovered. Whatever the details, the destruction was wholesale.[49]

Several objects in the British Museum may have come from the sack of Colchester. The first is a bronze head from an equestrian statue, which is now thought to be a young Nero (Plate 14). It was found in the River Alde in Suffolk and may have been an offering deposited in water by one of the rebels. The second item is an inlaid statue of Nero, also supposedly found in Suffolk and probably looted from Camulodunum. The damaged bronze helmet of a gladiator was ploughed up in 1965 at Hawkedon.[50] It could have been looted and used by a rebel in the war. Finally, at Hockwold-cum-Wilton, on the edge of the Fens in Norfolk, a hoard of five double-handled silver cups and two silver bowls was found (Plate 13). They date to the early period of occupation and may have been diplomatic gifts to Prasutagus or loot from Colchester or another town.

There is also considerable evidence for Boudican destruction in London, mainly consisting of burnt building debris filled with artefacts and coins dating to the period AD 50–60. At Verulamium there is evidence of some destruction in a row of workshops next to the theatre and buildings under the later *macellum* (market hall) but it is nothing like as extensive as in London and Camulodunum.[51]

London had not been distinguished with the title of *colonia*, but was a very busy centre for business and shipping. Paullinus was uncertain whether he should choose it as his theatre for the war; but, considering how few troops he had and the stark lesson learned from the Britons' response to Petilius' misjudged conduct, he decided to sacrifice this one town and so save the province as a whole. The inhabitants wept and begged him to help them, but this did not stop him giving the signal to depart. Those who could were allowed to march out with him; any who stayed behind, either because they were women or because they were too old or too attached to the place, were massacred by the enemy.[52]

With London smoking and in ruins, the Britons, buoyed by their successes, turned to the northwest and Verulamium (St Albans), the fledgling capital of the Catuvellauni, who may well have been considered by the rebels to be collaborators. Bypassing the military forts, whose grateful garrisons remained shut in behind their tight-closed gates,[53] Boudica and her people ransacked the city and the surrounding countryside, seizing rich pickings from defenceless homes and public buildings, unleashing terror on the inhabitants. By now the loss of life among the Romans and their allies was estimated at between 70,000 and 80,000 people. For the Britons took no prisoners. Instead, they tortured and butchered anyone they found. It was an orgy of violence and bloodshed. As Tacitus observed:

> Slaughter and the gibbet; fire and the cross; for all these they were eager, like men soon to be punished, but for the moment seeking instant vengeance.[54]

That day of punishment was already drawing near. Somewhere in the southern Midlands,[55] Paullinus was mustering what troops he could: the Ninth Legion was needed in the north to secure the frontier there, but the Fourteenth was on hand, with such detachments of the Twentieth who were not in Wales on garrison duty; and with them were a number of auxiliary units too, a total, writes Tacitus, of close on 10,000 men. Of those whom he had summoned, only the Second Legion had still not appeared. Based far to the southwest at Exeter they may themselves have been pinned down by a rebellion among the Durotriges. Whatever the reason, when he heard the outcome of the ensuing battle, the legion's camp commandant, Poenius Postumus, ashamed that he had not been present, fell on his sword.[56]

Meanwhile, Paullinus was preparing for the final showdown.

> [Paullinus] chose a position fronted by a narrow defile, and shut in
> at the rear by a wood. He made sure that none of the enemy was any-
> where except in his front, where the ground was open and there was
> no risk of ambush.[57]

Down the valley, Paullinus with his force of around 10,000 men saw an incalculable sea of British warriors. The historian Dio estimates their number as 230,000 and even allowing for exaggeration, as well as for his inclusion of the vast number of camp followers in Boudica's baggage train, the Romans were significantly outnumbered. Paullinus knew he had no option but to fight. His sudden unexpected march south had meant that he had had no time to organize logistics, and now supplies were running dangerously low. If his men did not join battle, they might soon starve, and then they would be sitting targets.[58]

So at the head of the valley Paullinus drew up his men for battle. In the centre were the legionaries, men of the Twentieth and the Fourteenth; on either side of them the lightly armed auxiliary infantry; and, massed on the wings, the cavalry. With the infantry line stretched to its maximum, the Roman legionaries could have presented a battle line some 2,460 ft (750 m) long,[59] but Dio suggests that this is not how Paullinus disposed his troops. He writes that:

> Paullinus could not stretch out his army to cover the whole of the
> enemy line – they were so heavily outnumbered that they would not
> have achieved this even with a line just one man deep – and he did
> not dare to fight in a single unit through fear of being surrounded
> and massacred; so he divided his army into three with the intention
> of fighting on several fronts at once and drew up each division in
> close formation to make it difficult to break up.[60]

Quite what he means is hard to tell. Perhaps he is simply referring to the division into three distinct groups of the legionaries, auxiliaries and cavalry, each with their own dedicated orders to obey. And obey they would. Their discipline and training were second to none. Even if they were outnumbered twenty to one, they would not flinch. Besides, they had faith in their general, Paullinus. They had heard how he had campaigned in Mauretania; they had seen how he had fought in Wales. So, stoically they waited for the order and they watched the enemy.

Across the valley they could see the British forces, infantry and cavalry, milling excitedly about, and riding in her chariot before them, their leader Boudica, assigning their positions, whipping up her troops into a frenzy. Such was their confidence, the Romans saw, that the British warriors had brought their families with them, arranging them in carts around the edges of the plain, in vantage places from where they best could view the battle.[61] Yet, compared to the legionaries, they were an unruly rabble, some in their ancestral fighting gear, others no doubt dressed in armour scavenged from the still-warm corpses of Cerealis' soldiers of the Ninth, or from the butchered veterans of Camulodunum. Although they lacked cohesion as a fighting force, they made up for it in grim determination. Every man and woman there had but one desire: to rid their island of her Roman overlords.

Parading her violated daughters in front of her men, Boudica goaded her troops to wild excitement. The speech, which Tacitus claims she made, is probably invented, but its content, while stirringly egalitarian, is far from improbable:

> It is not as the daughter of a noble family that I fight now, avenging my lost kingdom and my wealth; but rather as a woman of the people, avenging our lost liberty, my own scourged body, and my daughters' rape. The lusts of the Romans have gone so far that they can leave nothing unpolluted – not our bodies, not our old age, not our virginity. But the gods are on the side of just revenge; the legion, which dared stand up to us in battle, is destroyed; the rest are hiding in their camps, or planning their escape. They will not stand before the roar and thunder of so many thousands, let alone when we attack them and fight hand-to-hand. Think of how many warriors you are, think why you fight, and know that you must either win here on this battlefield or die. I am a woman; this is my resolve. Let my men live and be slaves if that is what they wish.[62]

It is stirring stuff. On the Roman side, Tacitus has Paullinus make a contrastingly measured speech,[63] stressing the enemy's lack of discipline, playing down the discrepancy in numbers, and finishing with the order:

> Only keep close in your ranks, throw your javelins and then keep on fighting and killing with your shields and swords. Put all thought of plunder from your minds; with victory, everything will be yours.[64]

There are two accounts of the battle. Dio's was written over a century after the events it purports to describe. His is a dramatic narrative: the two sides closing on each other; Roman legions falling on the British infantry; Paullinus' archers firing volley after volley at the charging chariots; the brutal ebb and flow of fighting as first one side, then the next prevailed. It was, he wrote, 'a mighty battle and equal spirit and daring were shown by both sides'.[65]

But Tacitus, who may well have heard eye-witness accounts, paints a much more clinical picture, and one which, given the geography and the imbalance in the numbers, is much more likely to be true:

> At first the legion stayed where it was, keeping to the security of the narrow defile, and only when they had launched their javelins with deadly accuracy at the close-advancing enemy did they burst forward in the wedge formation. The auxiliary infantry attacked in the same way, while the cavalry, with their lances levelled, broke through all those who put up any strong resistance.[66]

The battle turned into a rout. The lie of the land, their own British land, and the disposition of their wagons hampered the escaping Britons.

> The rest turned their backs and fled, but their escape was hampered by the surrounding wagons which now blocked their exits. Our soldiers did not spare even women, and baggage animals too, run through with spears, swelled the heaps of bodies...Some sources say that just under 80,000 Britons died; while we lost about about 400 dead, with just over that number wounded.[67]

Now it was the Britons' turn to flee for safety. Among their number was their leader, Boudica. But before long, she too was dead. Dio, somewhat prosaically, claims that she fell ill and died. Tacitus, however, tells us that she killed herself with poison. If she indeed knew that her cause had failed, she would not have allowed herself to live. She would have known that, like Caratacus before her, she would be taken in a captive's cage to Rome, and there paraded round the streets in triumph by her braggart conquerors before being strangled by the public executioner. She may have known, too, how another queen just ninety years before, the Egyptian Cleopatra, had taken poison to avoid such a degrading fate.[68] She and her daughters had already suffered enough humiliation at the hands of Rome. She would not suffer more.

The Britons, Dio informs us, 'missed her greatly and bestowed on her a costly funeral; but believing that they now were finally defeated they dispersed to their homes'.[69]

✧ ✧ ✧

Once the rebellion ended, it was time for the reprisals to begin. Those British men who had been captured were now most likely executed, their wives and children sold into slavery and shipped across the Channel far from Britain. For those allowed to live still in their homeland, conditions became harsh indeed. Cattle and other animals were no doubt confiscated. Horses and ponies, which might be ridden in battle or yoked to war chariots, were commandeered to join those captured by the Romans in the war. Some would have been sold at market; others were trained for use by Roman cavalry.

At around this time at The Lunt, a cavalry fort near modern Coventry, there was built a circular enclosure, 110 ft (33.5 m) in diameter, its levelled surface smoothed with sand and gravel and surrounded by an 8 ft (2.4 m) high wooden fence. This so-called *Gyrus* is a feature unique to this Roman fort, and it is believed that it was built to break and train the horses taken by the Roman army after the revolt.[70] Now even Britain's animals were to be Romanized.

The Britons defeated, Paullinus was bent on revenge. After all, he had come to Britain in the expectation of great glory, of exceeding the achievements of his rival Corbulo (see p. 74), of pushing back the boundaries of Rome's dominion, of extending the new province through conquest – not to preside over the destruction of three Roman towns or the massacre of Roman veterans and civilians and troops. Besides, it might be thought in Rome that the rebellion had happened because he, Paullinus, had failed to assess the situation correctly and that, on his watch, he had let things slide. If there was any blame to mete out (and under Nero there was always blame) it would not attach to him. No, it was the Britons who must bear the blame, and now they were going to suffer. So the man, who in Africa had taken time to study elephants and trees, now turned his whole attention to paying back the rebel British with a Roman reign of terror.

Reinforcements arrived from Germany: two thousand legionaries (perhaps commanded by Vespasian's son, the future emperor Titus), eight cohorts of auxiliary infantry and a thousand cavalry. At the same time

Paullinus built forts around the lands of the Iceni at Ixworth and Codden-ham (Baylham House), with a major fortress for a strong detachment barracked at Great Chesterford.[71] And as he did so, he unleashed his vengeance: 'whatever tribes still wavered in their allegiance or were openly hostile were destroyed by fire and sword'.[72]

As far away as Somerset, the hillfort of South Cadbury may bear signs of Paullinus' ruthlessness. Close to the alleyway, which led down to the gate, were found remains of thirty people, women and children as well as men, butchered and left to lie there to be picked apart by scavenging birds and animals. A little later, Roman troops systematically dismantled the gateway itself and erected their own huts in regular rows within the fort.[73]

For the Britons there was worse to come. Tacitus records that:

> It was famine which caused the natives the greatest hardship, since they had neglected to sow their crops, calling up men of every age to fight, and intending to take over our food supplies for themselves.[74]

Yet as winter came and went and Paullinus and his well-fed legionaries watched the tribesfolk starve, in his newly rebuilt offices in London, Julius Classicianus, successor to the loathsome Decianus Catus, was worried. For Paullinus' vengeance was not only threatening the future of the native populations, it was threatening the revenues of Rome; the harder that the Romans harried Britain, the less produce there would be to tax.

Ideologically, the two men, Classicianus and Paullinus, could not agree. Personally, they loathed each other. Their feud was even blamed by Tacitus for prolonging the last vestiges of resistance among the British.

> Classicianus spread the idea that they should wait for a new gover-nor, who had neither the wrath of an enemy or the arrogance of a conqueror and so would deal sympathetically with those who sur-rendered. At the same time, he wrote to Rome saying that they could expect no end to hostilities unless Paullinus were replaced. He put Paullinus' failures down to recalcitrance and his successes to good luck.[75]

In Rome, Classicianus' complaints were taken seriously. Nero re-sponded by despatching to Britain one of his high-ranking freedmen, Polyclitus. He was charged with conducting an enquiry and, if possible, with engineering the conditions by which governor and procurator could at least work together in some sort of harmony. His arrival sent shivers

JULIUS CLASSICIANUS, PROCURATOR

Tacitus might have provided our only knowledge of Classicianus had it not been for two chance discoveries in London. In 1852, while construction work was taking place by the Thames at Trinity House, among much Roman stonework was found a large block, part of a tomb inscription. In 1935, another block was found. This made it certain that the tombstone was that of Julius Classicianus, the Roman procurator. It is now reconstructed in the British Museum. The full inscription reads: DIS MANIBVS / C.IVL.C.F.FAB.ALPINI.CLASSICIANI. /..../ PROC.PROVINC. BRITANNIAE/IVLIA.INDI.FILIA.PACATA.INDVTA / VXOR F. 'To the spirits of the departed (and) of Gaius Iulius Alpinus Classicianus, son of Gaius, of the Fabian voting tribe... Procurator of the Province of Britain, his wife Iulia Pacata Induta, daughter of Indus, had this built'.

The tombstone's location also tells us that Classicianus died in office in Britain, probably in the late 60s. The tomb would have stood outside the town. It was later desecrated – in the fourth century the stones were reused as part of a bastion built to strengthen the wall on London's east side. The tomb's presence in London supports the supposition that the procurator was based here from very early on, even though the governor's seat was at Colchester.[76]

8 Classicianus' tomb (AD 60s), now in the British Museum. The inscription reveals that his wife, Julia, was daughter to Indus, chief of the Gallic Treveri tribe. It is probable that Classicianus was of the same tribe and his family gained Roman citizenship under Julius Caesar or Augustus.

down the army's spine,[77] but in the end they had nothing to fear. Polyclitus filed an anodyne report, which couched the situation in the most favourable light possible, and for the time being Paullinus was kept in post. It was not to last. Clearly, this was simply a means of allowing the governor to save face, for at the earliest opportunity he was replaced.

If Paullinus feared the reception waiting for him back at Rome, he must have been relieved to find it curiously favourable. Perhaps at his debriefing his suspicions were confirmed that Nero had for some time been toying with the idea of pulling the troops out of Britain. Only the thought of the shame that it might bring to the reputation of his imperial family had stayed his hand. So, with his reputation as a general intact, Paullinus lived on, far from the scene of what he had feared would be his great humiliation.[78]

For Britain, on the other hand, the years of Paullinus' governorship would take a longer lasting toll. For the Iceni, so many of whose men had died in the rebellion, their former wealth and pride would not return. Now under direct Roman rule, but governed by a council of their elders, many were resettled in a new tribal capital at Caistor-by-Norwich. But Caistor never really grew as other towns did. In the decades to come, the heady days of civic expansion passed it by (AD 70–100), and throughout the entire period of occupation until the fifth century much of the old Iceni land may have been farmed not by wealthy landowners but under the direct supervision of the procurator's staff. It was only in the third and fourth centuries that the region bordering the Fens seems to have gained significant prosperity, but never on the grand scale suggested by the large palatial villas of the south and west.[79]

The Iceni were not alone. The Trinovantes, too, who had joined with the Iceni to wreak their vengeance on the veterans of their old capital, Camulodunum, had suffered heavy losses. It is possible that, to punish the Trinovantes for their treachery and to teach the other tribes a lesson, they had been virtually wiped out in a campaign of genocide. Certainly, the town to which the Trinovantes may have been relocated, Caesaromagus (Chelmsford), was allowed to stagnate. Even if there was the manpower, there was neither the will nor wealth left to construct a major town.[80]

In the years after the rebellion, other civic centres in the southeast languished too. All that was built in Camulodunum seems to have been a defensive wall; in London only a new quay; and much of Verulamium seems to have seen a total moratorium in building of up to fifteen years.

It was a lethargy that may have seeped from Rome itself. For Nero was, at best, indifferent to Britain. The biographer Suetonius comments:

> He was never at any time moved by any desire or hope of expanding the empire. He even considered withdrawing the army from Britain, and only held back from his purpose because he did not wish to be seen to detract from his father's glory... [81]

It was not until Vespasian was raised to emperor (AD 69–79) that urban growth in these towns began once more in earnest.[82] With him, a new vitality emerged and with it brave new possibilities. It was a time to push the boundaries once more. It was a time for new campaigning.

4
SHOCK AND AWE
VERSUS HEARTS AND MINDS

'Theft, slaughter, rape – the Romans call these "government"!' He paused for a moment to let the words sink in, to relish them, and as he did so he could almost smell the bracken and the heather. He could almost feel the warm breeze on his cheeks. In his imagination, he could almost see the Highland chieftain with his long hair and his grizzled beard, his craggy face, his narrowed piercing eyes. He could almost hear him rallying his men (in a rousing speech he almost certainly had never made and in a language which he did not understand). And down across the glen the Roman army, drawn up in its ranks, outnumbered, yet steadfast, the morning sunlight on their burnished armour, their scarlet tunics standing out as bright as poppies against the mountainside.

The scene had been described to him so vividly. Not only by Agricola, but by men who had served under him, campaign veterans come back home and all too glad to reminisce. Of course they would exaggerate. And who could blame them? He was not above the odd embroidery of facts himself. Like now, for instance. But it was, after all, a eulogy that he was writing, a work of tribute and of praise. His audience would hardly thank him for a history lesson!

His scribe, a good Greek slave, looked up and met his eyes. For a moment, his concentration faltered, and he was back in Rome, in his richly furnished villa where even the splashing of the fountain could not quite mask the city's din. Concentrate, Tacitus! Concentrate! He must not be distracted. 'Theft, slaughter, rape – the Romans call these "government"!' He allowed himself a wry smile. In his mind, the next sentence had formed. His audience would like this, he was sure. He signalled to his slave to write, as he dictated: 'They make a wasteland, and they call it "peace"'.

❖ ❖ ❖

THE Boudican revolt had left Britain reeling, and rewritten the rules of Roman occupation. The sheer level of violence perpetrated by both sides had seen to that. It may have taken a loss of tax revenue for Rome's central government to respond adequately to the governor Suetonius Paullinus' harsh regime of reprisals (see above), but with his recall (AD 61) there was put in place a policy aimed, for a time, more at consolidation than at aggression.

The historian Tacitus (writing, as he was, for a Roman audience, which admired the virtues of military expansionism and abhorred anything which might smack of woolly liberalism) was not kind to Paullinus' successors. As a result they can seem weak and passive. In fact, given the circumstances, they were probably exactly the right men for the job, carefully chosen not to rock the boat.

The first, Publius Petronius Turpilianus, an ex-consul from an illustrious family, served as governor for less than two years (AD 61–63). In writing that he 'neither aggravated the enemy, nor was he himself provoked',[1] Tacitus means to damn him with faint praise. In reality, however, what he describes is something of an achievement. For, in the aftermath of destruction, this was a time not only for laying down the law and establishing order but for rebuilding ruined Roman towns and, wherever possible, for winning British hearts and minds.

That Turpilianus was replaced so relatively quickly might seem to suggest dissatisfaction with his policies. In fact, if anything his successor Marcus Trebellius Maximus (AD 63–69) took them further. It may be that this Trebellius had commanded a legion in the Taurus mountains; it may be that he was a friend of Columella, who wrote a book on farming;[2] but it is certain that he was a senator, an ex-consul who had served with Seneca (AD 55), and who later (AD 61) had helped conduct a census in Gaul. Perhaps he was now charged with conducting a similar census in Britain – after all, now that so many thousands had been killed, it was important to know how many people were still left. How else could the tax they owed be properly calculated?

Trebellius, however, miscalculated. For, while he was conducting what Tacitus called his 'easy-going kind of administration [in which] the barbarians learned, like any Roman, to condone seductive vices', he neglected his own people, his army. By AD 66, the number of legions in Britain had fallen to three. The Fourteenth had been reassigned to duties on the continent and, although this might suggest that the level of security within the occupied territories was high, it also meant that the army's capacity to campaign was diminished.[3] If, as seems possible, this coincided with the Twentieth Legion's move back from Usk to Gloucester, it suggests an avoidance of over-stretch through a consolidation on the Welsh borders. To the soldiers, however, such a policy may have seemed like a retreat, and this, coupled with disgruntlement at their new peace-keeping role, led to resentment. They mutinied.

Trebellius fled. When, at last, he came out of hiding, he found that he had lost the confidence of his men and according to Tacitus:

> ...could command merely on sufferance. By a kind of tacit bargain the troops had licence to do as they pleased; the general had his life.[4]

It was an untenable situation. Probably now based in Gloucester, and still seething with resentment that the Twentieth Legion, of which he was legate, had been withdrawn from Wales, one Roscius Caelius was whipping up dissent. He accused Trebellius of reducing his men to poverty by denying them booty; Trebellius responded by charging Caelius with sedition and indiscipline; the troops went over to Caelius. With the jeers of his auxiliaries ringing in his ears (AD 69), Trebellius abandoned Britain and took ship for Gaul. Back in Rome, he managed to survive the turmoil which was then gripping the empire (see below) and by AD 72 he could be found serving in the priestly college of the Arval Brothers, one of whose duties was to sacrifice to the gods for a good harvest. For Trebellius, friend of the farmer Columella, it must have been precisely the retirement he had longed for.

By now the political face of Rome had changed significantly. Civil war had seen to that. In the year that Trebellius fled from Britain (AD 69), the empire suffered massive convulsions as one after another of a succession of would-be rulers was placed on the throne by legions loyal to them.[5] By January, the army on the Rhine had already proclaimed in favour of their popular commander, Vitellius. In a sign of surprising unity, the British legions to a man soon followed suit and, by April, when – to prevent more carnage – his rival for the throne had nobly fallen on his sword, Vitellius had been hailed emperor in Rome.

Uniquely, Britain was virtually unaffected by the turbulence on the continent. Tacitus, while claiming that its army's morale had been destroyed by Trebellius, nonetheless notes that, during the civil war:

...no other legions conducted themselves more correctly, whether this was because, at such distance, they were divided from the rest of the world by the Ocean, or because, hardened by frequent fighting, they hated the enemy more than each other.[6]

They knew, in other words, what the Britons might do if they, the Romans, presented anything less than a united front.[7]

Meanwhile in the province, if only by default, Trebellius' nemesis Roscius Caelius ruled supreme. In these troubled times, this was not an ideal situation. Britain needed a new governor, and so, to fill the post, the new emperor Vitellius sent Vettius Bolanus (AD 69–71), an ex-consul (AD 66), who had served as a legionary commander under Corbulo (see p. 74) in Armenia in AD 61. Perhaps he had even been the great general's second-in-command. Despite Bolanus' military credentials, Tacitus, with his expansionist fetishes, is scathing about him, accusing him of having 'too gentle a hand for a warlike province'.[8] Yet this was no time for a major military push, despite what the intelligentsia in Rome or the rank-and-file of the army in Britain might have thought. Instead, Bolanus did what he was sent to do and maintained order.

To achieve this, he had to exercise considerable logistical skill. Throughout AD 69, that incendiary year with its succession of emperors, legions were being first deployed then redeployed with startling rapidity. Vitellius himself withdrew no fewer than 8,000 men from Britain, replacing them shortly afterwards with a legion that had fought against him in the civil war. That it was the Fourteenth, withdrawn from Britain only three years earlier (see above),[9] suggests perhaps that Vitellius was not merely trying to banish a potentially unruly legion across the Channel, but that he was deliberately sending back men familiar with the workings of the province at a time when they might be needed on campaign. Vitellius soon regretted his decision; now he needed all the troops that he could muster.

For in July (AD 69) news came that the legions in the east had proclaimed a general of their own as a rival candidate for emperor, and their choice provoked serious soul-searching among the army stationed in Britain. The general was one of their own kind, a man who, with the Second Legion, had fought under Claudius and Aulus Plautius in the first years of the British campaign, winning thirty battles, pacifying two tribes, capturing not only over twenty settlements but the entire Isle of Wight and leading his men west to Exeter.[10] He was Vespasian (Fig. 9).

9 Marble head of Vespasian when emperor (AD 69–79), now in the British Museum.

Down-to-earth and honest, with a wry sense of humour, Vespasian had won his men's respect. Like most of them, he did not come from an aristocratic background; his family, the Flavians, were undistinguished. It was entirely through his own abilities (both military and diplomatic) that Vespasian fought his way up through the ranks. Under emperors as diverse as Tiberius, Caligula and Claudius, Vespasian's career had advanced rapidly, and by the time he had returned from Britain he had earned himself the coveted *ornamenta triumphalia*, the 'Triumphal Decorations'.[11] Now, twenty-five years later (AD 69), he was in Judaea, struggling to suppress a grim revolt, when his devoted legions, hostile to Vitellius, declared their wish to see Vespasian on the throne. Approval for their decision rippled through the eastern provinces, and within months (December AD 69) he received news that in Italy his army was victorious, Vitellius was dead and the Senate had declared him emperor.

The troops in Britain could congratulate themselves that they had played a part in Vespasian's success – by doing nothing. For Bolanus had deliberately ignored Vitellius' increasingly urgent requests for troops. Britain, he argued, was too volatile to spare them. In reality, however, although there were inevitably some (like Bolanus himself) who owed their positions to Vitellius, the legions almost to a man had come out in favour of Vespasian.[12]

Yet Bolanus' excuse of instability was, in fact, genuine. Ever alert to any upheavals on the continent that might distract the Roman army, one of the British tribes chose this auspicious moment to rebel.

The Brigantes were experiencing their own civil war. Their queen, Cartimandua, had remained loyal to Rome (see p. 67), but, perhaps intoxicated by the wealth that was lavished on her as a result, she rejected her husband Venutius and set up house with her lover.

At once her household was shaken to its foundations by this scandal. The people supported Venutius: all that supported the adulterer was the lust and savage temper of the queen. Venutius therefore summoned his supporters, and with the Brigantes rallying to him, Cartimandua was in grave danger. She asked for Roman protection. Our auxiliaries and cavalry fought with varying success, but at last rescued the queen from danger. The kingdom went to Venutius; we had a war to fight.[13]

This version of the story, told by Tacitus, suggests that Bolanus did little to confront Venutius. In fact, there is tantalizing evidence that he may have pursued the Brigantian king north, perhaps even as far as southern Scotland. Writing in honour of Bolanus' son some twenty-five years later, the poet Statius exclaims:

What glory will exalt the Caledonian plains,
When an agèd native of that fearsome land tells you:
'Here your father [Bolanus] used to administer justice; from this
        mound he addressed
His cavalry. He established lookout posts and forts far and wide
Look at them! – and surrounded these walls with a ditch.
Here are the gifts he dedicated to the gods of war, and here the weapons
(You can still make out the inscriptions). Here is the breast-plate he wore as
Battle called; here is another, which he wrenched from a British king.[14]

WHO WERE THE BRIGANTES?

The Brigantes, whose name meant either 'The High Ones' or 'The Hill Dwellers', were a confederacy of small tribes living in the north of England. Their territory may have included most of modern Yorkshire (except for east Yorkshire, home of the Parisi), Lancashire, Cumbria and Northumberland, and even parts of southwestern Scotland. In the northwest, the Carvetii, probably part of the Brigantian confederacy, had their capital at Carlisle on Hadrian's Wall, but the most significant pre-Roman centre in Brigantia seems to have been at Stanwick, where ditches and ramparts enclosed an area of 731 acres. However, in the Roman period, the tribal capital was the Roman town of Isurium Brigantium (Aldborough, north of York).[15]

Was that king Venutius? Was Bolanus the first Roman governor to set foot on Scottish soil? He certainly seems to have sent his fleet on a reconnaissance mission round its coast.[16]

However, in these new, more hostile, circumstances Vespasian, like Tacitus, did not consider Bolanus the right man for the job. After only two years in post, Bolanus was recalled to Rome (AD 71).[17] In his place the emperor sent out a man who not only shared his knowledge of the country, but who had first-hand experience of a British rebellion: Petilius Cerealis, the commander of the Ninth Legion, who had led out his men from Long-thorpe and had fled when they were cut down by the forces under Boudica. It is believed that, in the years that followed, Cerealis may have achieved a success to put such memories into the shade: he may well have married the daughter of Vespasian himself.

Nonetheless, he must have been a controversial choice. In the civil war, during which he had served with Vespasian's troops in Italy, he had not been entirely conspicuous for military success. Indeed, the one engagement that we hear he led resulted in defeat. Not that this hindered his career. Fresh from a consulship (AD 70), he was sent to the Rhineland to suppress a revolt. A Roman commander had joined forces with some Germanic and Gaulish tribes and risen against Vespasian. In the marshes round the Rhine, Cerealis fought with characteristic energy – and reckless-ness. Tacitus was not impressed.[18] He wrote wearily of how Cerealis could easily 'be intercepted on the way, as he rushed to and fro in response to the various alarms' – as, indeed, he had been previously in his encounter with Boudica.

Still, in the spring of AD 71, Cerealis sailed back to Britain as its gov-ernor. He had been successful on the Rhineland. Now he must prove his worth in Britain too. According to Tacitus, he:

> ...at once struck terror into their hearts by attacking the state of the Brigantes, which is said to be the most densely populated in the whole province. After many battles – many by no means bloodless – Cerealis had either fought in or won victory over the major part of their territory.[19]

Whether, like Bolanus before him, he went further, is open to question. For good family reasons, Tacitus denies that any Roman reached Scotland before the governorship of his father-in-law Agricola, but writing in his *Natural History*, Pliny the Elder claims that:

In almost thirty years [i.e. between AD 43 and 73], Roman arms have extended knowledge of Britain as far as the vicinity of the Caledonian Forest.[20]

The Caledonian Forest is, of course, in Scotland. Archaeology, too, might suggest that Cerealis pushed further north than Tacitus would have us think. The fort at Dalswinton in Dumfriesshire might date from Cerealis' time.[21]

Elsewhere in southern Britain, the campaign of winning hearts and minds to Roman ways, which would characterize Vespasian's rule, was already afoot. In London, an amphitheatre, that most Roman of constructions designed for those most Roman of entertainments, the gladiatorial games, was already in use by AD 71.[22] Civilization was truly taking root. So by the time that he was recalled to Rome (AD 73) and took his seat as consul (AD 74), Cerealis could feel duly satisfied. Not only had he managed not to bungle things, he had brought the Brigantes back into the fold and left Britain as a province better than he had found it. He had done rather well.[23]

CEREALIS IN NORTHERN ENGLAND

It was once suggested that the major showdown between Cerealis and the Brigantes occurred at Stanwick in Yorkshire, an area of 731 acres, delineated by a series of large banks. At the heart of this *oppidum* was a 17-acre enclosure, 'The Tofts', which was excavated originally by Sir Mortimer Wheeler, who thought it was Venutius' stronghold. However, the discovery of pre-Flavian Roman Samian-ware pottery and building materials shows direct contacts with the Roman world prior to the campaigns of Bolanus and Cerealis. This being the case, the alternative interpretation of the site is that it was in fact the capital of Cartimandua. The Roman artefacts might have been the result of trade, or even represented diplomatic gifts from Rome, a common feature in relationships with client rulers.

It is still quite possible that the prominent marching camp at Rey Cross on the A66 (which follows the course of the later Roman road) was from Cerealis' campaigns. Tree-ring analysis has dated the turf and timber fort at Carlisle to AD 72–73, placing its foundation firmly in Cerealis' governorship and confirming dates derived from pottery. One can assume that Cerealis campaigned over much new territory not covered by Bolanus, building forts such as the one at Carlisle in order to establish a permanent Roman presence.[24]

His successor, if anything, did even better. Sextus Julius Frontinus (governor from late AD 73 to 77) was a military man to the core. Not only did he employ successful stratagems in battle, he wrote a monograph about them, too, and the title he chose for his book betrayed his no-nonsense pragmatic approach to life: he called it *Stratagems*. So valuable a source-book was it, that it was consulted heavily by Aelian when that author came to write his own book on tactics (in a volume that he entitled *Tactics*).[25]

Like Cerealis (whom he probably knew well), Frontinus had fought on behalf of Vespasian against Vitellius on the Rhine. Here, among other successes, he had negotiated the surrender of 80,000 of the enemy, an achievement that modesty did not prevent him including in *Stratagems* as an example of a good military outcome. He was, in other words, a safe choice not only as a loyal servant, but as a negotiator and a fighter.

And fight he did. With the Brigantes in the north subdued, Frontinus turned his attention west to Wales and the Silures, that tribe which had been a thorn in the side of so many of his predecessors. It was a hard-fought campaign in difficult terrain against determined opposition, but nonetheless Frontinus pushed through to victory. After thirty years of resistance, the Silures were eventually defeated. Frontinus, who also knew good stratagems for peace-building, built a new fortress for the Second Legion at Caerleon, from which they could keep a watchful eye on Rome's new subjects.[26]

Frontinus may have campaigned elsewhere, too. Perhaps he founded the legionary fort at Chester; perhaps, like Bolanus and Cerealis, he campaigned in southern Scotland; we cannot tell for sure. In AD 77, he was transferred from Britain. Six years later (AD 83) he was fighting in Germany; the next year he was in Asia as proconsul; in AD 98 and again in AD 100 he would serve as consul. And throughout it all, he wrote. Not only *Stratagems*; he wrote on military science, too, in a treatise entitled *On Military Science*.[27] In AD 97, a year when he was in charge of Rome's aqueducts, he wrote a book called, unsurprisingly, *About Rome's Aqueducts*.[28]

✧ ✧ ✧

While Frontinus was agonizing over book titles, in Britain in the field his successor as governor was (wittingly or not) writing himself indelibly into the pages of the island's history. For not only did Gnaeus Julius Agricola show considerable energy and achieve significant success both on campaign and in the province's administration; but his actions were also to be recorded for posterity in the works of one of the greatest of all Rome's historians, Tacitus. What was more, Agricola was guaranteed favourable coverage, for Tacitus was his son-in-law. With his wife and her family reading his every word, woe betide the younger man if he stepped out of line. The 'inside story' of Agricola's administration, which has survived in Tacitus' accounts, may present us with a unique picture of the intimate workings of a provincial governor, but it must also be treated with exceptional care if we are not to be misled by bias.[29]

Like Cerealis, when he took up his post as governor, Agricola was no stranger to Britain. He had already been posted to the island twice: once, as a young man of twenty, during the Boudican revolt, when he had served as an enthusiastic member of the governor Suetonius Paullinus' senior staff; next, when he had commanded the Twentieth Legion on campaign under Petilius Cerealis (AD 70–73/4).[30] These latter years were something of an education for Agricola. According to Tacitus:

> At first Cerealis let him share only in hard work and danger; soon in glory, too. Often, to test him, he gave him the command of a detachment of the army; sometimes, when [Agricola] had proved his worth, of larger forces.[31]

What gave Agricola's appointment to command the Twentieth added significance was that it was this legion which, only months before (AD 69), under the leadership of Roscius Caelius, had been the first to mutiny against the governor Trebellius (see above). Clearly Agricola was trusted not only to be a safe pair of hands but to re-impose discipline. He did so, we hear, 'with rare modesty, doing his best to give the impression that no such measures had been necessary'.[32]

That he managed the task with such equanimity and success is particularly impressive, as he was still reeling from distressing news from home. His mother had been murdered. In the mayhem of the civil war, marauding sailors had put in at her estate on the Ligurian coast and slaughtered her. She was not the only member of Agricola's family to meet a violent death. Years earlier, when Agricola was only six months old (January AD 41), Caligula's men had come for his father, Julius Graecinus. A gentle, scholarly man from Forum Iulii (Fréjus) in southeastern Gaul, Graecinus was a second-generation Roman citizen who had risen to the rank of senator, having won his fame 'by his devotion to literature and philosophy'.[33] His particular interest was vines. Indeed, not only was his monograph on viticulture quoted by Trebellius' friend Columella (see p. 89), but his passion for working the soil may explain the name he gave his son: Agricola means 'farmer'. But none of these pastoral pursuits could protect Graecinus from the ruthless savagery of Caligula's regime. When Graecinus refused the emperor's command to impeach a fellow senator, Caligula ordered his execution.

Fatherless, the young Agricola had risen rapidly through Rome's political ranks. Destined as he was for the Senate, on his return from his first tour of duty in Britain he undertook a succession of increasingly high-ranking postings, ranging from serving as Tribune of the Plebs (AD 66) to making an inventory of temple possessions looted by Nero (AD 68). It was after his second British posting that his career truly flourished. Soon after his return to Rome he was granted the status of patrician and appointed governor of Aquitania (AD 74–76). Next came a consulship (AD 76), and then, at the age of only thirty-seven, the governorship of Britain. So now, with a retinue which included his wife and perhaps his daughter and his son-in-law Tacitus, serving as tribune,[34] Agricola crossed the Channel for the third time.

Once in place (AD 77), Agricola acted fast. Frontinus' campaigns in Wales had dealt with only one of Rome's enemies, the Silures. Another Welsh tribe, the Ordovices, had still not been subdued. In fact, only months before Agricola's arrival:

> The Ordovices had nearly completely annihilated a squadron of cavalry billeted in their territory, and this initial success had stirred up the province. Those who were eager for war welcomed the precedent, and waited to test the character of the new governor.[35]

The Britons had learned that periods of crossover between one governor and another were potentially vulnerable times for the Roman administration, good times therefore for a rebellion. Agricola needed to stamp his authority firmly and unequivocally both on the natives and on his own men. The Ordovices provided the ideal opportunity. So, against all expectation, because the summer was already late, he led his troops from barracks and into the mountains of Wales. He showed his mettle. He 'cut to pieces almost the whole fighting force of the tribe'.[36] At a stroke (or rather many strokes) of the legionary's short sword, the whole of Wales was brought within the fold of Rome's growing family.

Only Anglesey, the island off the northwest coast of Wales, where the massed tribes and their Druids had made their last stand (see above), remained untamed. It had been spared total occupation in AD 60 when Paullinus was forced to turn his troops back south to confront the ravages of Boudica. Now Agricola (who had perhaps served on that original campaign) returned. This time he would show no mercy. In a surprise attack, he sent a specialist detachment of his cavalry to swim across the Menai Straits. Before they knew it, the islanders had surrendered. Agricola had made his point. He had established his authority. At Caernarvon (Segontium), he founded a fort, probably for an infantry cohort of about 800 men; later rebuilt in stone, this fort was to be the longest occupied in Wales. For the next 300 years, Wales would give no trouble to the Romans.[37]

Shock and awe had proved successful. It was now time truly to win hearts and minds, and to turn the barbarous lands of Britain into a fully Romanized province. Although work had already begun under previous governors, a more consolidated building programme was now put in place to ensure that British urban centres, like those elsewhere in the empire, contained those true hallmarks of 'Romanitas', the forum and the public baths.[38]

The rich were encouraged to prove their worth by vying with one another to see who could show themselves most loyal to Rome. Togas became the rage,[39] Latin the language of choice, and a Roman education *de rigueur* for the sons of the elite. The Britons, Agricola assured them (demonstrating a keen awareness of their competitiveness with their cousins across the Channel) possessed so much more natural talent than the Gauls. So, as the world-weary Tacitus put it:

> The people were gradually led into the demoralizing temptations of porticoes and baths, and elegant dinner-parties. In their ignorance, they called these things 'civilization', when really they were part of their enslavement.[40]

For some, the chains of that enslavement were more golden than for others. Although Agricola improved the common people's lot by ensuring that tax abuses, ignored perhaps under the Frontinus administration, were now largely stamped out, it was the rich who benefited most from Rome's new regime. (However, a bronze corn measure, dating from the reign of Domitian, AD 81–96, and now in Chester Museum, bears an inscription that states the measure holds 17.5 *sextarii*, or 16.8 pints, when it actually

10 Tenants paying rent, on a tomb relief from a tomb at Neumagen, near Trier, second century AD. The relief is now in the Landesmuseum, Trier.

holds 20 pints. Each time the measure was used to collect corn from locals, the authorities effectively tricked the Britons into giving 20 per cent more than the stated amount.[41]

Villas began to appear, country-houses at the heart of farming estates, including several around Verulamium (St Albans).[42] One British villa in particular, completed during Agricola's governorship (AD 80), was on a scale sufficiently unique in northern Europe for it to be considered a palace. With its well-worked stone and brickwork, its imported marble and luxurious mosaics, Fishbourne proclaimed power, prestige and an almost psychotic desire to broadcast as extravagantly as possible its owner's allegiance to Rome. It is believed to have been built for a man who styled himself 'Tiberius Claudius Togidubnus, Great King of Britain'. This, at least, is the proud formula he had inscribed on the dedication plaque for the temple of Neptune and Minerva, whose construction he funded in nearby Chichester. A gold signet ring, bearing the inscription 'Tiberius Claudius Catuarus', was discovered nearby, suggesting that the palace was owned by a member of Togidubnus' family.[43]

This new palace at Fishbourne was not the only major Roman-style building that Togidubnus had commissioned. Already there had been a small villa on the same site, and other villas seem to have been built at Chichester and Silchester, where two other symbols of Romanitas were also constructed: a bath-house and an amphitheatre. At Silchester, tiles were stamped with the name of Nero – were these buildings directly funded by the emperor himself in recognition of Togidubnus' steadfast loyalty during the Boudican revolt?[44]

By now (AD 70s), Togidubnus, the 'Great King of Britain', was a very old man. His family had for a long time been useful to the Romans. Indeed, it was probably a relative of his, Verica, whose request to Claudius for help had furnished Rome with its excuse for the invasion of AD 43 (see p. 42). Accordingly, early in the occupation, Aulus Plautius, the first governor, had made the trusted collaborator Togidubnus a client king, ruling the lands of the Regini, Belgae and Atrebates from West Sussex up to Winchester and Silchester.[45] During the early days of occupation, this was crucial territory. For Vespasian, leading his Second Legion westwards, the stability that Togidubnus brought to the lands to his rear (lands which no doubt housed granaries and other key supply dumps) was particularly important. As emperor, Vespasian would not forget his old ally. After all, during the firestorm of Boudica's revolt, not to mention the many smaller uprisings, in over thirty years of Togidubnus' rule, the realm of the 'Great King of Britain' had been peaceful and without incident. With characteristic incisiveness, Tacitus summed up the old man's position:

> Certain territories were given to king Togidubnus (even within my memory, he stayed the most loyal of men), an example of the long-established custom of the Roman people to use even kings as instruments of enslavement.[46]

Yet Togidubnus was not to enjoy the full fruits of his loyalty. By the time the builders had moved out of Fishbourne (AD 80), he was already dead.[47] At least he died content, gratified by the reports of the new governor's success. For, hundreds of miles away, Agricola had been hard at work.

With Wales and the west firmly under Rome's control, it was time to look north to Scotland. Agricola spent the first full year of his governorship (AD 78) preparing for campaign. The territory of the Brigantes, still simmering after the civil war between Cartimandua and her estranged husband Venutius (see above), needed once and for all to be pacified. According to Tacitus, 'a ring of garrisoned forts was built to surround the Brigantes'.[48] If a reliable peace could not be achieved through placating the Brigantes, Agricola was prepared to take no chances.

By the spring of the next year (AD 79), everything was in place for a twin-pronged attack. In the east, on the appointed day, the Ninth Legion marched out from York, where it had been stationed since the days of

Cerealis, north along Dere Street and so on into Scotland. Mirroring them in the west, another legion pounded a similarly ancient road up from Carlisle through Annandale and on to Clydesdale. Each night they bivouacked in marching camps, temporary but far from makeshift forts, each with a ditch and earthen rampart bristling with sharpened wooden stakes. Each legionary carried two of these stakes as part of his equipment. Although not exclusive to Agricola, many of his camps (which range in size from 3.7 to 60 acres) had a distinctive defended gateway that can be used to trace his campaigns. In highland regions, these are particularly well preserved.[49]

At Newstead (Trimontium), strategically placed across the River Tweed from Eildon Hill, the tribal capital of the Selgovae, the Ninth Legion built and garrisoned a fort, first, as was usual, in turf and timber, then in stone. It would remain in service on and off for a hundred years. Agricola's ability to find the best location for a fort was legendary. It was to serve him well.[50]

By the end of the campaigning season, Agricola had pushed much further. According to Tacitus, his offensive had 'opened up new peoples; as we ravaged the native population as far as the estuary called the Tay'.[51]

It was a good time to stop and take stock. For elsewhere in the empire, the year had brought with it events of some significance. Not only had ash and lava from Vesuvius engulfed the towns of Stabiae, Pompeii and Herculaneum on the fashionable bay of Naples; but also a few months earlier (June AD 79) the emperor Vespasian had died. His son Titus had succeeded him, and, with regards to military policy in Britain, Titus was inclined to be wary.

Or so Tacitus claims.[52] The historian excuses Agricola's lack of aggression the next year by citing orders from on high, but it is just as likely that the general himself wanted to use the time to secure the territory he had won. With an entire infrastructure to create, there was much to do. Forts and supply dumps needed to be built, roads laid, traffic monitored – in one direction that of military personnel, in the other shuffling lines of captives herded south towards the Channel and the slave-markets of Rome. By the end of the year, with the isthmus fortified between the Clyde and Forth,[53] the whole of southern Scotland was in Roman hands. Except, that is, for the southwest.

It was to this region that Agricola now turned his attention (AD 81), crossing the River Annan and turning the might of Rome against the Novantae, a tribe which he had bypassed in his push north two years earlier. The

Novantae stood no chance. Standing on a crisp day on the western coast of Galloway, Agricola, his generals and troops looked longingly across the sea to Ireland. It seemed so tempting. Especially as (following the usual pattern in such circumstances) an exiled Irish prince had turned up in the Roman camp asking for help to restore him to his rightful throne, the classic plea which for so many years had given Rome a perfect pretext for conquest.[54] It was with enormous reluctance that Agricola tore himself away. It was perhaps the greatest regret of his governorship. There were so many reasons to sail; it would have been so easy. Or so he kept repeating to his son-in-law, Tacitus:

> I have often heard him say that Ireland could be defeated and held with one legion and a few auxiliaries; and that it would have a beneficial effect on Britain if it was completely surrounded by Roman armies, and freedom was banished from its sight.[55]

Whatever was responsible for his naivety (and perhaps it was deliberate misinformation from the Irish prince), it was as well he did not put it to the test.[56] Instead the next year he gave the order to continue the push north. His most famous campaign was about to begin.

Agricola had already completed a thorough reconnaissance of the coast of Scotland:

> The Roman fleet now sailed round the furthest shores for the first time, and so established that Britain is an island. At the same time it discovered and overthrew some islands, called the Orkneys, which until then had been unknown. Thule [now thought to be Iceland], too, was sighted...[57]

In fact, the fleet was to play a vital role throughout the course of the campaign, sailing ahead to reconnoitre harbours, shadowing the troops as they pressed forward on land, shipping supplies up from the south. Just as importantly, it was a useful tool in Agricola's arsenal for psychological warfare, as the sight of Rome's galleys plying up and down the eastern coast of Scotland, using its sea lanes and its anchorages and beaches as if they were their own, struck fear and dismay into the Caledonians' hearts.[58] Mile by mile and glen by glen the Caledonii fell back, waiting with increasing edginess for the right moment to attack.

Tensions were running high in Agricola's camp, too. A German cohort serving in the Roman army mutinied and fled in three small warships. The veterans who spoke to Tacitus described how to the troops on shore, who saw them out to sea, the vessels seemed like 'a ghostly apparition as they sailed along the coast'. But without pilots they lost their way; starvation forced the Germans into cannibalism; and at last they were shipwrecked and sold into slavery. Some made it back to the River Rhine, 'where they gained notoriety by telling the story of their wonderful adventure'.[59]

As Agricola's army marched ever northwards up the east coast, they began to meet serious resistance. Some of his officers were decidedly uneasy and began to lobby for a 'strategic retreat' behind the Forth. 'Evacuation,' they said, 'was preferable to expulsion'. But by now the Roman army had reached the Moray Firth.[60] For the Caledonii it was time to make a stand.

When Agricola learned of their plans, he split his troops into three divisions and advanced to meet them.[61] In the dead of night, news came to him. The enemy had struck. They had taken advantage of the fact that the Roman force had been divided and had launched a surprise attack on the Ninth Legion as it slept. There was fierce fighting. The Romans were sustaining heavy casualties. Immediately, Agricola sent his cavalry galloping into the darkness out of the fire-lit camp and to their aid; at the head of his infantry the governor marched after them. The legions' eagles gleaming in the half-light, the soldiers raised a guttural roar and launched their vicious attack. Dawn broke to all-out battle as the full force of the now reunited Roman army, shields linked and short swords drawn, engaged with the Caledonii. It was a bitter, bloody struggle, but at last the Caledonii gave way and ran. In the marshland and the woods the Romans could not catch them. For the moment they had escaped, but both sides knew that the war was not yet over. Autumn was too close for the Romans to march further, but next spring they would be back. It was time to get ready.

The next year (AD 83), with their fleet again out to sea shadowing them, the Roman army, 20,000 to 30,000 strong, tramped up the now familiar east coast towards the final battle. Somewhere in the mountains northwest of Aberdeen, on the slopes of Mons Graupius, they met their enemy.[62] By now the Caledonii had amassed a mighty force, some 30,000 men (so Tacitus declares) drawn from the glens of Scotland. At their head was a leader whose name has come down to us as Calgacus, and it was into his mouth that Tacitus put one of the most rousing speeches in Latin literature.

It was a speech that Calgacus almost certainly did not make, written by the historian in precisely the elegant and balanced language whose mastery

Plate 15 The cavalry parade helmet found, with other horse gear, buried under a barrack-room floor at Ribchester fort. Second century AD.

Plate 16 *overleaf* The Roman fort at Vindolanda, just south of Hadrian's Wall, from the air. The fort is in the background, the baths and *vicus* in the foreground.

Plate 17 Bronze head of the emperor Hadrian (AD 117–38) found in the River Thames (London).

Plate 18 *opposite above* Bust of Antinous as Zagreus-Bacchus, from Littlecote villa in Wiltshire. Late Roman.

Plate 19 *opposite below* Copper *as* of Domitian from the issue of AD 87, found in Suffolk. This issue is commonly found in Britain. (Diam. 30 mm)

Plate 20 Looking east along Hadrian's Wall at Housesteads Crags. Housesteads fort stood on the high ground, behind the trees, in the centre of the photo.

Plate 21 *opposite below* The Staffordshire Moorlands Pan, naming forts at the western end of Hadrian's Wall, second century AD.

Plate 22 *overleaf* Marble bust of the emperor Antoninus Pius (AD 138–61), wearing a military cloak.

he had earlier seen as one of the signs of Britain's enslavement. It painted a picture of an island pillaged and a people oppressed, where wealth was stripped through taxation and harvests appropriated to fill Roman granaries. It called to mind how a woman, Boudica, had come so close to driving the occupying army out of Britain. It praised the bravery of the Caledonii, suggesting that the Romans, 'a paltry band, gaping wide-eyed at a strange sky, at strange seas and forests', were 'frightened and bewildered'.[63] And it contained these lines, so stirring and so unforgettable:

> Beyond us there are no more peoples; there is nothing but the waves and rocks, and the Romans, deadlier by far than these – you can't escape from them; not by obedience or by submission. Robbers of the world, now that they have exhausted the land by their plunder, they are ransacking the very sea. If an enemy is rich, he excites their lust; if he is poor, their ambition. Neither the East nor West can satisfy them. Alone of all men, they lust alike for riches and for poverty. Theft, slaughter, rape: the Romans call these 'government'; they make a wasteland and they call it peace.[64]

How Tacitus' audience reacted when they heard him read out these words we do not know. The most powerful men in Rome, they may have chuckled.

The record of the speech that Agricola made is possibly more accurate. The bravest of the Britons were all dead, he claimed; the men who faced them were the dregs; this was the battle that his men had longed for, the last great battle of them all, their chance to show their mettle. But it was not everyone who was to have this chance. Agricola was later to claim that he kept his legions back, drawn up in ranks outside the ramparts of their camp, because he felt that victory would be more glorious if no Roman blood was shed.[65] Whatever the real reason, it was the auxiliaries, men from Batavia and Tungria (the modern Netherlands) as well as some from southern Britain, who were to bear the brunt of battle. Numbering 8,000, they formed the centre of the line; on their flanks, 3,000 Roman cavalry, now reining in their horses, were poised to charge. Dismounting from his own horse, Agricola took his place in front of the eagles.

Theoretically at least, the Caledonii were in the better position – on higher ground from where they could rain missiles down on the heads of the Romans. They had roused themselves into a state of frenzy. Tacitus, who must surely have interviewed veterans of the fight, describes them:

...shouting and singing and yelling discordant cries. Groups of warriors began to mill about and weapons flashed as the bravest stepped
forward, and all the time their battle-line was taking shape.[66]

Soon the missiles began to fly. As the Romans held their locked shields
high to protect them from the deadly rain, the Caledonii buffeted the
Roman javelins aside with their long swords and small round shields. Soon
the two sides were fighting hand to hand, and the Caledonii's long swords
proved their downfall. For in the tight-packed melée, these weapons were
difficult to wield. They soon were worse than useless. The Romans, on the
other hand, armed with short stabbing swords, could unleash mayhem. The
Batavians 'struck blow after blow, smiting the Caledonii with the bosses of
their shields and stabbing them in the face'.[67] On either flank, the Roman
cavalry had driven off the Caledonii's war chariots, which, even in the hands
of such skilled drivers, must have been desperately difficult to control on
such rough terrain. Now Roman cavalry plunged into the battle, crashing
like a wave against the Caledonii, hacking and stabbing at them from above.

Ironically for the Romans, this was the moment of greatest danger.
For advancing as they were up the steep hillside, the infantry were finding
it hard to maintain their footing, while the cavalry, their horses' hooves
slipping on the heather and the scree, were jostling against them. Nor was
this the only hazard:

> Often a runaway chariot or riderless horse careering about wildly
> in their terror came plunging into the ranks from the side or in
> head-on collision.[68]

It was now that the Caledonii advanced. With the Roman legions still
kept back, and taking no part in the battle, Agricola's troops seemed easy
prey. The Caledonii could surely surround them. But at this moment,
Agricola ordered four squadrons of cavalry, which he had been holding
in reserve, to gallop round behind the Caledonii and to attack them from
the rear. The Britons panicked. In a moment, the tide had turned. The
Romans regained the initiative; yet while whole groups of Caledonii fled,
others from their army stood their ground; men, some of whom had lost
their weapons, charged headlong against the Roman lines to certain death.

For the Romans, all was still not secure. In the forests to their rear,
the fleeing Caledonii regrouped. The first of their pursuers found themselves ambushed, surrounded, cut to pieces. Agricola, seeing the danger,

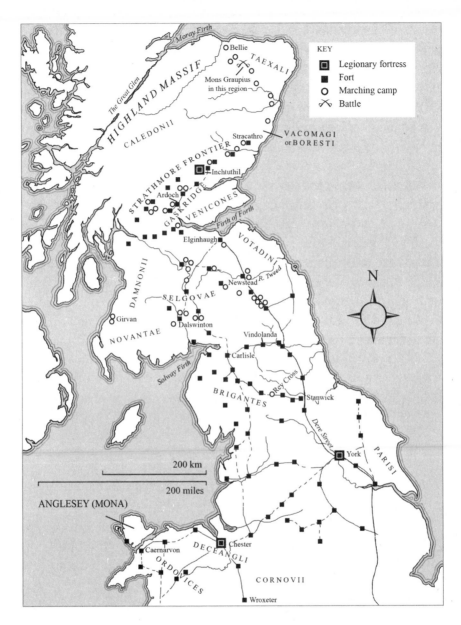

KEY

■ Legionary fortress
■ Fort
○ Marching camp
⚔ Battle

Moray Firth

Bellie

TAEXALI

Mons Graupius
in this region

The Great Glen

HIGHLAND MASSIF

CALEDONII

STRATHMORE FRONTIER

Stracathro

VACOMAGI
or BORESTI

Inchtuthil

Ardoch

GASK RIDGE

VENICONES

Firth of Forth

Elginhaugh

VOTADINI

Newstead

R. Tweed

DAMNONII

SELGOVAE

Girvan

Dalswinton

NOVANTAE

Vindolanda

Carlisle

Solway Firth

Rey Cross

BRIGANTES

Stanwick

Dere Street

200 km

200 miles

York

PARISI

ANGLESEY (MONA)

Chester

Caernarvon

DECEANGLI

ORDOVICES

CORNOVII

Wroxeter

N

11 Map showing major military sites in the Flavian period (AD 69–96), during the period of
military expansion north and into Scotland.

ran energetically from one detachment to the next, issuing orders, trying
to avert disaster. Soon he had seen to it that the forest was surrounded.
The Caledonii were trapped. Methodically and ruthlessly the infantry, in
line, scoured through the thickets; in the clearings the cavalry did likewise.

Those of the Caledonii who could escaped, melting into the mountains, leaving the corpses of perhaps 10,000 of their men strewn on the darkening hillside. The Roman losses were just 360, 'among them Aulus Atticus, the prefect of a cohort, whose youthful impetuosity and mettlesome horse carried him deep into the ranks of the enemy'.[69] That Atticus is named by Tacitus suggests he may have known him.

The Caledonii were broken. In the ghostly glens next day, Roman scouts found scenes of devastation: burnt and abandoned crofts, the bodies of whole families who had committed suicide. 'An awful silence reigned on every hand; the hills were deserted, houses smoking in the distance, and our scouts did not meet a soul.'[70]

It was too late in the summer for Agricola to consolidate his victory; but not too late to instil terror into the hearts of the conquered Caledonii. While the victorious Roman army marched south to winter quarters, their pace deliberately unhurried, a fleet of ships sailed round the north coast of Scotland before returning to its anchorage at Trucculensis Portus, somewhere on the Forth or on the Tay.

All Scotland, Agricola could claim, had now been conquered. Yet victory in battle is very different from the true subjugation of a nation. Wisely, Agricola chose not to return to the Highlands. Instead, he corralled

---

INCHTUTHIL, A LEGIONARY FORTRESS

Inchtuthil presents one of the best-preserved legionary fortress layouts from anywhere in the Roman empire. This is because of two unusual occurrences. First, the Roman army abandoned the fortress before it was complete (probably as a result of the withdrawal of the Second Legion Adiutrix from Britain); and second, there was no later settlement on the site.

Building began in AD 82 or 83 under Agricola and was still in progress when the site was evacuated, around AD 86/7 or slightly later (freshly minted coins of Domitian provide quite a precise date; see Plate 19). By that time, sixty-four barrack blocks, six granaries, a hospital, a headquarters building and a drill-hall were among the structures completed. Before the Romans left, despite its building having taken an estimated 2.7 million man hours, they levelled the entire site, burying tons of nails, either to hide them from the natives or with the intention of later retrieval.[71]

the Caledonii in the north, blocking the glens with a line of frontier forts. They were not to last for long. The legionary fortress at Inchtuthil was abandoned perhaps only four or five years later (after AD 86/87).

By AD 100 the line of forts and watchtowers slightly further to the south on the Gask Ridge had been abandoned too, as the Romans hunkered down in southern Scotland. Now Newstead (Trimontium), built by the Ninth Legion as Agricola advanced twenty years earlier (see p. 102), was Rome's most northerly outpost. Soon the Stanegate, farther to the south, would mark their frontier. Better to exploit the land they had than expend men and resources trying to annex Scotland. The rebuilding in stone of the legionary forts at Chester, Caerleon and York suggests acceptance of the status quo. With justification (at least with regards to the north), Tacitus could now write that 'Britain was conquered, then allowed to slip from our grasp'.[72]

Before the decision to retreat was made, Agricola himself had been recalled to Rome. His term of governorship had been long – seven years – more than twice that of any of his predecessors. He had left his province more peaceful and more prosperous than he had found it. He had reason to be satisfied. But by now Domitian, Vespasian's jealous and despotic younger son, was on the throne. For men of ability like Agricola, Rome was not a comfortable place to be. It might have been expected that a successful general and governor would be rewarded with an easy posting to a rich land: Africa or Asia. For Agricola, this was not to be. He chose rather to be inconspicuous, and in late August AD 93, ten years after his victory at Mons Graupius, he died. 'Even under bad emperors,' Tacitus observed, contrasting Domitian and Agricola, 'there can be great men'.[73]

✧   ✧   ✧

Of course, there were ordinary men as well as great ones, and a unique discovery has revealed much about their lives on Rome's northern frontier in the years after Agricola had been recalled. The so-called Vindolanda Tablets, found in waterlogged soil at one of the forts strung along the Stanegate (Plate 16), are a collection of more than 2,000 letters, records and other documents dating from c. AD 90 to AD 130.[74]

It is the sheer mundanity of the tablets' contents that makes the picture they paint so startlingly vivid. Lists of men available for duty show that at any given time many were often away from camp, serving on special assignments, while others were on sick leave, frequently suffering from conjunctivitis, the result of living in such smoky barracks. Some documents reveal how food and other goods were bought from local people or from military suppliers. One, written no doubt in the depths of winter, asks:

> The hides which you write are at Cataractonium (Catterick) – write that they be given to me and the wagon about which you write...I would have already been to collect them, except that I did not care to injure the animals while the roads are bad.[75]

Letters plead for references to aid promotion, request leave, appeal against punishment 'that an innocent man from overseas, about whose circumstances you may inquire, should not be bloodied with rods as if I had committed a crime'.[76] One memorandum talks of the Britons in scathing terms, noting that 'they have many cavalry. The cavalry do not use swords nor do the wretched little Brits (Brittunculi) mount in order to throw javelins'.[77]

One letter from a soldier starts:

> I want you to know that I am in good health, as I hope you are in turn, you neglectful man who have sent me not even one letter. But I think that I am behaving in a more considerate fashion in writing to you...[78]

Another (from back home, no doubt) tells its recipient that 'I have sent you socks, two pairs of sandals and two pairs of underpants'.[79] A cause for rejoicing, indeed.

It is about the life of the camp commandant, prefect of the Ninth Cohort of Batavians, Flavius Cerealis, that the tablets reveal the most. He was stationed at Vindolanda from around AD 97 to 103, and is mentioned in some sixty letters; his position suggests he came from a rich background, but it is his name that is most intriguing. The 'Flavius' element suggests that he (or perhaps his father) was granted Roman citizenship some time after AD 70, when Vespasian first established the Flavian dynasty. 'Cerealis', on the other hand, hints at a connection closer to the heart of Britain – with none other than Petillius Cerealis, the officer who had led his legionaries against Boudica and returned to the island as its governor (see above). It was usual for new citizens to take the name of Romans with whom they had been closely connected and to whom they now owed their status. Perhaps the prefect from Vindolanda (or his father) had served under Petillius Cerealis on the Rhine, during the civil war of AD 69, when the general was 'rushing to and fro in response to the various alarms'.

His wife, Sulpicia Lepidina, and children lived with him at the fort. Flavius Cerealis and his family led a curiously domestic life. While their sons reluctantly learned to write by copying out lines from Virgil (their tutor has written 'sloppy work', *seg*, in the margin of one poorly executed exercise),[80] Sulpicia was running a tight household. Lists have been found of foodstuffs and textiles, Celtic beer, fish-sauce and venison, egg-cups, bronze lamps, bed-spreads, tunics, robes. But it was not all hard work. At midwinter, the family celebrated the Saturnalia, a celebration that heavily influenced our Christmas festival, and excuses could always be found to socialize. The family of Flavius Cerealis was on very friendly terms with that of a nearby fort commander, Aelius Brocchus.[81] An invitation to Sulpicia from Brocchus' wife Claudia Severa is particularly touching:

Claudia Severa to her Lepidina, Greetings. My birthday is on 11 September, sister. Please accept my warm invitation to spend it with us, to make the day more enjoyable for me if you are there. Give my greetings to your Cerealis. My Aelius and my little son send their greetings. Farewell, my sister, my dearest soul, and may you prosper.[82]

The invitation speaks of a settled life, of a stable community where social norms were taking root and flourishing, of a province that, for the most part, had been tamed. Agricola's campaign of winning hearts and minds had worked. In what had once been the ancient tribal territory of the Brigantes, west to the conquered fastnesses of Wales, east to the devastated lands of the Iceni and the slaughtered Trinovantes, and south to the settled shires that Togidubnus had once ruled from Winchester and Silchester and Chichester, the Roman eagle stretched its wings, supreme. At Richborough, where Claudius had landed with his elephants back in the first year of the campaign, a great four-way triumphal arch towered 82 ft (25 m) into the Kent sky, a monumental gateway into Britain, a visible marker of an island pacified.[83]

Through it, in time, another emperor would ride, the energetic and obsessive Hadrian, when he came to Britain on an epic journey that would see him visit almost every province in the Roman world. His accession to the throne would bring a change of policy and have a major impact on the lives and landscape of the Britons.

5

THE LIMITS OF THE WORLD

A knot of men stands on the craggy ridge. Their scarlet cloaks flap and crack in the wind, which sighs, chilly from the north; late sunlight gleams on breastplates; and, a little way off, sleek horses snort and paw the hard ground, as their grooms try to settle them. At the edge of the group of men there are some, armed with bows and javelins, who restlessly scan the countryside around them...

If they feel the keen edge to the breeze, no one dares to show it. Not when they know that the emperor himself, Publius Aelius Hadrianus, is so inured to it. His reputation among the legionaries is awe-inspiring – how he will march with them, bareheaded in the baking sun or driving snow, how he will sleep on hard beds, share their rations, how he has stripped even the billets of commanding officers of every luxury.

Here, on the hilltop, where the land falls steeply through the bracken and the heather to the riverbed below, Hadrian seems in his element. Surrounded by the purple mountains, his lungs filled with pure crystal air, he is doing what he loves best: imposing order, setting limits, seeing his ideas come into fruition. He is building a wall.

✧ ✧ ✧

A LREADY forty-six years old, Hadrian had been born in AD 78 in Rome, of a family from Italica, near modern Seville in southern Spain.[1] Although not politically part of the elite, his family had grown rich from oil. Evidence of their business – shipping hundreds of thousands of amphorae of olive oil to Rome for use in cooking, lighting and cleansing – can still be seen today at Rome's Monte Testaccio, a huge artificial mound, the ancient dumping ground for empty amphorae.

However, it was not money that enabled Hadrian to become emperor. It was influence. Hadrian was only ten years old when his father died. He was adopted by a fellow Spaniard, a tough ambitious soldier, Trajan, and when Trajan became emperor in AD 98, Hadrian found himself moving in the highest and most rarefied circles of Roman society. Still, his future was not assured, and his early adult life was (for his class) unremarkable, as he filled the usual political offices and served his time in the army.

Indeed, his fellow senators seem to have viewed him with disdain, if not suspicion, mocking his provincial accent and his passion for all things Greek. They called him 'Greekling' (*Graeculus*), and his Greek-style beard, along with his interest in the arts and architecture, mysticism and philosophy, set him uneasily apart from his conservative Roman colleagues.

As the years dragged on and Trajan still refused to name him as his successor, Hadrian could count on one crucial ally: Trajan's wife Plotina. In August AD 117, as Trajan lay dangerously ill in Syria, Plotina produced a letter, written (so she claimed) by her husband, proclaiming Hadrian his heir. Days later, Trajan died. Or perhaps he had died already. A fourth-century biographer wrote:

> There are those who have recorded that it was through Plotina's faction (Trajan being already dead) that Hadrian was adopted; and that a substitute speaking in a tired voice impersonated Trajan.[2]

Hadrian at last was emperor.

It was the beginning of a reign that would be characterized by an almost superhuman energy, a restless refusal to stay put or be tied down to one discipline. A micro-manager, Hadrian did not underestimate his own abilities and from the start he appeared to court controversy. Within days of becoming emperor, he made his first and all-important decision. For centuries, Romans had believed it to be their destiny always to expand the territory they ruled. As their national epic, Virgil's *Aeneid*, had proclaimed:

Remember, Roman, bring the nations under your empire's rule;
For these are your special skills, to impose the ways of peace,
To spare the defeated and to defeat the proud.[3]

Now their empire stretched from Spain in the west to the borders of modern Iraq in the east, and from Britain in the north to the Sahara Desert in the south. When he died, Trajan had been trying to push those borders further to the east. Now, at a stroke, Hadrian reversed this policy. No longer was the Roman empire to expand. Instead, it would define its limits and defend its borders – and within those borders, harmony and civilization would flourish.

So, after a year spent consolidating the eastern provinces, Hadrian returned to Rome as emperor. His triumphant entry into the city in July AD 118 needed careful planning. He knew the Senate viewed him with hostility – and understandably so. Only weeks after his succession the year before, four of their number, all ex-consuls, had been executed for treason, on shaky legal grounds. The Senate's anger might be implacable.[4]

Hadrian's solution was characteristically clever. Immediately, he tried to buy the People's goodwill with a generous cash handout to every citizen. Then he wrote off all their debts, staging a dramatic bonfire of their IOUs in Trajan's Forum.[5] To the Senate he made a speech distancing himself from the executions of their colleagues and promising that this would never be repeated. But it still looked as if neither the Senate nor the People might be prepared to accept him, especially since they resented his new non-expansionist policy, which they thought cowardly and un-Roman.

So, seeking to establish himself as a second Augustus, and to demonstrate the benefits of peace to the empire and its capital, Hadrian embarked on the ambitious building projects that were to characterize his reign. Almost overnight there began a frenzy of activity. A huge double temple to Venus and Rome rose block by block beyond the Forum, while a great domed temple dedicated to all the gods, a newly remodelled Pantheon, took shape on what had once been the Field of Mars, close by the ancient voting pens of the Republic. And out in the hills at Tivoli, east of Rome, the very landscape was being moulded to accommodate a vast villa complex, Hadrian's imperial palace, with artificial lakes and fountains, frescoed walls and massive marble halls for state occasions, all linked by miles of subterranean service-tunnels, so that the slaves who managed it might not be seen.[6]

All these buildings, and many more which sprang up like flowers in a desert after rain, show signs of Hadrian's personal involvement. He was architecture-mad and, as in almost every other field, he thought that he knew best. Once, as a young man, he had tried to influence the architect Apollodorus, suggesting that he might like to incorporate some domes into his design. 'You and your pumpkins!', the architect had snarled. Now, as emperor, Hadrian had free rein. The story that he had Apollodorus killed is more than likely false, but domes did begin to mushroom across the empire.[7]

The greatest dome was that of the Pantheon, a building that more than any other reflected Hadrian's vision of heaven and earth. The sheer statistics are staggering. Some 142 ft (43 m) in diameter, the dome remains the largest made from unreinforced concrete anywhere in the world. Forming half of a perfect sphere, it was originally painted to represent the heavens, with a circular opening (or *oculus*) at its highest point, through which poured sunlight, the beams sweeping daily across the building's glittering interior, illuminating individual statues on its way. The material used in its construction came from every corner of the empire. It was truly pan-Roman, and it was here that Hadrian held court, seated symbolically at the very heart of his new world.[8]

✧ ✧ ✧

It was the fringes of the Roman world, and the provinces, which gripped Hadrian's imagination more than Rome. Indeed, he took every opportunity to absent himself from the teeming, scheming metropolis. No other emperor would travel as widely or for so long as he did – for more than ten years, half his reign, he was away from Rome.

Shortly after dedicating the foundations of the Temple of Venus and Rome in April AD 121, Hadrian at the head of his retinue set out for Germany and the Rhine. Here he supervised the building of a new frontier, a wooden palisade, which snaked across the landscape, to define the limits of his rule. To facilitate supplies, he had a 23 mile canal constructed between the River Maas and the River Rhine.[9]

Even if the army was not to face external enemies, it must still be kept in peak condition. A later biographer writes of Hadrian that 'although eager for peace rather than war, he trained his troops as if war was imminent...instilling into them the example of his own endurance'. For he led

12 Copper-alloy *as* of Hadrian showing Britannia as a warrior, AD 119–21. The coin is now in the British Museum.

by example, 'cheerfully eating camp fare out of doors, bacon and cheese and rough wine.'[10] It was a pattern of behaviour that would be repeated over and over wherever he went, whether on the Rhine or in North Africa – or Britain.

Britain was already high on Hadrian's agenda. There had been insurrection in the province early in his reign, with the north enduring heavy fighting. Such scant references as have come down to us tell of many Roman soldiers killed and fears that Britain could not be kept under Roman control, while a tombstone was set up at Vindolanda for a centurion of the First Cohort of Tungrians killed fighting the Britons in battle. It was only after the Roman legions had suffered serious losses that, in AD 119, the situation had been stabilized sufficiently to allow coins to be struck confidently depicting a Roman Britannia. It showed a female warrior, similar in many ways to Minerva herself, seated on a rocky crag armed with a shield and spear – a very different Britannia from the one whom Claudius was shown dragging by the hair at Aphrodisias, a new, proud and confident personification of the now settled province (Fig. 12; Plate 1).[11]

If Hadrian's new vision of an empire characterized by law, order and civilization within well-defined physical boundaries was to have any future, the touchstone of its success was to be Britain.

Preparations for Hadrian's visit were made well in advance, and by June AD 122, all was in place. It had to be. Along with the emperor came not only his own retinue, his wife Sabina, courtiers and civil servants, accompanied by a detachment of Praetorians and Horse Guards, but also 5,500 men of the Sixth Legion Victrix, 3,000 legionaries from Spain and Upper Germany,[12] and all of their support staff. To oversee his British projects he brought a new governor, Aulus Platorius Nepos.

Nepos was a close friend of the emperor. Roughly the same age as Hadrian, like him he had been born in southern Spain; like Hadrian, too, he had been in the east, serving as legate during Trajan's Parthian War. When Hadrian had risen to supreme power, Nepos had been rewarded first with the governorship of Thrace (AD 117–19) and then a consulship

(AD 119), before being sent to Lower Germany as governor. It was from here that he now accompanied Hadrian to Britain.[13]

If Hadrian was pleased to have his friend Nepos with him, his feelings about the presence of his wife, Sabina, may not have been so enthusiastic. The great-niece of Trajan, Sabina had been married to Hadrian in AD 100, when she was fourteen, and from the start it had been a disaster. The couple loathed each other, to such an extent that Sabina was said to have let it be well known that, to protect the human race, she had taken measures to ensure that she would never conceive a child by Hadrian. Hadrian meanwhile told friends that if he had not been emperor he would gladly have divorced Sabina; she was so moody and so difficult.[14]

It was, perhaps, to keep her out of Rome, where she might foment trouble, that Hadrian brought Sabina with him, and, although their official schedules were no doubt designed to let them spend as little time as possible together, Hadrian ensured that his wife was watched closely at all times. While the emperor headed north, Sabina may have toured the south, with stops perhaps in London and in Bath.[15]

THE IMAGE OF BRITANNIA

Britannia first appeared on Roman coins in the early years of Hadrian's reign, around AD 119. She is shown as a warlike warrior seated on rocks, holding a sceptre or spear and shield (Fig. 12).[16] This image conjures up a rugged, warlike province, an impression that was projected by Roman writers. The way in which Britannia is depicted is sometimes used as evidence for otherwise unrecorded events within the province itself. For example, although on one issue of coins struck by Antoninus Pius (AD 138–61) she is shown in a formal stance, on another of AD 154/5 she adopts a 'mournful' pose, perhaps suggesting that there has been rebellion or warfare in the province (Fig. 18).[17] She features briefly on the coinage of Commodus (AD 180–92) and probably on a coin of AD 211 celebrating victory in Scotland under Septimius Severus and Caracalla (Plate 25).[18] Then she does not reappear until the reign of Carausius (AD 286–93), when she welcomes the new emperor to Britain.[19] Here, she is not so warlike, but is dressed in flowing robes, greeting the long-awaited emperor (Plate 32). After Carausius, we have to wait about 1,350 years for Britannia to make a triumphant return on the coinage of Charles II (1660–85).

Already a well-established and sophisticated Roman spa town, Bath had been founded on the site of an ancient British shrine to the water goddess Sulis. Now, above her steaming sulphur springs, dedicated by the Romans to Sulis-Minerva, an elegant temple rose with fluted columns 24 ft (7.3 m) high, topped with a stylish pediment on which two winged victories flanked a Gorgon's head. Within the complex, in a vast rectangular pool, bathers enjoyed the water's natural warmth. In the inner sanctuary itself, where the scalding spring bubbled from the rock, rites of an altogether darker nature took place. For here in the subterranean gloom, with coals smoking on the altars, Sabina may have seen worshippers casting not only coins into the seething spring, but curses, too – prayers scratched in Latin on lead sheets calling on the goddess for vengeance:[20]

> Docilianus [son] of Brucerus to the most holy god Sulis. I curse him who has stolen my hooded cloak, whether man or woman, whether slave or free, that...the goddess Sulis inflict death upon...and not allow him sleep or children now and in the future, until he has brought my hooded cloak to the temple of her divinity.[21]

It may have been here, in the hot-house atmosphere of Bath, that Hadrian's spies finally uncovered scandal – a scandal so significant that it entailed a major reshuffle of the imperial court. Out went many of the top officials, including the imperial biographer Suetonius, who had held the post of Director of the Chancery. The reason given was that 'in their relations with [Hadrian's] wife Sabina, they behaved with greater familiarity than the etiquette of the court required'.[22] Quite what this means has been debated hotly ever since, but it marked a low point in Hadrian's already chilly conjugal arrangements.

It must have been with a sense of considerable relief that Hadrian escaped the tortured confines of domestic life and threw himself into the altogether more straightforward business of reforming Britain. Characteristically, he began by bolstering morale. On 17 July AD 122, he issued a document to the army veterans, possibly reflecting a speech made at a special ceremony on a parade-ground somewhere in the south of England. In it, he rewarded the troops who had subdued the uprisings three years earlier, granting to them:

> ...their children and descendants the citizenship and the right of legal marriage with the wife they had at the time that citizenship

was granted to them, or if they are unmarried, with the wife they subsequently marry (provided that each takes only one wife).[23]

Hadrian had not come to Britain merely to reward his soldiers or reform his civil service. Ensuring the province's stability was part of his agenda, yet to allow that stability to last he must first shore up the borders. He must go north.

Stories of the barbarians of Britain had been part of Hadrian's childhood. He had been seven when reports had reached the capital of the famous victory over Calgacus at Mons Graupius (see p. 104), and while he was on leave in Rome as a military tribune, twenty-one years old, he may have heard the great orator-historian Cornelius Tacitus recite his monograph in honour of Agricola. In Tacitus' *Histories* he may even have read how in the north of Britain 'a limit could be found' between the two seas, so that 'the enemy could be pushed out, as if into a different island'.[24]

As the newly implanted legionaries marched in from York, and the fleet nosed its way into the Tyne estuary, it was time for another ceremony. Together, Hadrian and his army dedicated two altars and made sacrifice to mark the construction of a new bridge, the *Pons Aelius*, named in honour of the emperor. With massive stone piers, each with cutwaters up- and down-stream, each built on a foundation of iron-shod piles driven deep into the riverbed, the bridge carried a roadway 18 ft (5.5 m) wide across the Tyne. It was a classic piece of Roman construction work.[25] But it was only the beginning.

A fragmentary inscription records what may have been the speech that Hadrian gave at the dedication ceremony. It mentions not only the restoration of security in Britain, but the construction of a barrier 'between the two shores of Ocean by the army of the province'.[26] It was time to build Hadrian's Wall (Plate 20). His biographer neatly sums it up:

> Having completely transformed the soldiers, in royal fashion he set out for Britain, where he corrected many things and was the first to build a wall 80 miles long to separate the barbarians and the Romans.[27]

Hadrian had not allowed topography to interfere with his design for the villa at Tivoli, nor his architect Apollodorus to advise him on the use of domes, and it seems that in his blueprint for the Wall the emperor was similarly stubborn. It is entirely in character that with a sweep of his stylus

he drew a line 80 miles in length from the Tyne Estuary to the Solway
Firth, just north of an existing road, the Stanegate, along which the Wall
would be laid out (Fig. 13). Every mile a fortlet or milecastle would be built,
and between each milecastle two turrets. It was an elegant design, but
often it completely ignored the lie of the land: some milecastles ended up
precariously placed on steep slopes, some turrets in deep dips and valleys.
Of course, no one dared to contradict the emperor, and before long the
great project was under way.[28] Later, when Hadrian was safely gone from
Britain, the garrison forts, such as that at Housesteads,[29] were moved from
the Stanegate to the line of the Wall itself. Behind the Wall a linear barrier
of a ditch and two embankments (*vallum*) was added, creating a demilita-
rized zone, perhaps to keep out disgruntled Brigantians.

Although to the far west there were stretches formed of turf, for the
most part the Wall was built of stone. A clay and rubble core was faced
with cut stone blocks, which were themselves rendered in plaster and
then whitewashed, as dazzling and clear a mark on the landscape as any
that the British tribes had carved into the chalky soil, a sign proclaiming
unequivocally to all who saw it that to the south lay the lands of Rome.
At the eastern end, between the Wall and the ditch to the north, sharpened wooden branches were set in pits to create an extra barrier. Along

13 Map of the Hadrianic frontier, after *c.* AD 130, showing the Wall, forts and roads.

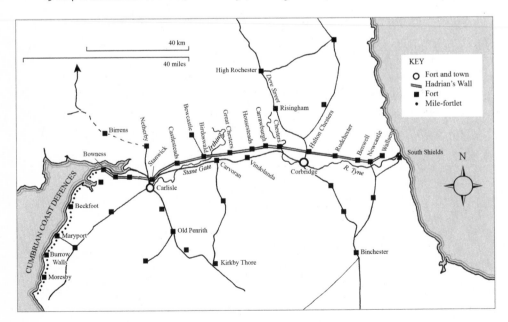

14 Soldiers building a fort during the Dacian campaign, from a relief on Trajan's Column, Rome, dedicated in AD 113.

the length of the Wall, its builders, men from all three British legions, left inscriptions commemorating their part in its construction. Three also bear the names of Nepos and Hadrian.[30]

However, the Wall was not the absolute limit of Roman power in Britain. There were still outposts further north to keep in check 'those pesky little Brits' (*Brittunculi*), as an officer stationed at Vindolanda had once referred to them (see p. 118). Indeed, for a long while the Wall may have served little more than a symbolic purpose, a shining white northern barrier, mirroring the cliffs of Dover to the south, albeit furnished with an array of crossing-points convenient for the collection of taxes and other dues. This was certainly part of the purpose of another of Hadrian's great walls, the *Fossatum Africae*, in modern Tunisia and Algeria.[31] In Britain, the monumental structure of the Wall left an impression on its garrison to the extent that tourist mementoes in the form of small pans were produced naming some of its forts (Plate 21).[32]

The Wall was not the only major project inaugurated during Hadrian's visit to Britain. Among the work probably begun in that remarkable year and continued throughout Hadrian's reign was the draining of the Fens, the marshland on the fringes of The Wash in Lincolnshire, Cambridge-shire and Norfolk. It was a scheme that would provide good income for the emperor, a new imperial estate run by the provincial procurator and his staff in London, with local offices like those in the administrative block near Stonea, Cambridgeshire. The newly reclaimed land was to produce a valuable supply of grain, which was probably shipped north in barges up the rivers Ouse and Tyne to feed the soldiers on the Wall.[33]

Mineral resources, too, caught the imperial eye. At the other side of the country in Wales, gold, silver and copper were all there for the taking. Even in the years immediately before Hadrian's visit to the island, a mile-stone had been set up on the north Welsh coast, 7 miles from the fort at Kanovium (Caerhun) on a road that led towards the mines. Agricola's subjugation of the Ordovices and Silures was paying rich dividends, some-thing that would have pleased the procurator Marcus Maenius Agrippa.[34] A friend of Hadrian, Maenius, may well have accompanied him to Britain to serve successively in three posts: prefect of the first Cohort of Spaniards at Maryport; prefect of the British fleet; and procurator.[35]

Further south, in the borderlands of Wales in modern Shropshire, the city of Viroconium (Wroxeter), the fourth largest in the province, was fur-nished with a new forum, a basilica, and baths.[36] An ancient tribal capital, Viroconium had been chosen as the site first of a temporary marching camp, then of a permanent military garrison. Now, under Hadrian, its status as a *civitas* capital, a town to rule the surrounding territory, a beacon of Roman civilization calculated to attract the local tribesfolk into the impe-rial fold, was secured. Elsewhere in the empire, in eastern cities such as Ephesus and Smyrna, Hadrian was to mark his visits by the distribution of funding for civic projects, the remission of taxes or the cancellation of existing debts. No doubt this, too, was the case at Viroconium.

It was part of Hadrian's grand plan to inject capital into local econo-mies, to help to boost a sense of pride and of belonging by creating new, gleaming Roman towns and cities – and nowhere was that sense of belonging more needed now than in Britain. So, generous funding poured into the regions to build new administrative capitals for some of the poorer and more peripheral tribes: Venta Silurum (Caerwent) in south Wales; Moridunum Demetarum (Carmarthen) in west Wales; Petuaria Pariso-rum (Brough-on-Humber) and Isurium Brigantum (Aldborough) in northeast England.[37] Throughout the province, tribal settlements were turning into Roman towns.

Hadrian and Hunting

One activity in which Hadrian undoubtedly participated was hunting – probably with his beloved horse Borysthenes, which 'used to fly over plains and marshes and hills and thickets...' A lion hunt in which he took part is described by the Alexandrian poet Pankrates, and Hadrian is shown hunting a bear, a boar and a lion on roundels on the Arch of Constantine in Rome (Fig. 15). The epitaph which Hadrian himself wrote for Borysthenes talks of 'boars with tusks foaming white', and in Britain, boar hunting was probably one of the most popular pursuits of the officer class. On Bollihope Common (County Durham) a cavalry officer dedicated an altar to the woodland deity Silvanus because he had managed to kill 'a wild boar of remarkable fineness which many of his predecessors had been unable to bag'.[38] For the wealthy, proximity to good hunting grounds was probably a major factor in choosing a villa location.

15 A roundel, reused in the Arch of Constantine in Rome, showing Hadrian and Antinous hunting a boar.

'After settling the situation in Britain, he crossed to Gaul.' So writes the ancient biographer of Hadrian.[39] No doubt, before he did leave, the emperor paid one last visit to London, now the provincial capital. It may have been to mark this final visit that a larger-than-life bronze statue was commissioned, to be erected somewhere near the River Thames (Plate 17).[40] It showed the emperor as he wished his British subjects to remember him: his head held high, his features strong and chiselled, his gaze implacably fixed on his now settled province. Unwittingly, it showed his weakness too – not in the impeccably groomed beard, which spoke of his pretensions as a Greek philosopher (though his Greek bent would forever alienate him from his Roman Senate); nor in his elegantly, almost effeminately coiffed hair (though allegations of inappropriate homosexual behaviour would dog him throughout his life); but in the tiny kinks on his earlobes, a potential indicator of coronary artery disease.[41]

✧ ✧ ✧

In the years that followed his brief time in Britain, Hadrian would turn his energies increasingly towards the east. Here was his spiritual homeland, and Athens was its spiritual capital. So, throughout the countries that today are Greece and Turkey, Armenia and Syria, Libya and Egypt, more buildings rose, more cities flourished. Everywhere he went, Hadrian's enquiring mind sought out new answers. He believed that he had found them in the 'mystery' religions of the east, in cults of death and rebirth such as those at Eleusis near Athens or on the Egyptian Nile.[42]

His quest found one fulfilment in his invention of a new god, Antinous, a chameleon creation promising rebirth, who combined elements of Greek and Roman deities such as Hermes, Pan and Dionysus as well as the Egyptian god Osiris. At the same time, he encouraged tales of how Antinous had been the emperor's companion, how he had drowned in the Nile, how in death he had become immortal – a carefully constructed matrix in which Antinous could be all things to all peoples, designed to bind the Roman world together in one universal belief. Of course, the new god's worship came to Britain, too. From Littlecote Villa in Wiltshire to Capel St Mary in Essex, worshippers adored their small bronze busts of Antinous as Bacchus (Dionysus; see Plate 18).[43]

Ironically, at the same time that Hadrian was creating this new god of harmony, a dangerous rebellion was erupting, the result of the emperor's uncharacteristically crass mishandling of another religion, Judaism. Tensions had been simmering for years, and, ever since Titus had torn the most sacred objects of the Jewish faith from the temple in Jerusalem and carried them in triumph through the streets of Rome (an event that he celebrated on the sculptures of his Arch at the western end of the Forum), it had been only a matter of time until resentment spilled over into violence. The spark was lit by Hadrian himself. Not only had he provoked the Jews empire-wide by issuing a ban on circumcision, in AD 130 he had turned Jerusalem into a full Roman city, building a massive temple of Jupiter in the Jewish sacred precinct and renaming the city Aelia Capitolina, a title which combined his own family name with one of the cult titles of Jupiter. To add insult to injury, on one of the gates facing the city of the pig-avoiding Jews, he had carved the image of a boar.[44]

Jewish resentment boiled over into violence. Shortly after the reported death of Antinous, a star had appeared in the sky, which Hadrian had interpreted as evidence of Antinous' divinity. The Jews saw it differently: it was a sign that they must shake off Roman rule. Led by the charismatic Simon Bar Kokhba, they fought Hadrian's legions for a bloody three-and-a-half years before their eventual inevitable defeat. According to one Roman historian, 'the whole of Judaea became a wasteland'.[45] Its consequence was the Jewish diaspora. Even today, when naming Hadrian, Jews will add 'may his bones rot in hell'.

Their curse may have taken effect in Hadrian's own lifetime. To it had been added another. In early AD 138, the emperor was dangerously ill and acting increasingly unpredictably and cruelly. His rule descended into one of terror, as, believing every rumour that reached his ears, he lashed out more and more at men whom he had once trusted. One was Nepos, the erstwhile British governor; another was his own brother-in-law Servianus. The historian Dio records that when Hadrian forced the old man to take his life, Servianus:

> ...demanded fire and, as he made an offering of incense, he cried
> out: 'Gods, you know that I am guilty of no wrong. But as for
> Hadrian, this is my one prayer: may he long for death but may
> death not come to him!'[46]

Servianus' dying prayers were answered. Eventually, his body racked with pain, Hadrian was taken to the seaside resort of Baiae, where he rallied sufficiently to write of his own feelings facing death. Addressing his own soul in terms so much more gentle than any which in the last years he had used to his friends, he mused:

> Sweet soul, sweet voyager, sweet charmer,
> You, guest and comrade of my earthly frame,
> Where are you going now on your journeying? To lands
> Of gloom and ice and fog –
> No laughter like there used to be.[47]

Hadrian may have established peace – at a price – throughout the empire, but in the years that followed, in those other lands that, to the Romans at any rate, were characterized by gloom and ice and fog, the lands of Britain, many of his policies would soon unravel.

6

BAND OF BROTHERS

It was natural that the men should grumble. He quite understood. This was not the sort of terrain in which anyone with any sense would choose to spend a day more than entirely necessary. The weather, the damp, the Caledonii: all so terribly tedious. And as for himself, an ex-consul, he could think of many other provinces that he would rather govern. Yet, orders were orders and, as sure as Antoninus was emperor, they must be obeyed.

The Caledonii! You did have to admire them. Even if grudgingly. Fighting and dying for a dank bit of hillside or a mist-wreathed glen. And the passion with which they fought. Reminded him of the zealots he had had to deal with in Judaea. Bitter campaign, that. High body count on both sides. Dragged on for years. At times it seemed there would be no end to all the butchering.

Needed to be done, though. Should have gone even further, in his opinion. Should have slaughtered the lot of them. Not left one alive. How could you let people follow a religion, which did not recognize the emperor as divine? Like the Druids, too – at least there were none of them left within the empire.

One thing to be said for Judaea, though: the sun had occasionally shone. Not like here. Still, the wetter the better for the turf sods. Made a good strong wall, they did. Just what was needed to keep out the Caledonii. Without them interfering it would be so much easier to bring the lowland tribes to heel once and for all. And maybe then he, Quintus Lollius Urbicus, could settle down to doing some governing.

✧ ✧ ✧

THE occupation of another's territory, like war itself, assumes a momentum of its own, and it is impossible for even the most far-sighted commander fully to predict future events. 'Unknown unknowns' are bound to occur, which will precipitate a major rethink in policy, leading it along paths unimaginable only a few years earlier.

Something of the sort seems to have happened within Britain a generation after the building of Hadrian's Wall. It led to an attempt to redefine the northern borders of the province, and involved the appointment of a succession of governors, many of whom had served in one of the bloodiest campaigns of Hadrian's rule: the suppression of the insurrection in Judaea (see Chapter 5).

It was in AD 132 that the Jewish Revolt erupted. In Britain seventy years earlier, religious and cultural insensitivities had helped to provoke the Boudican revolt. Now it was Judaea's turn. The country exploded in a welter of bloodshed. An entire legion was butchered and, with the situation worsening by the day, Hadrian hurriedly sent for his best general, Sextus Julius Severus.[1] It must have been a hard and headlong dash for him to reach Judaea, for when he received his order from the emperor, Julius Severus was 2,500 miles away in Britain, where he was serving as governor.[2]

From humble origins in the Dalmatian *colonia* of Aequum (Citluk in modern Croatia), Julius Severus had enjoyed a meteoric rise to power. The first of his family to take a seat in the Senate, he was soon commanding the Fourteenth Legion in the frontier province of Pannonia, before being appointed governor first of Dacia (AD 119–26) and then, after a consulship, of Lower Moesia (*c.* AD 128–30). All of these provinces were on the edges of the empire, where the Danube and the Rhine defined the limits of the Roman world, so it was natural that Julius Severus' next posting should be to Britain. Perhaps this came as the direct result of insurrection on the island – a later letter written to the emperor Marcus Aurelius might suggest that troops had been lost in Britain at this time[3] – or perhaps it was simply the obvious next step in his career path.

He was not to stay long. Judaea was in flames, and he was needed. So, with his son Julius Verus perhaps riding at his side, he made the long dash east to battle. For four years (AD 132–36) the rebels fought the legions hard, but in the end, with the loss of 580,000 of their people,[4] they were defeated. Julius Severus had proved his mettle. Back in Rome he was honoured with the *ornamenta triumphalia* before being sent, as a reward, to govern Syria. In the years to come, three of the officers who had fought beside him in Judaea – Lollius Urbicus, Marcus Statius Priscus and his own son Julius Verus – would be appointed governors, too, but of a very different province: Britain.

Just two years after the revolt in Judaea had been quelled, the emperor Hadrian died (AD 138). His successor, Antoninus Pius (AD 138–61), was a man with a reputation for shunning warfare unless absolutely necessary (Plate 22).[5] Yet, with an army to keep occupied and generals to placate, it was occasionally politic even for a man of peace to engineer necessities for war. After all, there would be those in Rome who remembered all too well men like the British governor Trebellius (see Chapter 4) whose inaction had prompted his troops to mutiny. A situation such as that must not be allowed to recur.

Perhaps it was for such a reason that Antoninus Pius chose Britain as the theatre for his only real campaign. As the man to lead it, he appointed (in AD 139) Quintus Lollius Urbicus, a seasoned soldier, who had served in Judaea as Julius Severus' second-in-command. His conduct there had earned him the 'pure spear and golden crown'.[6] This, however, was merely the latest in a string of successes in a brilliant career, which had seen him serve as a tribune in Mainz, a quaestor at Rome, a legate to the governor of Asia, a Tribune of the Plebs and praetor back in Rome and a legionary commander in Vienna. The Judaean campaign over, he was rewarded with an appointment to the consulship (AD 135 or 136) before being sent as governor to Lower Germany.[7]

Now, only months into the reign of Antoninus Pius, Lollius Urbicus arrived in Britain, tasked with a special mission: to push back the northern boundaries once more beyond Hadrian's Wall and into Scotland; to create a new frontier. The reasons for this move are far from clear. Without fresh evidence, they will remain so. It may indeed be that the emperor saw the need to keep the British troops engaged – there were so many of them, after all. Or perhaps, like Claudius a century before, he wished to prove his military worth – what better theatre for a spectacular campaign than Britain's frontier, with its notoriously fierce tribes? It was a theatre, moreover, sufficiently far from Rome that news of his legions' victories could be embellished in their telling. Indeed, at the campaign's conclusion some three years later, Antoninus Pius was hailed *imperator*, an event he marked at Rome with victory coins,[8] while allowing his grateful subjects to observe that:

Although the emperor committed the operations to others while remaining in the palace at Rome, yet like the helmsman at the tiller of a warship, the glory of the whole navigation and voyage belongs to him.[9]

On the other hand, however, it may be that explanations such as these are too simplistic. It is not impossible that the countryside around the Wall was, indeed, in confusion. In a passage of the travel-writer Pausanias, we read:

> In Britain, too, [Antoninus Pius] removed most of their territory from the Brigantes, because they too had begun a war on the province of Genunia, which is subject to the Romans.[10]

Such a situation would, indeed, require a rapid response. With Hadrian's Wall slicing through the ancient lands of the Brigantes there was perhaps good reason why their disgruntled warriors would rise up against the occupying troops, and such a rebellion could well have sucked in disaffected tribesmen from further north.[11] The problem lies in Pausanias' reference to Genunia, a region that lay not in Britain but in Raetia (modern Switzerland and Bavaria), the home of another tribe also (confusingly) called the Brigantes. Did Pausanias muddle his geography? It is entirely possible that he did, that he wrote 'Genunia' in error, and that it was indeed the British Brigantes who were rebelling.[12] On the other hand, the revolt may not have been in Britain at all, but in far-off Raetia. Archaeology provides no evidence for fighting round the Wall, and there may simply have been a tactical acceptance in Rome that Hadrian had sited his frontier in the wrong place and that the narrow strip of land between the rivers Forth and Clyde could be more easily defended. As Tacitus had pointed out, what lay beyond was 'virtually another island'.[13]

If the reasons for the advance north are obscure, the physical evidence for its taking place is clear. With troops drawn from all three legions based in Britain – the Second, Sixth and Twentieth – Urbicus marched once more into southern Scotland, covering the land with a network of forts, some new, others, like Trimontium[14] from previous campaigns, restrengthened and reoccupied. How much the lowland tribes resisted them we cannot tell, though a relief from Bridgeness is instructive (Fig. 16). On it a Roman cavalryman spurs on his horse as it tramples cowering British tribesmen, one of whom has already been decapitated.[15] Of course, it is impossible to tell just who these tribesmen were. Perhaps they were Brigantes, or Selgovae from the south of Scotland, or Caledonii from the north, maybe come down as allies to their lowland cousins.[16] Whoever they were, we know that Urbicus defeated them. A biography of Antoninus Pius informs us:

> Through the agency of Lollius Urbicus, a legate, he defeated the Britons, and when the barbarians had been removed from the area he had another wall constructed, of turf.[17]

16 A Roman soldier riding down barbarians, from a relief on the Bridgeness Slab from the east end of the Antonine Wall. Now in the National Museum of Scotland.

Stretching for 37 miles between the Forth and Clyde, this is the boundary we know as the Antonine Wall, and two inscriptions set up at Balmuildy (in Strathclyde), one of the four major forts of the new frontier, proclaim that its building was begun by Urbicus.[18] Like the western sector of Hadrian's Wall, this new construction was in turf. In parts augmented with clay blocks, it rose from its foundation of un-mortared rubble, 14 ft (4.25 m) wide and 9 to 10 ft (2.7 to 3 m) high, topped by a timber breastwork, itself some 6 ft (1.8 m) high. For most of its length, the Wall was fronted to the north by a deep ditch, 40 ft (12 m) wide, from which it was separated by a berm, a levelled strip of land, which served in part to reduce the pressure on both ditch and wall and so prevent them from collapsing. As a barrier it was formidable.

The Wall did not exist alone: along its length were strung as many as twenty-nine small fortlets and up to nineteen larger forts (Fig. 17). In size, they varied greatly. Only two (at Castlecary and Balmuildy) were built of stone; the rest were made from turf and timber. With its garrison of 6,000 to 7,000 troops, this new frontier was more densely manned than Hadrian's Wall had ever been. With signalling platforms and, no doubt, watchtowers too, each sector of the new Wall was in close contact with the next.[19] In addition, for the full length of the south side of the Wall there was a military road, along which troops could be moved with swift efficiency. Another road ran from the eastern flank north to the re-commissioned

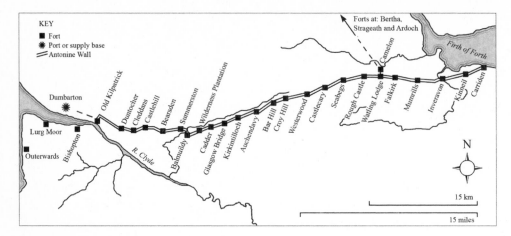

17 Map of the Antonine frontier, *c.* AD 142–58, showing the Wall, forts and roads.

forts of Bertha, Ardoch and Strathgeath, its line proclaiming all too clearly who the major threat was deemed to be: the Caledonii.

Perhaps in the years when Hadrian's Wall stood as Rome's most northerly frontier, the Caledonii had seized the chance to make inroads into Scotland's southern lowlands, forming alliances with other tribes to the south as well as those of the Brigantes who had been cut off from their native lands. Perhaps the building of the new Wall was designed to put an end to such incursions, keeping the Caledonii at bay, while kettling the lowland tribes and the troublesome Brigantes between barriers both to the south and to the north, and so enabling the Roman legions to cleanse the region of their irritating presence.

Whatever the purpose of the operation, by AD 142 it was over. Coins were struck to mark a victory and Urbicus, his mission complete, returned to Rome.[20] For around sixteen years, Antoninus' new Wall marked the frontier. To the south, Hadrian's old Wall was decommissioned, its forts abandoned and its garrisons dispersed across the south of Scotland or to the new forts of the north. It is a period from which little evidence of any kind survives. Archaeology provides no overt traces of warfare, and only an issue of base metal coins hints at disturbances of any kind. Struck in Rome in AD 154–55 and issued only within Britain, these depict the island's personification, Britannia, in mourning (Fig. 18).[21] For whom, or what, we cannot tell.

Around AD 158, again for reasons about which we can only speculate, the Antonine Wall was abandoned, probably in a process that lasted several years. Ironically, the governor who coordinated the withdrawal of the troops from the Wall was Gnaeus Julius Verus, the son of the same Julius Severus who had possibly recommended its building.[22]

Since his days of fighting in Judaea, Verus' career had taken him not only to Rome, first as prefect of the treasury and then as consul (?AD 151), but also to Lower Germany, where paradoxically the frontier of the empire was in the process of being extended. Indeed, when he took up his governorship of Britain in AD 157, he may well have brought back with him contingents from the legions, based on the island, which had been fighting under him on the newly extended German frontier.[23]

Verus' task may have been a frustrating one, but he conducted it with exemplary efficiency. Not only did he successfully withdraw the forces from the north, but he also initiated building work at the fort at Brough-on-Noe (in the Pennines), at the outpost fort of Birrens

18 Copper-alloy *as* of Antoninus Pius, showing Britannia in a mournful, or pensive, manner. The coin comes from Rome, AD 154–55; it was found in Essex.

THE ABANDONMENT OF THE ANTONINE WALL

It was traditionally thought, from the study of Samian pottery found on the frontier, that the Antonine Wall was occupied until around AD 155–58, that it was then evacuated, reoccupied around AD 158–61 and finally abandoned in AD 162. However, a reappraisal of the archaeological evidence has suggested that the Wall was in fact abandoned, in an orderly manner, around AD 158 without any reoccupation. This evacuation could have taken several years.[24] The reason for the abandonment of the frontier, so soon after it was constructed, is not known. Perhaps it was because of unrest further south, or perhaps because the cost of servicing such a northerly frontier outweighed any benefits that accrued from occupying southern Scotland. However, the discovery of a later altar, dedicated to Mercury, at Castlecary, and finds of later Roman coins at Mumrills and Kirkintilloch, do suggest that there were probably some Roman troops garrisoned or patrolling in the area after the frontier was abandoned.[25]

and at Corbridge, all of which were part of the great master plan to reoccupy Hadrian's Wall. His reward for this, and for subsequently fighting with great bravery against the Parthians, was (like his father, Sextus Julius Severus, before him) to be appointed governor of Syria.[26]

✧ ✧ ✧

Verus was not to be the last of the veterans of the Jewish campaign who would govern Britain. His immediate successor served only a few months. Perhaps he died in office. At any rate, he was soon to be replaced (AD 161) by Marcus Statius Priscus Licinius Italicus, fresh from a brief spell as governor of Upper Moesia, the latest triumph in a rich and varied career.[27]

Serving as a young man in Britain under Julius Severus, Priscus had accompanied the general to Judaea, where his prowess had earned him the 'military banner'. He was quickly promoted up the ranks, and his political career took off when he served as a procuratorial official in Gaul, collecting inheritance tax. But it was perhaps thanks to the patronage of his brother-in-arms, Lollius Urbicus, that he made the ultimate step and became a member of the Roman Senate.[28] The Jewish campaign had clearly forged close bonds between those who fought in it; in the coming years they would ensure that they helped each other in whatever ways they could.

More glory followed: Priscus was appointed quaestor, Tribune of the Plebs and praetor, priest of the Deified Vespasian and Titus, commander first of the Fourteenth Legion then of the Thirteenth, governor of Dacia (AD 156–58), consul (AD 159), and, to crown it all, curator of the Tiber and the Roman sewers (AD 160), posts which, as a young man, he could not have dared imagine even in his wildest dreams. And now, early in the reign of the new emperors, Marcus Aurelius and Lucius Verus (AD 161), he was returning to Britain as its governor.

Almost as soon as he arrived, he had to leave again. There was trouble in the east. The Parthians had invaded. Before his bags could be unpacked, Priscus, the last of the band of brothers who had fought against Bar Kokhba, was heading back along the roads he had just travelled, east to Armenia and to new glories.

The Britain he left behind was far from at peace. War, we are told, was threatening, and a new governor was sent to wage it.[29] It was in AD 161 or 162 that Sextus Calpurnius Agricola arrived to take up his post. Possibly from Numidia, he had been consul in AD 154 before going on to govern

Upper Germany. Now, in Britain, a province suffering no doubt from the usual upheavals associated with a rapid turnover of governors, he threw his energies into re-establishing the peace. In the north, on and near Hadrian's Wall – the restored frontier now that the army had withdrawn from Scotland – he took care to oversee a number of new projects and record his part in them in a series of inscriptions.[30]

With the Brigantian problem resolved and the threat of the southern tribesmen joining forces with their cousins to the north removed, the *vallum* to the south of the Wall was filled in. At the same time, a military road was constructed to run behind the Wall and link the forts, while the western sector of the Wall, which had before been made from turf, was now rebuilt in stone. To reinforce the barrier still further, some of the milecastles had their gateways narrowed, poorly sited turrets were abandoned and the number of troops now garrisoned along the Wall seems to have been increased. The *status quo* of twenty years before had been restored. Hadrian's Wall once more marked the northern bounds of Britain.

There were still forts beyond it, scattered in the hills of northern England and southern Scotland, manned by troops on constant watch, keeping a sharp eye on the tribes there, reporting anything in the slightest untoward back to the officers on the Wall. As far north as the Wall of Antoninus, and as late perhaps as AD 190, soldiers of the Sixth Legion were dedicating an altar to Mercury at the old stone fort of Castlecary, while at Mumrills and at Kirkintilloch others may have cursed the loss of coins. Even further north, small bands of scouts, the *exploratores*,[31] were no doubt practising their tradecraft in the foothills of the Grampians, striking as deep as possible into the native heartlands.

Such news as they were sending back cannot have been too reassuring. Already as the emperor Lucius Verus lay dying (AD 169), 'the Britons were on the verge of war'.[32] For a while the situation was contained; for almost thirty years, despite severe provocation, no Roman general marched north beyond the Wall. But patience can be tried only so far. The problem of the Caledonii remained and soon it would need to be addressed.

7

THE SCOURGE OF SCOTLAND

*'Let no one escape utter destruction at our hands; let not the infant
still carried in its mother's womb, if it be male, escape its fate.'*[1]

*Even in the January half-light of York's icy parade ground, where the breath
of soldiers, muffled in their winter uniforms, plumed chilly in the frosty air,
the words of the dying Septimius Severus must have sent a shiver down the
spine of those who heard them. Yet those who saw their emperor that day
must have seen the steely determination etched into his face. Despite his age
and illness, and despite the crippling pain, which now made even standing
difficult, he was blazing with incandescent rage.*

*Only hours earlier, a messenger had been admitted into the imperial
presence. His news was dire. The year before, Severus had concluded treaties with the Scottish tribes, the Maeatae and the Caledonii. Propagandist
headlines struck on victory coins in Rome gave him and his two sons the
honorific title of 'Britannicus'. There was cause for celebration: the boundaries of Roman dominance had been pushed still further north. But now,
all that was dashed. The tribal elders had reneged on their agreement. The
northern frontier was in meltdown.*

*Now, at York, a hasty meeting was convened. With the emperor were
not only his legions' top generals but his two sons, Caracalla and Geta,
unreliable men both of them, and a cause of great concern to Severus. For
he knew that, racked as he was with pain from the acute arthritis which
had spread inexorably across his body, and unable now to walk, he had no
choice but to entrust command of the forthcoming expedition to the elder of
his two sons, Caracalla. He suspected, too, that Caracalla had already tried
to kill him. And, superstitious as he was, he remembered the prophecy that
he himself would never return from Britain alive. It was now seven years
since he had celebrated Rome's seventh Secular Games and, for him, seven
was a number loaded with an ominous significance. He knew he had not
long to live. Now, as he gazed across the darkling parade ground, he may
have reflected on the long road that had brought him here.*

S EPTIMIUS Severus was born in AD 145 in North Africa, in the glittering coastal city of Lepcis Magna.² Visit it today, and you can still enjoy one of the finest views in the entire Roman world. Stand at the top of the theatre's auditorium, and there below you the columns of the stage building still shine white against a dark sea stretching far to the horizon. Look south and you can see the magnificent triumphal arch; turn slightly to the east and you will gaze on the Imperial Forum, a gift to his home city from its favourite son, the emperor Septimius Severus.

For four generations, the Septimii had been Roman citizens, ever since the time of Severus' great-grandfather, a grandee of Lepcis Magna, who owned estates near Veii north of Rome and made his wealth from olive oil and trans-Saharan trading. Like many new men, he understood the value of a good education, so he raised his son Lucius (Severus' grandfather) in Italy, made sure that he lost any trace of a provincial accent, and gave him the best classical schooling possible – including lessons in rhetoric from the famous Quintilian, the teacher of the younger Pliny. Admitted into the equestrian class, Lucius returned to Lepcis. The city, too, was prospering. In the early second century it was elevated to the status of *colonia*. They were exciting times, when anything seemed possible, and the Septimii made sure that they were at the heart of their city's expansion, while still keeping close ties with Rome. For here, too, they were making their influence felt. Politically ambitious, the family set its sights on one of the highest prizes of all, and in AD 160 they won it. For in this year, one of Lucius' sons became consul.

Two years later (AD 162), when young Septimius Severus was seventeen, his father sent him from Lepcis to Rome, to the house of his uncle, to begin his own political career. Short, stocky, but physically strong, Severus was possessed already of an active and enquiring mind and an almost inexhaustible energy.³ In time, with his squat face and small nose, his dark complexion, and his long luxurious beard, he would become immediately recognizable to citizens and senators alike (Plate 23). For now, a new boy in Rome, he had to work hard to make his mark. Of course, family connections helped, and (no doubt through his uncle's agency) he was awarded by the emperor Marcus Aurelius himself the honour of wearing the toga with the broad purple stripe, an indication that he was indeed on course for a senatorial career. Now, as a magistrate, he was truly in the public eye, and only seven years later (AD 169), at the age of twenty-four, the energetic Severus took his seat in the Senate.

From now on, the entire Roman empire would be Severus' stage. In the capital, he had already heard reports from the provinces – not least, perhaps, from his own brother, who had served in Britain with Calpurnius Agricola, as a tribune in the Second Legion based at Caerleon. But now, it was time for Severus himself to travel. His first posting came in Sardinia, but soon (AD 173) he was called to Africa to serve as legate under its new proconsul – his uncle, the ex-consul. The next year he was back in Rome, appointed Tribune of the Plebs as the emperor's own candidate before serving as a praetor, probably presiding over one of the city's law courts. Soon, as a judicial officer, he was in Spain (AD 176–80), where the army was engaged in quelling a Moorish uprising.

In AD 180, Marcus Aurelius died, and it was under his successor, the cruel and eccentric Commodus, that Severus received his first military command. As luck would have it he was sent to Syria to serve as legionary commander under the governor Publius Helvius Pertinax.[4] It was a fateful meeting, for, in the years that followed, the two men's lives would become curiously entwined.

Pertinax's own public career had been meteoric. The son of a freed-man, he had embarked first on a career in teaching, but, as can so often happen, he soon found himself looking for alternative employment. His first attempt (to gain a commission as a legionary centurion) failed, but he did succeed in being appointed prefect of a cohort of Gauls serving in Syria (AD 160). Indeed, he served with such distinction that a few years later he was promoted and sent to Britain as tribune of the Sixth Legion, based in York under the governorship of Calpurnius Agricola (at roughly the same time as Severus' own brother was serving at Caerleon). Perhaps Pertinax worked out of Corbridge, just to the south of Hadrian's Wall, which was at that time a major fort and supply depot. Before long, he was on the Wall itself, commanding an auxiliary unit, probably the First Cohort of Tungrians, at Housesteads. A succession of postings followed and in AD 172, Pertinax found himself commanding the First Legion Adiutrix in Pannonia. It was now that he entered military folklore, when, on campaign, his troops were surrounded by the enemy, without access to water. Just as the situation was becoming dire, the heavens opened. Pertinax's men drank deep, while the enemy was cowed by hail and thunder. Of course, the emperor took the credit for this meteorological miracle, but nonethe-less Pertinax himself was soon made consul, and now in AD 180 he had been appointed governor of Syria, one of the richest provinces in the empire.

It was the sort of place a man such as Pertinax's new lieutenant Severus must have relished. No doubt he seized the opportunity to travel widely throughout the province. Perhaps he visited the oasis city of Palmyra and the outpost fort at Dura Europos on the Euphrates. He certainly visited Emesa, where Elagabal, the 'god of the mountain', was worshipped, for it was here that Severus met Julia Domna, the daughter of the priest, Julius Bassianus. Severus was bewitched. Not only was she brilliant and beautiful; not only was her family fabulously rich; but her horoscope foretold a heady future: she was destined to marry a king. Severus, who already had a wife, resolved to bide his time.

In AD 182, any hopes that Severus might have entertained of frequent visits to Emesa were dashed when first Pertinax was dismissed as governor and then he himself was relieved of his command. For several years, Severus' career, which until now had seemed so promising, appeared to stall. Deprived of office, he spent much of his time in Athens, still one of the cultural hearts of the empire and a major seat of learning. For three years Severus kicked his heels, but in AD 185 the long-awaited call eventually came: he had been appointed governor of Gallia Lugdunensis (central and northwest France). It was not the only change his life would take. Within months his wife was dead, and, when the proper period had passed for mourning, Severus sent a messenger in haste east to Emesa to request Julia Domna's hand in marriage.

From the moment she arrived in Gaul (AD 187), the Syrian never left her husband's side, constantly supporting him as events began to take on a momentum all their own. Within a year (AD 188), she bore their first son, Caracalla. The next year (AD 189), she bore their second, Geta (Plate 24). By now the family were in Sicily, where Severus was governor; by AD 191, they had all moved again, this time to Upper Pannonia; but on New Year's Day AD 193, the Roman world was plunged deep into chaos – and the man at the heart of it was Pertinax.

✧   ✧   ✧

When Severus and he had parted ten years earlier in Syria, it had seemed for a while as if Pertinax's career too was over. Forced into an unwelcome retirement in his native Liguria, like Severus he kicked his heels. Like Severus, too, he received his recall in AD 185, and as his one-time deputy rode out to Gallia Lugdunensis, Pertinax himself set forth for Britain and the governorship. The province was in turmoil, thanks in no small part to Pertinax's predecessor, Ulpius Marcellus. Five years before (AD 180), following the massacre of a Roman army and its general, Marcellus had restored the northern frontier, pushing deep into the Scottish lowlands where he may have reoccupied the fort at Cramond and built another at Carpow,[5] where the River Earn joins the Tay. However, Marcellus was a hard task-master, who would make a point of sending orders to his officers to read during the night to prove to them how little sleep he needed. Unsurprisingly, they mutinied, and in the confusion that ensued, they proclaimed their legionary commander, Priscus, as their emperor. As Commodus' biographer tells us:

> Commodus was even named 'Britannicus' by flatterers, although the Britons wanted to choose an emperor in opposition to him.[6]

There was further turmoil. Priscus was removed and a legal official, who served under Marcellus, appears to have been made acting governor.[7] Sources are unclear, and we read of a bizarre episode in which 1,500 'javelin men' from the British army turned up outside Rome to complain to Commodus. Their grievance seems to have involved the Praetorian prefect, Perennis, whom they accused of meddling unduly in British affairs. Whatever the truth of the story, Perennis was handed over to the army and lynched.[8]

The mutinous situation in Britain could not be left unchecked, and it was now that Pertinax was called to his command. With characteristic fearlessness and energy, and after only narrowly escaping death, Pertinax put down the mutiny. Indeed, so completely did he gain his troops' respect that they may even have offered to make him emperor. But for Pertinax the time had not yet come. Instead (and to scotch any imperial suspicions of his own motivations), he proved his loyalty to Commodus by writing him a letter, in which he exposed a plot against the throne, masterminded by the emperor's own brother-in-law. It may be that this letter was sent from the villa at Lullingstone, a few miles south of London, for evidence is mounting to suggest that it was here, at Lullingstone, that the governor had his country residence. A bust found in the subterranean shrine may be a representation of Pertinax himself (Fig. 19), while an intaglio discovered nearby bears a device reminiscent of the coins struck to commemorate Rome's victory in the Parthian Wars (AD 160s), a campaign in which Pertinax had served.[9]

Still, Pertinax was not comfortable. He sensed the British legions' resentment, and he asked to be transferred. A posting to Africa as proconsul was followed by his recall to Rome, where, a popular figure in the Senate, he became not only consul for the year (AD 192) but city prefect, too. However, Rome was soon in turmoil. On New Year's Eve the highly unloved emperor Commodus was assassinated and, within hours, the Senate and a wary army had acknowledged his successor. It was Pertinax.

Despite his undoubted virtues and the enthusiasm with which his rule was greeted by the people, Pertinax was hated by the powerful Praetorian Guard. Only months after he took the throne, Pertinax was cut down in the palace by disaffected guardsmen and his head lopped off in triumph (28 March AD 193).

19 Marble bust, identified as being Pertinax (AD 193), found at Lullingstone Villa, Kent and presently on display in the British Museum.

As ever in such muddled situations, the killing of the emperor unleashed a messy, bloody and protracted struggle for power. In this case, it was rendered all the more undignified by two senatorial plutocrats, Julianus and Sulpicianus, who sought to buy the army's loyalty by offering increasingly extravagant bribes. In the end, the auction was won by Julianus, but it was clear he would not rule for long. The legions did not respect him; the Senate loathed him; and in the provinces preparations were already under way to oust him from the throne.

There were three generals who felt the empire should be theirs. One, Pescennius Niger, commanded legions in the east. A second, Clodius Albinus (Plate 26), was governor of that most troublesome of provinces, Britain. The third was Septimius Severus, and taking the title Imperator Caesar Lucius Septimius Severus Pertinax Augustus, he marched on Rome. Thanks to some clever political manoeuvring, and by offering him the role of his deputy ('Caesar'), he succeeded in gaining the support of one of his rivals, Albinus. Then, from Ravenna, he won over the Senate. However, before he assumed the throne he set himself one final duty: to seek down and kill the assassins of his erstwhile friend and colleague Pertinax and to disband the existing Praetorian Guard. This he achieved by luring them into an ambush, and when they were surrounded he bitterly harangued them for their treachery to Pertinax, relieved them of their arms and sent them, scattered, into the hills. The stage was now set for Severus' triumphal entry into Rome. Dio, the historian, was an eye-witness:

> Severus rode up to the gates on horseback dressed in cavalry uniform, but after that he changed into civilian clothing and walked on foot. The whole army, infantry and cavalry alike, accompanied him in full ceremonial armour. It was the most brilliant spectacle that I have ever seen: the entire city had been draped with garlands of flowers and laurel leaves and hung with richly woven fabrics; and it glittered with torches and incense. The people were dressed in white, and showed their joy with loud cheers, while the troops marched in rank under arms, as if in a festive procession, and we [the senators] too walked about in our ceremonial robes.[10]

The mood of jubilation did not last long. A service of remembrance in honour of Pertinax and a ceremony to deify the dead emperor made public Severus' respect for his murdered friend. From now on, however, Severus' behaviour would show increasingly that seeing how his one-time colleague had been killed by those he ought to have been able to trust most had taught him a bitter lesson. It had taught him to be ruthless.

Severus surrounded himself with a new Praetorian Guard drawn from the most brutish soldiers from across the empire – 'most savage in appearance, most terrifying in their talk, most uncultured to associate with', as Dio (who rubbed shoulders with them) commented – and purged the Senate of any who might oppose him. Then, with the city put on notice that he would brook no opposition, he turned his attention east towards his one remaining rival, Niger. With lightning speed, Severus led his legions to Asia and two victories. By the time he had reached Antioch, Niger had fled, but Severus' cavalry caught up with him at last on the road which led to the Euphrates, and it was not long before his head was rolling in the dust at the feet of the new emperor.

Soon Severus' legions were pounding that same road eastwards to the Euphrates, and then across the river deep into the ancient lands of

Mesopotamia, where they defeated the last remnants of Niger's troops and received the surrender of the region's Arab princes. Back in Rome, he could demonstrate to the Senate and the People that he had annexed a new kingdom, and created a new province, and although he refused a triumph (on the grounds that he did not want to celebrate a victory in a civil war) he did accept an arch, which still stands at the north end of the Roman Forum. His victory was met with general rejoicing, but when he proclaimed Caracalla, the elder of his two sons, Caesar it became evident to all that a dynasty was being established, that his so-called deputy Albinus, governor of Britain and Severus' fellow consul, was being passed over, and that another war was brewing. A carefully staged demonstration by the masses in the hippodrome[11] and an edict from the Senate declaring Albinus a public enemy (AD 195) precipitated matters further, and before long the legions were on the march again – this time northwest to Gaul.

By now, the British governor had crossed the Channel at the head of a massive army. Troops drawn from three legions, as well as 35,000 auxiliaries and perhaps 5,000 cavalry were under his command, and together they wound their way south to Lyons. Here Albinus declared himself Augustus and set up a mint. Here, too, he met Severus, his enemy, in battle. It was a hideous, blood-drenched fight, this struggle for the empire. On their right flank, Severus' men broke through, routing the enemy back to their tents and to their slaughter. On the left flank, though, they suffered horribly, falling into hidden trenches, crushed by the momentum of their own attack, mown down by spears and arrows. When they tried to retreat, Severus' troops found themselves slipping uncontrollably into a deep ravine, where, trapped in the mud and unable to move forward or back, the men and horses perished in a storm of missiles. Severus himself, his horse cut down beneath him, rallied his new Praetorians, and at last the tables turned. A cavalry charge, a final push, and Severus' men had won the day. Albinus, cornered, killed himself. His head was sent to Rome to be exhibited upon a cross; his body was ritually trampled by the hooves of Severus' horse as the emperor repeatedly rode over it; his family were thrown into the Rhone.

Back in Rome, the increasingly harsh Severus made a speech before the Senate, praising the cruelty and severity of men like Commodus and Marius and Sulla, and to underline the new tone of his rule, he wreaked his revenge on any senator who had supported Albinus. He executed almost thirty and confiscated their estates. Then, to demonstrate exactly where his power base lay, he imposed crippling taxes on the populace and almost doubled every soldier's pay.[12] And then he went to war.

Leaving his deputy, the ruthless Plautianus, to rule Rome, Severus himself returned to the east, to his new province of Mesopotamia where the Parthians had already been encroaching. With remorseless efficiency he swept south to their capital at Ctesiphon (AD 198), where he unleashed his soldiers to plunder the whole city and himself took lavish booty and 100,000 prisoners. It was a victory to celebrate, and celebrate he did, giving himself the title 'Parthicus Maximus' and raising his elder son Caracalla to be his co-Augustus, while his younger son Geta was elevated to the rank of Caesar. At the head of their legions and with their snaking wagon trains weighed down with plunder, the new imperial dynasty rode west to Egypt. Despite encountering at least one setback (he failed to take the Arab town of Hatra),[13] Severus nonetheless maintained his harsh authority, occasionally executing a more popular lieutenant either out of jealousy or *pour encourager les autres*.

As they passed the tomb of Pompey, murdered centuries before by one Lucius Septimius, the army paused to sacrifice; in Alexandria, on the other hand, Severus closed the monument that housed the tomb of Alexander the Great so that, from then on, no one could gaze upon his body or (more importantly) read from the secret books which had been housed there. For in Egypt, to the Romans that most mysterious of lands, Severus' passion for things mystical could be allowed full rein. As he sailed up the Nile, past the pyramids, the Sphinx, and on to Thebes and the twin Colossi of Memnon, Severus avidly sought out arcane texts and greedily annexed them to his own collection. In his palace in Rome, he adorned the ceilings of the two rooms in which he was accustomed to hold court with paintings of the stars under which he had been born – all except those of the very hour of his birth, for in the correct interpretation of these lay the most jealously guarded secret of all: the moment and manner of his death.

In Rome, Severus celebrated the tenth anniversary of his rule (AD 203), distributing his largesse to all the citizens but especially to the Praetorian Guard, to each of whom he gave ten gold coins. It was time, too, for a dynastic wedding, an alliance between the families of Severus and the vile Plautianus, whose daughter Plautilla married the young co-Augustus Caracalla. (This union would end eight years later with the bridegroom's brutal murder of his wife.) But life could not all be pleasure, and the same year Severus led his troops across the sea to Africa, where he led a new

Plate 28 The gateway of the
Saxon Shore Fort at Pevensey in
Sussex, probably built by Allectus
(AD 293–96).

Plate 29 *right* The Roman lighthouse (*pharos*) in the grounds of Dover Castle. It is the tallest surviving Roman building in Britain.

Plate 30 An unsorted group of late third-century coins from the Frome hoard, found in 2010.

Plate 31 Gold *aureus* of Carausius (AD 286–93) struck at Rouen on his accession. Found in Derbyshire. (Diam. 20 mm)

Plate 32 Silver *denarius* of Carausius from the Frome hoard, struck at London with the RSR mark. It shows Britannia greeting Carausius with a quotation from Virgil: 'Welcome, O long-awaited one.' (Diam. 18 mm)

Plate 33 Silver *denarius* of Carausius from the Frome hoard, showing the emperor riding into London. (Diam. 20 mm)

Plate 34 *overleaf* The 'Arras Medallion', showing Constantius I being greeted by the personification of London (or Britannia) as he and his fleet arrive at the city in AD 296. (Diam. 41 mm)

campaign south, deep into the Sahara, to check and control the tribes of the oases, and so protect the fringes of the province that contained his native Lepcis. It was now that his grateful fellow-citizens erected the triumphal arch in honour of their favourite son, while Severus himself paid for the building of the Basilica and the Imperial Forum. At the same time, he enforced a deal to gain free oil supplies for Rome.

Whoever was the emperor, the urban poor of Rome needed to be kept onside. Almost as soon as Severus returned to the capital (late summer AD 203), preparations began for the lavish public spectacles associated with the next year's celebration of the Seventh Secular Games: for seven days across the city were held religious ceremonies, races, gladiator bouts and the slaughter of 700 wild and tame beasts. Beneath the surface, though, trouble was beginning to boil. A massive eruption of Vesuvius was taken by some to presage political upheavals, and, indeed, it was not long before Plautianus at last fell out of favour. Only the personal intervention of Severus stopped Caracalla himself from killing him, but it did not prevent Plautianus' death. Other executions followed. One man's last words particularly haunted Severus, for, as this senator prepared to die, he burnt incense and said: 'I make the same prayer that Servianus made for Hadrian' (see p. 133). In so doing, he cursed Severus and wished on him a prolonged and painful death.

If the Senate was cowed, there were others who were not. Among them were Severus' sons, whose stay among the fleshpots of Rome was rendering them ill-disciplined. Meanwhile, the countryside of Italy was plagued by brigandage, and it was only with the utmost difficulty that it had been brought under control. More disturbing than any of this was the news from Britain. The historian Herodian sums up the situation:

> Severus was distressed by his sons' way of life, and by their unseemly passion for the popular shows. Under such circumstances, a message came from the governor of Britain with news of a rebellion among the barbarians, who were laying waste to the countryside with pillaging and widespread destruction. To defend the province required further troops or the presence of the emperor himself.[14]

✧ ✧ ✧

Ever since the time of Commodus, the peoples of northern Britain had been actively resisting Roman rule. In the early AD 180s the Caledonii, perhaps with help from the Maeatae, had breached Hadrian's Wall, pushing south down Dere Street, torching the forts of Halton, Chesters, Rudchester and Corbridge and killing a Roman general.[15] It was against these incursions that the martinet Marcellus had for a short time been successful (see p. 148). But Clodius Albinus' redeployment of the legions into Gaul in his bid to take the throne, and the subsequent slaughter of so many of his men at Lyons, meant that in Britain itself there had been severe reductions in troop numbers. This was precisely the situation that the Caledonii had been waiting for, and by AD 197 they had broken whatever treaties they had made with Marcellus and were again joining forces with the Maeatae, harassing the northern frontier and taking hostages. With the bulk of the Roman army fighting in the eastern Parthian War, the British governor, Virius Lupus, had no choice but to pour enormous sums of money into buying peace.[16] How stable this peace was, and how long it lasted, is far from clear, but the evidence for the enormous scale of Severus' response to the unrest in Britain is incontrovertible (AD 210).

The planning and logistics were on a quite colossal scale. The fort at Arbeia (modern South Shields) on the River Tyne, some 70 miles north of York, was chosen as the key supply depot.[17] Here vast granaries were built, bringing the number up to twenty-four in all with a combined capacity of over 2,500 tonnes, enough to feed 50,000 men for up to two months.[18] From here grain could be hauled in barges up the Tyne and thence to forts along Hadrian's Wall but, just as importantly, it could be loaded onto ships and ferried up the coast, so as to supply the army as it marched north into Scotland. That such a volume of grain was needed points to the sheer size of the army. Three legions (the Second, Sixth and Twentieth) were at hand already in the province and these may have been joined by the Second Legion Parthica, which had been based near Rome. In addition, vexillations from other legions stationed in both Gaul and Germany were probably joined by as many as 35,000 auxiliaries as well as Severus' own Praetorian Guard. It was the largest imperial expedition to be mounted in Britain since Claudius' invasion almost two centuries before, and it required an immense budget. To service this, the expedition was accompanied by heavy-laden wagons of coin and bullion.[19]

Not only were the treasury and army on the move, the court was too. York became the new imperial capital. Here Severus' Syrian empress,

Julia Domna, and her retinue would stay for the duration of the war, dazzling the locals with their sophisticated continental fashions (Plate 24). Face-pots discovered from the time suggest that Domna's famous crimped coiffure may have become *de rigeur* in York society, and anecdote suggests a vigorous relationship between the empress and local wives.[20] One famously sought to demonstrate the moral superiority of the British by remarking to Domna that: 'We fulfil the demands of nature in a much better way than you Roman women. We have intercourse openly with the best men – you allow yourselves to be seduced in secret by the worst.'[21]

It was not only Domna who stayed behind in York. Geta, Severus' younger son, remained there, too, to conduct the day-to-day affairs of state, assisted (naturally) by the most senior imperial officials and advisers. Meanwhile, Caracalla was perhaps at South Shields, overseeing preparations, taking care that his own power was appreciated (Plate 27).[22] When all was ready he was joined by Severus himself, at sixty-two a sick man plagued not only with arthritis but with gout. There is no doubt he was in considerable pain. Mobility was becoming increasingly difficult and for

SEVERAN COINS

A very large number of Severan-period coins have been found in Britain, struck for all of the imperial family: Severus, Julia Domna, Caracalla, Plautilla and Geta. Some are found in hoards, such as those from Shapwick (Somerset) and Falkirk and Birnie (Scotland). Many others, however, are single finds from across the province. The fact that Severan coins are more numerous in Britain than in other provinces of the northwestern empire seems to corroborate Dio's statement about Severus having a large amount of money in his train.

One phenomenon that is being increasingly noted by finds recorded with the Portable Antiquities Scheme is the high proportion of plated and baser silver coins in circulation in Britain. It is highly probable that many of these coins were made by people in Britain and were intended to deceive. However, some of them may have come from official sources, being produced for example in military workshops at Piercebridge. It is also possible that the population were not so easily fooled and that these coins were actually used in transactions at a lower value than the full *denarius*. Whatever the case, Severus' imperial expedition seems to have had a major impact on the monetary economy of Britain.[23]

an active man like him this must have caused great distress. Perhaps he remembered the curse called down upon him that he, like Hadrian, should endure a protracted and painful death. Perhaps it was in part to hasten the inevitable end that he had set out for Britain, a country from which, his astrologers had told him, he would never return.

The Caledonii made overtures for peace. Severus rejected them. Peace did not suit him. Instead, Herodian writes, he wanted to:

> ...prolong his time in Britain and not return hurriedly to Rome, while entertaining his ambition to add to his victories and titles by a campaign against the British, so he sent the delegates away empty-handed, and put everything in order for the war.[24]

At last, all was ready; supplies were loaded onto grain-ships for the voyage north and the legionaries, cavalry and all the polyglot auxiliaries set out along the old road bound for Scotland. As each day drew to its close they stopped to build their marching camps, each one covering some 165 acres. This vast size is a testament to the sheer scale of the whole operation.

Ransacking all the hackneyed stock motifs, reports sent back to Rome spoke of dark, gloomy swamps, of rivers, mists and marshes inhabited by fierce sub-human creatures, naked and tattooed, their bodies hung with iron. These beings, they said, could stand for days on end up to their necks in icy water, while eating nothing more than bark and roots. They armed themselves with shields and spears and fought, or so the bulletins implausibly proclaimed, from chariots. Like many military assessments, written with an eye to an audience back home, this was (to say they least) a skewed, exaggerated and eccentric evaluation of the Maetae and the Caledonii. But it was just what the Senate and people of Rome wanted to hear, aggrandizing as it did the bravery of Roman troops by adding a mystique to the extremities of empire.

Yet into this forbidding country, with its ragged coastline, its steep bracken-covered mountains and its dark and gloomy woods, marched men accustomed to the searing heat of Africa and the east. They laid wooden trackways across marshes, built pontoon bridges across the rivers, and, with Severus himself borne on a litter in their midst, they slowly struggled north in search of battle (Fig. 20). Two axes of advance, a pincer movement in the making, pushed inexorably forward, one to the east, the other to the west. But neither made contact with the enemy. A century of studying the Romans' tactics had taught the Scottish tribes not to engage in formal

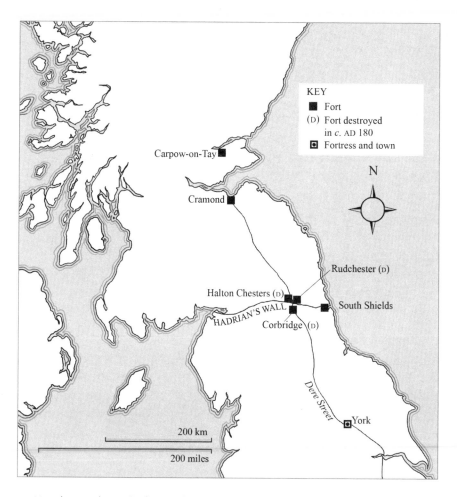

KEY
- ■ Fort
- (D) Fort destroyed in *c.* AD 180
- ▣ Fortress and town

N

Carpow-on-Tay ■

Cramond ■

Rudchester (D)

Halton Chesters (D)

South Shields

HADRIAN'S WALL

Corbridge (D)

Dere Street

York

200 km

200 miles

20 Map showing the north of Britain during the Severan campaigns against the Scottish tribes (AD 208–11).

battle – Calgacus' defeat at Mons Graupius (AD 83) at the hands of a much smaller force had entered folklore. Instead, they adopted guerrilla tactics, melting into marshes, moors and mountains, using sheep and cattle as a bait to lure the Romans into ambush.

Their tactics may have worked. The Scottish strategy, we hear from Herodian, 'told against the Romans and prolonged the war' with casualties on the Roman side of 50,000 dead.[25] Certainly, by the time that Severus had reached the Moray Firth, both he and his elusive enemy were ready to make terms. Ironically, however, as the moment came for peace to be negotiated, domestic hatreds and resentments raised their heads with an attempt at parricide. For some time, Caracalla had been nursing deep

grievances against his father (and co-Augustus) Severus. Now those grievances exploded into violence:

> Both men were riding to meet the Caledonii in order to receive their
> weapons and discuss the terms of a truce when Caracalla openly
> tried to kill his father with his own hand. They were riding their
> horses – Severus' feet were somewhat weakened by his illness but
> he was nonetheless on horseback – while the rest of the army fol-
> lowed behind. The enemy's army, too, was in full view. At that very
> moment, a moment of silence and ceremony, Caracalla reined in
> his horse and drew his sword, as if to strike his father in the back.
> When they saw what was happening, their fellow horsemen who
> were with them shouted out. [Caracalla] was startled and stayed his
> hand. Their shout made Severus turn round. He saw the sword, but
> said nothing and climbed up onto the tribunal. He completed his
> business, and returned to the general's tent.[26]

The terms of the treaty appear to have included an agreement from the
Caledonii and Maeatae that they would abandon part of their territory to
the Romans. Whatever Severus offered in return, it was enough to allow
him to proclaim a famous victory (Plate 25). In York a lavish ceremony was
no doubt staged (AD 210), and coins were struck which gave to Severus,
Caracalla and Geta the title of 'Britannicus'.[27] It seemed as if at last the
'barbarian problem' had been well and truly solved.

Nevertheless there were still two major issues plaguing Severus: his
own deteriorating health, and the obvious instability of his treacherous son
Caracalla. The attempt against his life in Scotland had been bad enough,
conducted as it had been in full view of the troops; but there were now
suspicions that Caracalla was plotting to have his father's doctors and
attendants poison him. As the year (AD 210) drew to a close, Severus tried
to dissipate Caracalla's ambitions. In a further ceremonial, the emperor
may have proclaimed the elevation of Geta, his younger son, to the role of
co-Augustus.[28] But even so, he was uneasy. Weak and in constant pain, he
knew that death was near, and he whispered to a confidant:

> I took over the republic in a disturbed condition everywhere, and
> I leave it pacified, even among the Britons. Now an old man crip-
> pled in the feet, I bequeath to my sons a stable empire if they will be
> good, a weak one if bad.[29]

In believing Britain pacified, however, he was mistaken, and early in AD 211 the news came that the Maetae and Caledonii were in revolt. Hastily, a fresh campaign against them was prepared, but this time Severus knew that his health would not permit him to ride with it. Instead he must entrust its leadership to Caracalla. Before much in the way of military might could be unleashed, Severus' health deteriorated still further. Calling his sons to him he urged them to 'agree with each other, make the soldiers rich, and ignore everyone else',[30] an illuminating reflection on the basis of his own rule, but advice which Caracalla was in part to ignore. On 4 February AD 211, Severus died in York: 'in pain', one ancient chronicler observed, 'but mostly in grief'.[31] After the proper period of lying in state, his body was cremated with full military honours on the banks of the Ouse, and his ashes packed into a golden urn. The imperial family would accompany them back to Rome.

Caracalla, of course, aborted the campaign to Scotland; the forts his father had established there were abandoned (if, that is, they had ever truly been occupied) and a hasty treaty was concluded with the enemy.[32] And yet the treaty lasted a surprisingly long time – almost a hundred years. Study of the archaeology might reveal why. There is good evidence that the great granaries at South Shields continued to be used throughout the century. Now, some of the grain was needed for the garrisons on Hadrian's Wall and the other military installations of the north – some, but by no means all. This raises an intriguing possibility. Did Caracalla buy the northern tribesmen off? Was his treaty with them predicated on Rome's giving them cheap (or even, perhaps, free) grain in return for a promise of peace? If so, it was astute negotiating, and as the imperial family's ship put out from South Shields, the new emperors could congratulate themselves not only that they had left behind them dedications for their well-being from their subjects,[33] but that they had secured an understanding and agreement with their age-old enemies.

In Rome, Severus' ashes were deposited in the mausoleum of Hadrian. In a short time they were joined by those of Geta, murdered by his brother Caracalla – and a few years later by the ashes of the empress, Julia Domna. For in AD 217, Caracalla was cut down by a rival while on campaign in Parthia. In resignation, Domna killed herself. Her horoscope had told her she would marry a king. She had followed him from the sands of Syria to the ice-bound snowfields of Rome's northernmost frontier. With him she had created a dynasty. And now she had seen it destroyed.[34]

8

THE BRITANNIC EMPIRE

It had been a successful raid, classically executed. Under the cover of night and fog, the German vessel had nosed silently into the creek and tied up to the jetty. Leaving a few men to guard the boat, the rest of the crew had soon found their objective – a poorly guarded villa just a stone's throw away. They had known what to do. A few deft slashes of their knives had dealt with any opposition. Thereafter, it had taken only minutes to identify the choicest plate and find the strong-box, to breach the store-room and to drag the bulging sacks of grain down to the jetty.

And now they were away already, back in the open water of the Channel, sail hoisted, tacking east and north again towards their home-land, job well done. They did not see the fast boats following them, gaining on them, pulling up alongside. They did not see them till too late, these Roman rapid-response ships, their sails dyed deep blue, and their rigging, too, their hulls all coated with wax as dark as the night waves, their sailors dressed in their new-issue camouflage.[1]

Now it was the Germans who were taken by surprise. Within moments, their ship was swarming with armed men; before they could so much as blink they were completely overpowered. And now they were aware of a new presence on their deck, a tall dark burly man with curly hair and a raffish beard – he might have been a pirate chief himself; he might have been King Neptune. They had never seen him, but they'd heard of him, of course. He was the scourge of the seas, the terror of the Germans; moreover he had stood up to the court at Rome itself and had proclaimed himself as emperor; he was a legend and his word was law; he was Carausius.

❖　❖　❖

21 Map showing the main settlements of Roman Britain from the late third to the early fifth century.

T HE years after Septimius Severus had died in York and his sons, Caracalla and Geta, had ridden south to their squabbles and their deaths had almost spelled disaster for the Roman world. Its borders were under increasing threat. Far to the east, Sasanian Persians had made inroads as far as Antioch in northern Syria (AD 252). Eight years later the Roman emperor Valerian, at the head of legions now severely depleted by plague, was defeated in battle, and in subsequent negotiations he was him-self the victim of treachery. Captured by his enemy, the Sasanian emperor Shapur I, he was kept a prisoner for the rest of his life. It was reported that Shapur delighted in parading him in front of the Persian army, dressed in his imperial purple, but in chains, forcing Valerian down onto his hands and knees beside his horse that he might use the vanquished Roman as

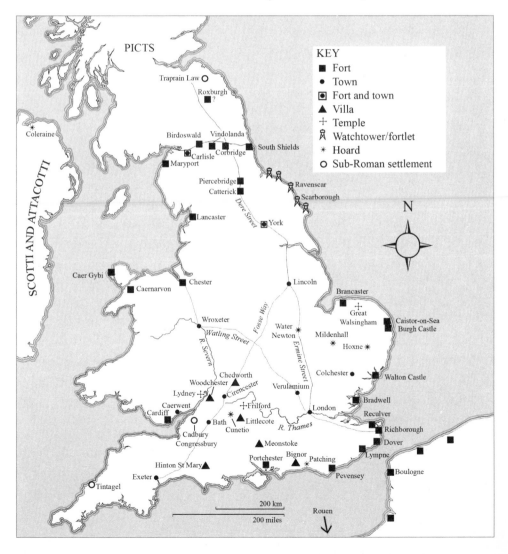

a mounting block. When Valerian died, executed – it was claimed – by having molten gold poured down his throat, Shapur was said to have had his one-time rival skinned and stuffed with straw, a trophy to take pride of place in the temple of the greatest Persian god.[2] Only when the eastern frontier was eventually restored in the reign of Aurelian (AD 270–75) was the gruesome relic removed, and the remains given proper Roman burial.

Elsewhere, to the west, the Danube frontier was breached too, when Gothic tribesmen crossed the river and swept south, bringing chaos to the Balkans and launching seaborne raids around the Aegean coastline. The military response took time to be effective, and when order was at last restored (AD 270s), it was at a cost: the Roman province of Dacia (modern Romania), so hard won in the centuries before, was abandoned to the Goths.

As if all this were not enough, Germany and Gaul too were in turmoil. In AD 259, the Alamanni crossed the Rhine and pushed south into Italy. At Milan that year they were defeated, but in the decade that followed, they devastated much of Gaul, leaving ruin in their wake.[3] In AD 275 the Franks crossed into the lands which had so recently been Roman – but by now, the vast swathe of territory between the Danube and the Rhine, the so-called Agri Decumates, had been (like Dacia) deserted. The Roman empire was contracting. The barbarians were at the gates.

Within the empire there was chronic instability. Emperors came and went with alarming regularity, and, if he had a solution to the problems pressing in on every side, none was able to impose his will for long enough for it to have any meaningful effect. At the same time, petty squabbling and civil wars seemed set to tear down the tottering edifice that was Rome.

The front-line provinces of Gaul and Germany, Spain and Britain responded in the only way they could. Faced with barbarian invasions from across the borders and what seemed to be implosion throughout the rest of the Roman world, they formed a breakaway 'Gallic empire' ruled from Trier. It lasted fourteen years (AD 260–74),[4] and, by the time that Probus became emperor in Rome (r. AD 276–82) and reasserted some authority, the wider empire had been so bruised and battered that its nature had been changed forever.

One of these changes had a profound effect in Britain. Since Republican times, Rome had understood the need for efficient food production and a reliable supply network throughout the territories that it controlled. Now, with the Agri Decumates lost to the barbarians and the great agricultural estates to the west of the Rhine frontier no doubt seriously damaged, the new emperor Probus faced a crisis: how to ensure sufficiently secure supplies of food for the garrisons on the Rhine frontier? One source reveals part of his answer: '[Probus] gave permission to all the Gauls, Spaniards and Britons to grow vines and make wine'.[5]

Even more important than wine, of course, was grain, and it was now that Britain became increasingly crucial as a source of food for the continent. Grain had been among the commodities exported from the island since the Iron Age, one of the list of goods recorded by Strabo,[6] but it was only now that the full potential of the British soil began to be exploited.

Britain attracted Probus' eye for other reasons, too. One of his solutions to the problem of the barbarians was to offer them land in Gaul in return for military service. In addition, despite having to contend with a rebellious British governor, he settled some defeated barbarian troops – Burgundians and Vandals[7] – in Britain.

It seems likely that these were not the only people crossing the Channel into Britain. Around the AD 270s, a period of intensive villa building and enlargement began in southern Britain, coinciding perhaps with a demand for luxury housing from high-ranking Romano-Britons who had served in continental Europe and the Rhineland, or possibly with rich Gauls relocating to Britain to enjoy the relative safety of a province largely unaffected by barbarian invasions.[8] In the late third and early fourth centuries BC,

22 Copper-alloy statuette of a plough-team from Piercebridge (County Durham), now in the British Museum. The ploughman wears a *birrus* (a hooded cloak).

villas such as Rockbourne (Hampshire), Lullingstone (Kent), Woodchester and Chedworth (both in Gloucestershire) were built with the province's growing agricultural wealth.⁹ Indeed, in the fourth century AD one of the richest regions north of the Alps (along with the hinterland of Trier and the Bordeaux region of southwest Gaul) seems to have been the villa belt of the West Country, the modern counties of Somerset, Gloucestershire, Oxfordshire, Hampshire and Wiltshire.¹⁰ By the end of the third century, it was possible for poets to write ecstatically (and no doubt hyperbolically) of the agricultural wealth of Britain:

> Without doubt Britain...was a land that the state could ill afford to lose, so rich are its harvests, so countless the pasturelands in which it delights, so many the metals whose seams pervade it, so great the wealth which comes from its taxes, so many the harbours which encompass it, so great an area it covers.¹¹

If it was an agricultural boom time, it was one that required careful management and protection. During the reign of Probus himself there was a flurry of activity in northern Britain. Milestones bearing Probus' name have been found close to Bowes in County Durham as well as near Hadrian's Wall, while the Fourth Cohort of Gauls, stationed at Vindolanda, took the title 'Probiana' in the emperor's honour.¹² In the years following Probus' death (AD 282), it is likely that his successor Carinus, too, paid a visit to the province.

✧ ✧ ✧

DID CARINUS CAMPAIGN IN BRITAIN?

There is no firm unequivocal evidence that Carinus (AD 283–85) visited Britain, though circumstances strongly suggest that he did. One of his titles, 'Britannicus', implies victories in the province, while in a poem Nemesianus congratulated him on his success in recent 'wars under the north star'. Archaeology, too, points to his presence. Not only has a dedication on stone to Carinus has been discovered in Hampshire, but a relatively high number of gold coins struck by Carinus have been found in Britain. In the later Roman period, such gold coins were increasingly distributed by the emperor himself.¹³

The threat from Germanic tribes across the Rhine had not gone away. The export route from Britain to the continent still needed close protection, and it is entirely possible that the Roman authorities began to construct the network of what are now called Saxon Shore Forts not only to provide bases for the navy, but also to stockpile food and corral livestock prior to their transportation across the Channel.[14] The first of these forts (Brancaster and Caistor-on-Sea in Norfolk and Reculver in Kent) were built in the early third century, and by the AD 270s – the same time as the intensive period of villa building – these had been joined by three more (Burgh Castle in Norfolk, Walton on the Suffolk/Essex border and Bradwell in Essex). In the 270s and 280s, Richborough, Dover and Lympne, all in Kent, appear to have been built. Later in the century, a fort was constructed at Portchester in Hampshire, possibly by Carausius, and another at Pevensey in Sussex, probably by Allectus (see p. 180 and Plate 28).[15]

On the west coast, too, a chain of forts faced the Atlantic. In the mid-third century AD, existing forts at Caernarvon, Chester, Ribchester, Ravenglass and Maryport were augmented by a large fort at Cardiff (c. AD 270s–80s) built in a similar style to the Saxon Shore Forts. Later two more were constructed, one at Holyhead (Caer Gybi) on Anglesey, the other at Lancaster. Meanwhile, probably from the reign of Probus (AD 276–82), coastal installations were also built on the continent from Oudenburg (Belgium) to Blaye (on the Gironde near Bordeaux) including the forts at Boulogne and Rouen.[16]

The need for protected coastal enclaves was clearly great, and nowhere more so than on the shores of the Channel and towards its eastern entrances. This was where the greatest threat lay, and it came from Saxons, Franks and Frisians. These were all Germanic peoples who had settled on the coastal lands outside the Roman empire, lands that are now called Holland, Germany and Denmark. To these ruthless bands of raiders in their fast low boats, Roman villages and villas by the sea or close to riverbanks were easy pickings. Lightning attacks were common and potential plunder substantial. Even more attractive to these hungry tribes-men than a villa's silverware[17] and fabrics, or a few rough rural slaves, were the slow convoys of grain ships plying the Channel seaways between Britain and the Rhine, the cargo of just one of which might feed a village for a year.

It was to quell such raiders from the sea that in the AD 280s the tough new emperor Maximian (r. AD 286–310), colleague of Diocletian, called on his brilliant young general Marcus Aurelius Mauseus Carausius.[18] An experienced ship's captain, Carausius had been born into a humble family in Menapia, the coastal territory of the Roman province of Gallia Belgica, which straddled parts of what are now France, Belgium and Holland. Crucially, Menapia bordered the Rhine estuary,[19] an area that had suffered more than most from barbarian incursions. Carausius himself may have remembered how the Franks and Alamanni launched a savage raid across the river in AD 260. He would certainly have been aware of the environmental catastrophe ten years later, when a rise in sea level caused widespread flooding, which permanently displaced large numbers of the region's population.[20] The sea, it seemed, was already an inescapable part of Carausius' life.

It is only with the accession of Maximian (AD 286) that Carausius steps out of the shadows and presents himself fully fledged as a major player in Gaul, striding onto the stage at a crucial time in its history. The desperate situation that had prevailed throughout the empire for years required desperate remedies, and the new emperor Diocletian was the man to administer them.[21] One of his first reforms was to divide the empire. Diocletian ruled the East; his co-emperor, the uncomplicated military genius Maximian, the West. Immediately Maximian turned the focus of his energies onto the internal affairs of Gaul, where law and order were effectively non-existent. Bands of so-called *bagaudae*[22] – escaped slaves, disaffected peasants and traitorous Roman soldiers – were roaming the countryside at will. The province was in turmoil, its economy destabilized, and many of its wealthiest inhabitants were probably deserting it for Britain. But the Bagaudae were no match for Maximian. Soon Gaul was safely back in Roman hands, and with internal stability restored, Maximian could concentrate on combating the threat which loomed beyond the empire's borders: the Germanic raiders from the sea.

Cue Carausius. As one Roman historian concisely put it:

In this war, Carausius, a citizen of Menapia, distinguished himself through his actions and as he was also considered to be an experienced helmsman (as a young man he had earned his living this way) they commissioned him to assemble a fleet and repulse the Germans who were infesting the seas.[23]

So Carausius set to work. Galleys, coastal boats and river craft were built or requisitioned,[24] and the ports and forts on both sides of the North

Sea and the Channel (including the Saxon Shore Forts) were placed on high alert. From his headquarters at Boulogne, Carausius began inexorably to impose his control upon the seas. Then something went badly wrong. The sources are vague and biased, so it is impossible to be certain of exactly what did happen, but somehow (and spectacularly) Carausius fell out of favour with Maximian. We hear from one historian how:

> [Carausius] had often captured many barbarians, but not given back the booty in its entirety to the provincials or sent it to the emperors, so there was a suspicion that he deliberately allowed the barbarians in, so that he could apprehend them as they passed with their booty, and in this way enrich himself.[25]

Another, drawing perhaps on a similar source, takes the story significantly further:

> Puffed up by his new appointment, although he intercepted many barbarians, [Carausius] did not return all the booty to the treasury, and fearing Maximian who (he learned) had ordered his death, he styled himself emperor and took control of Britain.[26]

It was now AD 286, a mere twelve years after the so-called Gallic empire had collapsed, and Britain was once again at the heart of a breakaway regime. It seems it was in Gaul, at Rouen, that Carausius, now with Maximian's death sentence on his head, was declared a rebel emperor. It was almost certainly here that he struck the first of the coins which were, in time, to speak so eloquently of his sense not only of his place in Roman history but, more importantly, of his ambitions. This first tranche ranged from coins of gold[27] to hurried crude base-metal 'radiate' coins (a modern term reflecting the fact that, on them, the emperor wears the radiate crown of the sun-god, Sol; see Plate 30). All the coins spoke of one thing: Carausius' need to reward his supporters and to buy the allegiance of his army. The legend that some coins proclaimed summed up his aspirations perfectly: it read CONCORDIA MILITUM, 'Harmony with the Army' (Plate 31).

How much of Gaul that army now controlled we do not know. Strategically it would have made sense for Carausius to try to hold on to as much as possible – and certainly the northern coastal strip, from which he had been operating so successfully against the Germanic raiders. We may perhaps surmise that he already held the area from Rouen through Amiens to Boulogne,[28] and we can infer, too, what his first most urgent task now was: to sail to Britain and secure the province. For without Britain, his new empire would be dead in the water. Sources hostile to Carausius describe his tactics:

> In that illegal usurpation, first the fleet, that once protected Gaul, was stolen by a pirate [Carausius] on the run, then many ships like ours were built, a Roman legion seized, some units of non-Roman soldiers commandeered, Gallic traders enlisted and vast forces of barbarians seduced by the loot of their own provinces...[29]

The breathlessness of this account suggests the speed and unexpectedness of his revolt. In the event, Carausius appears to have encountered little, if any, opposition in Britain. He quickly made London his capital, declaring his arrival (ADVENTVS) on some of his first coins (Plate 33).[30] Perhaps the disaffected province had never really wanted to be reintegrated into the wider Roman empire. It is not unlikely, after all, that at least some of those aspiring landowners, now lording it in their fine new villas, were less than happy to be exporting their produce at knock-down rates to a remote regime, unsympathetic to their local interests.[31] In the early days of his regime, Carausius would have had every incentive to stop such exports – feeding the hostile army on the Rhine was not on his agenda; supporting the economy of Britain was. And, just as in the days of the Gallic empire, that economy was once more booming.

Coins from Carausius' mints, both in his capital, London, and elsewhere, were soon flooding the province at least as far north as the River Trent, and even reached the continent.[32] The propagandist message that they circulated through their designs and legends was extraordinary. For alongside the images we might expect of Carausius himself – a powerfully built man with a long bushy beard and a mass of curly hair, the quintessential 'sea-dog' – were others, which, taken together with their inscriptions, reveal that Carausius' vision of his new empire had its roots deep in Rome's past.

One of the most common of his silver coins shows Carausius being greeted by the personification of Britannia herself, a usual enough pictorial trope, but it is the accompanying legend that sets it apart. It reads EXPEC-TATE VENI ('Come, O long awaited one'), a quotation from the *Aeneid*, the Augustan poet Virgil's iconic epic about the founding of Rome (written *c.* 29–19 BC; see Plate 32).[33] No other Roman ruler had ever quoted classical authors on their coinage, so, were this to be the only Virgilian quotation to appear on Carausius' coins, it would be significant enough. But it is not. Other coins from early in Carausius' rule bear the letters RSR, which have been recently and brilliantly deciphered as standing for REDEUNT SATURNIA REGNA ('the Golden Age returns'), words from Virgil's messianic Fourth Eclogue. Furthermore, on a unique Carausian medallion the next line of the poem also appears, abbreviated as INPCDA (IAM NOVA PROGENIES CAELO DEMITTITUR ALTO, 'Now a new progeny is sent down from heaven above').[34] The message is loud and clear. Carausius is a second Augustus. With him a new age of prosperity will begin.

Other coins take up the message. Alongside silver coins from London, repeating the desire he first expressed at Rouen for concord with the army (see p. 175), are others honouring the fleet and reading FELICITAS AVG ('Good fortune of Augustus/the emperor'), while others depict Carausius' protecting deity Neptune with the tag-line CONSERVATOR AVGVSTI ('Protector of Augustus/the emperor'). Nor is the British countryside forgotten. A coin bearing the word UBER[I]TAS ('fecundity') shows a milkmaid milking a cow.[35] The cities, too, are there. One coin commemorates Carausius' imperial arrival (ADVENTVS) in London while others record public vows (VOTO PVBLICO) made for the security of the state. Indeed, peace and security were the aspiration of the most common slogan found on Carausius'

CARAUSIUS' COINS

After the brief issuing of coins at Rouen, Carausius struck the rest of his coinage at two mints in Britain: London and another marked C or G. We do not know where the latter was situated, but numerous suggestions have been made. For many years C mint was identified as Camulodunum (Colchester), but other possibilities are Clausentum (Bitterne), near Southampton, Corinium (Cirencester), Colonia (York) and even Classis (a mint for the fleet). It does not seem that the location of the mint will ever be proved. It is possible that the C Mint was also in London.

Carausius struck very few gold coins, but a significant quantity of silver *denarii*, which were of better quality than any other coins being struck in the empire at this time, and unsurpassed since the reign of Nero (AD 54–68). Five unworn silver *denarii* were among the 52,503 coins recently discovered in the Frome hoard. The hoard also contains the largest single group of Carausius' common bronze 'radiate' coins (Plates 30, 32, 33).[36]

coins, PAX AVGVSTI ('Augustus'/the emperor's peace'), a phrase which resonated throughout Roman history and harked back to the days of the early empire, when the famous Ara Pacis Augustae (Altar of Augustan Peace) was dedicated in Rome in 9 BC. For Carausius, in other words, to be 'Augustus' was not merely to hold an imperial title; it was to be the re-embodiment of the first and greatest Roman emperor of all. Hence the slogans on his coins, which proclaimed him not only as the Restorer of Britain (RESTITVOR BRITANNIAE) but the Renewer of the Romans (RENO-VATOR ROMANORVM).[37]

It was not a situation that the legitimate Augusti (senior emperors), Diocletian and Maximian, could afford to ignore. Carausius knew it. He had inherited the chain of Saxon Shore Forts; now he may have added a new link to it at Portchester.[38] These forts were now to assume a new role: to defend Roman Britain against the rest of the Roman empire. Moreover, for the first time in her history, Britain would rely upon a fleet for her protection.

On each of the headlands overlooking the Dour Estuary between the Shakespeare Cliffs and the white cliffs of Dover stood lighthouses more than 80 ft (24 m) in height (Plate 29). In days gone by they had served as shipping beacons; now they became watchtowers, look-out posts for sentries scouring the horizon for a hostile fleet.[39] For it may have taken him three years to organize, but now at last Maximian was preparing his invasion (AD 289).

We would know nothing of Maximian's plans were it not for the survival of a panegyric written two years later (AD 291). In it (and in suitably fawning terms) the poet addresses Maximian himself, recalling how:

> Wonderful fleets were built and equipped, which all at once by every river sailed for Ocean; men vied in their work to finish them; the very rivers swelled to receive them. For close on a year, Your Majesty, you needed fair weather to build shipyards, to fell timber, to energize the workforce...[40]

The expedition was an abject failure. We hear no more about it, except for a tantalizing reference in a later panegyric of AD 297, which speaks of how 'the war was abandoned in despair' and a fleeting remark by an historian who writes that 'peace was arranged with Carausius after military operations against this expert strategist had been attempted without success'.[41] Indeed, at a meeting between Maximian and Diocletian in Milan in the winter of AD 290/1, protocol (or perhaps discretion) dictated that no mention was made of the aborted invasion. The whole business was quietly forgotten.

But not by Carausius. Instead he did what he enjoyed doing best. He issued a new series of coins. This time they proclaimed his association with his two 'colleagues' on the continent.[42] Some bore reverse inscriptions ending in the abbreviation AVGGG (the three Gs standing for the three Augusti: Diocletian, Maximian and Carausius). Others bore the names of Diocletian and Maximian.[43] Others still bore portraits of the three men, complete with the inscription CARAVSIVS ET FRATRES SVI ('Carausius and his brothers'; see the illustration on p. 1).

Sadly for Carausius, however, his brotherly feelings for the two legitimate Augusti were not reciprocated. Before long (AD 293), news came of the appointment of a Caesar to serve under Maximian in the west, one Constantius Chlorus. The message was loud and clear. Not only had Carausius not been consulted, the appointment was a direct challenge to his rule. Any doubt of this was swept away immediately when Chlorus marched on Carausius' strategic port in Gaul, Boulogne.

In Britain the mints producing coins proclaiming close fraternal love fell silent, while Boulogne echoed to the din of the building of military installations and of battle. A panegyricist takes up the story:

> The moment Constantius Chlorus was summoned to the throne, he cut off from Ocean the port, with its countless ships of the enemy fleet, and blockaded by both land and sea the army which occupied the shore at Boulogne. He built a mole across the sea's waves, so that contact with the sea, so nearby, was cut off from men whose city gates had been once been lapped by waves. The army which he had overcome by virtue he kept loyal by clemency.[44]

Boulogne had fallen (AD 293). Perhaps by now Carausius had fallen, too, murdered by his dour and dismal finance minister, Allectus.[45] The sources paint a wretched picture of Allectus. One, speaking of his treachery, tells how 'fear of his own crimes and of execution for them made Allectus usurp the imperial power'. Another accuses him of murdering Carausius in the hope of currying some favour with the legitimate emperors:

> ...and so the henchman killed his pirate chief, no longer afraid of a punishment they would both share, and thought his crime would be rewarded by imperial power.[46]

23 A copper-alloy coin of Allectus (AD 293–96), showing a war galley. Found in Leicestershire.

This was exactly what Chlorus wanted. With the charismatic ruler Carausius dead and Boulogne taken, Chlorus could now prepare to launch his troops across the Channel and into Britain. Even the dreary usurping Allectus did not take long to realize that this was the inevitable next move. In an attempt to emulate his murdered predecessor and to buy the support of the British people, Allectus minted patriotic coins, which soon found their way into the villas of the wealthy (Fig. 23). Many such coins are found in southern Britain.[47]

At the same time, it seems that, in anticipation of invasion, a timber wall was built on the banks of the Thames in London. Massive pile foundations, perhaps for one of the wall's towers,[48] have been found at Shadwell (City of London), and close to them 300 coins, most from the reigns of Carausius and Allectus. In addition, the next spring (AD 294), great trees were felled to be transported into London's southwestern sector for the construction of a major new administrative hub.[49] Nor was this flurry of activity confined to London. On the south coast – at Pevensey in Sussex and possibly Portchester in Hampshire – new shore forts were being built or strengthened (Plate 28).[50]

By AD 296, Constantius Chlorus' preparations were in place. He was now ready to embark for Britain. The invasion would be two-pronged, Chlorus himself setting sail from Boulogne, his Praetorian prefect, Julius Asclepiodotus, from the River Seine. The weather was filthy. Fog clung low to the grey waters of the Channel, and the murky drizzle cut down visibility still further. But for Asclepiodotus these were the perfect conditions. Silent and unseen, his ships slipped past the British fleet, which lay in ambush by the Isle of Wight, and so they came to land.

Once on shore, his troops and horses disembarked, Asclepiodotus gave the order to burn his ships, and, without stopping to construct any kind of encampment to which he could potentially retreat, he led his men inland. He may already have received intelligence reports that Allectus had fled in some confusion. At any rate, Asclepiodotus set out in pursuit. Somewhere near the Solent, perhaps near Portchester, Allectus and the army of the Britannic empire made their one last desperate stand. As a later writer, hostile to Allectus, triumphantly records, it was a massacre:

> I hear that it was only the sprawling corpses of our loathsome enemy that lay there on those fields and hills. Corpses, which their clothing and their thick red hair proclaimed as British natives, lay caked in dust and blood, scattered far and wide wherever they had stumbled in their wounded agony; among them was the flag-bearer of banditry himself [Allectus], the imperial robe he had, when he had lived, expropriated now calculatedly discarded, so that it was with difficulty that he was identified by one single piece of clothing.[51]

While Asclepiodotus was delivering the *coup de grâce* to the rebel army in Hampshire, Constantius Chlorus was sailing up the misty Thames. When they reached London, his troops met some resistance from the garrison of Frankish mercenaries, but in the ensuing bloodbath these were wiped out to a man. For the defeated, reality must have seemed a world away from the propaganda messages which soon were sweeping through the island – messages such as those on a medallion, whose slogan proclaimed Chlorus the 'Restorer of the Eternal Light'. It showed the fleet sailing in triumph up the Thames as Chlorus himself rode into London, with the personification of the city kneeling before him in submission (Plate 34).[52] A panegyric written for Chlorus the next year (AD 297) developed the image further:

> Euphoric, the Britons flocked to meet you with their wives and children. They gazed on you as if you had descended from the skies;[53] and not only you! They venerated even the sails and oars of the ship, in which your divine being had sailed; and they were ready to lie down and feel you walk on them. No wonder they were so ecstatic; after so many years of the harshest captivity, after the rape of their wives, after the humiliating enslavement of their children, now at last they were free; now at last they were Roman; now at last they were revived by the true light of our rule.[54]

In reality, it mattered little what the Britons felt. Whether they liked it or not, they were back in the Roman fold.

9

BLESSED ISLE

He'd ridden like the wind. He'd had no choice. His life depended on it. He'd known that if the enemy agents had caught up with him, they'd never have allowed him to survive. He'd had a day's start on them, true. But still it meant a mad dash across Europe, the hoofbeats of all the foam-flecked horses he had ridden thundering forever in his ears, their flying hooves pounding the long straight roads, which led him ever west.

They'd served him well, those horses. At each new staging post he'd picked out the best mount to carry him most quickly on his way. And then he'd rounded up the other horses, even the horse which had most lately brought him here, and slaughtered them. He'd had no option. He did not have the luxury of compassion. Fresh horses would be useful to those hunting him. He could not play into their hands.

And then, at last, after all the endless miles, the stretching limitless horizons, the dry roads and the dusty air, he sensed the moist tang of the sea. And then he saw the sea itself, wind-driven, grey. And the bellying sails of the merchant ships. And the walls of the port: Boulogne.

And he was riding through the gate. Dismounting. Handing the reins of this, the last horse, to the stable-boy that he might feed and water it. Then on into the headquarters complex, past the guards and to the inner chambers, where the Augustus, Constantius Chlorus, glanced up at the newcomer, this tall young man, whose hair was caked with dust, whose torn dishevelled clothing was streaked and stained with sweat, this young man who even now seemed like an apparition. But he was real and he was here, and Constantius Chlorus, emperor of Rome, stretched out his arms to greet his son, his Constantine.

✧ ✧ ✧

THE years following his triumphant entry into London (AD 296) had not been without incident for Constantius Chlorus, calling for him to exercise his skills to the utmost. He rose to the challenge. It had been, after all, his enviable aptitude in all areas military, diplomatic and administrative that had brought him to power in the first place.

Born in Illyricum (mostly modern Slovenia, Croatia and Serbia) in around AD 250, Constantius Chlorus had risen through the army's ranks, and by the time he was in his mid-thirties (c. AD 285) he had been appointed governor of Dalmatia (mostly modern Croatia). The years that followed saw major changes throughout the Roman world, for it was in AD 286 that, in an attempt to ensure both security and stability, the emperor Diocletian, himself a no-nonsense military careerist, formally divided the empire into two parts, east and west. Initially, each half was to be ruled by one man. As we have seen, Diocletian himself took the east, appointing his brother officer Maximian as Augustus of the West.

Almost immediately (AD 287), Maximian set out to secure the porous borders of the Rhine and Danube, and with him as a general he took Constantius Chlorus. It was a well-calculated choice – a panegyricist would later reflect that Chlorus had managed to protect the frontier 'not with forces of cavalry or infantry, but by the terror of [his] presence'.[1] The next year (AD 288), no doubt in part due to his successes on campaign, he was elevated to the rank of Praetorian prefect, effectively Maximian's second-in-command. Perhaps it was around this time that the Augustus of the West sought further to cement his ties with Chlorus by arranging a marriage between his new prefect and his daughter, Theodora.[2] For Chlorus, welcome though the union may well have been, it cannot but have interfered with his almost twenty-year relationship with the one-time barmaid[3] Helena, who long ago (c. AD 272) had given him a son, Constantinus (known universally today as Constantine), now nearing manhood.

Buoyed by his new marriage ties, Chlorus' role was further enhanced in AD 293 when Diocletian decreed that each of the two emperors (or Augusti) should have a deputy (or Caesar), who would serve under him and, in time, succeed him.[4] It came as no surprise to anyone that when the name of Maximian's Caesar was announced it was that of Constantius Chlorus.

We have already seen that Chlorus' duties as Caesar took him first west to Gaul and to Boulogne (AD 293), to win back Britain to the fold. The campaign took three years, but by AD 296, it was all over. As his propaganda proclaimed, the 'Eternal Light' of Roman rule shone once again across the hitherto benighted isle. Just how benighted it had in fact been, however, remains a subject of some controversy. Internally, Britain had been prospering (see Chapter 8), while even its northern borders may have been relatively quiet. A panegyric written for Chlorus exclaims:

> Beyond Ocean what was there except Britain? You took it back so utterly that even tribes who live at the island's furthest extremities now submit to your will.[5]

It is, of course, in the nature of panegyrics to be economical with the truth, but there is little evidence in the territory around Hadrian's Wall to suggest warlike incursions from the north. It is quite conceivable that detachments of troops were relocated south by Carausius and Allectus, as the rarity of coins from their reigns north of the River Trent perhaps suggests,[6] and this would in turn have led to a weakening of the Wall garrison. Indeed, at Birdoswald Fort, there seems to have been a run-down of activity and even a possible temporary abandonment.[7] Although the imperial log-book, the *Notitia Dignitatum*,[8] suggests no major withdrawals of units from the north, it is quite possible that detachments of units were sent south, denuding the frontier of part of its garrison. This is further suggested by later inscriptions from the time of Chlorus, made in the name of the Tetrarchs, the empire's four rulers (two Augusti and two Caesars). These inscriptions commemorate the repair of old structures on the Wall, which had 'fallen into ruin'.[9] The implication is that they had collapsed as a result not of violence but of neglect – and this in itself might suggest a degree of complacency born out of a period of relative calm.

Certainly the situation was sufficiently secure for Chlorus to turn his attention away from military campaigns to bureaucratic tinkering. Based perhaps on the model of the Tetrarchy itself, Britain became a *diocese* under the jurisdiction of a *vicarius*, himself answerable to the Prefect of Gaul.[10] It was subdivided into four provinces: Maxima Caesarensis was governed from London; Britannia Prima from Cirencester; Flavia Caesarensis from Lincoln; and Britannia Secunda from York.[11] The division of the province into smaller pockets was, in part, an attempt to prevent any repetition of the events of the previous decades, when strong generals had managed to establish power-bases with such relative ease and to use Britain in particular as a launch-pad from which to attack the greater empire. On the other hand, the new danger was that the inevitable increase in bureaucracy would make it harder to get anything achieved.

Not that Chlorus' life was now confined to pen pushing. The years around AD 300 saw him engaging in fierce fighting in the Rhineland against the Germanic tribesmen of the Alamanni, crushing some and offering terms to others. Among these, perhaps, was Crocus, an Alamannic king, whose floral name belies his bellicosity, and who would play such an important role in York at the end of Chlorus' life (see below).

By the autumn of AD 305 Chlorus was at Boulogne, preparing to return to Britain. Word had reached him that the situation in the territory around Hadrian's Wall had worsened. Determined warriors were threatening the frontier, men whom the Romans called the 'Painted Ones'. The Picts had entered history, and Chlorus meant to quash them.[12] But events were moving quickly. Already, earlier that year, the two Augusti, Diocletian and Maximian, had retired, and, following the plan laid down twelve years before, their Caesars were appointed in their place. Constantius Chlorus had thus become the western emperor, one of the two most powerful men in the Roman world. The Picts apart, two problems worried him. The first was his own health, which was deteriorating rapidly. The second was the safety of Constantine, his son. For Constantine was in the east, at the court of Chlorus' fellow emperor, Galerius. Galerius had for a long time harboured a bitter hatred for Constantine, and now, whether he was motivated from jealousy or fear, there was a real possibility that the eastern emperor would harm Chlorus' son. It was imperative that Constantine should join his father in the west.

It was when Chlorus had been appointed Caesar (AD 293) that Constantine had been sent east, to the court of Diocletian at Nicomedia. Perhaps Maximian did not wish his daughter Theodora to be constantly in the company of the child of Chlorus' previous union with the barmaid Helena. More likely, Diocletian wanted to prevent Constantine and Chlorus from entertaining any thoughts of starting a dynasty. At any rate, by keeping him in the east, Diocletian was effectively holding Constantine hostage. Not that Constantine was not useful in other ways, for he had inherited his father's skill as a soldier.

Which was more than seemed the case with Galerius – at least in the beginning. Constantine probably accompanied Galerius on his disastrous campaign against the Persian king Narses (AD 296), son of the notorious Shapur I who had so crushingly defeated and humiliated Valerian more than a generation earlier (see p. 169). Galerius' defeat at Narses' hands did not result in quite the same humiliation – but the disgrace dealt out to him by Diocletian was damning enough. Justified or not, Galerius was made to bear the full blame for his army's trouncing, and forced as punishment to enter Antioch on foot, a mile ahead of Diocletian's chariot, but still dressed in his full imperial raiment. Galerius got the message. Failure would not be tolerated. So the next year, he engaged his army once again with Narses. This time Galerius won. He captured Narses' family and many Persian nobles and kept them in gilded captivity in Nicomedia, a reminder to all of his success.

Whether campaigning on the eastern frontier or the Danube, Galerius seems to have used whatever opportunity arose to send his lieutenant Constantine on the most dangerous of missions – missions from which, perhaps, he hoped the young man would not return alive. It was not that Constantine was expendable; just that Galerius may already have wanted to expend him. An anonymous source states:

> Galerius put him in the way of many dangers. For even as a young cavalryman in the Sarmatian campaign he captured a fierce barbarian, seizing him by the hair, and brought him to the feet of the emperor Galerius. Another time, he was sent into a swamp by Galerius; he rode in on his horse and found a route to the Sarmatians, killed many of them and brought victory to Galerius.[13]

That Constantine survived is a mark of his good soldiery – and luck. Of course, the young man had time for other duties too, as well as opportunities to watch and learn. He would have witnessed, for example, two rebellions against the emperors in Egypt. Both failed, but the second was so serious that Diocletian was subsequently obliged to pay an imperial visit (AD 298), with Constantine most likely in his entourage.[14] But it was five years later that Diocletian felt moved to put down what he regarded as an even more insidious rebellion, that of the Christians, who, through their daily behaviour and professed beliefs, seemed to undermine the very fabric of the Roman world. The Great Persecution had a major impact on young Constantine, who seems to have been impressed with the way the Christians' network operated and at the same time shocked by how they now were forced to look for refuge among Rome's enemies. Surely this was not the most intelligent response the state could make. Surely there must be a more subtle solution.

Thoughts of religion were probably pushed far from Constantine's mind in AD 305, when, in an act unprecedented in the history of the

Roman empire, the two Augusti, Diocletian and Maximian, resigned. In the west, Constantine's father Chlorus became emperor, with Flavius Valerius Severus his Caesar; in the east Maximinus served as Caesar with the emperor Galerius. Not only did Constantine have no place in this new Tetrarchy; supreme power in the east, where he was stranded, was in the hands of his avowed enemy Galerius. It was essential that he should somehow manage to escape.

The opportunity came with a letter from Chlorus, announcing to Galerius that he was seriously ill and requesting that he allow Constantine to join him, that he might have his son at his side.[15] Galerius was unenthusiastic, but eventually compassion (or concern for how it might appear if he did otherwise) caused him to relent. Constantine left at once, which was just as well. Within hours Galerius changed his mind and sent men out in hot pursuit. But Constantine had a head start. He galloped across Europe, 'killing the post-horses along his route in order to frustrate those pursuing him', and so in late AD 305 he reached his father at Boulogne. Together they set sail for Britain.[16]

Despite his ill health and with his son Constantine beside him, Chlorus (like the dying Severus almost a hundred years before; see Chapter 7) led his army north, through the threatened gateways of the Wall, and so on into Scotland. We know little of the details, but we are told he pushed far into the lands of the Picts and Caledonii.[17] Pottery finds from the coastal forts of Cramond on the Forth and Carpow-on-Tay confirm what a knowledge of Roman tactics would anyway suggest, that significant use of the fleet was made to supply and support the army as it marched. Subsequent panegyrics proclaimed the expedition a resounding success, but even as they praised Chlorus they presaged the events to come:

> His last expedition was not in search of more trophies from Britain, as many people thought; rather, now that the gods were calling him to them, he advanced to the furthest outpost of the earth. With so many great deeds behind him, I know he had no need to conquer the forests and marshes of the Caledonians and other Picts, nor Hibernia which lies close to, nor far-off Thule, no!, nor even the Isles of the Blest, if they in fact exist.[18]

The campaign swiftly over, Chlorus returned (again, like Severus) to York. In AD 306 York, or Eburacum, was thriving. The capital of northern Britain (Britannia Inferior), it had enjoyed the status of *colonia* for almost seventy years.[19] Now, with its flourishing trade and the wealth it attracted as a garrison town, its citizens could well afford to erect fine public buildings, baths and temples on a scale to match the fine walls of the fortress with its eight magnificent towers.

Meanwhile, across the river from the fortress and the city, on the south bank of the Ouse there was a lavishly appointed building, constructed perhaps for Severus a century before or as the governor's official residence.[20] Its rooms contained ornate mosaics, including one that showed a fish-tailed bull. Near here were found two tablets made from silvered bronze, both bearing Greek inscriptions and dedications, one to Oceanus and Tethys, the other 'to the deities of the governor's headquarters'.[21]

THE NEW FORTRESS AT YORK

It is highly likely that the fortress on the north side of the River Ouse was modified some time in the late third and early fourth centuries. Although some people claim that the spectacular south wall, with eight towers,

was built in the Severan period, its style is closest to military fortifications found at Gamzigrad in Dacia Ripensis (Serbia) which surrounded two palatial residences, temples and a granary, an 11-acre site thought to have been intended as the retirement residence for the emperor Galerius (305–11), but never used. This places the rebuilding of York in the same period and we know that the *principia* (headquarters building) was rebuilt in the early years of the fourth century. A larger than life-size statue of Constantine stood either in the *principia* itself or in its courtyard, the head surviving as one of the most important treasures of the Yorkshire Museum.[22]

24 Marble head of Constantine the Great (AD 306–37) from the large statue that stood in the fortress at York. Now in the Yorkshire Museum.

No doubt in those early summer days of AD 306 there were some in the imperial household who made their prayers to these very deities. For even to those who were not admitted into the emperor's presence, it must have been clear from the hushed voices and the atmosphere of intrigue that Chlorus had not long to live. Whatever god they were addressed to, prayers proved fruitless, and some time in mid-July Constantius Chlorus died. The circumstances of his death are veiled in mystery. They soon became the stuff of legend, obfuscating the true history.

One Church historian, Eusebius, even seems to have invented circumstances whereby Constantine arrived in York in the last moments before Chlorus died. He continues:

> When [Constantius] saw the son he had not hoped to see standing in his presence, he rose quickly from his couch, threw his arms around him and said that he was now free of the one grief, his son's absence, which had prevented him from dying. ...He...gave thanks to God...bequeathed his part of the empire by natural succession to his eldest son, and so departed from the light.[23]

Setting aside the contrived drama of this description for the moment, the last sentence contains a crucial truth. Somehow, in the days that followed, Constantine himself was hailed as the new Augustus by his troops, the latest in a long succession of rebel British emperors. In proclaiming him, the army was deliberately flouting the new order that Diocletian had imposed, that Augusti should be succeeded by their Caesars. In more than one way the move was dangerously unconstitutional. But Constantine went on to become one of the most powerful Roman emperors of all, so it was in everyone's interests (including his own) to present his accession to the imperial throne in as positive and legitimate a light as possible. Hence the obfuscation and confusion.

Whatever the reality, the surviving accounts paint a dramatic picture. Most, if not all, agree that the decision to proclaim Constantine emperor was made while Chlorus was still alive. A later panegyric claims that Constantine was concerned about the legitimacy of the move, did his best to consult as many constitutional experts as possible, and, even then, showed himself to be suitably unwilling to accept the crown:

> The emperor [Constantius], ready to make his journey to Heaven, gazed on the heir he was leaving behind. As soon as he was released

from earthly life, the entire army gave you its approval, all thought of you, all looked at you, and though you had sought the decision of the senior officials about the supreme command, the fervour of the rest anticipated the considered agreement of the authorities which was to follow. As soon as they could, when you entered their presence, and despite your tears, the soldiers clothed you in imperial purple, thinking of the public interest if not your own feelings. For an emperor now consecrated as a god it was no longer proper that you should weep. The story is, unconquerable emperor, that you tried to escape the army's zeal as they acclaimed you, by spurring on your horse. In truth, this was an error of youth.[24]

If this reads like spin, that is probably because it is. But again and again the sources tell us that Constantine was proclaimed emperor 'by the will of all the soldiers' or 'in response to the pressure of all those present', while one adds the detail that it was Chlorus who 'commended Constantine to the troops and transmitted the imperial authority to him with his own hands'.[25] Another writes of the role of Crocus, the Alamannic king, whom Chlorus had recruited to his side while campaigning beyond the Rhine a few years earlier (see above).[26] His backing was significant:

With [Constantius] dead and with the approval of all who were present, but especially Crocus king of the Alamans a companion and supporter of Constantius, [Constantine] took the name of emperor.[27]

The influence of so-called barbarians was beginning to be felt not only in the military but in politics, too. It was a trend that would have major implications in the century to come.

Perhaps the sequence of events went something like this: knowing that death was near, Chlorus, Constantine, Crocus and the other commanders gathered in York held high-level meetings to discuss the future. Among their considerations must have been the fact that Constantine appeared to have no place in the official central hierarchy. Yet he was a seasoned soldier with an excellent military record and clearly popular not only with the troops but with the court.[28] Moreover, the eastern emperor Galerius clearly resented Constantine, and, with Chlorus dead and his protection gone, the young man might well find himself in a precarious and dangerous position. The stark reality of the situation pointed to one option only:

that Constantine himself should become emperor, without delay, before the legitimate successor, the Caesar, Flavius Valerius Severus, had time to act.

With the decision reached, the ailing Chlorus may have been transported in a litter across the River Ouse to the parade-ground, where he addressed his men.[29] The sight of their dying general entrusting his son's future to their care (and promising a monetary gift to all on Constantine's accession to the throne)[30] would have done much to fortify the troops' resolve, so that when the news of Chlorus' death reached them in their barracks they would have known instinctively what they must do. First, the solemn funerary rites must be observed.

If, as seems likely, it was in the governor's residence that Chlorus died, it would be here his body lay in state until his funeral. On the appointed day, it would have been conveyed with due solemnity across the bridge over the Ouse to the parade-ground where the emperor had so often addressed his troops. Here the courtiers and officers, the civil servants and the soldiers, all in their allotted places, would already have been drawn up in their ranks. In the centre of the parade-ground would be the pyre, a tall, ornate construction, decorated like a temple with statues and hung with garlands. With the catafalque containing Chlorus' body carried up the steps and placed on the pyre's high platform, those gathered for the ceremony would have processed around the structure one last time. Then, with due prayers and ritual, the fires would have been lit, and, as the inferno roared inexorably upwards, a trapdoor in a cage high on the pyre would have been sprung to release an eagle, symbol of the emperor's divinity, which soared up, far above the flames into the summer sky.

Perhaps it was at this point, at the climax of the ceremony, that the army began chanting for Constantine to be proclaimed Augustus of the West. Perhaps it was now that Constantine, in what must have been a calculated sham, turned his horse's head and made as if to ride away. Whatever happened, it was not long before he was addressing the assembly as their emperor. Constantine's biographer sums up:

He led the funeral procession accompanied by a great crowd of his father's friends, some walking in front, others following, and performed the last rites for the pious deceased with the greatest magnificence. All paid honour to this most blessed emperor with acclamations and praises, and as one, they proclaimed that his reign was born again in that of his son; so they immediately hailed [Constantine] cheering him and calling him, New Emperor, Imperial and Worshipful Augustus. In this way by praising the son, they honoured his dead father.[31]

In truth, even if his British subjects rejoiced at the news of Constantine's succession,[32] it was not an emotion universally shared. The rebel emperor's old enemy, Galerius, was furious, but given Constantine's undoubted popularity and the sheer geographical distance between them, there was little he could do. He tried to compromise by recognizing Constantine as Caesar under Flavius Valerius Severus, but even this backfired. The Roman world was plunged into a squalid period of infighting and power games as one pretender to the western throne after another sought to seize control. At last there were two left: Maxentius, the son of Diocletian's co-emperor Maximian, and Constantine.

✧ ✧ ✧

In late October AD 312, the armies of Maximian and Constantine met a little to the north of Rome by the Milvian Bridge, which spanned the River Tiber. Before the battle, Constantine prayed – not to the ancient gods of Rome itself but to the Christian God. As his biographer, the (Christian) Eusebius records, his resultant vision was to change the course of history:

> While the emperor was praying and making his fervent devotions, a remarkable vision came to him from God. If anyone else had told [the story], it might not have been so readily believed. But, as the victorious emperor himself related it, many years later, to the writer of this present work (when he was honoured to know him and enjoy his company), and since he swore the truth of it on oath, who could not believe his evidence? He said that at about midday, when the sun had already passed its highest, he saw with his own eyes, in the sky above the sun, the sign of the cross, along with the words: 'With this, be victorious'. When he saw the vision, he was struck with awe – as was his whole army, which witnessed the miracle, too.[33]

The following night Constantine claimed to have had a dream in which Christ Himself appeared before him, urging him to have a new banner made, a Christian standard (the Labarum) to replace the ancient imperial eagle behind which every army from the time of Marius had marched and whose potency had inspired the legionaries of Caesar to jump into the churning sea off Walmer Beach (see p. 25).

(see p. 25)

> A long gilded spear with a horizontal bar formed the sign of the cross. At the top was a circlet of gold and costly jewels, in the centre of which was the symbol of our Saviour's name: the first two letters of the name of Christ, the letter Rho [P] being crossed through with the letter Chi [X]. Later, the emperor would always wear these letters on his helmet. From the crossbar of the spear hung a royal banner, richly embroidered and shimmering with precious stones, all lavishly stitched with gold thread. It is impossible to describe its beauty or its effect on those who saw it. The banner was square. On its upper part, beneath the sign of the cross and immediately above the embroidered panel, it bore a half-length portrait of the devout emperor with his children.[34]

In the years ahead, the Chi-Rho symbol would be flanked in religious iconography by two other letters, Alpha [A] and Omega [Ω], which also symbolized Christ.[35] Read together they somewhat appropriately spell 'APXΩ', a Greek word meaning 'I rule'. By nailing his colours to the Christian mast, Constantine was taking a gamble, but one which, if it worked, might lead to greater stability than the Roman world had known for well over a century. He ordered his men to paint the Christian symbol on their shields, and, under the new Christian banner, led them into battle. It was a rout. Constantine's men pushed back the enemy, forcing them down into the waters of the Tiber, hacking at them, butchering until the waters ran red with blood. The body of Maxentius himself was found among the dead, his head hacked off and carried high in triumph through the streets of Rome. The Christian empire had been born.

Not that an immediate conversion was imposed throughout the Roman world. Instead, Constantine and his imperial colleague Licinius – by AD 313 (now that the eastern Augustus had conveniently died) the sole rulers of the empire – chose to conduct a quieter revolution. With the Edict of Toleration, issued at Milan that year, they brought an end to Christian persecution of the sort that had so troubled Constantine only ten years earlier. Instead, the new religion began actively to be supported and promoted not only by the emperor and his immediate court, but by many of the richest and most powerful families of the empire.[36] Interestingly, however, Constantine continued to strike coins honouring Sol, the sun god, who was closely associated with the eastern deity Mithras, popular among soldiers and merchants.

Not least among the provinces to embrace the newly legalized religion was Britain. Indeed, evidence suggests that in the years before the battle of the Milvian Bridge and afterwards, Constantine himself paid more than one official visit to the land in which he had first been proclaimed as emperor.[37] One such visit is suggested by a rare coin struck in London in the summer of AD 307 depicting Constantine on horseback, and accompanied by the word ADVENTUS ('Arrival'), while a larger issue of coins points to a longer and more major tour which took place (or at any rate was planned) in AD 310–12. A third and last return to Britain in AD 313–14 (by which time Constantine was ruling as the undisputed emperor of both west and east) is suggested by a rare ADVENTUS coin,[38] as well as by a number of gold coins (see box, p. 196).

Significantly, too, around this time Constantine began to use the title 'Britannicus Maximus',[39] which suggests a military victory in the province. Indeed, concealed in his biography is an oblique and tantalizing reference to just such a victory: 'he sailed across to Britain, which lies in the very bosom of Ocean, and reduced it to submission'.[40]

The identity of these people, whom Constantine was forced to reduce to submission, is not known. Perhaps they were the tribesmen from the north, the Picts and Caledonii, against whom Constantine had campaigned

---

MITHRAS

Mithraism originated in ancient Persia, but spread westwards into the Roman empire where it was adopted and adapted to suit local needs. Mithras was a sun-god whose slaying of the bull gave rise to creation, a scene commonly depicted as the main sculpture in a Mithraeum (temple of Mithras). Mithras was popular with the army and with merchants, and Mithraea were built across the empire. The largest number of extant examples are found in Ostia, the port of Rome, although many were built in Britain, and two can still be seen, one in London, and one at Carrawburgh on Hadrian's Wall. Mithraism offered a moral code, participation in rituals for its adherents and the promise of eternal life. However, it was only open to men. It was strongest in the second and third centuries, but waned with the rise of Christianity in the fourth century.[41]

years before with his father Chlorus. Or perhaps, more insidiously, they were people within the province itself, malcontents among the British tribes, or, even worse, within the army. For, as a rebel emperor himself, Constantine would have been all too aware of the troubled history of Britain and its legacy of rising up against the central authority of Rome. It was something he could ill afford to overlook. Archaeological evidence might suggest that part of his policy of consolidation in the north may well have been to abandon the outpost forts beyond Hadrian's Wall.[42]

✧ ✧ ✧

Now, with peace restored, Britain was to enter its most prosperous phase. Even the way the province was described by urbane Romans would undergo a sea change. No longer was it the mist-drenched boggy wilderness of years gone by. Now it was the darling of the panegyricists. They had a field day:

> How blessed is Britain, more blessed than any other land, that first saw Constantine as Caesar! Nature bestowed on you quite properly every advantage of climate and of soil. The winters are not too cold, nor the summers too hot. The fecund harvests bring their double gifts of Ceres and of Bacchus [Dionysus]. No savage creatures haunt the forests, nor deadly snakes the earth, no, but an immense abundance of domesticated animals with udders full of milk, or backs rich with fleeces.[43]

Palatial country residences (villas) sprang up all across the south, and everywhere the province's elite landowners began to spend their growing wealth on lavish bath complexes, wall-paintings and mosaics. Nor was it only the agricultural upturn that they had to thank. It seems unlikely that Constantine forgot the province which had first supported his illegal claim to the throne, but rather that his gratitude (and need to prevent dissension) was translated into tax incentives and imperial largesse.

Thus the mosaics, which were laid down in courtyard villas, such as those at Bignor, Woodchester and Chedworth and Low Ham (Plate 36), were the product not only of the riches of the fecund countryside but of the favoured political situation that the province now enjoyed.[44] It may be that one villa owner later honoured Constantine himself on a mosaic, if the face depicted on a floor at Hinton St Mary is indeed that of the emperor and not Christ (Plate 39).[45]

From Cumbria to north Wales, Worcestershire to Worthing, roads were improved and milestones erected[46] as the economic boom rippled throughout the countryside. In the cities, perhaps, its effect was more muted. There is little evidence of major building or expansion in any of the major urban centres. But many smaller towns did flourish, no doubt because of the increased activity within their regions. One such market town, Water Newton (Durobrivae), at the edge of the Fens, was home to a flourishing pottery industry and iron works, and the wealth of at least some of its inhabitants was staggering. The hoard of silver, which one of them concealed in an unhappier time in the late fourth or early fifth century, suggests that (here at least) the new religious tolerance and economic growth found no problem in advancing hand in hand. It is the earliest collection of Christian silver from anywhere within the Roman empire (Plate 38).[47]

GOLD COINS OF LICINIUS IN BRITAIN

A special series of gold coins or medallions, weighing one and a half *solidi* (just over 0.175 oz or 5 g), was struck between 313 and 315 at Trier in the names of the joint emperors, Constantine I and Licinius I. One particular issue of this series, struck for Licinius I, shows the standing emperor holding spear and globe with seated captives either side, together with the caption 'universal victories'. Until recently, it was known from only four specimens, three in British museums, and one found before 1847 in Cambridgeshire. Since the inception of the Portable Antiquities Scheme, two further examples have been found in Britain, one in Wiltshire, the other in Northamptonshire. It is possible that a batch of this particular issue came to Britain, to be distributed by the emperor; gold was increasingly becoming controlled by the imperial authorities. If this was the case, it would also suggest that there was another imperial visit by Constantine around 313–14, during which he gave out largesse consisting of these gold coins.[48]

25 Gold coin of Licinius, found in Wiltshire.

Of course, not every Christian was rich. Bishops from London, York and perhaps Lincoln who attended the Council of Arles in AD 314, required their journey and accommodation to be subsidized.[49] But in time such figures became wealthy and important local leaders. As pagan temples lost their state aid, many found their treasuries being appropriated by the Church. The world was changing. Christian churches were beginning to spring up across the empire. The identification of Christian churches in Britain is quite difficult – some have been potentially identified at places such as Colchester, Lincoln, Canterbury and Silchester; however, there is no doubt about the existence of a house-church at Lullingstone (Plate 41).[50] Meanwhile, pagan shrines were falling into ruin.

The driving force was Constantine. If he did come back to Britain in AD 313/314, it was his final visit. From now on, his attention would be focused on the east. In time, he and Licinius would quarrel and war break out between them. By AD 324, Licinius would be dead. Constantine would not appoint another co-Augustus. Instead, that same year, he would turn his energies into the creation of a city that would bear his name, the new Christian capital, Constantinople. It was here, thirteen years later (AD 337), in a porphyry sarcophagus beneath the great dome of his mausoleum, that Constantine, at last baptized a Christian in his dying hours, would be laid to rest by eastern bishops dressed in jewel-encrusted robes. It was all so far removed from Britain, and yet, even on his deathbed, Constantine remembered where his imperial journey had begun:

> So beginning at the far Britannic ocean, and the regions where, according to Nature's law, the sun sinks beyond the horizon, with the help of God I banished and removed completely every form of evil, in the hope that the human race, enlightened through me, might be brought back to a proper observance of the holy laws of God, and at the same time our most blessed faith might prosper under the guidance of His almighty hand.[51]

10

TURMOIL

Midwinter, and the seas were rough. For many days now, volley upon icy volley of hail as hard as any arrow-tip had been pouring ceaselessly from leaden skies, as gales drove chilly from the northern wastes and great grey rollers washed inexorably through the Channel. It was no time to be sailing.

Even in the harbour at Boulogne the waves were heaving. Tall tarry hulls were scraping against one another; timbers creaking; ropes and rigging slapping rhythmically as the storm screeched through them. With terrifying regularity a deluge of white water would explode into the spray-soaked air as a huge wave crashed its deafening boom against the outer harbour wall. It was no time to be putting out to sea.

And yet the order had been given. Even now the ropes were being cast off; even now the bucking ships were nudging out into the maelstrom. Among themselves (not openly), the crews had questioned the decision. Some had half-heartedly protested that they would not sail. And yet it must be safe. The emperor himself was sailing with them. Surely he would not risk his own life senselessly. Maybe, a few had speculated, being the Anointed One, he had the power to calm the waves, just as he had the power to pacify his people, just as (so it was rumoured) he was now leading them to Britain to quell the storms of insurrection. So many rumours. So many maybes. It was clearly time to put them to the test.

✧ ✧ ✧

I	N the years of Constantine's reign, Britain had reached the high water
	mark of its prosperity. The small towns, villages and villas of the south
	and east were flourishing, as they basked in the glow of an economic
boom time. Yet only six years after Constantine's state funeral in his new
eastern Christian capital (AD 337), it seems the situation in the province
had broken down so badly that his successor Constans was forced to make
a hurried winter crossing of the Channel. A mere eleven years thereafter
(AD 354), Constans' brother would unleash a reign of terror on the island,
so devastating that the Roman province would never truly recover.

That this reversal in Britain's fortunes happened in so short a time is
largely incontrovertible. Why and how it happened is somewhat harder to
explain, partly because of the paucity of evidence and partly because what
literary sources survive are far from reliable, many of them being clearly
written for propaganda purposes. What we can reconstruct, however, paints
a bleak picture.

After the death of Constantine the Great, the Roman world was split
between his three sons. The eldest, named after his father, Constantine
II, took the west; the youngest, Constans, took Italy, Illyricum and Africa;
while the middle brother, Constantius II, took the east. The arrangement
did not last long. Constantine II resented what he perceived as Constans'
unfair share and, in an attempt to seize it for himself, marched into
Italy. The two armies met at Aquileia (AD 340). It was a victory for young
Constans, still only seventeen; in an ambush, Constantine II was killed.
Constans had gained the western empire, but among his newly won subjects there may well have been many who resented him.

These were the followers of his defeated brother, Constantine II, many
of whom may well have been high-ranking Britons.[1] It is not unlikely that
British soldiers had fought for Constantine II at Aquileia; but that this
support for their defeated emperor went deeper, permeating not only all
ranks of Britain's military but of her civil society as well, is suggested by
Constans' movements less than three years later. For in the first weeks of
AD 343, in the treacherous storms of winter, the twenty-year-old Constans
braved the Channel for what was apparently an unannounced and unexpected visit.

In truth, the reasons for this crossing are so hidden in the fudge and
confusion of contemporary sources that they can only be conjectured. The
Greek sophist Libanius (a pagan pillar of the establishment who cultivated
influential Christians) oozed the reassuring view that 'affairs in Britain

were settled'. There had, he gushed, been no recent invasion or rebellion in the province, but rather Constans crossed to Britain purely to fulfil his heart's desire to 'set his hand to everything'.[2] His praise of Constans is so fulsome that it almost invites disbelief. Equally fawning are the words of the Christian astrologer Julius Firmius Maternus, who, in reference to the winter voyage, wrote:

> The waves of a sea still barely known to us quaked beneath your oars, and the Briton shuddered before the face of an emperor he had not thought to see.[3]

But why did the Briton shudder? What was the real reason that Constans risked the seas in such an unlikely season? Sadly, the relevant section of the *Histories* of Ammianus Marcellinus no longer survives – here, surely, we would have found some explanation. However, all is not lost. In a later (extant) chapter, Ammianus writes of certain *areani*, frontier scouts tasked with patrolling the native tribes to the north of Hadrian's Wall, 'certain affairs referring to which I mentioned earlier in connection with the actions of Constans'.[4] The linkage of Constans to the *areani* might suggest a visit by Constans to the northern frontier, and could even point to his finding it necessary to take measures against the Picts.

Certainly it seems that by the early fourth century there was no longer any Roman military presence in the lands north of the Wall. Outpost forts at Birrens and Bewcastle, Netherby, High Rochester and Risingham had all already been abandoned. Even on the Wall itself, the garrisons may well have been considerably depleted, as troops may have been withdrawn by Constantine the Great to march with him on Italy in AD 312 (see Chapter 9). Perhaps by now the *areani*, based on the Wall itself, found that their mission had evolved into one that combined intelligence gathering with the maintenance of diplomatic links with the mostly friendly kingdoms in the south of Scotland.[5] Perhaps this was a buffer zone against the Picts. Certainly its kings were still content to call themselves by quaintly bastardized Roman names, such as Annwn (Antoninus) or Patern Pesrut (Paternus Red Cloak).[6]

Whatever the *areani*'s role, it seems that Constans may have felt the need to stiffen their resolve. That this involved a military encounter is suggested by a bronze medallion struck around this time, which shows the emperor in full military uniform, standing in a warship, threatening the sea with his spear (Fig. 26). Military standards adorn the stern, while Victory stands prominent at the prow. The legend on the medallion reads: BONONIA OCEANEN, a reference to the seas around Boulogne, where the emperor embarked that winter.[7]

That Constans wished to make a military expedition to the north of Britain does not fully explain either the urgency of his crossing to the island or the apparent need for it to be unannounced. These considerations might suggest a further reason: that there was disaffection within the higher echelons of the provincial government, who, had they been apprised of the forthcoming visit, might have opposed it. By arriving unexpectedly, Constans may have suc-

26 Copper-alloy medallion of Constans (AD 337–50), showing the emperor in warlike pose on a ship off the coast at Boulogne. Now in the Bibliothèque nationale de France.

ceeded in catching such malcontents unawares and quashing them.

Certainly, when he departed, Constans seems to have left behind a substantial military force. By the end of the decade (AD 340s) the province was being governed by a count (or *comes*), Gratian, whose children would one day be emperors;[8] counts were men of considerable rank, commanding many men. Certainly, too, by AD 348, Constans could issue coins proclaiming FELICIVM TEMPVS REPARATIO ('Happy Days Are Here Again'). But equally certainly, these words were hollow.

> Constans maltreated his subjects with the greatest cruelty, outdoing the most oppressive tyrant; he surrounded himself with handsome barbarians (either bought or held as hostages) and he let them treat his subjects as they wished, in return for them allowing him to corrupt their youth. So every land he ruled was reduced to utter wretchedness.[9]

So writes the later historian (himself a count), the pagan Zosimus. He is not alone. Another source tells how, still only in his mid-twenties, Constans:

> ...disabled in the feet and hands through a disease of the joints, was fortunate in mildness of climate, the richness of harvests, and the

lack of fear of a barbarian attack. He would have been more fortu-
nate still if he had appointed governors to provinces not for how
much they could bribe him, but for their good judgment.[10]

Another reports that:

> Constans' reign was for some time dynamic and just, but later when
> he became ill and was influenced by malicious friends he indulged
> in extreme vices; he became intolerable to the people of the prov-
> inces, and unpopular with the army...[11]

Some of his courtiers had had enough. At the 'university town' of
Autun in western Gaul, while Constans was out hunting, they staged a coup
against the 'cruel animal'. That evening (18 January AD 350), one of their
number, Magnentius – the commander of the Jovian and Herulian legions,
a giant of a man born of a British father[12] – appeared at a gathering dressed
in imperial robes to be acclaimed as emperor. Constans himself escaped
and fled for his life along the cold roads south and west. In the foothills of
the snowy Pyrenees, where the road began to climb towards the mountains,
his pursuers caught up with him at Helena (modern Elne). They dragged
him trembling from the temple where he was hiding and killed him.

Magnentius survived him by a mere three years, but his short reign
was to have far-reaching and serious repercussions in Britain. Although
he quickly gained the support of the provinces north of the Alps and so
moved into Italy and Rome, striking coins across his newly won empire
proclaiming himself a Christian (Plate 40),[13] Magnentius' wider propaganda machine was unconvincing. As a result of this, and because he was
an enemy of the victorious House of Constantine, most of the sources we
have for him are hostile. We hear how he was of barbarian descent, from
Amiens (Ambianum) in Gaul, how he had lived with the *laeti*, barbarian
peoples settled in the Roman empire with lesser rights than citizens,[14] how
(horror of horrors) 'he was inclined toward the study of reading':

> Sharp of tongue, with an arrogant personality, and extremely cow-
> ardly; he was, however, a master of masking terror with an
> appearance of boldness.[15]

Constantius II, brother of the murdered Constans and last surviving
son of Constantine the Great, of course could not tolerate Magnentius'
behaviour.[16] As soon as he could, he rode west at the head of a huge army.

They met at Mursa, in the valley of the Drava River in Pannonia (modern Croatia) on 1 March AD 351, in one of the bloodiest battles in the history of Rome. As many as 50,000 men may have died that day, men whom the empire could scarcely spare, threatened as it was with such a pressure on its borders.[17]

With his heavily depleted army, Magnentius limped westwards to try to regroup north of the Alps. But already the situation looked desperate. Although his brother, Decentius, was valiantly trying to deal with the barbarian threat from across the Roman borders, within them Magnentius' position was in meltdown. Constantius' supporters seized Trier, the imperial capital of the west; his support in Spain slipped steadily away; and on 11 August AD 353, after a defeat in battle at Mons Seleucus near Lyons, Magnentius killed himself:

> ...his side stabbed through with a sword smuggled to him, expediting matters by pushing against a wall (he was so huge) his blood gushing from the wound, his nostrils and his mouth.[18]

When Decentius heard the news, he hanged himself 'with a noose made of cloth swathe'.[19]

MAGNENTIUS AND THE HINTON ST MARY MOSAIC

The Hinton St Mary mosaic, found in Dorset, shows the facing bust of a man with the Christian Chi-Rho symbol behind his head. On either side are pomegranates, which were an ancient representation of eternal life. The figure is generally believed to be that of Christ, although it has been argued that it is Constantine. What is striking, though, is that the portrait and Chi-Rho symbol bear a close resemblance to the Christian coins of Magnentius (Plates 39, 40). The swept-back hair, the eyes, the nose and the chin of Christ are similar to those on the coins of Magnentius. The Chi-Rho from the reverse of the coin is also the same, although pomegranates have replaced the alpha and omega. Is it possible to suggest that the mosaicist used one of Magnentius' coins for a model when designing his schema? If so, it could help to date the mosaic to around the mid-350s. As luck would have it, a coin of the same type, pierced for use as a pendant, was found in a burial at Poundbury, outside the nearby Roman town at Dorchester.[20]

It all seems a long way off from Britain, yet the harsh revenge that Constantius and his lieutenants were to take on the inhabitants of the province suggests that many Britons had thrown themselves behind Magnentius and given him considerable support. Indeed, according to the historian Ammianus, what was to follow was nothing short of a reign of terror (AD 353/354):

> Any military officer or civil dignitary or anyone considered virtuous in society of whom there was even the faintest rumour that he had supported the opposing side was weighed down with chains and dragged off like a wild animal; it took no influence from an enemy; that he had been named or denounced or brought to court was enough to ensure that he was condemned to death or stripped of his property or exiled to a barren island.[21]

To conduct his campaign against Magnentius' followers in Britain, Constantius chose one of his most loyal and remorseless secretaries (*notarii*), the Spanish-born fanatic Paul, who, because of the subterfuge and ruthlessness with which he undertook his duties, soon earned himself the soubriquet Catena ('the Chain'). Ammianus describes him as a bully, going far beyond his brief to hunt out those 'officers who had been bold enough to join Magnentius' conspiracy', and, when he found the Britons powerless to resist:

> ...descending like a river in flood on both individuals and whole estates, spreading every kind of ruin and destruction, imprisoning freeborn men and even shackling them in handcuffs.[22]

Yet there were some brave, decent men who tried to stop him. Chief among these was Martin, the Prefect of the Provinces of Britain. Time and again, he tried to intervene, pleading on behalf of those he knew were innocent and threatening to precipitate what he naively thought would be a political crisis by offering his own high-profile resignation. But Paul did not play by Martin's rules. Instead, he accused the prefect of complicity with those so-called criminals whom he was trying to protect, and ordered his arrest. In desperation, Martin drew his sword and rushed at Paul, but his attempt to kill him failed. Instead, he turned his sword upon himself, and died, as he had lived, a noble Roman.

Paul sailed in triumph back to Gaul and to Constantius:

...steeped in blood and bringing with him many prisoners almost crushed with chains, and reduced to misery and squalor. When they arrived, the racks were made ready and the executioner prepared his hooks and instruments of torture. Many of these prisoners had their property confiscated, others were exiled, more still were killed.[23]

Eventually, Paul's grotesque cruelty caught up with him, but not for another seven years (AD 361). At last, in Chalcedon, across the Bosphorus from Constantinople, he was burnt alive by the apostate emperor Julian, a fate, as Ammianus candidly reflects, 'one must have wished for him'.[24]

That the pagan Julian and Paul did not see eye-to-eye perhaps betrays in part the motivation behind Paul's almost maniacal purge of Britain. For, despite Magnentius' public profession of Christianity on his coins (see p. 202), he showed a significant degree of tolerance towards paganism, and paganism seems to have maintained a presence in the island for some considerable time. Sadly, the evidence from archaeology is scarce, but a picture does emerge. Gadebridge Villa, apparently a centre of contemporary pagan worship close to Verulamium (St Albans), seems to have been destroyed around AD 360, perhaps as a result of Paul's plundering.[25] At the same time there is evidence of Christian activity, such as the mosaic laid down in at Hinton St Mary in Dorset (see box, p. 203 and Plate 39).[26]

Perhaps, though, Paul's purge can better be explained by Constantius' notorious vindictiveness.[27] It was, after all, the emperor's own brother that Magnentius and his fellow rebel officers had killed. That Britain had supported the revolt – indeed, that Magnentius himself had had a British father – may have provided Constantius, at a time when the imperial coffers were under pressure, with the perfect pretext for ravaging the now very wealthy province. In the bloodbath of Paul's reign of terror, many of the leading landowners, who lived in the lavish villas of the south and east, may have been dispossessed, their wealthy estates confiscated, sold or given to Constantius' own men.[28] Some may have been annexed as imperial estates, their profits flowing now directly to the emperor.

Again, the evidence of archaeology is scant. A change of ownership does not inevitably leave its trace, but evidence of a brief pause in occupancy has been suggested at villas throughout Gloucestershire and Somerset, Hampshire, Hertfordshire and northern Kent.[29] Some sites speak of a more significant upheaval. At Barnsley Park in Gloucestershire a massive change took place, with a new stone dwelling built that was surrounded by yards and enclosures for the livestock. It may be that this farm, so close to Cirencester, had now become part of an imperial estate.[30] At Thruxton Villa in Hampshire, the coin record suddenly ends with two pieces of Magnentius, evidence perhaps of a cleansing of its occupants by Constantius' ruthless proxy, Paul.[31] Perhaps his hand can be seen elsewhere in Hampshire at Meonstoke Villa, too, where the latest coins found under a collapsed barn wall date to about the year of Paul's arrival in the island, AD 353.[32]

Coins of Magnentius, in fact, were outlawed after his defeat, part of Constantius' drive to eradicate all memory of him (Plate 40).[33] Throughout Britain, people responded by burying their now illegal tender or cutting small coins out of larger ones.[34] At every level of society, from the richest villa owner to the poorest artisan, Britons were being made to suffer for supporting Magnentius. In the years following Paul's predations, the province went into a sharp decline, as Britain's towns and villas and once-thriving industries fell into disrepair.[35]

This was ironic, for in the years to come, the island was to be the saviour of the northwest empire. Grain, after all, and other produce were still flowing from this, 'the greatest island under the sun',[36] to the army of the Rhine. As time went on, this traffic became more and more essential.

✧ ✧ ✧

AD 356 saw the Alamanni make a major incursion into Roman territory. For Constantius and his newly appointed Caesar, his nephew Julian (Fig. 27), by then less than twelve months in office, it was the start of a bitter three-year campaign, as the Alamanni, Franks and other barbarian tribes poured into Germany and Gaul, looting, burning and destroying whole towns and cities. In time, Julian began to gain the upper hand and some of the invading tribesmen sued for peace. Among them were the Chamavi, whose lands lay at the mouth of the Rhine. Their cooperation was thus key. As one observer put it, 'they could prevent supplies from Britain reaching the Roman garrisons'.[37] In other words, they could cut off the grain supply.

The threat of attack now over, Julian addressed its consequences. Gaul was in chaos, its people destitute. Immediately, Julian attempted to revive the moribund economy. Taxes were slashed, while cities long since ruined and abandoned were rebuilt and fortified. Ammianus tells us that Julian took special care to replace 'burnt out granaries with new ones, so that they could house the corn which was regularly shipped from Britain'.[38] Quite simply, the fields of Germany and Gaul had been laid waste so utterly that their crops could no longer support their people. If starvation were to be averted, not least among the Roman army of the Rhine, Julian needed to act quickly and decisively.

He did. He unleashed a gaggle of accountants and inspectors into Britain, tasked with the job of bringing into line the corrupt army generals, in charge of the collection and export of grain, who had been siphoning off much of the profit. At the same time, he reopened the sea lanes and rebuilt the merchant navy.

> In the past, grain was shipped by sea from Britain and up the Rhine. But after the barbarians took control they did not let it pass. Most of the ships, dragged onto dry land long before, had rotted. A few did still sail, but these unloaded their cargo in coastal ports, so it was necessary for the grain to be transported on wagons instead of by river, which was very expensive. [Julian] thought that there would be problems if he was not able to restore the traditional means of grain-shipment, so he quickly built more ships than before, and put his mind to how the river could take receipt of the wheat...[39]

27 Roman statue of a priestly bearded figure with features resembling Julian the Apostate, now in the Louvre, Paris.

His efforts paid off. Libanius goes on to tell how 'he brought the boats into the Rhine, while those who hoped to stop him were choking with rage but unable to do anything about it'.[40] The sheer number of new ships he needed for the operation was staggering. In less than ten months, as Julian told the Senate and the people of Athens in a letter, 400 ships were built, to bring the fleet up to a total of 600.[41] According to the historian Zosimus (who puts the final number of new ships at 800) they were constructed on the River Rhine with timber felled from local forests.[42] So, by AD 359, just five years after Paul had shipped his captives back to Gaul in chains, heavily laden grain fleets were plying their way across the North Sea from Britain to the Rhine:

> Because the distance was so short, by continuous convoys, and by bringing the grain up the Rhine in river boats, he kept those who had gone back to their own towns well supplied not only with food, but with seed to sow in their fields, and with provisions to last until the harvest.[43]

Disaster had been averted: but at a price. Although food was the major cargo of these ships, it is quite likely that some carried soldiers, too, regiments now relocated from their British bases to shore up the Rhineland garrison. The result of this, of course, was that the troops left on the island were significantly reduced in number. Ever alert to such movements of Roman military personnel, the Picts in Scotland and the Scots from Ireland soon reneged on the terms of an earlier treaty and launched a renewed attack (AD 360).[44] Ammianus writes:

> The savage tribes of Scots and Picts had broken the terms of the treaty and were conducting raids into Britain, laying waste those areas close to the frontiers. Fear permeated the provinces, exhausted already by all the disasters of previous years. Julian was over-wintering in Paris and already had enough worries of his own; he was loath to cross the sea to help (as I mentioned earlier that Constans did) as that would have meant leaving Gaul without a ruler, and the Alamanni had already made preparations for a bitter war.[45]

In his place, Julian sent his *magister equitum*, Flavius Lupicinus. It was a mission noteworthy as much for its ending as for anything that it achieved, and its denouement eloquently shows how Britain was still seen as a potential seedbed for revolt or counter-revolution.

Lupicinus does not get a good press from Ammianus, a friend of Julian but the best historian of the day. Lupicinus was, we hear, a:

> ...warlike man and skilled in military affairs, but apt to boast and talk in the style of a tragic hero. It was long a matter of debate whether his greed predominated over his cruelty or the reverse.[46]

Whatever his faults, a lack of energy and commitment were not among them. Crossing the Channel in the depths of winter (in itself a sign that he had no time to lose), Lupicinus rapidly marched his troops, a light-armed force of Herulians and Batavians, together with two units of Moesians, from Richborough to London. With him he may have brought chests filled with silver coins. Certainly there was a major influx of such money into Britain at this time, payment perhaps for the army there or for those loyal suppliers of corn destined for the Rhineland troops.[47]

From London it seems highly likely that Lupicinus quickly struck out to the borders of the province, where the Picts were once more raiding from the north, while Scots and Attacotti were harrying the western coastal lands from across the Irish Sea. But suddenly news came from another of the empire's borders, which threatened to stall any progress Lupicinus may have made. Far to the east, the Sassanid king Shapur II had torn up a treaty made a generation earlier (AD 297) and launched an attack deep into Mesopotamia. Constantius, the Roman emperor, was in urgent need of troops. He sent a request to transfer Lupicinus' light-armed Batavians and Heruli to the east. In the west, this did not go down well. Not only did the troops stay put; but also in Paris the army acclaimed Julian full emperor ('Augustus'). It was a direct challenge to Constantius.

There were still supporters of the old regime, and Lupicinus was one of them. Before news of Julian's promotion could reach him, and with bewildering rapidity, he found himself recalled across the Channel, and, on arrival at Boulogne, arrested. It was only from his jailers that he heard what had happened.

The account of the episode by Ammianus Marcellinus contains a clue as to why Julian needed to recall his lieutenant so quickly:

> Lupicinus was an arrogant man with ideas above his station, and there were concerns that if he heard the news from across the Channel he might try to stage a coup. So an official was dispatched to Boulogne to keep close watch and stop anyone from crossing the Channel. As a result Lupicinus returned before he could learn what had happened and was unable to cause any unrest.[48]

Not that Lupicinus is thought to have intended declaring himself emperor. Rather, being loyal to Constantius, he was likely to have rallied the army in Britain against the usurper Julian, a risk Julian could not afford to take. Whether, as Julian went on to claim, Constantius had already ordered Lupicinus to arrest the rebel Augustus, we cannot know, but the fact that Lupicinus returned to Gaul and was himself so easily arrested there suggests his ignorance of Julian's elevation.

There is another tantalizing piece of evidence, which may shed light on Lupicinus' sudden return to Gaul: the so-called Mildenhall Treasure. For this dazzling collection of silverware, hidden some time in the late Roman period in Suffolk, may have belonged to Lupicinus himself.[49] The star piece of the hoard, a massive circular platter known as the Great Dish, depicts the drinking contest between the pagan gods Bacchus (Dionysus) and Hercules, accompanied by wild revellers (Plate 35), but it is on the reverse of two smaller platters that the name Eutherios is inscribed in Greek letters.[50] Now, there was a eunuch called Eutherios, who served under both Constantine the Great and Constans before becoming Grand Chamberlain (*Praepositus Sacri Cubiculi*) under Julian in Gaul from AD 355 to 361. As eunuchs went, he was unusually loyal and trustworthy. Indeed, the normally hard-headed Ammianus was so impressed by how unlike other eunuchs Eutherios was, that he was moved almost to poetic flights of fancy, rhapsodizing how 'roses grow in the midst of thorns and among wild beasts there are some that grow tame'.[51] The speculation is that it was Eutherios who gave the two Bacchic dishes to Lupicinus as a gift in Gaul, and that Lupicinus then took them with him among his other tableware to Britain. In the confusion of his recall across the Channel, which required him to move swiftly and lightly (and because he sensed a looming danger), Lupicinus, or someone in his entourage, buried these burdensome valuables in the corner of a Suffolk field and never returned to reclaim them.[52] He did, however, live to tell the tale, for he was freed from the jailhouse in Boulogne, and went on to give sterling service under two further emperors, for both of whom his efficiency outweighed his arrogance.

If the Bacchic plates of the Mildenhall Treasure, with their exuberantly pagan scenes, really did belong to Lupicinus, he may have found their subject matter somewhat offensive. For Lupicinus was an ardent Christian, and it may have been his beliefs that contributed to the less than trusting relationship that existed between him and Julian. The new emperor was famously an apostate, a man who turned his back on the Church and who did his best to reverse the decline in pagan worship. Since his youth, Julian had been a committed Neoplatonist, combining the beliefs of those proponents of the revived and revised philosophy of Plato, professors of which he had studied with both at Ephesus and at Athens, with the worship of the pantheon of pagan gods.

Practically this meant that, for a few brief years, the Church saw its status diminished, while moves were planned for the state to borrow some of the more clearly effective elements of Christianity, such as its practice of charity. This, thought Julian, was insidious in the extreme. 'These impious Galileans not only feed their own poor,' he wrote, 'but ours also; welcoming them into their fold, they attract them, as children are attracted, with cakes.'[53] At the same time, Julian encouraged the rebuilding of the pagan temples. In Britain there was a bustle of renewed, if short-term, activity at pagan sites such as the healing shrine of Nodens at Lydney in Gloucestershire, Nettleton in Wiltshire, Frilford in Oxfordshire and probably also Great Walsingham in Norfolk. At Cirencester, the governor in a fit of pagan zeal erected a great column to Jupiter, whilst at Littlecote in Wiltshire a splendid mosaic was laid in an Orphic shrine (Plate 37).[54] Throughout the land, the local aristocracy and landowners were no doubt delighted, and nowhere more than in the West Country and Norfolk, the seat more than anywhere, it seems, of pagan conservatism.

Yet it was not to last. In the spring of AD 363, news came to Britain that Julian's brief reign was over. As sole Augustus of the empire, now that Constantius had died (AD 361), it had fallen to Julian to protect the eastern borders. So he had led his army out against Shapur II, deep into Mesopotamia, but at Samarra he had been wounded by a spear and died. The pagan renaissance was over. Soon, a new Christian emperor was on the throne (AD 364), the son of Gratian who had once been governor of Britain, Valentinian. In the years that followed, in the face of growing turmoil in the province, Valentinian would send across the Channel his toughest general, Theodosius, a man who would himself beget a dynasty of emperors. But for Roman Britain, that dynasty would be its last. Time was already running out. In less than fifty years, Rome's jurisdiction over Britain would be at an end.

11
MELTDOWN

Here, on the Wall, there had been some protection. Hunkered down in one of its remaining towers, a few men could perhaps endure a passing raid. But they had always known that they could not go on like this forever. A few days earlier the news had come which they had all been dreading for so long. It may have been inevitable, but, when they heard it, an icy chill had run down each man's spine. The rebel emperor, the man the army had so recently elected, Constantine III, had mustered most of the last troops remaining in this god-forsaken land, and with them he had sailed to Gaul.

Only a few men had been left behind, a token force tasked with a mission every one of them knew all too well was doomed: to try to stop the tribesmen from across the borders bursting through and ravaging the land they once had called Britannia. But there were so many of them, these vicious, cold barbarians with their lust for Roman blood. Even their names brought terror: the Saxons and the Picts, the Scots and Attacotti.

But here, on the Wall, in the tower, there was a closer threat. Late in the last afternoon, the watchman had seen movement in the whin across the valley. Even in the dying sunlight he had no doubt who they were. Their painted bodies, blue against the darker shadows of the hill; their sinuous and cat-like movement; the dull glint of the sunset on their spears. The Picts had come. And now the Romans in the tower knew that they were surrounded, and this time it was no passing raid. For the news that the army had departed had already seeped across the border. Britannia lay open for the taking, and even on the Wall the towers no longer could provide protection.

✧ ✧ ✧

I N AD 364, at a time of crisis, the new Christian emperor Valentinian became Augustus of the West, sharing his rule with his brother Valens in the east. Their predecessor Julian's experiment of a return to the old religion was over, and within the borders of the empire, such faltering moves as he had made towards returning to a pagan status quo needed to be reversed. At the same time, from outside the empire, danger threatened.

In Britain, these external pressures, coupled with a total breakdown of the reach of central government, meant that the province was – or soon would be – fast descending into anarchy. In what may be a literary commonplace (it being pleasingly convenient for an historian to present his reader with a new ruler facing a chaotic situation, which he then goes on to settle) Ammianus writes how early in Valentinian's reign 'the Picts, Saxons, Scots and Attacotti were bringing continual misery upon Britain'. By AD 367, the threat was all too real. In what has become known as the 'Great Barbarian Conspiracy', a 'concerted attack' had brought the province to the 'verge of ruin'. The *comes* of the coastal regions had been killed, as possibly had the army's general. It was time for a serious intervention.[1]

After a fumbled start, Valentinian sent Flavius Jovinus, his *magister equitum* (one of the most senior generals), to take charge.[2] Jovinus soon realized the enormous scale of the task facing him. He sent for massive reinforcements, and also for a tough and seasoned general to lead them: Theodosius, a Spaniard who had risen through the ranks to reach the status of *comes rei militarium*, the 'Count in Charge of Military Affairs'. The situation facing him was dire, as Ammianus explains:

> There were two tribes of Picts, the Dicalydones and Verturiones, and they, along with the warlike peoples of the Attacotti and the Scots,[3] were roaming far and wide and causing great destruction. In addition the Franks and Saxons were seizing the opportunity to raid those parts of Gaul nearest to them by land and sea, pillaging and burning and killing anyone they captured.[4]

Before he could even begin to tackle these raiders from outside the province's frontiers, Count Theodosius discovered that he must first restore order to the towns and countryside of Britain itself. For, having crossed the Channel from Boulogne by the normal route to Richborough, and riding north up Watling Street at the head of his 2,000 men to London, he soon encountered 'roving bands of plunderers...weighed down by their spoils and driving before them prisoners and cattle'.[5] Although no match for Count Theodosius and his troops,[6] these looters nonetheless worried him. It seems likely that, as well as a smattering of Franks and Saxons, these roaming robbers (*bagaudae*) included in their number members of the island's dispossessed: poor labourers or artisans, runaway slaves, soldiers seizing any opportunity that anarchy provided, deserters, even, from the Roman army.

How Theodosius dealt with them speaks volumes. He promised them immunity. In the days of the high empire this would have been unthinkable – the punishment for such offences would automatically have been death. But now, in straitened times, and seeing the sheer numbers of the men involved, Count Theodosius made the only real decision that he could. After all, he needed them back in the army. He needed them onside. In return, he asked for information, intelligence about the 'scattered and wildly ferocious peoples of the various tribes', and he discovered that they could be defeated by only one means: a strategy of stealth and of surprise.

So, having made every effort to restore most of the plunder to its rightful owners (albeit keeping back a little for his 'exhausted troops'), Count Theodosius rode triumphant at the head not only of his army, but of his newly recruited rag-tag force of plunderers and robbers, into a London that genuinely welcomed him as its saviour. At his side, and sharing in the citizens' acclaim, was his twenty-year-old son and namesake, a man who, as Theodosius I (r. AD 379–95), would be the last Augustus of the West to die still ruling over Britain.[7]

Quickly, the Count assembled an impressive government with a new governor, a certain Civilis, 'a man of fiery temper but uncompromising integrity', and a new general in charge of the British garrisons, Dulcitius.[8] With them in place, he himself could turn his attention to the rest of the province (AD 368). Following the advice he had received the year before, he matched his tactics to his enemy and launched a series of swift attacks with himself at their head. The result was just as he had hoped:

He scattered and put to flight various tribes, whose impatience to attack anything Roman was inflamed by the belief that they could act with impunity.[9]

The tribesmen were not Count Theodosius' only enemy. There was in Britain a Roman exile, Valentinus, a member of a family of high rank. His odious brother back in Rome was even now climbing up the ladder of preferment, which in time would take him to the heady heights first of city prefect, then of Praetorian Prefect of Gaul (AD 371–76).[10] Valentinus himself had committed an offence. What it was, we do not know, but it was so serious that it merited banishment to a remote island (a common enough penalty in the Roman world). The island chosen for his punishment was Britain. Here, Valentinus, with nothing more to lose, tried to weave together an alliance of fellow exiles and disaffected troops with the intention of staging a coup d'état against Count Theodosius. It failed. The Count got wind of it and Valentinus and his fellow ringleaders were sent to General Dulcitius for execution. But that was all that happened. On Theodosius' express orders, there was no further inquiry. It seems that the conspiracy had gone so deep that it was thought more politic to turn a blind eye than to pursue each lead to its inevitable and troublesome conclusion. Indeed, by showing clemency, the Count no doubt believed that he could win the support of the provincials.

This much we know. However, the true significance of Valentinus and his plot is much less certain. The normally reliable Ammianus suggests that the Valentine conspiracy was only partially to blame for the chaos faced by Theodosius. In his *Histories*, he stresses the part that barbarian invasions played,[11] and it is, indeed, likely that there was extreme pressure from beyond the borders at this time, especially if it was known that, internally, the province was in meltdown. Ammianus, though, may have wished to downplay Valentinus' role in order to decrease his kudos, and also to minimize the part played by disaffected civilian provincials.

Ammianus' version of the facts is not the only one. Jordanes, Jerome and Zosimus all claim that Valentinus was at the root of all the lawlessness in Britain.[12] Follow their accounts and another picture emerges, according to which Valentinus led a large and significant section of Romano-British society in rebellion: landowners and their workforces, who felt increasingly exploited to produce more food to be exported to the continent; townsmen, forced to billet soldiers in their homes, while at the same time shouldering the burden of increased taxation; dissatisfied and treacherous soldiers, disgruntled at the way the province was being run, aggrieved at what they saw as unfair pay and squalid conditions.[13] It represents a powerful cocktail, and one that could easily spill over into violence and the breakdown of effective government. So, yes, perhaps Count Theodosius did have to deal with raiders from beyond Britain's borders, but perhaps the reason they were raiding in the first place was because the province had descended into anarchy.

Among the seditious troops with whom Theodosius had to deal were the *areani*, the frontier scouts who patrolled the territory far to the north of Hadrian's Wall (see p. 200). Part of their responsibility had been to gather intelligence from native tribes, but now it seems they had been turned. They had 'become corrupt'.[14] They had been selling military secrets to the enemy, providing them with useful information about troop movements, defences and strategy. At a stroke, Theodosius disbanded them. Yet it seems that he did not leave the lands beyond the Wall completely without troops. Large quantities of bronze coins, found at Kelso (Roxburghshire), from the House of Valentinian (r. AD 364–79) and later, suggest that there was a military presence here for some years to come, perhaps a rapid response unit of cavalry.[15]

Having crushed the rebellion, reinstated order and beaten off the barbarians, Theodosius proceeded to 'protect the borders with guard-posts and defence works' and to restore those 'towns and forts, which had suffered

---

THE NORTH UNDER COUNT THEODOSIUS

The written sources are very quiet about northern Britain, so it is difficult to ascertain what Count Theodosius did in the region. However, it is possible that Roman forces were concentrated at fewer, nodal, points. The significant number of Valentinianic coins found at Corbridge and Piercebridge suggests that Dere Street, the road that ran north from York to Hadrian's Wall, was a major artery for Theodosius' troops. Furthermore, one can assume that Valentinianic coins at South Shields show that the military used seaborne routes on the east coast. In addition, it appears that Theodosius initiated the building of the fortlets, sometimes called watchtowers, on the Yorkshire coast (at Huntcliff, Goldsborough, Ravenscar, Scarborough and Filey). On the west coast, Valentinianic coins are common at Caernarvon and further research will almost certainly show that Maryport, on the Cumbrian coast, was also an important military base at this time. There is also evidence for late activity at Carlisle further north. Most of the other forts in the north of England, for example at Housesteads on Hadrian's Wall, have very few Valentinianic coins, so can we envisage the Romans holding the territory with fleets on both coasts and highly mobile, probably cavalry, units operating from major forts in the territory between?[16]

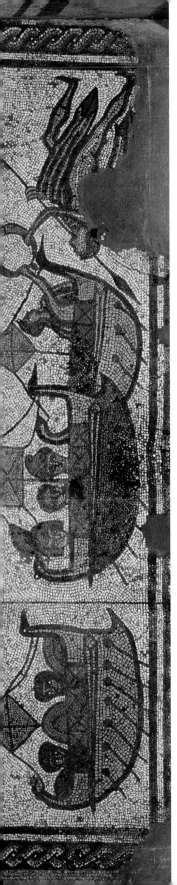

Plate 35 *previous page*
The Mildenhall Great Dish,
buried in the late fourth or
early fifth century AD, showing
the drinking contest between
Dionysus and Hercules.

Plate 36 *left* The Low Ham
Mosaic (Somerset) showing
various scenes, including Dido
embracing Aeneas. Fourth
century AD.

Plate 37 *above* The Orphic
mosaic at Littlecote in Wiltshire,
showing Orpheus with the
four seasons riding around him.
Mid-fourth century AD.

Plate 38 *overleaf* The hoard
of Christian silver found at Water
Newton. This is the earliest
set of Christian silver to survive
anywhere in the Roman empire,
dating from *c*. AD 350 or later.

Plate 39 *top* The central part of the
Hinton St Mary mosaic, depicting
either Christ or Constantine I.
Made in the AD 350s.

Plate 40 *bottom* Bronze coin of
Magnentius, showing the Chi-Rho,
struck at Amiens, AD 352–53.
(Diam. 27 mm)

Plate 41 Part of a wall-painting from Lullingstone Villa, showing Christian worshippers, c. AD 360.

Plate 42 *overleaf* A silver pepper-pot, with gilding, from the Hoxne hoard (Suffolk). It is in the form of a late Roman empress. Late fourth to early fifth century AD.

a series of calamities', according to Ammianus.[17] Exactly what Theodosius did build or restore, however, has proved difficult to unravel – direct archaeological evidence is highly elusive. It is almost certain that it was Theodosius who built, or any rate initiated, a series of watchtowers on the east Yorkshire coast,[18] defence, it is thought, against the Picts. They had recently changed their tactics: rather than conducting their raids overland, where they were forced to cross the Wall and face its (albeit depleted) garrisons, they had begun to take to boats and sail down the east coast, to raid settlements not only by the sea and river-mouths but further inland too. Even in times of huge upheaval, the Romans were adapting swiftly to new pressures with new defensive systems.

From Hadrian's Wall itself comes an intriguing set of inscriptions, which record how sections were rebuilt by peoples from the *civitates* further south: the Durotriges (probably from Ilchester in Somerset); the Dumnonii (from around Exeter); the once great Catuvellauni (from the lands around St Albans); and the Yorkshire men of the Brigantes.[19] Uprooting gangs of labourers from their own lands and bringing them north to the Wall must have resulted in no little upheaval: a short-term solution to a medium-term problem, which may have had long-term and unforeseen implications. For free men to be used, in effect, as slave gangs would hardly improve their opinion of their Roman masters. If, as is possible because the dating of these inscriptions from the Wall is difficult, this happened before Theodosius arrived, these men may have been among those all too ready to nail their colours to the mast of Valentinus' insurrection. No matter their precise date, though, the inscriptions bear stark witness to an increasingly high-handed treatment of the native people by the Roman administration.

It is now thought that at this time (after AD 367) there was major rebuilding at Halton Chesters and Rudchester; there was also less substantial work at Housesteads and Vindolanda, which is dated to this general period. Reconstruction work was certainly carried out on the Wall at Birdoswald Fort. It may be that it was now that the civilian settlements (*vici*), which had sprung up outside the forts, were abandoned, their inhabitants moving inside the walls for safety.[20] For the most part, however, activity around the Wall seems to have been relatively lacklustre: very little coinage has been found, except at a few strategic posts such as Corbridge and South Shields. South Shields was, in fact, a major naval base. The *Notitia Dignitatum* records a unit of bargemen serving in the Tyne Estuary, recruited far to the east on the River Tigris in Mesopotamia.[21]

A few miles south of the Wall, Piercebridge remained a key hub late into the fourth century AD. It may have been the base for a rapid reaction cavalry unit, a vital part of the new military order, now that, with manpower heavily reduced, units on the ground were much more thinly spread. Certainly, spurs found on the site suggest a cavalry presence. In fact, Piercebridge may well have been one of the last bastions of Roman power in the north; there is even evidence to suggest that it was newly fortified in the early years of the fifth century.[22]

We do not know if great parades were ever held here, but Ammianus' description of military displays from Rome gives some idea of what these cavalrymen, with their dragon standards, the heirs of Marius' eagles (see p. 16), looked like:

> He rode surrounded by dragon-standards woven out of purple cloth and fastened to the tops of gold and jewelled spears. As the breeze blew through the gaping mouths of the dragon standards, they seemed to hiss as if roused to anger, and their long tails snaked behind them in the wind....They were accompanied by cavalry in full armour, wearing masks and breastplates, and encased in metal plate and mail, so that they could have been mistaken for statues rather than living men.[23]

In Britain on the west coast, too, it seems work was afoot. Forts such as Maryport were strengthened and some Cumbrian mile fortlets were reoccupied.[24] At sites such as Holyhead and Caernarvon, installations were being fortified and strengthened, while in Gloucestershire, at Lydney, at the temple of Nodens, an inscription dedicated by a government official suggests the presence in the area of naval dockyards. At the same time, far to the south, at the naval base of Bitterne on the Solent, the mudflats were ringing to the sound of major building work.[25]

If a ring of defences was being shored up around the British coast, it was, of course, to protect the agricultural heartlands of the island's south, the vital supply source for the army of the Rhine. There must have been a grimly focused bustle of activity as Theodosius worked hard to regain control and trust among those landowners and farmers who, through desperation, had thrown in their lot with Valentinus. Lest that trust should break down, however, Theodosius, it seems, built massive fortifications, heavily protected compounds for officials and soldiers (including units, perhaps, of the mobile field army), in towns such as Kenchester and

28 Front and back views of a copper-alloy zoomorphic (animal-shaped) buckle, late fourth to fifth century AD, found in Somerset, and now in the Museum of Somerset, Taunton.

Alcester. Or such as Cunetio in Wiltshire, by the River Kennet, where towering walls with sturdy buttresses, similar in their design to shore-forts, were raised above the old town. Here, in the safety of their compound at Cunetio, the tax-collectors and the troops gathered in the *annona*, the tax-in-kind of crops and foodstuffs, which from there would be transported in slow barges pulled by oxen downstream to the Thames and on to London, stored for a time, perhaps in an enormous granary, and then shipped out across the sea bound for the continent.[26]

Not only these areas, but the West Country, too, as well as the great swathe of rich farmland that stretches all the way along the east coast from east Yorkshire down to Lincolnshire and to the Wash, saw heavy troop movement. At least, this is what the dense concentration of contemporary bronze coinage discovered here suggests – on the continent, such coins are found in their highest quantities in frontier zones where the army operated and was based.[27] Across the south and east of Britain, too, bronze belt-buckles have been found with intricate animal-inspired designs (Fig. 28). For a long time it was thought that these belonged to German mercenaries, but now it is believed that they may well have been worn, too, by Roman soldiers and administrators, such as tax collectors, or by civilians who had formed local militias.[28] Perhaps the military activity which all of this suggests included some campaigning, as Theodosius fought to regain control of regions that had so recently rebelled under Valentinus.

Eventually, Theodosius restored order. That he worked hard to do so not only through military force, but by diplomacy, can be seen perhaps from how he appears to have treated Britain's pagan population, who may well still have been basking in the afterglow of the apostate Julian's reign.[29] Instead of persecuting them, the Christian Count Theodosius seems to have done his best to gain their backing – in such a volatile province it did not pay to be too choosy where one garnered one's support.

In recognition that Britain was once more back in the Roman fold, the emperor Valentinian (who had played no active part in its pacification) celebrated by renaming the province, or part of it, after himself. As the historian Ammianus records:

> The repossession of a province which had fallen into the hands of the enemy was now so complete that it had, in his own words, a lawful governor. The emperor considering the affair a triumph, ordered that from then on it should be known as Valentia.[30]

Mission accomplished, Count Theodosius received his orders to return across the Channel (AD 368). He did so in triumph:

> After his excellent management of these affairs and others like them, Theodosius was recalled to court. ...So great was his popularity that a large crowd escorted him to the Channel, which he crossed with a smooth voyage. He was welcomed at the imperial headquarters with rejoicing and congratulations, and promoted to the rank of commander of the cavalry in place of Jovinus, who was considered lax.[31]

Unfortunately for Theodosius, such celebrations did not last. The next years were to see him fighting doggedly against the Alamanni (AD 370 and 372) before being sent south to North Africa, to Mauretania, where he was charged with the task of putting down the insurrection of a Moorish prince (AD 373). It was a long and arduous campaign in hot and arid mountains, and by the time that it was concluded, the emperor Valentinian was dead (AD 375). His brother Valens was now senior Augustus, and – unknown to Theodosius – this regime change was to spell his death. For Valens, years before, had been told in a prophecy that he would be succeeded as emperor by a man, the first two syllables of whose name would be 'Theod'. Now, mindful of this ominous prediction, nervous, perhaps, of Theodosius' power and prestige throughout the west, and scornful of the Count's religious views, Valens vowed to obliterate his rival. At Carthage, Theodosius was killed.[32]

However, they had killed the wrong Theodosius. Three years later, when, during the catastrophic battle with the Visigoths, Valens was slain at Hadrianople (AD 378), his successor Gratian summoned out of premature retirement a general who would rapidly inherit the title of Augustus. It was the dead Count's son, his namesake, Theodosius, who had ridden into London at his father's side eleven years before (see above). The prophecy had been fulfilled.

✧ ✧ ✧

In the hagiography of the new dynasty, Count Theodosius' deeds would become legend. A generation later (AD 398), the court poet Claudian would weave fact into fawning fiction to produce his eulogistic flights of fancy, which described the Count as:

> The conqueror of Britain's coast, who laid waste north
>   and south alike.
> What use the everlasting cold, the icy weather,
>   and the unknown sea?
> The Orcades ran red with slaughtered Saxon blood,
>   the blood of Picts thawed Thule,
> And icy Hiberne mourned the mounds of Scotti dead.[33]

Even by the time that Claudian was honing his deathless purple verse, the situation in Britain had changed significantly. Just over a decade after Count Theodosius had left the island, a new military commander was appointed there, who had once served under him. Like Theodosius, Magnus Maximus was a Spaniard.[34] Indeed, the two men may well have been related, or at least, from an early stage, have known each other in some way. A panegyricist of the Count's son, Theodosius I (who, as we shall see, had no reason to love Magnus Maximus), writes damningly of how '[Maximus] was once a disobedient little house-born slave to your family, an attendant who stood in waiting at the tables of your slaves'.[35]

In fact, most of what we know about Maximus comes from hostile sources; and, apart from the knowledge that he served under Count Theodosius (and with his son, the future emperor Theodosius I) in Britain (AD 367–68), the details of much of his early life are unclear. It may be that he served in the Count's North African campaign (AD 373), after which he was appointed *dux* (commander) in Moesia (a Balkan province, today including parts of Macedonia, Serbia, Bulgaria and Moldova). If this is indeed the case, he may well have been one of the 'flawed characters' who so mismanaged the crossing of the Danube by the Goths in the winter of AD 376–77, an episode which, more than many, hastened the internal disintegration of the Roman empire.[36] Intriguingly, his colleague in this ruinous disaster may well have been another player in Britain's story, the man whose treasure was already lying forgotten at Mildenhall in Suffolk, Lupicinus (see above). Ammianus writes of their soldiers, 'at their head were Lupicinus and Maximus, the one commander in Thrace, the other a useless general, both equally careless'.[37]

It is back in Britain that Magnus Maximus eventually steps into the spotlight. In AD 381, three years after the disastrous battle of Hadrianople (which his bungling policies may well have helped provoke, and in which the emperor Valens died) and two years after his erstwhile colleague, now Theodosius I, had been appointed Augustus, we find Maximus in Britain serving either as *dux Britanniarum* (the senior military commander of the garrisons) or as *comes litoris Saxonici* (Count of the Saxon Shore), commanding the forts along the island's southeast coast.

Within a year (AD 382), Maximus' military skills were being put to the test. The Picts and Scots were on the move again. The northern borders were in peril. With troop numbers now stretched to breaking point, reinforcements had to be brought in from Germany. So an Alammanic king, Fraomarius, together with a large contingent of his men, crossed into Britain. The campaign was successful. The invading Picts and Scots were 'energetically subdued', to mark which Maximus appears later to have awarded himself the title 'Britannicus Maximus'.[38]

Yet whatever his success or rank, it seems that Magnus Maximus was far from happy. To be made to return to far-flung Britain while his former colleague Theodosius lorded it as emperor seems to have rankled. If Maximus was disaffected, he soon found that his mood chimed well with that of the army. After the battle of Hadrianople, Gratian (Theodosius I's co-Augustus of the West) had taken somewhat eccentrically, if not insensitively, to dressing in Gothic costume. If his identification with the peoples who had slaughtered so many Romans were not distressing enough, he was also perceived as preferring so-called barbarian regiments over Roman troops. Recently, indeed, he had received some Alan deserters into the army and 'lavished them with gifts', according to the historian Zosimus.[39] This went down particularly badly with the army in Britain. Given their track record, their subsequent course of action can hardly have come as much of a surprise. They appointed their own rebel emperor, Magnus Maximus:

[Gratian's behaviour] bred in his soldiers a hatred of the emperor, which smouldered and grew, provoking especially those stationed in the British islands (they were the most stubborn and violent) to revolt. They were encouraged by Maximus, a Spaniard who campaigned in Britain with Theodosius. He resented that Theodosius had been considered worthy of becoming emperor, while he himself had not even been given a decent command, so he whipped up the army's hatred of the emperor. They mutinied and acclaimed Maximus emperor, dressing him in the purple and the diadem; then they sailed across the Ocean and anchored at the mouth of the Rhine.[40]

Such, of course, was the view of establishment Rome. Only the Church historian Orosius presents another side. To him, his fellow-Christian, the equally zealous Maximus, was 'an energetic man to be sure, and upright, and worthy of being an Augustus', who had 'not risen through usurpation against his oath of loyalty, but was made emperor by the army in Britain almost against his will'.[41] One wonders.

He certainly took care to make a good impression on his troops, hastily reopening the mint at London (or Augusta, as the city was now called) and striking gold and silver coins, donatives to pay his followers before they left for the continent. Once in Germany, Maximus marched into Gaul. Perhaps hearing the newly minted coins jangling in their British colleague's bags, 'the armies in Germany reacted gladly to the news', and before long the rebel Maximus and the emperor Gratian's men were facing one another in battle. For five days there was skirmishing. Then Gratian's command disintegrated. 'First of all the Moorish horse deserted him, acclaiming Maximus their emperor, then gradually the other troops followed suit,' writes Zosimus.[42]

Like Constans before him, when faced with the victorious rebel Magnentius (see p. 202), Gratian fled south. Like Constans, too, he was pursued. They caught him as he tried to cross a bridge near Lyons. He did not survive the encounter (August AD 383).

For four years, Magnus Maximus ruled as emperor from Trier, the imperial capital in Gaul, striking coins both here and at Arles and Lyons, with which to pay his men (Fig. 29). Perhaps at some stage he returned to Britain – certainly, later in his reign, the London mint was issuing gold coins, and traditionally these tended to be struck only when the emperor

29 Gold coin of Magnus Maximus (383–88), struck at Trier.

was in residence – and in the land of his appointment to the throne it seems he ruled for the most part effectively, though it has been argued that he may have over-taxed and confiscated more than was judicious.[43]

For much of his rule, the rebel emperor was even recognized by the two legitimate Augusti, young Valentinian II (Gratian's successor) and Maximus' old messmate Theodosius I, who, we are told by Zosimus:

...thought him worthy of sharing his statues and his imperial title, but in secret prepared for war while outmanoeuvring him with every kind of flattery and kindness.[44]

Maximus chose the year of his victory over Gratian (AD 383) not only to be baptized but to demonstrate the fervour of his religious beliefs. It certainly seemed to work for him. He wrote to Siricius, the Bishop of Rome, telling how he had ascended 'straight from the font of salvation to the throne', and it was Ambrose, Bishop of Milan, who was instrumental in arranging for Maximus to be recognized as emperor. He even managed to find time to intervene in doctrinal matters, banishing a band of strictly ascetic heretics to an exile in the Scilly Isles.[45] Despite his best efforts, though, (like Theodosius I) he still could not avoid upsetting Ambrose. Maximus condemned to death some fellow Christians for burning down a synagogue. For Ambrose such treatment of the faithful was unforgivable.[46]

At last, Maximus' innate dissatisfaction with his present lot caused him to act. In AD 387, using as his pretext a dispute over ecclesiastical niceties,[47] he crossed the Alps and marched on Rome. In his train was a rag-tag but ruthless army, its core of Roman soldiers swollen by Gauls and Britons, Celts and other tribesmen. The young Valentinian II fled to Theodosius. This was the moment Theodosius had been waiting for. He mobilized his men and marched out against Maximus. The final battle came at Aquileia (AD 388). Close to its newly finished church, adorned by wondrous mosaics proclaiming the miracle of Christian forgiveness, the defeated Maximus pleaded for his life. To no avail. He was stripped of his royal clothing and condemned to death. Far off in Gaul, in obedience to an imperial command, his son would soon be butchered by a Frankish general.[48]

In some ways, it was not just Maximus' reign that ended at Aquileia, but the security of Roman Britain, too. For, despite the fact that Maximus would enter Welsh folklore as a legendary hero, there is no doubt that he was responsible for dangerously denuding the island of its garrison. We hear that, when Maximus first sailed to Gaul and then invaded Italy, he had with him a significant number of troops from Britain.[49] We read of such troop movements everywhere:

> Maximus set sail from Britain, with all British troops, and killed Gratian.[50]

> After this, Britain was robbed of all her armed forces, her military supplies, her rulers, brutal though they were, her robust young men. They followed in the steps of the usurper Magnus Maximus, and never came back again.[51]

At the same time, soldiers from Segontium (Caernarvon) are mentioned in the records as being stationed in Illyricum.[52]

MAGNUS MAXIMUS IN LATER TRADITION

It may have been Magnus Maximus who settled the Irish *foederati* in Wales, possibly giving them the territory of the Demetae tribe (Dyfed). These *foederati* may have been the same Attacotti who had been raiding Britain since the AD 360s. Later, Maximus, a hero of both English and Breton legend, was to enter Welsh folklore as Macsen Wledig, and on the Pillar of Eliseg, erected by Cyngen ap Cadell, King of Powys (died AD 855) it is claimed that one of Maximus' daughters was married to the sub-Roman warlord, Vortigern ('High King'), who ruled in Britain at some time in the 420s–440s. The inscription on the Pillar of Eliseg, which stands near Valle Crucis Abbey in Denbighshire, is no longer legible, but it was recorded by antiquarians as reading: 'Britu, son of Vortigern, whom Germanus blessed, and whom Severa bore to him, daughter of Maximus the king, who killed the king of the Romans.'[53]

It was no time for Britain to have been stripped of such crucial defences. The later historian Gildas may well be unreliable, but his account of what happened next is far from unlikely. Emptied of soldiery, the province was easy prey, and, with the news of Maximus' death (AD 388), the hostile tribes from beyond the borders struck:

> Completely ignorant of the art of war, Britain groaned for many years in shock, exposed for the first time to the cruelty of two foreign tribes, the Scots from the northwest, the Picts from the north. Unable to bear these attacks and the terrible oppression, the Britons sent ambassadors to Rome with letters, making emotional appeals for an armed protection force, and promising loyal and whole-hearted submission to the authority of Rome, if only they would drive out the enemy. Forgetting the previous rebellion, Rome sent a well-equipped legion. It crossed over Ocean to Britain in ships and engaged the fierce enemy, slaughtering a great many of them and driving them all out. So the battered peoples were freed from the bloody slavery which had threatened them.[54]

To protect them, Gildas goes on, the Britons were instructed 'to build a wall from sea to sea across the island' (c. AD 390). Perhaps Hadrian's Wall was indeed strengthened at this time, though there is no evidence from archaeology to bear this out. Whatever the measures that now were put in place, it seems that for the time being peace was restored.

It would not last. Within five years (AD 395), Theodosius I was dead, and, while his son, the weak Honorius, was growing up, the ruling of the western empire was entrusted to the implacable half-Vandal general, Flavius Stilicho. Chronology is difficult, but it seems possible that Stilicho was redeploying the same troops that had been sent to fight the Picts and Scots in Britain after Maximus' death. Gildas writes:

> When all at once, like starved and ravening wolves that leap with hungry jaws into the sheepfold when the shepherd is away, the old enemy burst across the frontier. They slaughtered everything... Again, the Britons sent ambassadors to Rome...The Romans, moved as much as men can be by such accounts of horror, swiftly sent their cavalry by land and their sailors by sea. Like eagles they plunged the talons of their sword-points into the shoulders of their enemies...[55]

Certainly Stilicho took the credit for the victory. There is no evidence that the general himself ever set foot on the island, but this did not stop the fulsome Claudian from exuding more flattering verses. Britain was safe, he said in AD 399; the seas secure.[56] A year later he could paint what (even for him) was a bizarre, outlandish picture. In it, he imagined the province's personification, Britannia, in a way quite alien to anything that had been visualized before:

> Then, wrapped in the skin of a Caledonian beast, her cheeks tattooed, her sky-blue garments like the waves of Ocean falling round her feet, Britannia spoke: 'My neighbours would have killed me, but Stilicho protected me – for the Scot roused all Ireland against me and the sea foamed under their hostile oars. Now, thanks to Stilicho, I need not fear the Scottic javelin nor tremble at the Pict, nor scour suspiciously each wind along my coast for the approaching Saxon.'[57]

She has come a long way, this Britannia, from her cool, classical, Minerva-like depictions of the centuries before. Now, in the mind's eyes of Romans at the heart of empire, she is as wild and barbaric as the tribes against which she needs to be kept safe. She is not so much Britannia as Boudica reborn, not Roman any more but alien, barbarian. At a time when even the heart of empire was under threat, how much longer could Britain really count on Rome for her protection?

Already, the last days were fast approaching. In the east, the Visi-goths, for many years treated with such patronizing scorn by their Roman over-lords, had elected a new king, Alaric, a general who had cut his teeth fighting side by side with Stilicho for Theodosius and who now wanted a homeland. From him would come the threat which would occupy the central Roman establishment for years to come, and in Italy, with the Visigoths a mere few hundred miles away, Britain began to seem decid-edly distant. Indeed, when the inevitable military conflict came, as at the battle of Pollentia (AD 402), we hear from Claudian that Stilicho had already begun the final withdrawal of troops from Britain's shores. For among his victorious army was:

> A legion that had been stationed among the far-off Britons, which had reined in the fierce Scot and had scanned the strange patterns tattooed on the dying Pict.[58]

Against these Picts and other hostile tribesmen, in Britain itself, defences were rapidly being built. Gildas once more writes of a wall constructed across the country, perhaps a stock response by an unreliable historian,[59] but chiming with another comment that:

> They built towers, too, overlooking the sea at intervals on the coast to the south where they kept their ships, since there too they feared the savage barbarian beast.[60]

If only Gildas were more trustworthy. These may be new towers, or, of course, they may simply refer to the existing Saxon Shore Forts or the Yorkshire Signal Towers built when Count Theodosius was in Britain. As for Stilicho himself, he may well have appointed a new military commander for the island, the *Comes Britanniarum*, but he did little else.

By AD 406, isolation and the feeling of having been abandoned by central government meant that the rump of the army now left in Britain felt that it had no option but to act. Evidence for what actually happened in those fraught months is scanty, yet the sketchy account of one late fifth-century historian is enough to paint a grim picture. For, over on the continent:

> The Vandals joined forces with the Suebi and Alans and, sweeping across these lands, they ravaged the Transalpine tribes. So widespread was the slaughter they carried out that even the Roman army in Britain was afraid: indeed such was its fear that the barbarians might attack, that it was forced to appoint the usurper emperors, Marcus and Gratian...[61]

About this Marcus and Gratian we know next to nothing except that neither lasted long. Indeed, the situation was so volatile that, within weeks, each was removed from power and executed by the very army that had raised them up.[62] Clearly the troops were looking for a strong leader who would present them with a clear and immediate solution, a military stratagem to instill in them some faith that they could meet and defeat an imminent barbarian onslaught.

If morale could have deteriorated any further, it surely did so in the early days of AD 407. For some time soon after the New Year, news came to Britain to chill the blood. The winter had been harsh, the river Danube frozen, and on the last day of the old year an incalculable number of barbarian tribesmen, Alans and Suevi, Vandals and Burgundians, had crossed the ice and broken through to Gaul. The Roman army had been powerless to stop them. Indeed, it may be that many troops had already been redeployed away from this crucial boundary – to guard the Channel against a potential crossing by a rebel emperor from Britain.

That their choice in rebel emperor had so far failed to inspire did not deter the army in Britain. They searched for another candidate. They found him in one of their own rank, a man with an auspicious name: Constantine. The Church historian, Orosius, pours scorn upon him, sneering that he:

> ...was elected from the lowest ranks of the military, simply because his name seemed propitious, and not because of any bravery he might have had.[63]

Perhaps the army was, indeed, clutching at straws, though the fact that this Constantine had named his two sons Constans and Julian suggests that he did at least have an eye for history. The soldiers both in Britain and in the western provinces knew him, too, and thanks to his auspicious name they trusted him.[64]

The newly proclaimed Augustus, Constantine III, repaid that trust. He did not hesitate. He had weighed up the threat, and realized already that the future lay in Gaul, the lands that Caesar had so brilliantly annexed almost half a millennium before. Unless that province was secure, the Roman empire in the west was nothing. So, without delay, he appointed his generals[65] and, the army's dragon standards hissing in the Channel breeze, embarked his men on what even then he may have realized would be the last Roman fleet to sail from Britain. He ordered his helmsmen to set course for Boulogne.

With him, Constantine may well have had the entire British field army, a force of perhaps around 6,000 men. Only a handful of the once massive occupation force were left behind, a few forlorn frontier troops to stand against what they all surely must have known to be quite irresistible numbers of hostile tribesmen pressing hard against the borders.[66]

For the first time in almost 400 years, Britain had no real Roman military presence. Of course, reports must have reached the cities and the villas from across the Channel of how the army in Gaul had gone over to Constantine, how the usurper emperor had repelled attacks not only from barbarians but from Stilicho's general, how Constantine was now ensconced in Arles, and in control (in name at least) of the Gallic prefecture whose jurisdiction embraced Britain. But by the time that they might have heard of how first Constantine had been recognized by the true emperor Honorius, then how he faced rebellion from his own commanders, then finally how he had been cut down, executed on the orders of Honorius on the road to Ravenna – by then, the British people had more pressing problems of their own.

In AD 409, according to the Gallic Chronicle, 'the Britons were devastated by an incursion of the Saxons'.[67] The floodgates had opened. Zosimus describes the bitter consequences:

> The barbarians caused such suffering among the inhabitants of Britain as well as some of the Gallic peoples that they revolted from the Roman empire. They no longer recognized Roman law, but reverted to their native customs. So the Britons armed themselves and took many risks to ensure their own safety and keep their cities free from barbarian attacks. The other Gallic provinces followed the Britons and freed themselves in the same way, by expelling the Roman magistrates and forming the style of government they wanted.[68]

By then there can have been no one who believed the Roman army would ever come back, no one, indeed, who would have seriously petitioned central command to help to save them. For many years there has been a belief that a sentence in the histories of Zosimus spells the moment of the end. Referring to events of AD 410, it was thought to read, 'Honorius sent letters to the cities in Britain, urging them to fend for themselves'. Now, though, it seems that these letters were addressed to Bruttium in Italy or even to Bologna.[69] Why, anyway, would Honorius be writing to the British cities, when (as he had himself agreed) the island came under the jurisdiction of Constantine III? As it was, by now even Constantine seemed to have turned his back on them, and by now he may have had good reason (see below).

In truth, Britain had already slipped away from the rule and even from the interest of what still remained of the Roman empire. In the minds of many, it was once more reverting to that distant fog-bound island far across the Ocean, as remote as it had ever been in the days before the legions came. Nevertheless, in Britain itself there was still a population who lived and worked as they had done for centuries, whose lifestyle had been influenced irrevocably by the Roman presence, and for many of them Rome was in their blood.

12

Praying for the Coming
of the Once and Future King

They had conferred on him the duty of writing the letter. Not that anyone really believed it would have much effect, but it needed to be written. It was a last ditch effort, and perhaps for a few brief weeks it would buy them hope. And he knew how desperately hope was needed.

He had travelled from the west, where they still clung on as best they could to what they called the civilized old ways. Before setting out, he had eaten his last meal with them from treasured antique Roman plates. But those heirlooms had served only to remind him of what was lost, of an old world, which never would return.

With every mile of his journey that old world had seemed ever further distant. He had had to travel in the twilight or at night-time, sleeping fitfully by day wherever he could find shelter, but even then the signs were everywhere: burnt-out basilicas, warehouses empty and decayed, ruined villas, whose rotten roofs let in the winter rain, where pigs were rooting up the once so lovely gardens. Several times he had woken in terror, thinking there was somebody outside – a robber, a rough local youth, his face concealed beneath a tattered hooded cloak, or even worse, a Saxon. But it had been nothing more than a fox or feral dog, and it had, thank God, ignored him.

The candle was already guttering as he took up his stylus. Already a pale dawn was breaking far across the salt flats and the haunting cry of curlews was carried on the chilly morning air. He knew it would be useless, but nonetheless he wrote: 'To the Roman, Aetius, in his third consulship. Listen to the lamentations of the Britons, and come to our aid. The barbarians are driving us to the sea; the sea is driving us back to the barbarians; between barbarians and sea we are being drowned or slaughtered...' Yes, the scribe knew it would be useless. The Romans would not return. What Britain needed was a strong king of its own it could believe in, and perhaps he knew already who that strong king would be.

THE departure of the dragon standards of the Roman army in
AD 407, accompanied as it was by the fast disintegration of the last
vestiges of security and order, must have sent Britain into rapid
freefall. Across the country, Roman soldiers and officials had bolstered
up the entire infrastructure of the thriving agricultural economy, which
had relied so heavily not only upon farming, but also on haulage to the
depots on the estuaries and coasts, before the freight was shipped out in
the transport vessels to the continent. With this infrastructure gone, the
whole edifice must quickly have collapsed.[1]

The evidence from archaeology is clear. By the early decades of the
fifth century, Roman Britain's material culture, which had already been
decaying, was coming to an end. Forums and baths, theatres and amphi-
theatres: as the urban populations went into steep decline, all were
increasingly abandoned, or reused for agricultural purposes.[2] Such new
buildings as appeared were no longer in stone, but often in those ancient
and pre-Roman materials, wattle and daub. In Wroxeter, where there was
some attempt at least to maintain urban life, timber buildings were erected
where once there had been masonry structures, while in Caerwent in
South Wales, an important centre right until the end, stonework was used
– but only to block the gates to the south and north to make the city more
secure.[3]

POPULATION DECLINE

The shrinkage in the number of settlements in the fifth century suggests
a population decline. Gildas mentions plagues twice, although there is no
other evidence for such outbreaks in Britain.[4] There are signs of farming
being centred within towns, for example at Cirencester, possibly suggesting
that rural settlements were becoming increasingly vulnerable in an unstable society.[5] Furthermore, in towns 'dark earth' is found in late Roman
layers across the province. This can represent decaying organic material
from buildings, but possibly shows farming or market gardening taking
place within town walls.[6] The picture presented is one of an increasingly
insecure world in which it is quite likely that the amount of land farmed
was in decline. This in turn would lead to a decline in population. Much
of this, however, is speculation and ongoing research into post-Roman
Britain will probably present new findings in the coming decades.

Elsewhere, as in the valley of the Nene, the factories fell silent as once-booming industries such as pottery and iron found their old markets gone. In the countryside, too, some of the villas, which, with their intricate mosaics and wall-paintings, had been the jewels of the West Country and the south, fell into disrepair. In others, entire wings were closed down and allowed to moulder, as landed families tried hard to retrench, to save on heating and repairs, by living and working in a smaller space, or as the dispossessed sought refuge in the peeling rooms of empty and decaying country houses.[7]

That this happened relatively quickly is not surprising. Quite simply, Britain had been both a military and a service state, providing goods to the continent. Once it had ceased to trade and the army was withdrawn, next to no money came into the island from outside. A short time after Constantine III left, such soldiers or officials who had stayed behind soon found that they were no longer being paid.[8] No matter how much the Britons may have wished to keep their Romanized lifestyle, without the law and order and the centralized administrative infrastructure to keep it all afloat, they must have found it more difficult by the day. So they were forced to improvise.

In different parts of Britain, people responded to the atmosphere of growing unrest in different ways. To the north, at South Shields on the ancient Hadrianic frontier, savage destruction may well suggest that they were taken unprepared. Early in the fifth century, corpses were buried beneath the *praetorium* (commander's house), the result perhaps of a sudden Pictish raid. Further to the west at Birdoswald, the people built a large timber hall over the granaries to be the seat, some think, of a local warlord (perhaps the fort commander, forced to take control as best he could now that the flow of pay-chests from the continent had ceased).[9] The hall remained in use for close on a hundred years. Across the country, there were many situations in which sub-Roman leaders organized local militias, which would in time give rise to new political bodies. Recent excavations have shown that there was still occupation of parts of the fort at Vindolanda up until the eighth century.[10]

In its appearance, the warlord's hall at Birdoswald was similar to another hall far to the south at Cadbury Congresbury in Somerset, built in the confines of an Iron Age hillfort, reoccupied now that the Roman army had withdrawn. Perhaps the inhabitants of local rural settlements, aristocrats from rich villas forming a necessary if unlikely alliance with workers from humble farmsteads, came here to find security behind its ancient earthen ramparts and keep something of the Roman way of life alive. Within the earthworks, in their homes of timber or of stone reclaimed from ruined villa sites, they were still using treasured antique Roman glassware, pottery and brooches (some as many as a hundred years old), when a trickle of trade with the Mediterranean resumed in the sixth century and new fine tableware and amphorae were proudly brought into the site.Such goods came to Tintagel, too, and Dinas Powys, and Dumbarton Rock, and Bantham Beach in Devon; and with them came Byzantine coins. Which begs the question: what (or whom) were the Britons trading in return?[11]

LATE ROMAN SILVER CURRENCY

Across much of south and east England, from east Yorkshire to Somerset, there is strong evidence for the continuation of a silver currency for some years after 407–11. The coin in question was called the *siliqua*. Many of these coins were clipped so that their size and weight were reduced, often drastically; this clipping was a very British phenomenon. The clippings could be used to make local copies of *siliquae* (suggesting a continued need for currency) or were melted down to make ingots. It is generally accepted that the practice post-dated 402, and might have continued beyond 411. Not only are these coins found in many hoards across Britain, such as the enormous Hoxne hoard (Plate 42), they have also been recorded as single finds across the country. It is highly likely that these coins, along with hacksilver (cut up pieces of silver plate) and ingots, continued to be used as currency, perhaps up to around 430. The Coleraine hoard is an excellent example of a cache of such items from this period. Recently, a hoard of clipped *siliquae* has been found in the foothills of the Pyrenees in France – these were surely coins taken by British troops serving in the army of Constantine III (AD 407–11) on the continent.[12]

30 Clipped-silver *siliqua* of Constantine III (AD 407–11), struck at Lyons, AD 407–8. From the Coleraine hoard, British Museum.

The Roman empire may have given up on Britain, but in the west of the country at least its people still clung on to what they could of Roman ways. After all, it was a way of life that had for centuries provided them with not only stability, but security. It may be that they started to revert to ancient tribal boundaries, as earthworks such as Wansdyke (Wiltshire) might suggest. Still, across much of the south and east, from Somerset north to east Yorkshire, they attempted to buy and sell with Roman silver currency for some years after Constantine had sailed for Gaul. Yet, who these people were and how they lived becomes increasingly difficult to know.[13]

✧ ✧ ✧

Only a few names stand out in this period.[14] Of these some of the most significant do still belong to Romans trying to impose some order upon British lives; but these men are no longer state officials or military commanders. Instead, they are priests of the Roman Church. One such was Germanus, and he came to Britain to suppress a heresy.

Britain already had a history of non-conformity when it came to Christianity. In many parts, the Fens and West Country for example, the grip of paganism was still tight and the final decades of the fourth century had seen a resurgence in the old beliefs. Even the celebrated Water Newton treasure, the Christian hoard buried in the early fifth century at the latest, contains a whiff of paganism (Plate 38). One silver gilt plaque bears a dedication to Christ from a woman called Iamcilla (a variant, perhaps of *Ancilla*, the Latin word for 'maidservant'): 'Iamcilla fulfilled the vow that she had promised'.[15]

It sounds innocuous enough, but in fact the formula is pagan to the core, as pagan as the curse tablets from Bath so many centuries before (see p. 126). For it implies that Iamcilla had promised her God an offering on condition that He brought her good fortune. In Christianity, however, the concept of God's grace should render such contracts meaningless. It implies that the notion of God's universal, unconditional grace was something that Iamcilla and people like her found it difficult to come to terms with...which brings us to Pelagius.

Pelagius was born in Britain around AD 350. His parents were sufficiently rich to educate him well, and when he was in his late twenties and already a priest, he went to Rome. Here he found favour with Augustine and his fellow Church Elders: but not for long. For Pelagius began to argue passionately against the concepts both of 'grace' and of 'original sin'.

Instead, he suggested that mankind possessed free will, and that people could choose to win salvation through their own good deeds and actions. This, the Church Elders did not like at all. In AD 415 they accused Pelagius of heresy. The next year he was excommunicated by the Pope, and in AD 418 the emperor Honorius was sufficiently moved to denounce him.[16] Pelagius himself now departs from the pages of history. His heresy, however, does not. For by AD 429, a Pelagian disciple, Agricola, was preaching the dissenting doctrine in Britain.

The Pope was not amused. Free will was not on his agenda. So he sent to Britain his representatives, Germanus, Bishop of Auxerre, and Lupus, Bishop of Troyes, to bring the island back into line.[17] The later *Life of Germanus* describes both men in breathless terms as 'shining lights of the Faith' and 'saintly paragons' – but it makes sure that it is Germanus who receives the credit for what happened next, and it begins the story of his mission with an oddly familiar description.

For we read that the saintly paragon, now in his early fifties, a qualified lawyer, an ex-provincial governor, and now, of course, a bishop, was sailing in his ship in mid-Channel when a sudden storm boiled up. It is worth quoting the passage at some length:

> The ocean was attacked by the savagery of demons, who detest religion, and who were now livid with malice at the sight of such great men hurrying to bring salvation to the nations. They piled up every danger, whipped up gales, concealed the heavens and the day beneath a night of clouds, and filled the solid darkness with the terrors of the sea and air. The sails were not proof against the fury of the winds and the fragile boat could hardly bear the weight of all the water. Helpless, the sailors abandoned their efforts; the boat was steered by prayer, not brawn. And it was now that their leader himself, the bishop, his body aching and exhausted, went to sleep.
>
> Now the storm unleashed its full force; it was as if the hand which had restrained it had now gone. Soon the boat was swamped by the waves that crashed over it. At last the blessed Lupus and all the anxious crew aroused their leader, that he might stand against the raging tempest. The enormity of the danger made him more resolute. In the name of Christ he chastized the ocean, using the name of religion to quell the savagery of the winds. Then he took some oil and, in the name of the Trinity, lightly sprinkled it onto the

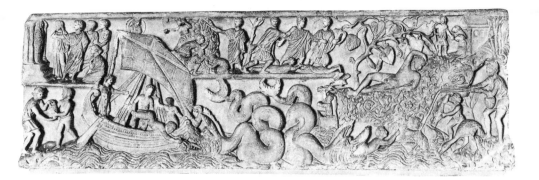

31 A stone sarcophagus (coffin) showing the story of Jonah and the whale, third century AD, now in the Vatican Museum, Rome. The scene is reminiscent of the description of St Germanus' Channel crossing.

waves and so quelled their fury. Turning to his colleague, he called everybody together; and with one voice all prayed.

And there was God! The enemies of souls were routed, the air cleared and was calm, the opposing winds were turned to help their voyage, and the current changed to ease the passage of the ship. In this way the great distances were covered and soon all were enjoying rest on the shore they had so longed for.[18]

The trope of the Channel crossing is by now as familiar as that of the swamps and bogs and fogs of the island with which earlier military commanders had to contend. A stormy voyage, heroically endured and followed by a peaceful landing, presages the hero's triumphant quelling of barbarian attack or British insurrection. Here, in Germanus' case, it is not only the elements but demons, haters of religion, heretics, no doubt, that try to drown him. But now there are new weapons in the armoury against cross-Channel mayhem – holy oils and prayer – that can be used to calm the seas. For the reader, at least, the omens are exceedingly favourable.

Perhaps there was indeed a storm, which miraculously did abate; perhaps large crowds did gather to receive the bishops as Germanus' biographer avows; perhaps the island really was awash with miracles:

...since every day they were hemmed in by crowds, the word of God was preached, not just in churches, but at crossroads and in fields and lanes. Everywhere faithful Catholics were strengthened in their faith and those who had lapsed found the way back to the truth.[19]

Whatever really happened, the showdown came at Verulamium (St Albans). According to Germanus' biographer, here the Pelagian heretics, led perhaps by the disciple Agricola himself, 'flaunting their wealth and dressed in dazzling robes' confronted the two bishops (Plate 41). Then, in turn, each side spoke, and according to the biographer, it was the assembled Britons who were allowed to judge the outcome. The heretics put their side first. The bishops replied:

> ...mingling their own eloquence with the thunders of apostles and the Gospels, for their own words were interwoven with the inspired writings and their strongest assertions were supported by the testimony of Scripture.[20]

The people's jury was about to give its judgment, when:

> Suddenly a man of the high military rank of tribune, accompanied by his wife, stepped into their midst and set into the arms of the bishops his ten-year-old daughter, who was blind. The bishops told him to take her to their opponents. But they were pricked by conscience and not a little alarmed, so they joined the parents in begging the bishops to cure the little girl. The bishops saw that the people were expectant and their opponents in a more deferential frame of mind, so they offered up a short prayer. Then Germanus, filled with the Holy Spirit and in the name of the Trinity, took from his neck the reliquary that always hung at his side and – in full view of everybody – raised it to the child's eyes. Immediately it drove out the darkness from them and replenished them with light and truth. The parents were filled with joy at the miracle and the onlookers with awe. From that day on, the false doctrine was so completely uprooted from men's minds that they looked to the bishops for teaching, with thirsty souls.[21]

The story seems so contrived, the miracle potentially so stage-managed, that it seems almost pointless to ask who the tribune was, whose daughter was miraculously cured. Might he have been a soldier who had served with Rome but had then stayed on in Britain? Was he a still-serving soldier? Was he in the bishops' entourage? Did old Roman ranks linger on in sub-Roman Britain? Or is it yet another trope, a revisiting of the story of how Christ cured the centurion's servant, an episode thrown in to prove Germanus' saintliness?[22]

Germanus was not yet through with miracles. With the girl's sight now restored, 'the bishops visited the shrine of the blessed martyr Alban, to give thanks to God through him'. Already St Alban's shrine was a focus of veneration in the city that would take his name. On the hill above Roman Verulamium, perhaps where the present Abbey stands, the saint, a Roman soldier punished for protecting a fugitive priest and then converting to Christianity, had been decapitated.[23] (Interestingly, St Alban's executioner is said to have experienced a somewhat unwelcome miracle of his own, which, in a neat reversal of the tribune's daughter's fate, involved his eyes. At the moment that he struck the fatal blow, they fell out of their sockets.) Now, we are told, Germanus, still flushed from his own ophthalmological triumph:

> ...tore up a lump of earth from the very place where the martyr's blood had been spilt. This desecration was justified, since the stain of his blood could still be seen. This great sign was revealed to all men, how the martyr's blood had reddened the earth, and his persecutor grew pale.[24]

In fact (as he no doubt already knew) Germanus simply held up, in the words of a modern archaeological report, 'the local clay with flints subsoil, which, distinctively orange in its upper, oxidized levels, occurs locally within a few centimetres of the surface'.[25] When conducting a miracle, it pays to be prepared.

Little could have prepared Germanus for his final, and perhaps greatest, miracle on British soil – except perhaps a knowledge of acoustics. We read how, having suffered a hurt ankle and survived a house fire, the now limping bishop found himself involved in military action. According to his biographer, an army of Britons had been surrounded by a combined force of Picts and Saxons. Seeing that they were greatly outnumbered, they sent for Lupus and Germanus. Germanus naturally knew what to do. He baptized the soldiers, celebrated Easter, and announced that he would lead the army into battle.[26]

> By now the enemy's savage troops were close by. Germanus swiftly circulated the command that everyone should repeat together the call he would give as a battle-cry. Then, with the enemy believing that their attack was unexpected, the bishops chanted the Alleluia three times. All to a man repeated it and the shout they raised rang

through the air to be echoed many times in the confined space between the mountains. The enemy were panic-stricken – they believed that all the rocks around them and the sky itself were falling in on them. So terrified were they that they seemed unable to run fast enough to save themselves. They ran off in every direction, throwing down their weapons, grateful that they could save their skins. Many threw themselves into the river which they had just crossed easily, and were drowned in it.[27]

Alleluia, indeed. Germanus returned across the Channel, safe in the knowledge that Britain, 'this most wealthy island, with the defeat of both its spiritual and its human foes, was rendered secure in every sense'. Back in Gaul he founded a monastery on the banks of the Yonne and involved himself in politics before dying, at last, in Ravenna (AD 447–48). He was subsequently canonized.[28]

Britain was capable of producing its own saints, too. The most famous of the period, perhaps, was Patrick, and it may well be that he studied under Germanus himself. Despite his fame and the plethora of stories that surround him, the facts about his life are few. Many come from his own writings. In his *Confessio*, for example, he tells us that he was born the grandson of a presbyter and son of a deacon, who owned a small villa near the settlement of Bannaven Taburniae. Sadly, the location of this place is unknown and recent attempts at locating it have suggested sites as far apart as the western region of Hadrian's Wall and west Somerset.[29]

When Patrick was about sixteen, he was captured by raiders and taken to captivity in Ireland, where he was put to work as a shepherd. In time he returned to Britain, but, one day while reading a letter from Ireland, he heard the voice of those 'beside the forest of Foclut in County Mayo, crying: "We beg you, holy youth, that you shall come and shall walk again amongst us."'[30] He did, and played an important role in that island's conversion. And so the missionary work went on. Columba sailed from Ireland to Iona (AD 563); and, from Iona, Aidan travelled to Northumberland to found the monastery on Lindisfarne (Holy Island AD 635).

The journey had gone almost full circle. By now, in written records as in the minds (no doubt) of many of their authors, historical fact and religious fantasy were becoming seriously intertwined. Whereas Caesar, writing six centuries or so before, might have been trying to impress his audience with his skills as a soldier or a politician, now authors had a new agenda: to show that everything that happened was the will of God, that good was triumphing, that the Kingdom was coming.

✧ ✧ ✧

In the real world, what had once been part of a great empire was fast disintegrating. Into the dangerous vacuum left by the departed Roman army, local warlords stepped, and internecine strife erupted over territory and resources, as communities 'plundered one another for the meagre provisions the wretched citizens possessed as a short-term means of sustenance'.[31] For a time (?AD 420s–440s), they may have had a ruler to unite them: Vortigern, whose name means 'High King'. Perhaps, like Cunobelin before him (see Chapter 2), he exercised wide power; or perhaps his rule was much more localized.[32] But his was a troubled kingship.

Still the Picts were harrying the northern marches, while to the west the Scots remained a constant threat. On the Rhine the Roman general Aetius, campaigning year on year from AD 425 to 450,[33] may well have cast an acquisitive eye across the sea to Britain. After all, Britain had fed the army in the century before. There may, indeed, have been some form of Roman mission to the island in these years, possibly even the one led by Germanus. Five scattered copper coins struck between AD 425 and 435 and found as far apart as Richborough and Wroxeter perhaps suggest the visit of an official Roman delegation.[34]

Under pressure from all sides, Vortigern convened a council. Its options limited, it resolved to send for Saxon mercenaries. It could not have made a worse decision. Under the leadership of warlords known to us now as Hengist and Horsa,[35] the Saxons soon turned on their British masters. Gildas' near-contemporary description is still chilling:

> Then the litter of cubs bursts out of the lair of the barbaric lioness, carried in three 'cylae' (keels), as they call their longboats....On the tyrant's [Vortigern's] orders they first latched their terrible claws in the eastern part of the island as if meaning to fight to protect the country, but in fact to attack it. To these the mother lioness, learning her first contingent has prospered, sends another larger contingent of accomplice dogs....Then the barbarians, sent into the island, contrive to have provisions given to them as if they were soldiers about to suffer great danger on behalf of their good hosts – such were their lies....Again they complain that the monthly rations they are

given are not enough, deliberately exaggerating their case, and they declare that unless greater generosity is heaped upon them, they will break their treaty and plunder the whole island. Without delay they follow up their threats with deeds...[36]

The Saxon conquest had begun. By now, the old world of Roman Britain had gone forever. In some places, it is true, they still tried to cling on and there was one last vain appeal to the Roman army to protect them (AD 446). We read of:

> The miserable remains of a letter sent to Aetius, a man of great power among the Romans, in the following terms: 'To Aetius, consul for the third time, come the groans of the Britons' ... 'The barbarians drive us to the sea; the sea drives us back to the barbarians; between these two forms of death we are either slaughtered or drowned.'[37]

Aetius did not come and it was left to the Britons to resist as best they could. There were some successes, for example the famous victory at Mons Badonicus (some time between AD 490 and 520) recorded by Gildas:

> Under the leadership of Ambrosius Aurelianus, a modest man... they recovered their strength and challenged the victorious Saxons to battle. The Lord gave His assent and victory was theirs.[38]

By now, the history of Roman Britain had entered the world of legend. For fighting in the shield wall alongside Ambrosius, helping to stem the Saxon tide, was said to be a man whose father, Uther, had been born beneath the dragon standard of the Roman army, the son, some said, of Constantine III himself. This was perhaps how Uther had received his second name, 'The Dragon's Son', 'Pendragon'. But if Uther still had vestiges of Rome about him, his son would be proclaimed to be entirely British.

So, it was as a purely British hero that he strode into the world of folklore and mythology and shaped, more than any Roman ever had, the island's psyche. Even in death this British grandson of a rebel Roman emperor would fire his people's spirits. For centuries he was their once and future king. Today we know him as King Arthur, and it would be his story, along with that of Guinevere and Galahad and Lancelot and Merlin, which would lend to Britain her new, indomitable character.

Epilogue

In AD 577, in the bloody aftermath of the British defeat at Dyrham, the towns of Cirencester, Bath and Gloucester fell to the Saxons. The final death blow had been dealt to Roman Britain.

Two centuries later, inspired perhaps by the dilapidated Roman spa at Bath, someone (we do not know who) wrote one of the most famous of all Anglo-Saxon poems, 'The Ruin'. By then, the men who had once built the now crumbling porticoes and shrines had been forgotten. Such was the chasm which had opened up between Roman and Anglo-Saxon Britain that the poet could believe only that the buildings must have been the work of giants, of great antiquity, fifty generations in the past:

> Well-wrought this wall: Weirds broke it.
> The stronghold burst...

> Snapped rooftrees, towers fallen,
> the work of the Giants, the stonesmiths,
> mouldereth.

> Rime scoureth gatetowers
> rime on mortar.

> Shattered the showershields, roofs ruined,
> age under-ate them.

> And the wielders and wrights?
> Earthgrip holds them – gone, long gone,
> fast in gravegrasp while fifty fathers
> and sons have passed.[1]

Timeline of Roman Britain

Bold type = emperor (e.g. **Claudius**)

Bold italic type = governor (e.g. ***Aulus Plautius***)

BC

55	Caesar's first expedition to Britain
54	Caesar's second expedition to Britain
c. 51	Commius flees to Britain
34	Octavian (later Augustus) considers invasion of Britain
27	**Augustus** becomes emperor of Rome
27/26	**Augustus** considers invasion of Britain
by *c.* 25	Commius dies
16–15	Augustus in Gaul; possible treaty with Tincomarus

AD

c. 40	Adminius flees to **Caligula**; Caligula's abortive invasion of Britain
41–54	**Claudius** emperor
c. 43	Verica flees to Claudius
43	Claudian invasion of Britain under Aulus Plautius and Cnaius Sentius
43–7	***Aulus Plautius*** governor
47–52	***Ostorius Scapula*** governor
47/8	Icenian 'dis-arming' revolt
48/9	Camulodunum (Colchester) made a *colonia*; Cartimandua supported by Rome in Brigantia
51	Caratacus handed over to Rome by Cartimandua
51/2	Silures aggression; death of O. Scapula
52–57	***Aulus Didius Gallus*** governor
54–68	**Nero** emperor
57–58	***Quintus Veranius Nepos*** governor
58–61	***Gaius Suetonius Paullinus*** governor
60	Druids defeated on Anglesey
60–1	Boudican revolt
61–*c.* 69	Julius Classicianus procurator
61–63	***Petronius Turpilianus*** governor
63–69	***Marcus Trebellius Maximus*** governor
68–69	Civil war: **Galba**, **Otho**, and **Vitellius** emperors; mutiny of Roscius Caelius (Twentieth Legion)
69–79	**Vespasian** emperor
69–71	***Vettius Bolanus*** governor; Cartimandua rescued; Romans reach Scotland?

71–74	*Quintus Petillius Cerealis* governor; campaigns in Brigantia
74–77	*Sextus Julius Frontinus* governor; Silures finally conquered
77–83/4	*Gaius Julius Agricola* governor
77	Ordovices defeated; Anglesey occupied
78	Brigantia occupied
79–81	**Titus** emperor
79–83	Scottish campaigns, culminating in Battle of Mons Graupius (83)
81–96	**Domitian** emperor
c. 84–90	Strathmore line of forts and Inchuthil legionary fortress built; then abandoned after withdrawal of Second Legion Adiutrix
c. 90–130	Period when Vindolanda Tablets written
98–117	**Trajan** emperor
c. 100	Caerleon, Chester and York legionary fortresses rebuilt in stone
by *c.* 105	Northern frontier based on the Stanegate Road between Solway and Tyne
c. 114	Ninth Legion withdrawn from Britain
117–38	**Hadrian** emperor
c. 117–19	War in northern Britain
c. 119–21	Britannia first appears on Roman coins (Hadrian)
122	**Hadrian,** *Julius Nepos* and Sixth Legion arrive in Britain; Hadrian's Wall begun
122–?25	*Aulus Platorius Nepos* governor
c. 131–32/3	*Sextus Julius Severus* governor
132–35	Second Jewish revolt
138–61	**Antoninus Pius** emperor
c. 139–?44	*Quintus Lollius Urbicus* governor; advance into Scotland and construction of the Antonine Wall
c. 153–55	Large output of 'Coins of British Association' from mint at Rome
c. 157–60	*Gnaeus Julius Verus* governor
c. 158–63	Withdrawal from the Antonine Wall, probably gradual
161–80	**Marcus Aurelius** emperor
c. 161–62	*Marcus Statius Priscus* governor
c. 163–66	*Sextus Calpurnius Agricola* governor
180–92	**Commodus** emperor
c. 180	Part of Hadrian's Wall overrun and Roman army defeated
c. 180	*Ulpius Marcellus* governor: restores order in Britain
185–?87	*Publius Helvius Pertinax* governor
191/2–3	*Decimus Clodius Albinus* governor
193–211	**Septimius Severus** emperor
193–96	**Clodius Albinus** junior emperor
196	Septimius Severus defeats and kills Clodius Albinus near Lyons
197–201/2	*Virius Lupus* governor

197	Maeatae tribe in Scotland bought off by Rome
206/7–?	**Lucius Alfensus Senecio** governor; calls for aid from Severus against the Maeatae and Caledonians
208–11	Imperial expedition to Britain under **Septimius Severus**, **Caracalla** and **Geta**
211–17	**Caracalla** emperor; murders joint-emperor **Geta** in 212
c. 211	Province split into Britannia Superior (capital at London) and Britannia Inferior (capital at York)
212	*Constitutio Antoniniana* – all free-born men in the Roman empire made citizens
260s–70s	Series of major invasions across the Roman empire
260–74	Britain part of the breakaway Gallic empire
270–75	**Aurelian** emperor; brings Gallic empire back into the fold
276–82	**Probus** emperor; encourages viticulture in Britain
c. 270s	British villas start to expand, a process that continues into the fourth century
282–84	**Carinus** emperor; takes title 'Britannicus'
270s–80s	Several 'Saxon Shore Forts' constructed
284–305	**Diocletian** emperor
286–93	**Carausius** emperor in Britain and parts of northern Gaul; Portchester Shore Fort built in this reign?; coins struck at London and 'C' mint
c. 290	Carausius repels continental emperor **Maximian** (286–310)
293	**Allectus** assassinates **Carausius** and becomes emperor in Britain; Boulogne lost to continental emperor **Constantius I Chlorus** (293–306); Pevensey Saxon Shore Fort built
296	Allectus defeated by invasion force of **Constantius Chlorus**
301	British woollen goods and beer mentioned in **Diocletian**'s Price Edict
306	**Constantius I** campaigns against the Picts and then dies in York; **Constantine I** declared emperor at York
306–37	**Constantine I** emperor; period of great prosperity in Britain
312	Constantine has Christian vision before his victory over **Maxentius** at the Battle of the Milvian Bridge outside Rome
by 313	Britannia becomes a *diocese*, now split into four smaller provinces
313	Edict of Toleration at Milan ends persecution of the Christians
314	British Bishops of London, York and Lincoln attend the Council of Arles
315	Constantine titled 'Britannicus Maximus'; outpost forts beyond Hadrian's Wall abandoned around this time
324	Mint at London closes
330	Dedication of the new city of Constantinople
337–50	**Constans** emperor in the west
337–61	**Constantius II** emperor in the east
343	Constans visits Britain in the winter
350–53	**Magnentius** emperor in the west (with **Decentius**, 351–53)
353–54	Paul the Chain's pogrom in Britain

355–63	**Julian** emperor first in the west, and then of entire empire (361–63)
357–58	Julian drives the barbarians back across the Rhine; he increases the size of the fleet supplying the Roman troops in Germany with British grain
360	Scotti, Attacotti, Picti and Saxons raid Britain; Lupicinus sent to Britain
364–78	**Valentinian I** (364–75) and **Valens** (364–78) emperors
367–83	**Gratian** emperor
367	'Great Barbarian Conspiracy' and revolt of Valentinus
368–70	Count Theodosius restores order in Britain
379–95	**Theodosius I** emperor
383–88	**Magnus Maximus** emperor; takes much of the army to the continent
395–423	**Honorius** emperor in the west
c. 401	British troops withdrawn by Stilicho
407–11	**Constantine III** emperor; takes remaining field army from Britain to the continent in 407
409	Britons revolt against Rome; effective end of Roman rule in Britain?
410	Sack of Rome by Alaric the Goth; traditional date for end of Roman Britain, erroneously based upon a letter of Honorius
429	St Germanus' visit to Britain and the Alleluia Victory near Verulamium (St Albans)
?420s–40s	Vortigern holds power
c. 440s	Major Saxon invasions begin
c. 446 –	British appeals to Aetius fall on deaf ears
c. 490–520	Battle of Mons Badonicus
577	Battle of Dyrham

Glossary of Roman Administrative Terms and Titles

Augustus The title bestowed on Octavian in 27 BC. It became a common title for an emperor, often a senior emperor (see 'Caesar').

Caesar Octavian took the name of his adoptive father, Julius Caesar, before he was titled Augustus in 27 BC. The term 'Caesar' became a common title for an emperor, often a junior emperor (see 'Augustus'). Clodius Albinus, governor of Britain in AD 193, was given the rank 'Caesar' by Septimius Severus.

comes **(count)** A high-ranking military commander (*comes rei militaris*) in the late Roman period. The *comes* normally commanded the elite field army (*comitatenses*). Count Theodosius, who quelled 'The Great Barbarian Conspiracy' of AD 367, is the best-known holder of the rank to serve in Britain. In Britain, there was also a Count of the Saxon Shore (*comes litoris Saxonici*).

colonia A high-status town occupied by Roman citizens, often originally veterans, and administered under Roman law. For details about the *colonia* at Camulodunum, see pp. 65–66.

civitas **(pl. *civitates*)** An administrative unit or canton within a Roman province. It would ultimately be under the jurisdiction of Rome, but it was administered by native councillors (*decuriones*) from a town (*civitas* capital) which had a form of government based upon that of Roman towns, such as the *colonia* at Camulodunum.

consul In the Roman Republic two consuls were elected annually by the people from nominees put forward from the Senate. Although the office lost most of its power after Augustus' time, the consulship was still a prized office in the imperial period. Most governors of Britain also held the consulship during their career.

dictator Traditionally, in the Roman Republican period, a *dictator* could be appointed for six months, normally to hold military power in a time of emergency. However, later in the Republic, the office began to be abused. Sulla held the dictatorship for two years (81–79 BC) and Caesar received the title in 48 and 46 BC, before he was made *Dictator Perpetuus* (Dictator Forever) in 44 BC.

diocese In the early fourth century Britain became a *diocese* under the control of a *vicarius*. The *diocese* was split into four provinces.

dux **(duke)** A military commander in the late Roman period. He normally had control of the low status frontier troops (*limitanei*). The *Dux Britanniarum* probably controlled the Hadrianic frontier, other forces in the north and possibly in Wales.

imperator Successful generals in the Roman Republican period were hailed as *imperator*. Claudius was hailed *imperator* several times at Colchester in AD 43. Augustus was to use the title and from the reign of Otho (AD 69) *imperator* became the formulaic first-name (*praenomen*) of the emperors. When a new emperor was declared, the army would proclaim him *imperator*, the title acknowledging the emperor's hold on power.

legion A legion consisted of around 5,500 men, mostly infantry. There were around thirty legions. In Britain, there were four for much of the first century, three thereafter: Second Legion Augusta, Sixth Legion Victrix and Twentieth Legion Valeria Victrix. Each legion had a title, sometimes received after a victory – the Twentieth received the title Victrix after the Boudican rebellion.

ovatio An *ovatio* was a minor triumph held by a general who could not claim a complete victory or commanded a force under an emperor. The general would process on foot or horseback, not in a chariot. The last recorded *ovatio* was for Aulus Plautius in AD 47.

praetor Praetors were magistrates with responsibility for the administration of justice in Rome and across the empire.

prefect (*praefectus*) A title used for a variety of senior posts in the Roman empire. Prefects were drawn from the equestrian class (one lower than the senatorial class). They commanded the Praetorian Guard, various other military units and naval fleets. The Prefect of the City (Rome) was the senior official in the city, a position held by a senator.

procurator An official of equestrian class (one lower than the senatorial class) responsible for provincial expenditure and taxes. He oversaw other economic activities, such as the mining of metals and the supervision of imperial estates. Although the governor was the senior official in the province, he did not have control over the procurator, who was directly answerable to the emperor. We witness a conflict between procurator and governor when Julius Classicianus reported Suetonius Paullinus to Nero.

proconsul Proconsuls were governors of senatorial provinces. The governors of Asia and Africa had to be ex-consuls. After their year's term, consuls could be appointed as proconsuls to govern the senatorial provinces of Asia and Africa. The governors Vettius Bolanus and Julius Frontinus both became proconsuls of Asia.

quaestor Quaestors were junior magistrates, often with financial responsibilities. Some quaestors were appointed by senior officials to act as assistants in a variety of activities.

tribune Military tribunes were junior commissioned officers, of senatorial rank, in the legions. They performed this service early in their career. Agricola served as tribune in Britain at the time of the Boudican revolt (AD 60/1). The commander of a double-size auxiliary unit was also a tribune.

vexillation A vexillation was a detachment of a legion. In the first century especially, legions were often split into smaller forces so as to cover the ground more effectively.

Notes

Introduction
Re-Imagining Roman Britain (pp. 6–11)

[1] For example at Vindolanda (Bowman 1994, Birley 2009), Wroxeter (White and Barker 1998), Silchester (Fulford 1989, 2003 and 2008; Fulford and Timby 2000), Fishbourne (Cunliffe 1998; Manley and Rudkin 2003), Piercebridge (Cool and Mason 2008), Lincoln (Jones 2002), Verulamium (Niblett 2001), Housesteads (Crow 1995) and Birdoswald (Wilmott 2001).

[2] For art: Henig 1995; for women: Allason-Jones 1989.

[3] Challenging the traditional view: Reece 1988, Millet (1990), Laycock (2008), Laycock and Russell (2010). General synthesis: Mattingly 2006 and de la Bédoyère 2006.

[4] For more information about the Portable Antiquities Scheme, visit its website: www.finds.org.uk

[5] Moorhead, Booth and Bland 2010.

[6] Taylor 2007.

[7] Although one should not substitute modern study with antiquarianism, it is interesting that some of the earlier, seminal, books on Roman Britain did appreciate the role of personalities in shaping the past. Many early books are rendered obsolete because of recent discoveries and research, but they still contain interpretations that should not be overlooked. See Horsley 1733; Haverfield and MacDonald 1924; Collingwood and Myres 1937; Collingwood and Richmond 1969.

1 To Boldly Go...
(pp. 12–38)

[1] The main source for Caesar's invasion is his own De Bello Gallico. Useful secondary sources are Berresford Ellis 1978, Ridd 1993, Southern 2001.

[2] Caesar, De Bello Gallico 4.20.

[3] Caesar, De Bello Gallico 2.4.

[4] Caesar, De Bello Gallico 4.21; that Volusenus missed the natural harbour at Richborough, where Claudius' invasion was to land 100 years later, was a major omission.

[5] Caesar, De Bello Gallico 4.21.

[6] Caesar, De Bello Gallico 5.12–14.

[7] The loss of legionary standards to the Parthians after the defeat of Crassus at Carrhae, 53 BC, caused great pain at Rome; their return in the reign of Augustus, celebration.

[8] This alliance between Pompey, Crassus and Caesar is sometimes called the First Triumvirate, although this is misleading because it was not an official alliance.

[9] It has been argued that Gallo-Belgic gold staters, Classes C & E, might represent payment to British mercenaries for fighting in Gaul. These coins are commonly found in southeast Britain, but it is just as likely that they represent trading, dynastic and diplomatic contacts between Britain and Gaul. Van Arsdell 1989, 6 and 67ff; ABC nos 13 and 16.

[10] Cunliffe 1984; Cunliffe 2001, 77ff; Cunliffe argues that the ancient trading emporium of Ictis should be identified as Mount Batten; coins from northern Gaul have been found across southern Britain (for an extensive sample, see www.finds.org.uk, which records around 40,000 Iron Age coins found in Britain).

[11] Gold and silver: Cicero, Letters to Friends 7, 7, 1 (to Trebatius, June 54); Tacitus, Agricola 12; pearls: Suetonius, Deified Julius 47.

[12] Doggedly putting his trust in Commius' own version of events, Caesar tells us that his British agent had been arrested and bound. De Bello Gallico 5.1.

[13] Caesar, De Bello Gallico 4.23.

[14] Past St Margaret's at Cliffe and on to Oldstairs Bay, where the cliffs run out down to a shingle beach at Walmer.

[15] Caesar, De Bello Gallico 4.24.

[16] Suetonius, Deified Julius 62.

[17] Caesar, De Bello Gallico 4.26.

[18] Caesar, De Bello Gallico 3.19.

[19] Caesar, De Bello Gallico 4.28.

[20] Caesar, De Bello Gallico 4.32.

[21] Caesar, De Bello Gallico 4.33.

[22] Caesar, De Bello Gallico 4.36.

[23] Caesar, De Bello Gallico 4.38.

[24] Caesar, De Bello Gallico 5.2.

[25] Caesar, De Bello Gallico 5.9.

[26] Caesar, De Bello Gallico 5.15.

[27] Caesar, De Bello Gallico 5.16.

[28] Caesar, De Bello Gallico 5.17.

[29] Caesar, De Bello Gallico 5.18.

[30] Wheeler and Wheeler 1936, 19–22.

[31] Niblett 1985, 13–15, Niblett 2001, 48–49; Wacher 1979, 9.

[32] Caesar, De Bello Gallico 5.20.

[33] Caesar, De Bello Gallico 5.21.

[34] It has been argued that to pay this tribute a large issue of 'Whaddon Chase' gold staters (British LA type) was struck by Cassivellaunus (Sills 1996, 334–35).

[35] Cicero, Letters to Friends 7,7,1 – to Trebatius, June 54.

[36] Cicero, Letters to Atticus 4,17,6 – July 54 BC.

[37] Cicero, Letters to Atticus 4,18,5 – Oct./Nov. 54 BC.

[38] Frontinus, Stratagems, 2.13.11.

[39] Virgil, Eclogue I, 66.

[40] Tacitus, Agricola 13.

[41] BMC IA 724–7 and 730; ABC 1022 and 1025. Note that on his coins, Commius uses the Greek form of his name.

[42] Tibullus III, 7, 147f.

[43] Dio 49.38.2

[44] Ibid. 53.22.5

[45] Ibid. 53.25.2

[46] Augustus, Res Gestae 32

[47] Propertius II, 27, 5f.

48 Horace, *Odes* III, 5, 1–4.

49 Horace, *Odes* I, 35, 29f.

50 We do not know with any real certainty when Commius died.

51 Augustus, *Res Gestae* 32.

52 *BMC IA* 761–5 and 766ff; *ABC* 1049–67.

53 For a recent coverage of the late Iron Age period in Britain, see Creighton 2006.

2 ELEPHANTS AND CASTLES (PP. 39–63)

1 Polyaenus, *Stratagems* VIII, 23.5.

2 It has been suggested that there were continental merchants at sites such as Skeleton Green and Braughing (Partridge 1979 and 1981; Cunliffe 1984).

3 Strabo, *Geography* 4.5.2. Strabo is incorrect about Britain producing silver. The technology for the cupellation of lead to extract silver was not available in Britain until after the Roman invasion of AD 43.

4 Outside Camulodunum, in a burial mound at Lexden, a rich royal burial was found, possibly for the king Addedomaros, in which was found much imported Roman metalware and a silver medallion of Augustus himself (Crummy 1997, 22–25).

5 Augustus tells us in his *Res Gestae*: 'the following kings sought refuge with me as suppliants:... Dumnovellaunus and Tincom[arus], Kings of the Britons...' (*Res Gestae* 32).

6 Such 'trinkets' are represented by silver goblets, bronze vessels and glassware found in graves such as the royal burial at Lexden and the high status burial at Welwyn Garden City (Foster 1986 and Stead 1967). See Plate 2.

7 Strabo, *Geography* 4.5.3.

8 Suetonius, *Gaius Caligula* 44.2. It is possible that Adminius' brothers, Togodumnus and Caratacus, had a role in his banishment.

9 Probably at Boulogne (Gesoriacum/Bononia).

10 Suetonius, *Gaius Caligula*, 22.

11 See *BMC IA* 1159ff. and 1772ff.

12 Suetonius, *Gaius Caligula*, 9.

13 Suetonius, *Gaius Caligula* 46; Dio 59.25.1–3.

14 The abortion of the mission was perhaps a lucky escape – the potential defeat of such an ill-disciplined force, coinciding as it would have done with the subsequent assassination of Gaius (in AD 41), might have set back the Romans' ambitions for Britain to such an extent that they might never have been realized.

15 On his coins he, too, declared himself an heir of Caesar's one-time ally, Commius (*ABC* no. 1181ff).

16 These probably included Verica and Adminius. Suetonius, *Deified Claudius* 17.1.

17 Claudius was ruthless in his suppression of all opponents. A number of high-ranking Romans died during his reign. Levick 1990, 53ff.

18 See Tacitus, *Agricola* 12.

19 For more on the family background and life of Aulus Plautius, see Birley 2005, 17ff.

20 Claudius subsequently divorced Plautius' sister when he discovered her adulterous conduct. Plautius' wife Pomponia Graecina was a close friend of Tiberius' granddaughter Julia, who died in AD 41 as a result of the intrigues of Messalina (Claudius' second wife). Graecina went into mourning for the rest of her life. Tacitus, *Annals* 13.32.2–3.

21 The revolt was hatched by Furius Camillus Scribonianus, but it faltered after five days for religious reasons.

22 Second Legion Augusta; Ninth Hispania; Fourteenth Gemina; and Twentieth Valeria.

23 Frere and Fulford 2001, 47. Alternative ports that might

have been used include Liane, Boulogne and ports at the mouth of the Seine, Somme and Canche (Hind 1989, 13).

24 *Praepositus ab epistulis.*

25 The hoard contained thirty-seven gold *aurei*, the latest being struck in AD 41–42, at the start of Claudius' reign (Robertson 2000, p. 6, no. 22). Whatever Narcissus' exact methods, he was to receive an award after the conquest of Britain – Narcissus depicted himself as '*dominus* of the *dominus* himself' (*Epitome of the Caesars* 4).

26 Dio 60, 19. 4ff.

27 Forts have been recently identified at Canterbury and Faversham (Frere and Fulford 2001, 48). Also, the discovery of the Bredgar hoard (see above) on this route does suggest that it was a line of advance for the Roman army.

28 Juvenal *Satire* IV, 141 and Lucian VI, 67. Accounts of the invasion that assume Richborough was the main landing site: Peddie 1987, Webster 1993a and Frere and Fulford 2001. Accounts that suggest Chichester as a possible landing site: Hind 1989, Bird 2000 and Black 2000.

29 Dio 60.20.2 writes that the Bodounni were won over; scholars generally agree that he was referring to the Dobunni tribe of Gloucestershire and neighbouring counties.

30 The Medway: Webster 1993b, 97–100; Peddie 1987, 66ff and Frere and Fulford 2001 47ff, all of whom provide an analysis of the action. With the advent of the alternative argument for the landings in the Chichester region, other rivers have been suggested, most notably the Arun in West Sussex (Hind 1989, 17), although this seems unlikely.

31 Dio 60, 20. 2ff.

32 It is argued that Sabinus and Vespasian were each commanding legions at the battle and that after a day of indecisive struggle it was the sending in of a third legion under

Hosidius Geta that finally won the day. This does suggest that it was a major battle and that the Britons had mustered a very large force (Frere and Fulford 2001, 47).

33 Unsuccessful attempts to follow: Dio 60, 20. 5f; possibly the Higham to East Tilbury ford: Frere and Fulford 2001, 48; bridge may have been at Staines: Hind 1989, 17–18.

34 Dio 60, 21.1f; there is evidence for an early Roman marching camp at Fenchurch Street and Duke's Place (Frere and Fulford 2001, 49).

35 Suetonius, *Deified Claudius*, 17.

36 Josephus, *Jewish War* III.4 (written during Vespasian's reign, which explains why he gives prominence to Vespasian instead of Aulus Plautius).

37 Levick 1990, 58.

38 For an account of the war against Caratacus, see Webster 1993b.

39 Wacher 1995, 207ff.

40 Suetonius, *Deified Claudius*, 21.

41 This might have been Prasutagus, the king of the Iceni whose death precipitated the Boudican revolt in AD 60 (see below).

42 Bullied by tutor: Suetonius, *Deified Claudius*, 2; disparaged by family, *ibid*. 3; butt of jokes, *ibid*. 8.

43 Dio 60, 21.4f.

44 Dio 60, 21.

45 Dio 60, 22.

46 Suetonius, *Deified Claudius*, 17.

47 Suetonius, *Deified Claudius*, 28.

48 Dio 60.23.1.

49 Pliny, *Nat. Hist.* III, 119.

50 Seneca, *Apocolocyntosis* 12.3.

51 Eutropius, *Breviarium* 7.13.2.

52 Black 2000, 1.

53 *Ibid*. and Frere and Fulford 2001, 50–51.

54 Potter and Johns 1992, 41.

55 A gold *aureus* and a silver *denarius* (*RIC* I, nos 33–34) and a silver *didrachm* (*RIC* I, 122).

56 *Aurum coronarium*: Pliny, *Nat. Hist.* xxxiii, 54. A papyrus he sent to athletes from Antioch, thanking them for a golden crown, survives in the British Library. P. Lond 3.215; *LACTOR* 4, 21.

57 *CIL* 6, no. 920.

58 Eutropius, *Breviarium* vii, xiii, 2–3.

59 Tacitus, *Annals*, 12, 36f.

60 Dio 61, 33, 3.

61 Seneca satirized Claudius' wish to see Gauls, Greeks and Britons wearing togas. Seneca, *Apocolocyntosis* 3.3; Levick 1990, 91.

3 REVOLT
(PP. 64–87)

1 The recently discovered fortress at Alchester (Oxfordshire) has tree-ring dates for October 44 to March 45 (Sauer 2002).

2 Suetonius, *Deified Vespasian* 4.1; Levick 1999, 14ff; it is reckoned that the Second Legion Augusta advanced all the way down to Devon and Cornwall, founding the legionary fortress at Exeter (Peddie, 1987, 130ff).

3 The Fosse Way is seen by many scholars today as a dividing line in Roman Britain between different zones of military, economic and social activity over the next 350 years; see Walton, forthcoming.

4 Tacitus, *Agricola* 14.

5 Maiden Castle: Wheeler 1943 (however, Wheeler's interpretation is now questioned); Sharples 1991, 124–25. Hod Hill: Hogg 1975, 228; Johnson 1983, 241ff.

6 In the Vatican Museum, a funerary monument for Gnaeus Munatius Aurelius Bassus, who rose to be a procurator of the emperor, tells us that as a younger man he had been the 'census officer for the *Colonia Victricensis* [City of Victory] which is in Britain at *Camulodunum*' (*CIL* xiv. 3955; Crummy 1997, 53).

7 Little is known about Ostorius Scapula; he may have come from the mountainous regions of central Italy (Birley 2005, 28).

8 Tacitus, *Annals* 14.23.

9 Tacitus, *Agricola* 14.

10 Tacitus, *Annals* 12.31 and 39.

11 Tacitus, *Annals*, 12.40.

12 Tacitus, *Agricola* 14.1; for more on Gallus, see Birley 2005, 32–35.

13 One of the aqueducts is the Aqua Claudia, which can still be seen running to the Palatine Hill.

14 Birley 2005, 35, citing Quintilian 6.3.38.

15 Tacitus, *Annals*, 12.40.

16 Tacitus, *Agricola* 14.

17 Birley 2005, 38–39.

18 Onasander, *Strategicus*.

19 Tacitus, *Annals* 14.29.

20 The Second Legion also probably had a fort at Lake Farm, Dorset (Peddie 1987, 146); Exeter bath-house: Wacher 1995, 337. Restormel and Calstock have only been recently discovered (Thorpe 2007; Claughton and Smart 2008).

21 Recent finds of Roman Republican and early imperial *denarii* in the West Midlands do attest to a heavy military presence at this time. A very high number of early *denarii* have been recorded with the Portable Antiquities Scheme from this region (Walton, forthcoming).

22 A lead ingot, dated to AD 49, from the Mendips, attests to early exploitation of Britain's mineral reserves. *RIB* 2404.

23 The foundations of the temple of Claudius still survive as large vaults under the present Colchester Castle (Crummy 1997, 59–60; Fishwick 1995). The arch is now known as the Balkerne Gate (Crummy 1997, 60–61).

24 There is no way of telling who these people were, but they are testament to the Romans resorting to brutal measures when they deemed it necessary. However, one surmises that these are more likely to be Britons than Romans and, in the years prior to AD 60, such a display was bound to heighten

tensions in a newly conquered territory (Crummy 1997, 54).

25 Tacitus, *Annals* 14.31.

26 Tacitus, *Annals* 14.31.

27 Tacitus, *Annals* 12.31–32.

28 It has been suggested by some scholars, from coin evidence, that the king of the Iceni in 43 was Antedius, and that he was replaced by Prasutagus after the 'dis-arming revolt' of 47/8, although this now seems unlikely (Wacher 1995, 243). Gallow's Hill: there was also a Roman belt-plate found, suggesting a Roman military presence. Was this lost during looting of the site in AD 60 or during reprisals after the rebellion? The site was systematically destroyed after the rebellion (Robinson and Gregory 1987, 44–47; Gregory 1991). Another potential Iceni centre has been identified at Saham Toney in Norfolk, which has Iron Age and Roman artefacts (Bates 2000).

29 Suetonius, *Nero*, 32; Justinian's *Digest* (1.19.1) states that it was the duty of the procurator to take possession of an inheritance in Caesar's name.

30 Dio 62.2.1.

31 A good summary of client rulers is provided in Braund 1984.

32 Tacitus, *Annals*, 14.31.

33 Tacitus, *Annals*, 14.31.

34 Some of the Catuvellauni might have had a hand in the destruction of London and Verulamium. A massacre at Cadbury Hillfort and a destruction layer at Winchester might suggest a rebellion by the Durotriges (Hogg 1975, 275; Salway 1981, 121; Jones and Mattingly 1990, 71; Frere 1987, 72 and 80 n.38). Did the Durotriges pin down the Second Legion at Exeter? See Tacitus, *Annals*, 14.37, and below.

35 Rome persecuted Druidism, along with Judaism and Christianity. Modern interpretations of the Druids range from priests to philosophers (Chadwick 1966; Piggott 1985; Webster 1986, 24–27;

Henig 1984, 19–20). Caesar's description, based on Posidonius, suggests that Druidism originated in Britain but later had its centre in the Carnutes tribe in Gaul. Identifying Druids in the archaeological record is difficult, but some believe that one Iron Age spoon type might have been associated with Druidic practices (Parfitt 2011; Cunliffe 1991, 509). A male burial at Mill Hill, Kent might have been a Druid (Stead 1995; Parfitt 1995 and 2011) and the bog body known as Lindow Man may have been a Druidic sacrifice, associated with the Roman invasion (Brothwell 1986; Ross and Robins 1991; Turner and Scaife 1995). It is clear that the Druids were involved in the British resistance against Rome.

36 Dio 60.9.1; For the career of Suetonius Paullinus, see Birley 2005, 43–50.

37 Pliny, *Nat. Hist.*, V, 14–15.

38 Tacitus, *Annals*, 14.29.

39 Tacitus, *Agricola*, 14.

40 Tacitus, *Annals*, 14.29–30.

41 Tacitus, *Agricola*, 14; Tacitus, *Annals*, 14.30.

42 It has become fashionable for some modern revisionist scholars to question Boudica's involvement in the revolt (and even her existence): Braund 1996, 118ff; J.D. Hill pers. comm.

43 Dio 62, 2. It would have been quite expected for a classical writer to give a northern ruler a torc. In this case, almost certainly unbeknown to Dio, many finds of torcs have been made in Iceni territory, notably those found at Snettisham (Joy forthcoming).

44 Dio 62.2.2–62.3.1.

45 Tacitus, *Annals* 14.32. Perhaps there was a fifth column of Britons in Colchester who threw down the statue and started psychological warfare on the veterans. We know that there were those who 'secretly knew of the rebellion'. Dio (62.9.2) tells us Colchester was betrayed.

46 Tacitus, *Annals* 14.32.

47 It seems likely that part of the Ninth Legion was based at Longthorpe, but a fort may have been founded at Lincoln (Jones 2002, 33–34; Birley 2005, 65).

48 Tacitus, *Annals* 14.32.

49 It appears that the Boudican rebels literally defaced a tomb-sculpture of Longinus from the First Cavalry Regiment of Thracians. The tombstone was then broken and thrown over. Only recently has the head of Longinus been discovered and reunited with the sculpture (*RIB* 201).

50 The Hawkedon helmet is probably first-century and might have been made in the famous gladiatorial region of Campania in Italy. The British Museum has recently acquired the visor of this piece, which has been reunited with the helmet on display.

51 Destruction at Colchester: Crummy 1997, 79–84; head of Claudius or Nero: Hobbs and Jackson 2010, 34–35; statue of Nero: *ibid.* 37; Hawkedon helmet: Webster 1993c, 126; Hockwold-cum-Wilton silver cups: Potter and Johns 1992, 10 and 128–29 and Webster 1993c, 125–26. All of these objects are on display in the British Museum. For destruction at London, see Milne 1995, 42; Perring 1991, 22; for Verulamium, see Niblett 2001, 67.

52 Tacitus, *Annals* 14.33. The concentration of the destruction suggests that the centre of the city was the Cornhill (Milne 1995, 42; Perring 1991, 22).

53 It is not obvious where these forts were, or if Tacitus is merely fabricating this detail for dramatic effect.

54 Casualty figures: 70,000 = Tacitus, *Annals* 14.33; 80,000 = Dio 62.1; slaughter and the gibbet: Tacitus, *Annals*, 14.33.

55 The battle between Paullinus and Boudica probably took place between Mancetter (north Warwickshire) and Verulamium. At Mancetter there is an early

Roman fort and the topography matches Tacitus' description; excavations in the area have uncovered ditches with Neronian pottery and a hoard of sixteen copper asses, common imitations of official coins of Claudius, in use at the time. However, it is hard to believe that Boudica's army could have moved so far north without interception. Also, the small settlement at Towcester (Lactodurum, Northamptonshire) remained unscathed, suggesting that the Britons did not reach this far north. Indeed, local legend speaks of a battle site at Cuttle Mill, south of Towcester, where Watling Street crosses a valley; and the topography does match the scene described by Tacitus. Webster, 1993c; Evans 2001, 25–33.

[56] Tacitus, *Annals* 14.34. It is possible that Paullinus' force was slightly larger, even nearer 13,000 (Evans 2001). Postumus' suicide: Tacitus, *Annals* 14.37.

[57] Tacitus, *Annals*, 14.34.

[58] Estimate of numbers: Dio 67.8.2; supplies running low: Dio 62.8.1.

[59] Tacitus, *Annals*, 14.34; Evans 2001, 30.

[60] Dio 62.8.2–3.

[61] Tacitus, *Annals*, 14.34.

[62] Tacitus, *Annals* 14.35.

[63] Agricola was a tribune in the army in Britain at the time, although we do not know in which legion he served. It is just possible that he was a source for his son-in-law Tacitus about the revolt; if he was present at the battle, he may have reported the gist of what Paullinus said. It is also possible that Agricola heard a report from another soldier serving at the battle.

[64] Tacitus, *Annals* 14.36.

[65] Dio 62.12.1–6.

[66] Tacitus, *Annals* 14.37.

[67] *Ibid.*

[68] Illness: Dio 62.12.6; poison: Tacitus, *Annals* 14.37; Cleopatra:

see Stuttard and Moorhead, forthcoming 2012.

[69] Dio 62.12.6.

[70] For a discussion of the Lunt Gyrus, see Webster 1993c, 107–11. When the Lunt was decreased in size, the new ramparts curved especially to protect the Gyrus, which remained in use, suggesting that the fort retained a small force of soldiers explicitly for the purpose of breaking and training horses for the Roman army.

[71] The legionaries replaced the men lost in the *vexillatio* (detachment) of the Ninth Legion under Petilius Cerealis. It is suggested that the commander of the *vexillatio* was none other than Titus, the son of Vespasian and future emperor (AD 79–81). We know that he served in Britain and that many statues were erected for him in the province (Webster 1993c, 101; Suetonius, *Deified Titus* 4). Military reinforcements: Tacitus, *Annals* 14.38; fort-building: Webster 1993c, 106; Frere and St Joseph 1983, 92–95; Jones and Mattingly 1990, 70–71.

[72] Tacitus, *Annals* 14.38.

[73] Hogg 1975, 275; Salway 1981, 121; Jones and Mattingly 1990, 71.

[74] Tacitus, *Annals* 14.38.

[75] Tacitus, *Annals* 14.38.

[76] For the text of the Classicianus inscription, see Grasby and Tomlin 2002; *RIB* 12; Ireland 1995, p. 71, 80 and *LACTOR* 4, 24. For a broader discussion, see Webster 1993c, 127–28.

[77] Tacitus claims that to the Britons he was a laughing-stock: 'For them the flame of liberty still burned, and as yet they knew nothing of the power of the freedman; they were amazed that a commander and an army which had brought so great a war to a successful conclusion should obey a slave.' (Tacitus, *Annals* 14.39). In fact, this tells us more about Tacitus' hatred of freedmen. The Britons probably had no idea of Polyclitus' background.

[78] Suetonius, *Nero* 18. It is possible that Nero considered pulling out of Britain closer to the start of his reign in the governorships of Aulus Didius Gallus or Quintus Veranius. It is equally possible that the Boudican revolt tested Nero's patience to its limit. We shall never know, but it is clear that Britain was regarded as a potential liability at this time and that a continued Roman presence could not be taken for granted. Reputation: Tacitus, *Histories* 2.32; Birley 2005, 50.

[79] For a discussion of Caistor, see Wacher 1995, 243–55. Given that an enormous number of men would have been killed in the revolt, it is possible that in the following years a Roman official, a *praefectus civitatis*, would have performed this role of government. Another tribal town that did not grow was Caerwent, the capital of the unruly Silures. Excavations at Stonea Grange in the Cambridgeshire Fens have shown that a probable official administrative building was erected in the second century, possibly in the reign of Hadrian (Jackson and Potter 1996).

[80] Wacher 1995, 207–14. Caesaromagus only received a large *mansio* (official inn) in Hadrian's reign.

[81] Suetonius, *Nero* 18.

[82] Fulford 2008, 9–10.

4 SHOCK AND AWE VERSUS HEARTS AND MINDS (PP. 88–119)

[1] Tacitus, *Annals* 14.39.

[2] For background on Trebellius Maximus, see Birley 2005, 52–56.

[3] Style of administration: Tacitus, *Agricola* 16; Fourteenth Legion: Tacitus, *Histories* 2.11 and 2.27. It is probable that eight Batavian cohorts went with them.

[4] Tacitus, *Agricola* 16.

[5] Galba (AD 68–69), Otho (AD 69), Vitellius (AD 69), Vespasian (AD 69–79).

[6] Tacitus, *Histories* 1.9.

7 Morale destroyed: Tacitus, *Histories* 1, 59–60; unity in the face of the enemy: Tacitus, *Histories* 1.9.

8 Legionary commander under Corbulo: Tacitus, *Annals* 15.3; Corbulo's second-in-command: Statius, *Silvae* 5.2.48; Tacitus' scathing remarks: Tacitus, *Agricola* 8. He goes on to report 'paralysis in the camp and inaction in the face of the enemy', though there is no evidence of British victories at this time. For more on the career of Vettius Bolanus, see Birley 2005, 57–62 and Shotter 2002.

9 Vitellius withdraws 8,000 men: Tacitus, *Histories* 2.57.1; Fourteenth Legion: Tacitus, *Histories* 2.66. The Fourteenth had fought for Otho at the Battle of Bedriacum (16 April AD 69), where they were defeated by Vitellius' troops.

10 Suetonius, *Deified Vespasian* 4. See Levick 1999.

11 Undistinguished Flavians: Suetonius, *Deified Vespasian* 1 (see Levick 1999); triumph: Suetonius, *Deified Vespasian* 4.

12 Britain volatile: Tacitus, *Histories* 2.97; Vitellius' appointees: Tacitus, *Histories* 3.44.

13 Tacitus, *Histories* 3.45.

14 Statius, *Silvae* 5.2, 142f.

15 See Hartley and Fitts 1988; Wacher 1995, 401ff.

16 Statius (*Silvae* 53–56) again addressed to Bolanus' son, declares: 'your own mighty father, who, carrying out his commission, penetrated to Thule, barrier of the western waters, where always Hyperion grows weary.' Thule has sometimes been identified as the Shetland Islands, but it is more commonly reckoned to be Iceland. Cunliffe 2001, 116–33. Hyperion grows weary because in the summer he does not set.

17 But not to dishonour. He was made first a patrician (?AD 73–74) and then proconsul of Asia, where coins were struck in his name at Smyrna (*BMCG* pp. 272–73, nos 294–301).

18 Defeat: Tacitus, *Histories* 3.78–79; the precise date of Cerealis' consulship is uncertain: Tacitus, *Agricola* 8; Tacitus not impressed: Tacitus, *Histories* 5.20.

19 Tacitus, *Agricola* 17.

20 Pliny, *Nat. Hist.* 4.102.

21 That Cerealis did reach Scotland is a view shared by prominent scholars: Birley 1961; Hanson 1987, Shotter 2000 and 2002. The arguments for the dating of Dalswinton are contained in Hanson 1987, 61 and 63.

22 Wilmott 2008, 49.

23 Even Tacitus has to admit this: *Agricola* 17.

24 For a discussion of Stanwick: Hanson 1987, 59–60 and Hartley and Fitts 1988, 7 *passim*. For Rey Cross camp: Frere and St. Joseph 1983, 23–25. For Carlisle: McCarthy 2002, 69 and Birley 1961, 40.

25 Aelian, *Tactics* Preface 3.

26 Victory in Wales: Tacitus, *Agricola* 17; Caerleon is a few miles south of the earlier fortress at Usk. It was to remain the base for the legion well into the third century, possibly beyond (Knight 2003, 8–9).

27 Legionary fortress at Chester: de la Bédoyère 2001, 52; fighting in Germany: Birley 2005, 70; proconsul in Asia: an inscription from Hierapolis in Phrygia tells us that he was present as proconsul of Asia in 84–85, a fact supported by the issuing of coins from Smyrna with his name (*BMCG* p. 250, no. 133). *On Military Science*: *De re militari*, a work quarried by Vegetius. Frontinus' book does not survive.

28 *De Aqueductibus Urbis Romae*.

29 Several works discuss the *Agricola*, Agricola and his period: Furneaux and Anderson 1922; Mothersole 1927; Ogilvie and Richmond 1967; Hanson 1987; Birley 2005, 71–95. The most recent work by Birley has the most up to date material and is the ultimate guide to this section. There are two popular translations of *Agricola*

in print today: Mattingly and Handford 1970; Birley, A.R. 1999.

30 Senior staff: Tacitus, *Agricola* 5; Twentieth Legion: Tacitus, *Agricola* 8.

31 Tacitus, *Agricola* 8.

32 Tacitus, *Agricola* 7.

33 Mother's murder: Tacitus, *Agricola* 6. Forum Iulii, in Gallia Narbonensis, had been founded by Julius Caesar for veterans of the Eighth Legion and was re-founded by Augustus, with the name Colonia Octavanorum Pacensis (or Pacata) Classica Forum Iuli. Most of these veterans would have been Italian-born and would have aspired to the creation of their own 'Rome' in Gaul. However, some could have been Gauls. Indeed, Agricola's family name (*nomen*) Iulius suggests that a paternal ancestor was enfranchised by Caesar himself. Agricola had three generations of Roman citizenship behind him: his grandfathers were *equites*, both serving as procurators. Father: Tacitus, *Agricola* 4.

34 Tribune of the Plebs: Tacitus, *Agricola* 5; Tacitus in Britain: Birley 2005, 77.

35 Tacitus, *Agricola* 18.

36 Tacitus, *Agricola* 18.

37 Wilson 2002, 346–47; Hanson 1987, 54. Another fort at Pen Llystyn in North Wales is also reckoned to be Agricolan (Hanson 1987, 53).

38 It is possible that the forum at Exeter was started in Agricola's governorship (Wacher 1995, 337), but the forum and basilica at Verulamium, which bore his name on an inscription (*LACTOR* 4, 28; *JRS* 46 (1956), 146–47), and the forum at Cirencester were probably started earlier, probably under Frontinus (Wacher 1995, 304ff; Hanson 1987, 79). The forum at Wroxeter was started after his governorship, c. 90 (Wacher 1995, 363ff). London's first forum is early Flavian (Perring 1991, 23–26) and we know now that the amphitheatre was built under Cerealis in AD 70–71 (Wilmott

2008, 49). We have no specific evidence for temples built under Agricola and most town-houses were modest affairs before the second century.

39 Seneca tells us that Claudius 'wanted to see every Briton in a toga' – Seneca, *Apocolocyntosis* 3.3.

40 Tacitus, *Agricola* 21.

41 Tacitus, *Agricola* 19. Archaeological evidence for Roman officials profiteering comes from the fort at Carvoran on Hadrian's Wall (Liversidge 1968, 177–78).

42 Niblett 1995, 77ff.

43 Chichester inscription: discovered in 1723 (*RIB* 91; Bogaers 1979; Tomlin 1997; Cunliffe 1998, 21–23); signet ring: Tomlin 1997. For Fishbourne see Cunliffe 1998; Manley and Rudkin 2003. Fishbourne had earlier origins. There had been settlement in the region before 43, but just after the Roman army arrived in 43, two timber granaries were constructed at Fishbourne; a legionary helmet was dredged up in the harbour, and many Claudian period coins were found (Cunliffe 1998, 25–32). In the Neronian period a small timber house was built and then replaced by a much larger 'proto-palace' (*ibid.* 33–47). It has been suggested that Togidubnus might have been educated in the imperial court in Rome, as had been the case with a number of provincial children since the time of Augustus (Cunliffe 1998, 22). Famous examples include Cleopatra Selene (daughter of Cleopatra) and Juba II, who subsequently married and ruled in Mauretania, and Herod Agrippa who went on to rule in Judaea.

44 Fulford 2008.

45 Togidubnus' title of *Rex Magnus* ('Great King') probably gave rise to the name of the tribal region in West Sussex, the Regini and to their capital at *Noviomagus Regnensium* (Chichester) (Cunliffe 1998, 22).

46 Tacitus, *Agricola* 14.

47 It is suggested that his death precipitated the arrival of a special legal agent, an *iuridicus*, called Gaius Salvius Liberalis Nonnius Bassus (Birley 2005, 468). If Salvius was sent to sort out the estate of Togidubnus after his death, then the conversion of the client kingdom into apparently three tribal or administrative units (*civitates*) – the Atrebates, Belgae and Regini/Regnenses – went off without any problems that have been recorded, unlike the storm that was unleashed in AD 60.

48 Tacitus, *Agricola* 20. This has led people to assume that many forts in the region are Agricolan. There was already a fort at Carlisle, built in the governorship of Cerealis in AD 72–73 (see above). It was once claimed that Carlisle was an Agricolan foundation, so one has to ask whether other forts attributed to him at Brough-under-Stainmore, Binchester, Ebchester and Red House (near Corbridge) are not also earlier. One would expect forts south of Carlisle, such as Brough, to be earlier than Agricola, and it would not be surprising if Red House, on the course of Dere Street running north from York, was not of a similar date to Carlisle. It is also likely that Agricola entered southern Scotland, where his predecessors had already campaigned. It is probable that about this time, lead water pipes were laid at the legionary fortress of Chester, one bearing an inscription for Agricola (*RIB* 2.3.2434.1). Furthermore, it is possible that Chester was earmarked to play a major role, possibly as a capital of a separate northern province. Excavations have revealed an unusual elliptical building, with twelve bays, within the fortress, which has been interpreted by some as representing Rome and her empire (Shotter 2004, 3).

49 It is probable under Cerealis that the Second Legion Adiutrix moved to Lincoln, and the Ninth Legion to York, although the precise date is not known. Ottaway 1993, 19ff. Marching camps: Hanson 1987, 124. A fine example of these camps with 'Stracathro-type' entrances is at Dalginross, near Perth (Frere and St. Joseph 1983, 129–31).

50 Trimontium: Frere and St. Joseph 1983, 120–22; Tacitus, *Agricola* 22, but the description of fort siting is sycophantic.

51 Tacitus, *Agricola* 22.

52 Tacitus, *Agricola* 23.

53 Agricolan forts are known at Mollins and Barochan, with a more recently excavated fort at Elginhaugh, south of the Forth (Hanson 1987, 99 and *passim*).

54 It is possible that the Irish prince was Tuathal Teachtmhar, who was exiled to Britain for twenty years before returning to avenge his father's death. This event is dated to AD 76 in the Irish Annals (Rance 2001, 250; Warner 1995).

55 Tacitus, *Agricola* 24.

56 In fact, no Roman army ever ventured into Ireland, although contact between Britain and Ireland did occur. A significant selection of Roman objects, mostly coins, has been found on the promontory of Drumanagh, 16 miles north of Dublin, but has not yet been fully published (Warner 1996). Ironically, Ireland was to be a major sanctuary for the maintenance of classical learning after the fall of Roman Britain in the fifth century.

57 Tacitus, *Agricola* 10; Thule as Iceland: Cunliffe 2001, 166ff.

58 Tacitus, *Agricola* 25.

59 Tacitus, *Agricola* 28.

60 Evacuation preferable to defeat: Tacitus, *Agricola* 25; marching camps have been found at Bellie, Muiryfold and Auchinove (Hanson 1987, 125–36).

61 Tacitus, *Agricola* 26.

62 The site of the battle is not known, but is probably in the vicinity of the marching camps between Raedykes and Durno, and Auchinove and Muiryfold. Hanson 1987, 130–37; Fraser 2005; Campbell 2010.

63 Tacitus, *Agricola* 32.

64 Tacitus, *Agricola* 30.

[65] Tacitus, *Agricola* 33–35.

[66] Tacitus, *Agricola* 33.

[67] Tacitus, *Agricola* 36.

[68] Tacitus, *Agricola* 36.

[69] Tacitus, *Agricola* 37.

[70] Tacitus, *Agricola* 39.

[71] Hanson 1987, 143ff; Pitts and St. Joseph 1985; Shirley 2001; Wilson 2002, 596–8.

[72] Fortress rebuilding: see *RIB* 330 and 665; Britain allowed to slip: Tacitus, *Histories* 1.2.

[73] Province more peaceful: Tacitus, *Agricola* 40; great men under bad emperors: Tacitus, *Agricola* 42.

[74] The first Vindolanda Tablet was discovered in 1973; the most comprehensive introduction to the letters is Bowman 1994.

[75] Bowman 1994, 136, no. 32.

[76] Promotion: Bowman 1994, 124–25, no. 19. Beating: Bowman 1994, 138, no. 33.

[77] Bowman 1994, 106, no. 3.

[78] Bowman 1994, 133–34, no. 29.

[79] Bowman 1994, 139–40, no. 34.

[80] Virgil '*seg*' tablet: http://www. britishmuseum.org/explore/ highlights/highlight_objects/ pe_prb/w/tablet_with_a_line_ from_virgil.aspx

[81] Sulpicia's name might suggest that her family gained its citizenship during the reign of Galba – Servius Sulpicius Galba – in AD 68. Children's footwear has been discovered at Vindolanda, perhaps belonging to Cerealis' family. Saturnalia tablet: Bowman 1994, 57–58. Brocchus: from an inscription, we know that Brocchus moved to command a cavalry unit in Pannonia (*ibid.* 55)

[82] Bowman 1994, 127 no. 21.

[83] It must have been intended to be a monumental gateway into the province. However, only the square base and fragments of the monument survive (Frere and St. Joseph 1983, 78–79). Various candidates, from Claudius to Domitian, have been suggested as its initiator. However, it seems highly likely that Vespasian built the monument, thereby linking himself with Claudius, the conqueror of the province (Shotter 2004, 5–6).

5 THE LIMITS OF THE WORLD
(PP. 120–34)

[1] There are many books on Hadrian. The main original source is the *Scriptores Historiae Augustae* (*SHA*), written in the late fourth century. The most comprehensive biography: Birley 1997. Hadrian's travels: Speller 2002. Lavishly illustrated catalogue of the 2008 British Museum exhibition: Opper 2008.

[2] *SHA Hadrian* 4.10.

[3] Virgil, *Aeneid* 6.851ff.

[4] *SHA Hadrian* 6.

[5] A relief showing a bonfire of these documents survives at Chatsworth House in the Devonshire Collection (Opper 2008, 57 fig. 39).

[6] Building programme: Birley 1997, 111f; Opper 2008, 126–27; Pantheon: Opper 2008, 110–25; Tivoli: Opper 2008, 130–65; Macdonald and Pinto 1995.

[7] Apollodorus incurred Hadrian's wrath by pointing out that when the seated statues of Venus and Roma stood up, their heads would have gone through the roof of their temple. Dio 69.4.1–5; Opper 2008, 102–3; Birley 1997, 56.

[8] Opper 2008, 110–25; the columns in the portico came from Mons Claudianus in the eastern desert of Egypt and from Aswan on the River Nile.

[9] Birley 1997, 117.

[10] *SHA Hadrian* 10; coins were struck celebrating the 'Emperor's Discipline' showing Hadrian with an officer and standard bearers (*RIC* II nos 746–47).

[11] References to number of Romans killed: Fronto, *Letter to Marcus on the Parthian War* (*LACTOR* 11.29); fears about Roman control: *SHA Hadrian* 5.1–2; Tungrian centurion: Birley 1998.

[12] The Sixth Legion may have erected altars to Neptune and Oceanus on the Roman bridge over the Tyne at Newcastle to commemorate their safe arrival (*RIB* XIII nos 19–20; Birley 2005, 121). It is possible that the 3,000 legionaries from Spain and Germany came to Britain as reinforcements in around AD 119, although they may equally possibly have come with Hadrian in AD 122 (Birley 2005, 118).

[13] Birley 2005, 119–24.

[14] *SHA Hadrian* 11.

[15] Birley 1997, 125.

[16] *RIC* II Hadrian nos 577 and 845.

[17] *RIC* III Antoninus Pius nos 742 and 934.

[18] *RIC* III Commodus no. 437; *RIC* IV, pt 1, Caracalla 483b.

[19] *RIC* V, pt 2, Carausius nos 554–58.

[20] Gorgon's head: Cunliffe 1995, 31ff; Henig 1995, 39–41; coals: Cunliffe 1995, 16; Gaius Julius Solinus, *Collectanea Rerum Memorabilium* 22.11; coins: among these were pieces struck for Hadrian (Walker 1988, 314–15), including many of the Britannia coins mentioned earlier; curses: Tomlin 1988.

[21] Tomlin 1988, 122 no 10; one can surmise that this cloak was stolen from the changing room.

[22] *SHA Hadrian* 11.2–3.

[23] *CIL* xvi 69; Birley 1997, 127.

[24] Tacitus, *Agricola* 14.

[25] It was on this bridge that the Sixth Legion erected their altars to Neptune and Oceanus (see note 12 above).

[26] Birley 1997, 133.

[27] *SHA Hadrian* 11.2.

[28] The most commonly cited book on Hadrian's Wall is Breeze and Dobson 2000; but see also Davies 1974; Breeze 1982; Embleton and Graham 1984; Johnson 1989; Wilson 2002, 439ff; Collingwood Bruce 2006. There

is also an excellent map of the Wall (Ordnance Survey 2009).

29 Crow 1995.

30 A similar technique of using sharpened branches was employed by Caesar at the siege of Alesia in Gaul (Caesar, *De Bello Gallico* 7.72). Legionary builders: *RIB* 1308 *passim*; Nepos and Hadrian: *RIB* 1634,1637–8. It was not until the nineteenth century and the recognition of these inscriptions that the Wall was attributed to Hadrian; previously, because of inscriptions recording repair work, it was thought the Wall was built during the reign of Septimius Severus (AD 193–211).

31 Cherry 1998. It is quite likely that this African frontier was built to control the movement of the desert nomads and their goats, which were a potential threat to the fertile farmland to the north, much of it recently reclaimed by Hadrian.

32 The most recent example is the Staffordshire Moorlands Pan (Tomlin and Hassall, 2004; Worrell, 2004; www.finds.org.uk: WMID-3FE965). See Plate 21.

33 Jackson and Potter 1996. The structure at Stonea was monumental, probably of a similar plan to a surviving Hadrianic building near Anguillara, now called Le Mura di Santo Stefano, just to the north of Rome. There is no doubt that the building at Stonea would have dominated the landscape (*ibid*. p. 679).

34 The milestone is on display at the British Museum: *RIB* 2265; for mining in north Wales see Jones and Mattingley 1990, 179ff; in the Silures' territory the gold mine at Dolaucothi was being exploited (*ibid*. 180–84; Burnham and Davies 1990, 161–71).

35 We can assume he served at Maryport for four years because he set up four altars to Jupiter Optimus Maximus, which were erected as an annual oath of allegiance by the soldiers (*RIB* 823–6; Breeze 1997, 72). Procurator: *CIL* 11.5632 (*LACTOR* 4

46); there is a great deal of debate about the exact chronology of Maenius Agrippa's career (see Birley 2005, 307–10).

36 An inscription by the main entrance to the Forum notes that the basilica was constructed under Hadrian (*RIB* 288).

37 Wacher 1995, 378ff.

38 Opper 2008, 171–73; Birley 1997, 145; *CIL* 12,1122; *RIB* 1041.

39 *SHA Hadrian* 12.1.

40 This statue was later pulled down and flung into the River Thames. The head was recovered in 1834 and is on display at the British Museum.

41 Opper 2008, 59 fig. 42; 81 fig. 64.

42 Birley 1997, 151ff.

43 Antinous the god: Birley 1997, 235ff; Opper 2008, 166ff; Littlecote Antinous: Walters and Henig 1988; Henig 1995, 70–71; Worrell 2008, 363 no 13.

44 Booty from the sack of Jerusalem is depicted on reliefs on the vault of the Arch of Titus in the Roman Forum. Boar on gate: Birley 1997, 268ff; Opper 2008, 89–97.

45 Dio 69.12.

46 Dio 69.17.2.

47 *SHA Hadrian* 25.9.

6 BAND OF BROTHERS
(PP. 135–43)

1 Dio 69.13.2.

2 It is likely that Severus crossed the Channel in a ship from the *Classis Britannica*, which we know at this time was commanded by L. Aufidius Pantera, who erected an altar at the naval base at Lympne (Kent) (*RIB* 66). This altar is on display at the British Museum.

3 Fronto, *Letter to Marcus Aurelius on the Parthian War*, 2 (*LACTOR* 11, 29). Fronto might well have been referring to the beginning of Hadrian's reign and it has been argued that the great size of the army in Britain justified the

appointment of such a man as Severus (Salway 1981, 182).

4 Dio 69.13.3; Goodman 2007, 487ff; Opper 2008, 89ff.

5 'Antoninus never willingly made war; but when the Moors took up arms against Rome, he drove them from the whole of their territory...' (Pausanias, *Description of Greece* 8.43.3).

6 *CIL* 8, 6706.

7 For the career of Lollius Urbicus, see Birley 2005, 136–40.

8 *RIC* III, 743–5.

9 *Pan. Lat.* 8(5), 14.2 (citing Fronto).

10 Pausanias, *Description of Greece* 8.43.4.

11 The Brigantes extended beyond the western part of Hadrian's Wall, their territory probably being a partial reason for the construction of the outpost forts of Birrens, Bewcastle and Netherby. A relief of Brigantia was discovered at Birrens (*RIB* 2091).

12 Salway 1981, 199; Hanson and Maxwell 1986, 62; also note that the passage in Pausanias might refer to the 150s, in the twilight years of the Antonine Wall (see below).

13 Tacitus, *Agricola* 23.

14 Near to which a milestone was erected on Dere Street at this time (Ireland 1986, 92, no. 141).

15 *RIB* 2139.

16 The lack of Roman forts on the southeast coast of Scotland suggests that the Votadini tribe were not hostile.

17 *SHA Antoninus Pius* 5.4.

18 *RIB* 2191–2. The construction of the wall by the three legions was commemorated by a series of building slabs informing us how much each legion built in their particular sections (Keppie 1979, 9ff; e.g. *RIB* 2139; 2173; 2184–6; 2193–4; 2196–8; 2200; 2204–6; 2208; 2199; 2207). For full descriptions and discussion of the Antonine Wall, see Breeze 1982,

97ff; Hanson and Maxwell 1986; Breeze and Dobson 2000, 88ff; Breeze 2006.

[19] There was a greater density of troops at the western end, where the frontier had no outpost forts. Signal towers have not yet been discovered in the archaeological record.

[20] Urbicus went on to be the Prefect of Rome, possibly in AD 146.

[21] Walker 1988, 293ff. These are one of several base metal types dating between 153 and 155, which were sent to Britain in vast numbers. To suggest that they were to help finance military activity is stretching the evidence too far, but it does seem that they were sent for a reason, which still eludes us.

[22] For the career of Julius Verus, see Birley 2005, 145–49.

[23] An inscription at Newcastle records the troops' return with the governor (RIB 1322). Had there been serious trouble in Britain, it is doubtful that these troops would have been sent to Germany.

[24] Breeze 1996, 94–95; Hodgson 1995; Breeze and Dobson 2000, 128–29; Breeze 2006, 166–67.

[25] Altar to Mercury: RIB 2145 and Lactor 4, 73; coins: Abdy 2002, 200 and 206; frontier scouts were called exploratores, later to be known as areani.

[26] Fort building: RIB 283, 1132, 2110 and 1389. Julius Verus probably left Britain around AD 160. After governing Syria, he returned to Italy to oversee the recruitment of troops for two new legions, the Second and Third Italicae. He was granted a second consulship in AD 180, but died before he could take up the post in AD 179.

[27] For more on the career of Statius Priscus, see Birley 2005, 151–55.

[28] Birley 2005, 153.

[29] SHA Marcus Aurelius 8.7; for more on the career of Calpurnius Agricola, see Birley 2005, 155–57.

[30] Thus we find that the Sixth and Twentieth Legions were at work

in Corbridge, a Syrian unit at Carvoran, and other units at Vindolanda, Hardknott and Ribchester (RIB 1137 and 1149; 1792; 1703; 793; 589).

[31] See note 25.

[32] SHA Marcus Aurelius 22.1.

7 THE SCOURGE OF SCOTLAND (PP. 144–67)

[1] Dio 76.15.1.

[2] The most comprehensive biography of Severus is Birley 1999. For Lepcis Magna see Kenrick 2009, 89ff.

[3] Dio 77.16–17.

[4] Birley 2005, 172–74.

[5] Casey 2010, 225–35.

[6] SHA Commodus 8.4; Birley 2005, 169.

[7] Birley 2005, 170–71.

[8] Dio 79.9.22–23; Birley 2005, 169.

[9] The bust: Meates 1979, 36 and 185; it is on display at the British Museum. The intaglio: Meates 1987, 54–55; Henig 2007.

[10] Dio 74.1.

[11] Dio 75.4.

[12] From 300 to 500 denarii. This was also facilitated by the debasement of the silver coinage, with about 40% copper being added – this was a major step in the demise of the Augustan monetary system, introduced over 200 years earlier.

[13] The subsequent presence of a Roman garrison at Hatra does, however, suggest that Severus eventually managed to gain control of the town.

[14] Herodian 3,14,1.

[15] Breeze and Dobson 2000, 133–34.

[16] Dio 75.5.4.

[17] South Shields was quite a cosmopolitan centre. It is possibly around this time that a Palmyrene called Barates set up a tombstone for his wife Regina, an ex-slave from the Catuvellauni tribe (RIB 1065). Six imperial lead sealings of Severus, Caracalla and Geta have

been found at South Shields, confirming that it was a major Severan base (Hodgson 2001, 30).

[18] Bidwell and Hodgson 2001.

[19] Dio 76 11 1.

[20] Toynbee 1962, pl. 194, cat. no. 165.

[21] Dio 76 16 5.

[22] A cameo showing Caracalla as Hercules, found at South Shields, might suggest an imperial presence (Henig 1986).

[23] For the Shapwick hoard, see Abdy and Minnitt 2002; for Falkirk, see Robertson 2000, 90, no. 45; for Birnie, see Holmes 2006. For Severan coins on the Portable Antiquities Scheme database, go to www.finds.org.uk. For Piercebridge finds, see Walton, forthcoming.

[24] Herodian 3.14.4.

[25] Prolonging the war: Herodian 3,14,9; casualty figures, surely an exaggeration: Dio 76 13 2.

[26] Dio 76.14.

[27] For example, RIC IV, pt 1, p. 205, nos 833–34 and 837; ibid. p. 288, nos 464–45 and 467; p. 339 nos 166–67.

[28] Birley 1999, p. 218, n. 22. The traditional date for Geta's elevation is AD 209, but Birley suggests AD 210 and this fits well with the increasing surliness of Caracalla.

[29] SHA 23.

[30] Dio 76,15,1.

[31] Herodian 3.15.2.

[32] Forts abandoned: Casey 2010; South Shields: Hodgson 2001, 34–35.

[33] An inscription from South Shields, dedicated to the 'Preservers for the welfare of Caracalla and Geta' suggests that the imperial party started its journey home from the Tyne estuary. RIB 1054.

[34] Julia Domna's sister, Julia Maesa, had two grandchildren, Elagabalus and Severus Alexander, who were to continue the broader Severan dynasty from AD 218 to 235.

8 THE BRITANNIC EMPIRE
(PP. 168–81)

[1] Vegetius, *On Military Affairs* 4.37.

[2] Lactantius, *De Mortibus Persecutorum* 5.

[3] Gregory, *Historia Francorum* 1.32–4.

[4] It was the emperor Aurelian who retook the Gallic empire in AD 274.

[5] *Historia Augusta Probus* 18.8.

[6] Strabo, *Geography* 4.5.2.

[7] Zosimus, *New History* I.lxviii.3.

[8] This theory remains attractive, as the archaeological evidence (including that of coins) attests (Branigan 1976, 46–47; Wacher 1978, 116; Salway 1981, 278ff).

[9] Salway 1981, 279–80; it is possible that the large circuit walls at Gatcombe, surrounding an agricultural and industrial processing area, highlighted the insecurity of the age (Branigan 1977, 187ff).

[10] Esmonde Cleary, forthcoming.

[11] *Pan. Lat.*, ix(4), 11.1.

[12] *RIB* 2280 and 2300; we do not know exactly when the cohort was at Vindolanda (*RIB* 1710).

[13] Nemesianus, *Cynegetica* 63–70; Birley 2005, 367–68; *RIB* 98; Bland and Loriot 2010, 20; Shiel 1977a, 153.

[14] The most comprehensive coverage of the Saxon Shore Forts is Pearson 2002.

[15] Pearson 2002, 59–60; Wilson 2002, 54.

[16] Pearson 2002 63–64.

[17] A large number of hoards of silver plate are recorded in Gaul in the third century, possibly reflecting insecurity (Hobbs 2006, 36ff.).

[18] *RIB* 2291 = a milestone found near Carlisle; this is the only place where Carausius is given the name Mauseus. The name Marcus Aurelius is very common because many people who gained Roman citizenship as a result of the *Constitutio Antoniniana* of AD 212 took the name of the emperor

Caracalla, whose official name was Marcus Aurelius Antoninus Pius.

[19] The translation of *gubernandi gnarus* is normally 'helmsman', although some prefer 'pilot'; Menapia is situated between the Scheldt (northern Belgium) and the Waal (southern Holland), the heart of the territory lying between the Rivers Scheldt and Waal (Aurelius Victor 39, 20; Clotuche 2009).

[20] There is still much uncertainty and debate surrounding the extent and date of the Dutch marine transgression (Leon Geyskens pers. comm.). To learn more about the nature of coastal change in Britain, see Cracknell 2005.

[21] Moorhead and Stuttard 2010, ch. 2.

[22] The exact nature of the *bagaudae* will always be open to debate. It is quite likely that their composition varied from place to place.

[23] Aurelius Victor 39, 20.

[24] Vessels such as these are widely illustrated on the coinage of Carausius' successor, Allectus (Besly 2006, 65–67). See Fig. 23.

[25] Eutropius, *Breviarium* IX, 21.

[26] Aurelius Victor 39, 21.

[27] Of the twenty-five gold coins struck by Carausius that have survived, nine come from the first issues at Rouen (Huvelin 1985, 16; and recent discovery, Bland and Loriot 2010, 142, no. 133).

[28] There is no doubt that after the unsuccessful attempt to dislodge Carausius by Maximian in *c.* 290 Carausius did have some continental possessions, probably including Rouen, Boulogne and Amiens.

[29] *Pan. Lat.* viii(5), 12 (AD 297). Carausius probably took with him a number of units drawn from continental bases that had been in his army – it has even been suggested that part of the Thirtieth Legion from Xanten was with him (Casey 1994, 94–95). Furthermore, numismatic evidence suggests that he might have had vexillations from some other continental legions,

all of whom were honoured on the early coinage of Carausius: the First Minervia, Second Augusta, Second Parthica, Fourth Flavia, Seventh Claudia, Eighth Augusta, Twentieth Valeria Victrix, Twenty-Second Primigenia, Thirtieth Ulpia Victrix. The absence of the Sixth Legion Victrix (York) from coins is possibly due to the fact that this legion did not have vexillations serving on the continent as the Second Augusta and Twentieth Valeria Victrix did (Casey 1994, 92–95).

[30] The only inscription of Carausius from Britain, other than those on coins, is on a milestone from near Carlisle (see note 18 above).

[31] De la Bédoyère 1999, 38.

[32] Robertson 2000, p. l, map 16; Walton, forthcoming.

[33] For another Virgilian reference, see the depiction of Dido and Aeneas on the Low Ham mosaic, Plate 36.

[34] De la Bédoyère, 1999, 34–35; Richard Abdy has found that this very same inscription was included above the throne on an anonymous Restoration print depicting Charles II's coronation (British Museum, PD 1870, 0514.306). These coins presage a flowering of classical culture in fourth-century Britain, as shown by the Latin couplet inscribed on a mosaic at Lullingstone Villa that was an allusion to Virgil, written in the style of Ovid (Meates 1979, 77).

[35] Casey 1994, 58 notes the pun on udder (*ubera*) and *Uberitas* (plenty).

[36] Casey 1994, 55–88; *RIC* V pt 2, 426ff.; Moorhead, Booth and Bland, 2010.

[37] For the most comprehensive listing of Carausian silver *denarii* see *RIC* V pt 2, 508–16 and Shield 1977a, 94–165.

[38] Pearson 2002, 36–38.

[39] In the grounds of Dover Castle stands one of these lighthouses, the tallest surviving monument from Roman Britain, standing to 62 ft (19 m), of which 42½ ft (13 m) are genuine Roman work (Wilson 2002, 52).

40 *Pan. Lat.* x(2), 12.

41 War abandoned: *Pan. Lat.* viii(5), 12.1–2; peace arranged: Eutropius, *Breviarium* IX,22,2.

42 Casey 1994, 110 dates the coins to 292 in response to the nomination of Constantius I as Caesar. However, it is just as likely that the coins were struck before and ceased to be issued before, or just after, the promotion of Constantius.

43 Most are silver-washed radiates, but four gold *aurei* of Maximian survive (Huvelin 1985, 118).

44 *Pan. Lat.* vi(7), 5.2–3.

45 It is not known if Boulogne fell in Carausius' or Allectus' reign. In many ways it would make more sense were it towards the end of Allectus' reign. This might have even precipitated the building of the Shore Fort at Pevensey.

46 Allectus usurps imperial power: Aurelius Victor V.39; currying favour: *Pan. Lat.* viii(5), 12.

47 Allectus continued to strike coins at London and 'C' mint, even introducing a new 'half-radiate' coin with galleys on the reverse (Fig. 23), again referring to the effective power-base of the Britannic empire. His coins are found in similar regions to those of Carausius, although very few hoards are found north of the Wash – there is a concentration in the West Country, an area which was to become the richest part of Britain in the first half of the fourth century (Robertson 2000, p. li, map 17). Single finds are also very scarce in the north (Walton, forthcoming).

48 Perring 1991, 110; Casey 1994, 125; de la Bédoyère 1999, 29; Pearson 2002, 62.

49 Some scholars urge caution about linking the structure to Allectus, suggesting the timbers (dated to AD 294 by tree-ring dating) might have been allowed to season. See Williams 1989 and 1993; Casey 1994, 133; de la Bédoyère 1999, 40; Pearson 2002, 62.

50 Pearson 2002, 59–61.

51 *Pan. Lat.* viii(5), 16.4–5.

52 *RIC* VI, Trier 34.

53 Whether the panegyricist knew of the RSR INDPCA coins of Carausius (see p. 177) is not known, but the similarity of expression is ironic.

54 *Pan. Lat.* viii(5), 19.1–2.

9 BLESSED ISLE
(PP. 182–97)

1 *Pan. Lat.* viii(5), 13.3.

2 Or step-daughter.

3 *Constantine Byzantinus* 7.

4 This is the so-called Tetrarchy, or Rule of Four.

5 *Pan. Lat.* viii(5), 20.3–5.

6 Shiel 1977b, 75ff, supported by hoard evidence (Robertson 2000 p.li, map 17) and Portable Antiquities Scheme data (www.finds.org.uk; Walton, forthcoming).

7 Wilmott 2001, 114–15; this is also possibly the case at Halton Chesters and Rudchester (Breeze and Dobson 2000, 222–23).

8 This provides good (if not always reliable) information on the location of military units (Ireland 1996, 23ff; *LACTOR* 11, 56ff).

9 For example the Birdoswald and Housesteads restorations (*RIB* 1912; Breeze and Dobson 2000, 224–25).

10 The terms *vicarius* and *diocese* would, of course, later be adopted by the Christian Church.

11 Jones and Mattingley 1990, 148; Salway 1981 map vii.

12 This is the first time that the Picts are mentioned in the historical record (Rivet and Smith 1979, 438–40), although they might have been recorded in the late second or early third century as the 'Cruithentuath' (Rance 2001, 249 after Chadwick 1949, 71–72 and 139).

13 Anon., *Origo Constantini* II,2–3.

14 It was probably at this time that Constantine visited Memphis – we know that Diocletian had a fort erected around the Temple of Amun at Luxor, and among the Roman remains is a statue base of Constantius Chlorus and the other three Tetrarchs (Bagnall and Rathbone 2004, 191–92).

15 Lactantius, *De Mortibus Persecutorum* 24; Lactantius of Nicomedia was a Christian teacher of Latin at Nicomedia, the tutor of Constantine's eldest son, Crispus.

16 Killing horses: Aurelius Victor, 40, 2–3; sailing for Britain: Anon., *Origo Constantini* 2.4.

17 *Pan. Lat.* vi(7), 7.2.

18 *Pan. Lat.* vii(6), 7.1–2. Much of the description of the campaign suggests that earlier, Severan, sources were being used to embellish the record.

19 York and Lincoln are recorded as *coloniae* on an altar found in Bordeaux (*JRS* 11 (1921), 102).

20 Bidwell 2006 provides most of the most recent information used in this discussion of the governor's residence and fortress at York.

21 *RIB* 662–63. Although traditionally attributed to Demetrius of Tarsus in the Flavian period, it is now reckoned that these tablets are of another Demetrius and probably date to the third century (see Bidwell 2006, 33–34; *LACTOR* 4, 126). This is more evidence for the governor's residence being on the south side of the river. Reinterpretation of the features suggests that the structure was not a bath-house (as previously thought), but the hypocaust heating system for a hall or *aula* in the later Roman period, the type of room one would expect to find in an official residence of the period. The most famous example is the 'basilica' of Constantine, still standing in all its splendour at Trier.

22 For discussion of the fort, see Bidwell 2006, 36–39; for a description of the head of Constantine, see Hartley *et al* 2006, 120–21.

[23] Eusebius, *Vita Constantini* I.21.

[24] *Pan. Lat.* vii(6), 8.2–4).

[25] Anon., *Origo Constantini* II, 4; Aurelius Victor 40,4; Lactantius, *De Mortibus Persecutorum* 24.8.

[26] Crocus is discussed at length in Wood 2006 and Drinkwater 2009.

[27] *Epitome of the Caesars* 41.3.

[28] Eutropius, *Breviarium* X.2.2.

[29] This was probably north of the fortress. Ottaway 1993, 12 shows the area to the north of the fortress clear of settlement.

[30] Zosimus, *New History* II.9.1.

[31] Eusebius, *Vita Constantini* I.22.

[32] Constantine's acceptance as emperor was quickly acknowledged in Britain, as is attested by a series of milestones erected across the province in 306–7. Examples are known from near Carvoran on Hadrian's Wall (*RIB* 2310), near Chester (*RIB* 2303), Cambridgeshire (*RIB* 2237) and Cornwall (*RIB* 2233). On Gallows Hill, near Carlisle, a milestone of Carausius was upended and re-inscribed at the other end for Constantine, emphasizing the change of regime (*RIB* 2292). Many of the inscriptions underlined Constantine's parentage, stating he was the son of the 'divine Constantius Pius'. Furthermore, the mint at London, along with others on the continent, was swift to strike coins commemorating Constantius, as well as proclaiming the new emperor Constantine.

[33] Eusebius, *Vita Constantini* I.28.

[34] Eusebius, *Vita Constantini* I.31.

[35] 'I am the Alpha and Omega, the beginning and the end' (Revelation 21.6; 22.13).

[36] See Moorhead and Stuttard 2010, ch. 3 for an outline of the rise of Christianity in the fourth century.

[37] Casey 1978.

[38] For these ADVENTUS coins see *RIC* VI, 82; *RIC* VII, 133ff; *RIC* VII, 1.

[39] *ILS* 8942; Ireland 1996, 142, 243.

[40] Eusebius, *Vita Constantini* I.25.

[41] For Mithraism in general, see Clauss 2000 and Beck 2007; for the London Mithraeum, see Shepherd 1998.

[42] Breeze and Dobson 2000, 241–43.

[43] *Pan. Lat.* vi(7),9.1–2.

[44] De la Bédoyère 1999 elucidates the flowering of Roman Britain in the fourth century.

[45] Moorhead 2005; Pearce 2008.

[46] *RIB* 2220, 2242, 2239, 2249, 2267, 2285, 2288.

[47] The silver itself probably dates from the middle of the fourth century (Painter 1977a and 1999).

[48] *RIC* VII, 5: Hunterian, Glasgow; Ashmolean, Oxford; British Museum, London; Bland and Loriot 2010, 149 no. 169; PAS WILT-D86FB6, *BNJ* 78, 2008, 268, no. 42; PAS NARC-A1A418, *BNJ* 80, 2010, 214, no. 30.

[49] Salway 1981, 536.

[50] Churches: Watts 1991, 99ff.; Janes 2002, 123–24; Lullingstone: Meates 1979 and 1987.

[51] Eusebius, *Vita Constantini* II, 28.

10 TURMOIL
(PP. 198–211)

[1] Salway 1981, 348–49.

[2] Libanius, *Oratio* LIX, 141.

[3] Julius Firmicus Maternus, *De Errore Profanum Religionum* 28, 6.

[4] Ammianus 28.iii.8; Salway 1981, 351–52.

[5] Breeze and Dobson 2000, 235.

[6] *Ibid.* 242. The region north of Hadrian's Wall received very few Roman objects in the fourth century, suggesting less Roman presence in southern Scotland (Hunter 2010).

[7] *RIC* VIII, p. 283, no. 338; Alföldi 1942–43, pl. II, no. 12. In AD 348, Constans and Constantius reformed the coinage across the Roman world. In the west, Constans' dominion, there was a popular design that showed the emperor on a galley, holding Victory or a phoenix or Victory and a Christian standard, the ship being steered by Victory. (*RIC* VIII, pl. 2, no. 214 and pl. 6, no. 128). Although this design can be seen as a stock motif showing the emperor commanding the 'ship of state', and although the phoenix alludes to Rome's 1,100th anniversary in 348, the coin may also have been inspired by Constans' earlier medallion, and therefore ultimately by the mid-winter voyage to Britain (*RIC* VIII, p. 35).

[8] Valentinian I (364–75) and Valens (364–78).

[9] Zosimus, *New History* 2.43.1.

[10] *Epitome of the Caesars* 41.24.

[11] Eutropius, *Breviarium* 10.9.

[12] Cruel animal: Zosimus, *New History* 2.47.3; giant of a man: *Epitome of the Caesars* 42.6; British father: Zonaras 13.6B; Scholian on Julian's *Oration*, 2.95C; Drinkwater 2000, 139.

[13] Magnentius began to strike coins at the existing Gallic mints of Trier, Arles and Lyons, but opened another mint at Amiens. This might have been because it was his home town, but it might have also been needed to supply coinage to the northern part of Gaul, and even Britain, where much of his most loyal support might have been. He struck a massive issue of coins, which featured the Chi-Rho between an Alpha and Omega (e.g. *RIC* VIII, p. 123, nos 34–45). See Plate 40.

[14] Barbarian descent: *Epitome of the Caesars* 42.6. *Laeti*: Zosimus 2.54.1; see Drinkwater 2000, 131–45.

[15] *Epitome of the Caesars* 42.7.

[16] Another emperor, Vetranio, was declared by the Balkan army in AD 350 but he abdicated in favour of Constantius.

[17] Zonaras xiii 8.17.

[18] *Epitome of the Caesars* 42.6.

[19] *Epitome of the Caesars* 42.8.

20 Moorhead 2005; Pearce 2008.

21 Ammianus 14.5.3.

22 Ammianus 14.5.6.

23 Ammianus 14.5.9.

24 Ammianus 22.3.11–12.

25 Webster 1983, 248–50.

26 Moorhead 2005.

27 Ammianus 14.5.1.

28 A wealthy heiress, Melania, owned estates across the Roman world in Italy, Sicily, Africa, Spain and Britain (Salway 1981, 431; Clark 1985).

29 Webster 1983. Coin records for sites around Salisbury suggest that there was a hiatus in this region as well (Moorhead 2001, 95).

30 Webster 1983, 247.

31 Soffe and Henig 2002.

32 King 1996.

33 Codex Theodosianus 9.23.1; RIC VIII, pp. 64–65; Grierson and Mays 1992, 28.

34 Burying money: Robertson 2000, 317–28. Cutting coins: Boon suggests that this occurred later in the fourth century, but it could well have occurred in the period 355–63 when there was a rash of forging of small bronze coins in Britain (Boon 1988, p. 145 and pl. VIII, nos 148–49). Such pieces are increasingly being recorded with the Portable Antiquities Scheme (www.finds.org.uk).

35 This is most clearly shown in Faulkner 2001.

36 Libanius, Oratio 18.82.

37 Eunapius fr 12.

38 Ammianus 18.2.3.

39 Libanius, Oratio 18.82–3.

40 Libanius, Oratio 18.87.

41 Julian, Letters, 279D and 280A.

42 Zosimus, New History 3.5.2.

43 Zosimus, New History 3.5.2.

44 A treaty possibly made by Constans in 343 (see above), or even Constantius I in 306 (see above).

45 Ammianus 20.1.1.

46 Ammianus 20.1.2.

47 Portable Antiquities Scheme data shows that the period 357 to 363 has the highest proportion of silver siliquae in late Roman Britain, overturning the evidence of the hoards that had misleadingly suggested a time in the late fourth century (Bland, Moorhead and Walton, forthcoming).

48 Ammianus, 20.9.9.

49 Painter 1977b, 21–23.

50 Ibid. 26. The name appears in the genitive: ευθηριου.

51 Ammianus, 16.7 (which contains a full description of Eutherios).

52 In 1942, thirteen silver coins were published which might have been found with the hoard, but we will never know the truth. The latest coin is of Honorius and dates to 397–402, so had these coins been part of the hoard, then the treasure would have to have been buried later than the time of Lupicinus (Hobbs 2008, 408; Pearce 1942; Robertson 2000, no. 1592).

53 Julian, Letters, 89 (305C).

54 Lydney: Wheeler and Wheeler 1932 and Casey and Hoffman 1999; Nettleton: Wedlake 1982; Frilford: Hingley 1982 and Henig and Booth 2000, 19 passim; Great Walsingham: Davies and Gregory 1991, 70; Cirencester: RIB 103; Littlecote: Littlecote Roman Villa 1994.

II MELTDOWN
(PP. 212–38)

1 Ammianus 26.4.5; the cataclysm of AD 367 can be seen as a culmination of events rather than a sudden upheaval (Rance 2001, 244–45). There is very little evidence for destruction in the province, but up to thirty villas from Gloucester to Ilchester (Somerset) may have evidence for destruction from this period (Branigan and Fowler 1976, 136–39; Laycock 2008, 136).

2 It is interesting to note that in 367 Jovinus was consul alongside Lupicinus (see above).

3 The Scots were certainly based in Ireland; the Attacotti are also now thought to be from Ireland, rather than northern Scotland as scholars once believed (Rance 2001).

4 Ammianus 27.8.5. It should be noted that, although a fine historian, Ammianus was writing in the reign of Count Theodosius' son, Theodosius I (379–95). It is likely that Count Theodosius gets a very good press as a result, although it has been suggested that there are veiled criticisms in Ammianus' account (Seager 1997).

5 Ammianus 27.8.7.

6 Ammianus 27.8.7.

7 At Colchester House in London, archaeologists have uncovered a monumental late Roman building, which might have been a massive granary or Christian cathedral. Either alternative highlights the continuing importance of London in the late Roman period (Gerrard, forthcoming).

8 Ammianus 27.8.7–10.

9 Ammianus 28.3.2.

10 Ammianus 28.2.4; Birley 2005, 439, n.76; Salway 1981, 394–95.

11 Thompson 1990.

12 Jerome, Chronicle, 371, p. 246c; Jordanes, Romana 308; Zosimus 4.12.2; all in Birley 2005, 438–39.

13 Bartholomew 1984; Birley 2005, 430, n.61.

14 Ammianus 28.3.8.

15 These coins have been catalogued by Nick Holmes at the National Museum of Scotland, but are still to be published fully. Out of 225 coins, 49 came to the House of Valentinian (364–78) and 6 to the House of Theodosius (388–402) (Hunter 2010, 97–98). They are mentioned in Moffat 1999 (160–61).

16 Reece 1991, sites 112, 116, 121, 123 and 125; Jones and Mattingly 1990, 136; Cool 2008; RIB 955.

17 Ammianus 28.3.7; 28.3.2.

18 From north to south these are
at Huntcliff, Goldsborough,
Ravenscar, Scarborough and Filey.
At Ravenscar an officer, Justinianus,
caused an inscription to be raised
proclaiming how he 'built the
tower and fort from the ground up'
(RIB 721) though this may refer to
a later rebuilding. The coin evidence
from the watchtowers is consistent
with a Valentinianic date.

19 RIB 1672–73; 1843–44; 1962; 2022.

20 Breeze and Dobson 2000, 236–40;
Wilmott 2001,119–20.

21 Notitia Dignitatum Occ. xl, 22.

22 Cool 2008, 308–11.

23 Ammianus 16.10.6ff.

24 Potter 1977, 183; Laycock 2008, 113.

25 Salway 1981, 384.

26 Cunetio: Corney 1997; Moorhead
1997, 48–49; 2001, 95; 2009a, 158;
it is possible that a massive late-
Roman granary has been found in
London (Gerrard, forthcoming).

27 Cunetio, Kenchester and
Alcester are in a region (north
and east Somerset, Wiltshire,
Gloucestershire, Hampshire
and parts of Oxfordshire,
Buckinghamshire, Worcestershire
and Warwickshire) where there
is a high concentration of
Valentinianic bronze coinage
(Moorhead 2001 and 2009a).
In southeast England, on the
other hand, a region that Count
Theodosius brought under
his control without much difficulty,
coin-finds associated with the
army are relatively rare.

28 Laycock 2008, 113–16; Leahy 2007.

29 Very large numbers of Valentinianic
coins have been found on West
Country and Norfolk temple sites
(Moorhead 2001, 93).

30 Ammianus 28.3.7. There are many
interpretations of what area is
represented by the name 'Valentia',
ranging from new regions in
the north to the renaming of
an existing province, which had
seceded but been brought back

into the fold (Salway 1981, 392–96).
A recent argument suggests that it
was Maxima Caesariensis that was
renamed Valentia (de la Bédoyère
2006, 77).

31 Ammianus 28.3.8.

32 Zosimus, New History 4.15.4.
Theodosius was an Orthodox
Christian; Valens was an Arian,
a follower of a theologian
whose views had been branded
heretical by the Orthodox Church.
Ammianus does not mention
Theodosius' death, but does
compare Theodosius with two
famous generals who suffered
similar fates, Corbulo at the
hands of Nero, and Lucius
Quietus at the start of Hadrian's
reign. Ammianus 29.5.4; Birley
2005, 440.

33 Claudian, On the Fourth Consulship
of Honorius 24–33.

34 Zosimus, New History 4.35.3.

35 Pan. Lat. ii(12).31.1.

36 Maximus in Britain: Zosimus,
New History 4.35.3; John of Antioch
Fr. 186 in Birley 2005, 447; in
North Africa: Ammianus 29.5.6
and 21; note also that the Moorish
cavalry deserted Gratian for
Maximus in the final showdown
in 383 – Zosimus 4.35.5; at the
Danube: Moorhead and Stuttard
2010, ch 4.

37 Ammianus 31.4.9–10.

38 Fraomarius: Ammianus 29.4.7.
These might have been some of
the 'barbarians' that later Magnus
Maximus was said to have had
in his army; the title 'Britannicus
Maximus' depends on whether
the reading of a fragmentary
Italian inscription is correct
(Birley 2005, 449).

39 Zosimus, New History 4.35.2–4.

40 Zosimus, New History 4.35.3–4.

41 Orosius 7.34.9.

42 Augusta: Ammianus 28.3.1; coins
RIC IX, pp. 1–2, nos 1–4; army's
reaction: Zosimus, New History
4.35.4–5.

43 Salway 1981, 405.

44 Zosimus, New History 4.36.3.
One such statue was set up in
Alexandria: Birley 2005, 449.

45 Birley 2005, 449.

46 Ambrose, in Patrologia Latina
16–17 (1845), 40.

47 Gallic Chronicle of AD 452.

48 Count Arbogast – see Prosper Tiro,
Chronicon 1191, AD 388.

49 Sozomen VII.13.

50 Historia Brittonum 27 (written in
the ninth century); Gildas, De
Excidio (c. 540) goes even further,
saying that Maximus took all the
Roman troops, governors and
flower of its youth.

51 Gildas, De Excidio 14. Gildas should
be used with great care by
historians. He wrote in around 540
and his historical pronouncements
are often unsound. The present
statement is undoubtedly an
exaggeration.

52 Notitia Dignitatium Occ. v.65; Birley
2005, 449, n107.

53 Attacotti: Rance 2001; Snyder 1998,
12 passim; Dark 1994, 107 passim;
Nash-Williams 1950, Stone 182.

54 Gildas, De Excidio 14–15. Although
it is very difficult to use Gildas as
a reliable source for this period, his
evidence does suggest barbarian
invasions in the late 380s and late
390s. See Miller 1975, 141–45 and
Salway 1981, 419ff.

55 Gildas, De Excidio 16–17; it is
possible that Britain was further
destabilized by the usurpation
of Eugenius in Gaul (AD 392–94).

56 Claudian, Against Eutropius I, 391–
93; Milan, spring 399.

57 Claudian, second poem of Stilicho's
Consulship 261ff.; early January 400.

58 Claudian, De Bello Gothico, 416–18.
There is a debate about whether
this legion was taken from Britain
at this time, or later under
Constantine III, but we believe it
is highly likely that Stilicho would
have taken any troops that he
thought could be spared (see Birley
2005, 453).

59 This might just be a stock statement, to be compared with the similar description made after the previous victory (see above).

60 Gildas, *De Excidio* 17.

61 Zosimus, *New History* 6.3.1; there is possible evidence for destruction at the Yorkshire signal towers at Goldsborough and Huntcliff (Pearson 2006, 345).

62 Zosimus, *New History* 6.2.1–2.

63 Orosius, *Adversum Paganos*, 7.40.4.

64 Drinkwater 1998, 272. Julian was a monk at Constantine's accession.

65 Unlike Magnus Maximus, Constantine did not strike an issue of coins in Britain upon his succession. One of his generals may have been the Justinian whose name appears on the Ravenscar signal tower inscription (*RIB* 721, see above).

66 Drinkwater 1998, 275.

67 *Gallic Chronicle of 452* (iv. 62).

68 Zosimus, *New History* 6.5.3.

69 Zosimus, *New History* 6.10.2; Birley 2005, 461–62.

12 PRAYING FOR THE COMING OF THE ONCE AND FUTURE KING (PP. 239–50)

1 Laycock 2008, 201–2.

2 Material culture: Faulkner 2000, 121ff.

3 Wattle and daub: Dark and Dark 1997, 120–22; Laycock 2008, 161; Wroxeter: White and Barker 1998; Caerwent: a large number of late fourth-century bronze coins suggests official activity into the early fifth century; Nicholas Wells is currently re-cataloguing and appraising all the late Roman coin finds from Caerwent (Reece 1991, sites 51–52; Wacher 1995, 390).

4 Population decline: Faulkner 2000, 145. Plague: Gildas, *De Excidio* 2 and 22; no evidence for plague in Britain: Esmonde Cleary 1989, 174–75.

5 Wacher 1989, 111.

6 De la Bedoyère 1992, 121–22; Faulkner 2000, 124.

7 Many rooms were used for agricultural purposes (Esmonde Cleary 1989, 158; Laycock 2008, 164; Hostetter and Howe 1997, 373–74).

8 Early, but not late, silver coins of Constantine III are found in Britain, suggesting that payments to the province ended during his reign.

9 Wilmott 2001, 121–24.

10 'Vindolanda granaries occupied into the eighth century', *Current Archaeology* 221 (August 2008), 5.

11 Rahtz, Woodward and Burrow 1992; Fleming 2010, 32–35; an increasing number of Byzantine coins are being found in Britain (Moorhead 2009a).

12 Clipping: Burnett 1984, Guest 2005, 110–15, Bland, Moorhead and Walton, forthcoming; Hoxne hoard: Guest 2005 and Johns 2010; Coleraine hoard: Hobbs and Jackson 2010, 145; hoard in the Pyrenees: Berdeaux-Le Brazidec and Hollard 2008.

13 Clinging on to Roman ways: Dark 2000 and Harris 2003; Wansdyke: Laycock 2008, 141 *passim*.

14 It would be fascinating to know what role Aurelius Ursicinus, the man named on so many spoons found in the Hoxne hoard, played in late Roman Britain (Johns 2010).

15 *RIB* II, 3, 2431,1.

16 Cross 1974, 1058–59.

17 Constantius, *Vita Germani*, the source used by Bede (Bks 17–21), tells us that a synod of Gallic bishops initiated Germanus' mission. It is quite possible that the matter was causing agitation in Gaul and that this is how Rome heard as well. Who actually initiated Germanus' mission will never be known for certain.

18 Constantius, *Vita Germani* 13; Germanus' earlier position of authority is not clear – Constantius writes: '...the state promoted him to official rank by conferring on him the supreme office of *dux* and the rule over more than one province' (*Vita Germani* 1).

19 Constantius, *Vita Germani* 13–14.

20 *Ibid.* 14; it has been suggested that the description of rich clothing is a device to differentiate the materialistic enemy from the spiritual mission (Barrett 2009, 205), but it is quite possible that there were still people in Britain at this time who had splendid clothes which were heirlooms from their ancestors. The best representation of ecclesiastical garb from Roman Britain is on a fine wall-painting at Lullingstone villa (Plate 41), dating to around 360 (Salway 1981, 465; Abdy and Moorhead 2008, 48–49).

21 Constantius, *Vita Germani* 15.

22 Salway 1981, 466–67; Matthew 8:5–13; Luke 7:1–10.

23 Constantius, *Vita Germani* 16. The Abbey itself has much Roman brick re-used in its construction. Efforts to identify Christian churches at Verulamium have been generally unsuccessful, although a late Roman cemetery near to the present Abbey might have had a cemetery church (Niblett 2001, 136–40). The date of St Alban's martyrdom is disputed, traditionally being attributed to the persecution enacted by Diocletian in AD 303. However, now some scholars date it to *c.* 208–9 when Geta was Caesar in charge of civil affairs at York (Frere 1987, 164; Salway 1981, 720).

24 Constantius, *Vita Germani* 15.

25 Niblett 2001, 138.

26 Constantius, *Vita Germani* 17. Given the reference to Germanus serving as *dux* in Gaul (see *VG* I), it is possible that he did have military experience.

27 Constantius, *Vita Germani* 17. It is difficult to believe this account of the bloodless 'Alleluia Victory' but it does suggest that the Britain that Germanus visited was still threatened by external forces, in this case, the Picts and Saxons.

It also suggests that the Britons were in some cases able to hold their own (see below).

[28] Leaves Britain: Constantius, *Vita Germani* 18. In the *Vita Germani*, Germanus returns to Britain a second time to combat Pelagianism and this time heals the crippled son of a leading Briton, Elafius (*VG* 26). However, careful consideration of the sources by Anthony Barrett suggests strongly that this second mission never occurred and was probably the result of Constantius' using two separate sources that wrote about the same event in different ways (Barrett 2009, 205ff). Looking at both Prosper of Aquitaine and Constantius, it does appear that at the end of Germanus' (only) mission a number of heretics were driven from the island and some were handed over to priests from the Mediterranean.

[29] Even the dates of Patrick's life are uncertain. It is now thought by many that he was born in the late fourth century and died around AD 460. Studies under Germanus: Cross and Livingstone 1974, 1073; Patrick, *Confessio* 1: the only other work thought to be by Patrick's hand is a letter to Coroticus; Bannaven Taburniae: Patrick, *Confessio* 1; de la Bédoyère 2006, 260.

[30] Patrick, *Confessio* 23.

[31] Gildas, *De Excidio* 19. This is a central theme in an excellent work on the end of Roman Britain (Laycock 2008, ch. 6).

[32] Snyder 1998, 102–3.

[33] Salway 1981, 474.

[34] The coins were struck at Rome in the reign of Valentinian III and are of a type very rarely found north of the Alps. One was found at Richborough, two at St Albans, one at Dunstable, and one at Wroxeter (Abdy and Williams 2006, 31–32, nos 57–61).

[35] *Anglo-Saxon Chronicle* 449 and 455. These (probably legendary) Saxons are normally credited with arriving in Kent, and it is interesting that a very early Saxon cemetery has been recently excavated at Ringlemere, near Sandwich. The earliest material dates from around AD 450 (Hobbs and Jackson 2010, 155).

[36] Gildas, *De Excidio* 23.

[37] Gildas, *De Excidio* 20.

[38] Gildas, *De Excidio* 25; Morris 1973, 112–15; Snyder 1998, 43 *passim*. The last vestiges of contact with authority on the continent might be shown by the discovery of fifty gold and silver coins with fifty-four pieces of hacksilver and two rings at Patching. The coins are Roman, or continental imitations of Roman, coins, the latest dating from around AD 470 (Abdy 2006).

Epilogue
(P. 251)

[1] *The Earliest English Poems* translated and introduced by Michael Alexander (Penguin Classics 1966, Third edition 1991). Copyright © Michael Alexander, 1966, 1977, 1991. Reproduced by permission of Penguin Books Ltd.

Further Reading

Find Out More
Those wishing to take an active part in Romano-British studies are recommended to explore the benefits of membership of the Association for Roman Archaeology (www.associationromanarchaeology.org), which runs many events across the country. More comprehensive information about the latest discoveries, as well as research into Roman Britain, can be had by joining the Society for the Promotion of Roman Studies (www.romansociety.org), whose members receive the annual journal *Britannia*.

Abbreviations
ABC = E. Cottam, P. de Jersey, C. Rudd and J. Sills, *Ancient British Coins* (Aylsham: Chris Rudd, 2010)

BMCG = B. V. Head and R. S. Poole, *A Catalogue of the Greek Coins in the British Museum – Ionia* (London: British Museum Press, 1982)

BMC IA = R. Hobbs, *British Iron Age Coins in the British Museum* (London: British Museum Press, 1996)

BNJ = *British Numismatic Journal*

CIL = T. Momsen *et al.* (eds), *Corpus Inscriptionum Latinarum* (Walter de Gruyter & Co, Berlin, 1863–)

ILS = H. Dessau, *Inscriptiones Latinae Selectae* (1892–1916)

JRS = *Journal of Roman Studies*

LACTOR 4 = V. A. Maxfield and B. Dobson (eds), *Inscriptions of Roman Britain* (London Association of Classical Teachers, Vol. 4, 4th edn, 2006)

LACTOR 11 = J. C. Mann and R. G. Penman (eds), *Literary Sources for Roman Britain* (London Association of Classical Teachers, Vol. 11, 1985)

RIB = R. G. Collingwood and R. P. Wright, *The Roman Inscriptions of Britain* (2 vols with addenda and corrigenda by S. S. Frere, R. S. O. Tomlin and M. Roxan) (Stroud: Alan Sutton, 1990–95)

RIC = H. Mattingly *et al.*, *The Roman Imperial Coinage* (London: Spink, 1923–2007)

Original Sources
This book has drawn upon a very large number of ancient literary texts. The comprehensive listing can be found in Ireland (1996) and *LACTOR* 11. The more commonly read works are available as Penguin Classics and/or in the Loeb series of parallel texts. Also, many of the texts are now available both in their original form and as translations on the internet. A number of obscure texts are referred to in Birley 2005. Below, we list the original sources used in this book and give accessible sources where available.

In addition, we draw heavily upon inscriptions and these can be found in *RIB* and *LACTOR* 4. Archaeological sources are covered in the general bibliography.

English translations of quotations from ancient sources are the authors' own, unless otherwise noted.

Ambrose (see J. P. Migne, *Patrologia Latina*, Paris 1844–80)

Ammianus (Ammianus Marcellinus, *Histories*, Penguin Classics; Loeb)

Aelian, *Tactics* (H. Augustus, Viscount Dillion, *The Tactics of Aelian*, Cox & Bayles, London, 1814)

Anglo-Saxon Chronicle (G. N. Garmonsway, trans., J. M. Dent, London, 1953, and numerous later edns)

Anon., *Origo Constantini* (in S. N. C. Lieu and D. Montserrat, *From Constantine to Julian*, Routledge, 1996, 39–62)

Augustus, *Res Gestae* (Loeb)

Aurelius Victor (H.W. Bird, trans., Liverpool University Press, 1994)

Bede, *A History of the English Church and People* (Penguin Classics)

Caesar, *De Bello Gallico* (Penguin Classics; Loeb)

Cicero, *Letters to Friends; Letters to Atticus* (Penguin Classics; Loeb)

Claudian, *Poems* (Loeb)

Codex Theodosianus (Clyde Pharr, ed., Greenwood, 1952); available (in Latin) at: http://ancientrome.ru/ius/library/codex/theod/tituli.htm

Columella, *On Agriculture* (Loeb)

Constantius, *Vita Germani* (eds/trans. Thomas Noble and Thomas Head, in *Soldiers of Christ: Saints' Lives from Late Antiquity and the Early Middle Ages*, Pennsylvania State University Press, 1994)

Constantine Byzantinus (*The Anonymous Life of Constantine*, Lieu and Montserrat 1996, 97–146)

Dio (Cassius Dio, Penguin Classics, abridged; Loeb)

Epitome of the Caesars (http://www.roman-emperors.org/epitome.htm)

Eunapius = R. Bockley, *The Fragmentary Classicising Historians of the Later Roman Empire – Eunapius, Olympiodorus, Priscus and Malchus II* (text, translation and historiographical notes, ARCA Classical and Mediaeval Texts, Papers and Monographs 10, Francis Cairns 1983

Eusebius, *Vita Constantini* (Cameron and Hall, 1999)

Eusebius, *Historia Ecclesiastica* (Penguin Classics; Loeb)

Eutropius, *Breviarium* (H. W. Bird, Liverpool University Press, 1993)

Frontinus, *Stratagems* and *Aqueducts of Rome* (Loeb)

Fronto, *Letters to Marcus Aurelius* (Loeb)

Gaius Julius Solinus *Collectanea Rerum Memorabilium* (A. Golding, trans., *The Excellent and Pleasant Worke: Collectanea Rerum Memorabilium of Caius Julius Solinus*, Scholars Facsimiles & Reprints, New York, 1999)

Gallic Chronicle of AD 452 (Richard Burgess in Ralph W. Mathisen, Danuta Shanzer, *Society and Culture in Late Antique Gaul. Revisiting the Sources*, Aldershot 2001)

Gerontius, *Life of Melania* (Clark, 1985)

Gildas, *De Excidio et Conquestu Britanniae* (M. Winterbottom, *Arthurian Period Sources Vol. 7: Gildas: The Ruin of Britain and Other Documents*, v. 7, Phillimore 1980)

Gregory of Tours, *Historia Francorum* (E. Brehaut, trans., *A History of the Franks*, Digiread Com 2010)

Herodian (Loeb)

Historia Brittonum, once attributed to Nennius
(J. Morris, ed., Arthurian Period Sources Vol. 8, Nennius,
Phillimore 1980). Available at: www.fordham.edu/
halsall/basis/nennius-ful.html

Horace, Odes (Penguin Classics; Loeb)

Jerome, Chronicle (translation available at www.tertullian.
org/fathers/jerome_chronicle_00_eintro.htm)

Jordanes, Romana (available in Latin and English at www.
harbornet.com/folks/theedrich/Goths/Romana.htm)

Josephus, Antiquities (Loeb) and Jewish War (Penguin
Classics; Loeb)

Julian Letters and Orations (Loeb)

Julius Firmicus Maternus, De Errore Profanum Religionum
(C. A. Forbes, The Error of Pagan Religions, Newman
Press, 1970)

Justinian, Digest (Penguin Classics)

Juvenal, Satires (Penguin Classics; Loeb)

Lactantius, De Mortibus Persecutorum (J. L. Creed, ed.,
Oxford University Press, 1985)

Libanius, Oratio (Loeb)

Lucian (Penguin Classics; Loeb)

Nemesianus, Cynegetica (Loeb)

Notitia Dignitatum (see LACTOR 11 and Ireland 1996)

Olympiodorus = R. Bockley, The Fragmentary Classicising
Historians of the Later Roman Empire – Eunapius,
Olympiodorus, Priscus and Malchus II, text, translation
and historiographical notes, ARCA Classical
and Mediaeval Texts, Papers and Monographs 10,
Francis Cairns, 1983)

Onosander, Strategicus (Loeb)

Orosius, Adversum Paganos (http://tertullian.org/
fathers/philostorgius.htm)

Pan. Lat. = Panegyrici Latini (Nixon and Rodgers 1994)

Patrick, Confessio (J. Skinner, ed., Image, 1998)

Pausanias, Description of Greece (Penguin Classics; Loeb)

Pliny, Nat. Hist. = Pliny the Elder, Natural History
(Penguin Classics, abridged; Loeb)

Plutarch, Moralia (Loeb)

Polyaenus, Stratagems (English translation: http://www.
attalus.org/translate/polyaenus.html)

Propertius (Penguin Classics; Loeb)

Prosper Tiro, Chronicon (A. C. Murray, trans. and ed.,
From Roman to Merovingian Gaul: A Reader, UTP
Higher Education, Ontario, 2003, 62–76)

Quintilian, Institutio Oratoria (English translation: http://
honeyl/public.iastate.edu/quintilian/)

Seneca, Apocolocyntosis (P. T. Eden, ed., Cambridge Greek
and Latin Classics, 1984)

SHA: Scriptores Historiae Augustae or The Augustan
History (Penguin Classics, Lives of the Later Caesars; Loeb)

Sozomen (http://www.freewebs.com/vitaphone1/history/
sozomen.html)

Statius, Silvae (Loeb)

Strabo, Geography (Loeb)

Suetonius, Lives of the Twelve Caesars (Penguin Classics;
Loeb)

Tacitus, Agricola (Penguin Classics; Loeb)

Tacitus, Annals (Penguin Classics; Loeb)

Tacitus, Histories (Penguin Classics; Loeb)

Tibullus (Penguin Classics; Loeb)

Vegetius, On Military Affairs (N. P. Milner, Liverpool
University Press, 1995)

Virgil, Aeneid (Penguin Classics; Loeb)

Virgil, Aeneid and Eclogues (Penguin Classics; Loeb)

Zonaras (T. Banchich and E. Lane, The History of Zonaras:
From Alexander Severus through the Death of Theodosius
the Great, Routledge, 2009)

Zosimus, New History (R. T. Ridley, trans., University
of Sydney, 1982)

Bibliography

Abdy, R. A. 2002 'A survey of the coins from the Antonine
Wall', Britannia XXXIII, 189–218

Abdy, R. A. 2006 'After Patching; imported and recycled
coinage in fifth- and sixth-century Britain', in B. Cook
and G. Williams, Coinage and History in the North Sea
World, c. 500–1250 (Leiden: Brill)

Abdy, R. A. & Minnitt, S. 2006 'Shapwick Villa, Somerset:
9,328 denarii to AD 224', in R. A. Abdy, I. Leins and
J. Williams (eds), Coin Hoards from Roman Britain XI
(London: Royal Numismatic Society Special Publication
36), 169–233

Abdy, R. A. & Moorhead, S. 2008 'Triumph of the Cross',
British Museum Magazine 60, 46–49

Abdy, R. A. and Williams, G. 2006 'A catalogue of hoards
and single finds from the British Isles, c. AD 410–675',
in B. Cook and G. Williams (eds), Coinage and History
in the North Sea World, c. 500–1250 (Leiden: Brill), 11–74

Alföldi, A. 1942–43 Die Kontorniaten (Budapest: Magyar
Numizmatikai Társulat)

Allason-Jones, L. 1989 Women in Roman Britain (London:
British Museum Press)

Barrett, A. A. 2009 'Saint Germanus and the British
missions', Britannia XL, 197–218

Bagnall, R. S. and Rathbone, D. W. (eds) 2004 Egypt, from
Alexander to the Copts (London: British Museum Press)

Bartholomew, P. 1984 'Fourth-century Saxons', Britannia
XV, 169–86

Bates, S. 2000 'Excavations at Quidney Farm, Saham
Toney, Norfolk, 1995', Britannia XXXI, 201–38

Beck, R. 2007 The Religion of the Mithras Cult in the
Roman Empire: Mysteries of the Unconquered Sun
(Oxford and New York: Oxford University Press)

Berdeaux-Le Brazidec, M.-L. & Hollard, D. 2008 'Le dépôt
de siliques à Bédeilhac-et-Aynat (Ariège): un témoin
de la présence des troupes de Constantin III (407–411)
dans les Pyrénées', Cahier Numismatiques 177, 21–33.

Berresford Ellis, P. 1978 Caesar's Invasion of Britain
(London and New York: Orbis)

Besly, E. M. 2006 'The Rogiet hoard and the coinage
of Allectus', British Numismatic Journal 76, 45–146

Bidwell, P. 2006 'Constantius and Constantine at York',
in E. Hartley et al. (eds) 2006, 31–40

Bidwell, P. and Hodgson, N. 2001 'Port, supply-base and
naval base for the Roman northern frontier: evidence
for the maritime role of South Shields' (unpublished
draft, courtesy of N. Hodgson)

Bird, D. G. 2000 'The Claudian invasion campaign
reconsidered', Oxford Journal of Archaeology 19.1, 91–104.

Birley, A. R. 1997 *Hadrian, the Restless Emperor* (London and New York: Routledge)

Birley, A. R. 1999 *Septimius Severus, the African Emperor* (London and New York: Routledge)

Birley, A. R. 1999, *Tacitus, Agricola, Germania* (Oxford and New York: Oxford University Press)

Birley, A. R. 1998 'A New Tombstone from Vindolanda', *Britannia* XXIX, 299–306

Birley, A. R. 2005 *The Roman Government of Britain* (Oxford and New York: Oxford University Press)

Birley, E. 1961 *Roman Britain and the Roman Army* (Kendal: Titus Wilson and Son)

Birley, R. 2009 *Vindolanda, A Roman Frontier Fort on Hadrian's Wall* (Stroud: Amberley Publications)

Black, E. W. 2000 'Sentius Saturninus and the Roman invasion of Britain', *Britannia* XXXI, 1–10

Bland, R. and Loriot, X. 2010 *Roman and Early Byzantine Gold Coins found in Britain and Ireland* (Royal Numismatic Society Special Publication 46)

Bland, R., Moorhead, S. and Walton, P. forthcoming 'Finds of late Roman silver coins from Britain: the contribution of the Portable Antiquities Scheme', in F. Hunter and K. Painter (eds), *Late Roman Silver and the End of the Empire: The Traprain Law Treasure in Context* (Edinburgh: Society of Antiquaries of Scotland)

Bogaers, J. E. 1979 'King Cogidubnus: Another reading of *RIB* 91', *Britannia* 10, 243–54.

Boon, G. C. 1988 'Counterfeit coins in Roman Britain', in J. Casey and R. Reece (eds), *Coins and the Archaeologist* (London: Seaby), 102–88

Bourke, C. 1993 *Patrick – The Archaeology of a Saint* (Belfast: HMSO)

Bowman, A. K. 1994 *Life and Letters on the Roman Frontier* (London: British Museum Press)

Branigan, K. 1976 *The Roman Villa in South-West England* (Bradford-on-Avon : Moonraker)

Branigan, K. 1977 *Gatcombe: The Excavation and Study of a Romano-British Villa Estate 1967–1976* (British Archaeological Reports, British Series, 44)

Branigan, K. and Fowler, P. J. (eds) 1976 *The Roman West Country* (Newton Abbot: David and Charles)

Braund, D. C 1984 *Rome and the Friendly King* (London: Croom Helm and New York: St Martin's Press)

Braund, D. C. 1996 *Ruling Roman Britain: Kings, Queens, Governors and Emperors from Julius Caesar to Agricola* (London and New York: Routledge)

Breeze, D. J. 1982 *The Northern Frontiers of Roman Britain* (London: Batsford and New York: St Martin's Press)

Breeze, D. J. 1996 *Roman Scotland: Frontier Country* (London: Batsford)

Breeze, D. J. 1997 'The regiments stationed at Maryport and their commanders', in R. J. A. Wilson (ed.), *Roman Maryport and its Setting* (Senhouse Roman Museum, Maryport), 67–89

Breeze, D. J. 2006 *The Antonine Wall* (Edinburgh: John Donald/Historic Scotland)

Breeze, D. J. and Dobson, B. 2000 *Hadrian's Wall* (London: Penguin)

Brothwell, D. 1986 *The Bog Man and the Archaeology of People* (London: British Museum Press and Cambridge, MA: Harvard University Press)

Burnett, A. M. 1984 'Clipped *siliquae* and the end of Roman Britain', *Britannia* XV, 163–68

Burnham, B. C. & Davies, J. L. (eds) 1990 'Conquest, co-existence and change – recent work in Roman Wales', *Trivium* 25 (Lampeter: St David's University College)

Cameron, A. 2006 'Constantius and Constantine: An exercise in publicity', in E. Hartley *et al.* (eds) 2006, 18–30

Cameron A. and Hall, S. G. 1999 *Eusebius, Life of Constantine* (Oxford: Clarendon Press and New York: Oxford University Press)

Campbell, D. 2010 *Mons Graupius AD 83: Rome's Battle at the Edge of the World* (Oxford: Osprey)

Casey, P. J. 1978 'Constantine the Great in Britain – the evidence of the coinage of the London Mint, AD 312–314', in J. Bird, H. Chapman and J. Clark (eds), *Collectanea Londiniensia: Studies in London Archaeology and History Presented to Ralph Merrifield* (London and Middlesex Archaeological Society), 180–93

Casey, P. J. 1994 *Carausius and Allectus: The British Usurpers* (London: Batsford and New Haven: Yale University Press)

Casey, P. J. and Hoffman B. 1999 'Excavations at the Roman Temple in Lydney Park, Gloucestershire in 1980 and 1981', *The Antiquaries Journal* 79: 81–143

Casey, P. J. 2010 'Who built Carpow? A review of events in Britain in the reigns of Commodus and Septimius Severus', *Britannia* XLI, 225–35

Chadwick, H. M. 1949 *Early Scotland* (Cambridge: Cambridge University Press)

Chadwick, N. K. 1966 *The Druids* (Cardiff: Wales University Press)

Cherry, D. 1998 *Frontier and Society in Roman North Africa* (Oxford: Clarendon Press)

Clark, E. A. 1985 *Life of Melania the Younger: Introduction, Translation and Commentary* (New York: Edwin Mellen Press)

Claughton, P. and Smart C. 2008 'The Bere Ferrers Project and Discovery of a Roman fort at Calstock' (Exeter University): http://people.exeter.ac.uk/pfclaugh/mhinf/contents.htm

Clauss, M. 2000 *The Roman Cult of Mithras: The God and His Mysteries* (Edinburgh: Edinburgh University Press)

Clotuche, R. 2009 'The Scheldt Valley commercial activity zone: 350 hectares of the Gallo-Roman landscape', *Britannia* XL, 41–64

Collingwood, R. G. and Myres, J. N. L. 1937, *Roman Britain and the English Settlements* (Oxford: Clarendon Press)

Collingwood, R. G. and Richmond 1969 *The Archaeology of Roman Britain* (London: Methuen)

Collingwood Bruce, J. 2006 *A Handbook to the Roman Wall* (14th edn, ed. D. J. Breeze, Newcastle: Society of Antiquaries of Newcastle upon Tyne)

Cool, H. E. M. and Mason, D. J. P. (eds) 2008 *Roman Piercebridge* (Durham: The Architectural and

Archaeological Society of Durham and
Northumberland, Research Project 7)
Corney, M. 1997 'The origins and development of the
"Small Town" of *Cunetio*, Mildenhall, Wiltshire',
Britannia XXVIII, 337–50
Cracknell, B. E. 2005 *Outrageous Waves – Global Warming
and Coastal Change in Britain* (Chichester: Phillimore)
Creighton, J, 2006 *Britannia, The Creation of a Roman
Province* (London and New York: Routledge)
Cross F. L. and Livingstone, E. A. 1974 *The Oxford
Dictionary of the Christian Church* (London and New
York: Oxford University Press)
Crow, J. 1995 *Housesteads* (London: Batsford/English
Heritage)
Crummy, P. 1997 *City of Victory: The Story of Colchester
– Britain's First Town* (Colchester: Colchester
Archaeological Trust)
Cunliffe, B. 1984 'Relations between Britain and Gaul
in the first century B.C. and early first century A.D.', in
S. Macready and F. H. Thompson, *Cross-Channel Trade
between Gaul and Britain in the pre-Roman Iron Age*
(London: Society of Antiquaries)
Cunliffe, B. 1991 *Iron Age Communities in Britain* (3rd edn,
London and New York: Routledge)
Cunliffe, B. 1995 *Book of Roman Bath* (London: Batsford/
English Heritage)
Cunliffe, B. 1998 *Fishbourne Roman Palace* (Stroud: Tempus)
Cunliffe, B. 2001 *The Extraordinary Voyage of Pytheas the
Greek* (London and New York: Allen Lane)
Dark, K. R. 1994 *Civitas to Kingdom* (London: Leicester
University Press)
Dark, K. R. 2000 *Britain and the End of the Roman Empire*
(Stroud and Charleston, SC: Tempus)
Dark, K. R. and Dark, P. 1997 *The Landscape of Roman
Britain* (Stroud: Sutton)
Davies, H. 1974 *A Walk along the Wall* (London:
Weidenfeld & Nicolson)
Davies, J. A. and Gregory, A. 1991 'Coinage from a *Civitas*:
a survey of the Roman coins found in Norfolk and their
contribution to the archaeology of the *Civitas Icenorum*',
Britannia XXII, 65–102
de la Bédoyère, G. 1992 *Roman Towns in Britain* (London:
Batsford/English Heritage)
de la Bédoyère, G. 1999 *The Golden Age of Roman Britain*
(Stroud and Charleston, SC: Tempus)
de la Bédoyère, G. 2001 *Eagles over Britannia: The Roman
Army in Britain* (Stroud: Tempus)
de la Bédoyère, G. 2006 *Roman Britain: A New History*
(London and New York: Thames & Hudson)
Dörres, H. 1972 *Constantine the Great* (trans. R. H.
Bainton, New York: Harper & Row)
Drinkwater, J. F. 1998 'The usurpers Constantine III
(407–411) and Jovinus (411–413)', *Britannia* XXIX, 269–98.
Drinkwater, J. F. 2000 'The revolt and ethnic origin
of the usurper Magnentius (350–53), and the rebellion
of Vetranio (350)', *Chiron* 30, 131–59
Drinkwater, J. F. 2009 'Crocus, "King of the Alamanni"',
Britannia XL, 185–95
Embleton, R. and Graham, F. 1984 *Hadrian's Wall in the
Days of the Romans* (Newcastle: Frank Graham)

Esmonde Cleary, A. S. 1989 *The Ending of Roman
Britain* (London: Batsford and Savage, MD: Barnes &
Noble)
Esmonde Cleary, A. S. forthcoming *An Archaeology of
the Roman West*, AD 200–500 (Cambridge: Cambridge
University Press)
Evans, M. M. 2001 'Boudica's last battle', *Osprey Military
Journal* Vol 3, Issue 5, 25–34
Faulkner, N. 2000 *The Decline and Fall of Roman Britain*
(Stroud: Tempus)
Fishwick, D. 1995 'The Temple of Divus Claudius
at *Camulodunum*', *Britannia* XXVI, 11–28
Fleming, R. 2010 *Britain after Rome* (London and New
York: Allen Lane)
Foster, J. 1986 *The Lexden Tumulus – A Re-appraisal
of an Iron Age Burial from Colchester, Essex* (Oxford:
BAR series 156)
Fraser, J. E. 2005 *The Roman Conquest of Scotland:
The Battle of Mons Graupius AD 84* (Stroud: Tempus)
Frere, S. S. 1987 *Britannia* (3rd edn, London and New
York: Routledge and Kegan Paul)
Frere, S. S. and Fulford, M. 2001 'The Roman invasion
of AD 43', *Britannia* XXXII, 45–55
Frere S. S. and St Joseph, J. K. S. 1983 *Roman Britain from
the Air* (Cambridge and New York: Cambridge
University Press)
Fry, P. S. 1982 *Rebellion Against Rome* (Lavenham: Terence
Dalton)
Fulford, M. 1989 *The Silchester Amphitheatre: Excavations
of 1979–85* (London: Britannia Monograph 10)
Fulford, M. 2003 'Julio-Claudian and early Flavian
Calleva', in P. Wilson (ed.), *The Archaeology of Roman
Towns: Studies in Honour of John Wacher* (Oxford:
Oxbow), 95–104
Fulford, M. 2008 'Nero and Britain: the palace of
the client king at *Calleva* and imperial policy towards
the province after Boudicca', *Britannia* XXXIX, 1–13
Fulford, M. and Timby, J. 2000 *Late Iron Age and Roman
Silchester: Excavations on the Forum Basilica 1977*
(London: Britannia Monograph 15)
Furneaux, H. and Anderson, J. 1922 *Cornelii Taciti,
De Vita Agricolae* (Oxford: Clarendon Press)
Gerrard, J. forthcoming 'Cathedral or granary? The
Roman coins from Colchester House, City of London',
*Transactions of the London and Middlesex Archaeological
Society* 62.
Goodman, M. 2007 *Rome and Jerusalem* (London and
New York: Allen Lane)
Grasby, R. D and Tomlin, R. S. O., 2002 'The sepulchral
monument of the procurator C. Julius Classicianus',
Britannia XXXIII, 43–75
Gregory, T. 1991 *Excavations in Thetford, 1980–82: Fison
Way*, Vol. 1 (Dereham: Anglian Archaeology 53)
Grierson, P. and Mays, M. 1992 *Catalogue of Late Roman
Coins in the Dumbarton Oaks Collection and in the
Whittemore Collection* (Washington DC: Dumbarton
Oaks Research Library and Collection)
Guest, P. 2005 *The Late Roman Gold and Silver
Coins from the Hoxne Treasure* (London: British
Museum Press)

Hanson, W. and Maxwell, G. 1987 *Rome's North West Frontier: The Antonine Wall* (Edinburgh: Edinburgh University Press)

Harris, A. 2003 *Byzantium, Britain and the West: The Archaeology of Cultural Identity* (Stroud: Tempus)

Hartley, B. and Fitts, L. 1988 *The Brigantes* (Gloucester: Sutton)

Hartley, E. 2006 'Introduction' in E. Hartley *et al.* (eds) 2006, 15–16

Hartley, E., Hawkes, J., Henig, M. and F. Mee (eds) 2006 *Constantine the Great: York's Roman Emperor* (York: York Museums and Gallery Trust/Lund Humphries)

Haverfield, F. and MacDonald, G. 1924, *The Roman Occupation of Britain* (Oxford: Clarendon Press)

Henig, M. 1984 *Religion in Roman Britain* (London: Batsford and New York: St Martin's Press)

Henig, M. 1986, 'Caracalla as Hercules? A new cameo from South Shields', *Antiquaries Journal* 66, 378–80

Henig, M. 1995 *The Art of Roman Britain* (London: Batsford)

Henig, M. and Booth, P. 2000 *Roman Oxfordshire* (Stroud: Sutton)

Henig, M. 2007 'The victory-gem from Lullingstone Roman Villa', *Journal of the British Archaeological Association* 160, 1–7

Hind, J. G. F. 1989 'The invasion of Britain in A.D. 43', *Britannia* XX, 1–22

Hingley, R. 1982 'Recent discoveries of the Roman period at Noah's Ark Inn, Frilford, South Oxfordshire', *Britannia* XIII, 305–9

Hobbs, R. and Jackson, R. 2010 *Roman Britain: Life at the Edge of Empire* (London: British Museum Press)

Hobbs, R. 2006 *Late Roman Precious Metal Deposits, c. AD 200–700* (BAR International Series 1504)

Hobbs, R. 2008 'The secret history of the Mildenhall Treasure', *Antiquaries Journal* 88, 376–420

Hodgson, N. 1995 'Were there two Antonine occupations of Scotland?', *Britannia* XXVI, 29–50

Hodgson, N. 2001 'The origins and the development of the Roman military supply-base at South Shields: an interim report on the results of excavations in the eastern quadrant and central area, 1990–2000', *Arbeia Journal* 6–7, 25–36

Hogg, A. H. A. 1975 *Hill-Forts of Britain* (London: Hart-Davis, MacGibbon)

Holmes, N. M. McQ., 2006 'Two *denarius* hoards from Birnie, Moray', *British Numismatic Journal* 76, 1–44

Holt, W. C. 2003 'The evidence of the coinage of Poemenius' revolt of Trier', *American Journal of Numismatics* 15 (New York: American Numismatic Society), 61–76

Horsley, J. 1733 *Britannia Romana, or the Roman Antiquities of Britain* (1974 facsimile, Newcastle: Frank Graham)

Hostetter E. and Howe, T. N. 1997 *The Romano-British Villa at Castle Copse, Great Bedwyn* (Bloomington: Indiana University Press)

Hunter, F. 1999 *Fieldwork at Birnie, Moray, 1998* (National Museum of Scotland – http:/repository.nms. ac.uk/33)

Hunter, F. 2002 'Birnie', *Britannia* XXXIII, 284

Hunter, F. 2010 'Beyond the frontier: interpreting late Roman Iron Age indigenous and imported material culture' in R. Collins and L. Allason-Jones (eds) *Finds from the Frontier: Material Culture in the 4th and 5th centuries* (CBA Research Project), 96–109

Huvelin, H. 1985 'Classement et chronologie du monnayage d'or de Carausius', *Revue Numismatique,* Series VI, Vol. XXVII, 107–19

Ireland, S. 1996 *Roman Britain – A Sourcebook* (London: Routledge)

Jackson, R. P. J and Potter, T. W. 1996 *Excavations at Stonea* (London: British Museum Press)

Janes, D. 2002 *Romans and Christians* (Stroud and Charleston, SC: Tempus)

Johns, C. M. 2010 *The Hoxne Late Roman Treasure* (London: British Museum Press)

Johnson, A. 1983 *Roman Forts of the 1st and 2nd Centuries AD in Britain and the German Provinces* (London: A & C Black)

Johnson, S. 1989 *Hadrian's Wall* (London: Batsford/English Heritage)

Johnson, S. 1976 *The Roman Forts of the Saxon Shore* (London: Elek and New York: St Martin's Press)

Jones, A. H. M. 1948 *Constantine and the Conversion of Europe* (London: Hodder & Stoughton)

Jones, B. and Mattingly, D. 1990 *An Atlas of Roman Britain* (Oxford and Cambridge, MA: Basil Blackwell)

Jones, M. 2002 *Roman Lincoln: Conquest, Colony and Capital* (Stroud and Charleston SC: Tempus)

Joy, J. forthcoming *The Snettisham Treasure* (London: British Museum Press)

Kenrick, P. 2009 *Tripolitania* (London: Society for Libyan Studies)

Keppie, L. 1979 *Roman Distance Slabs from the Antonine Wall: A Brief Guide* (Glasgow: Hunterian Museum)

King, A. (drawings by S. Crummy) 1996 'The south-east façade of Meonstoke aisled building', in P. Johnson and I. Haynes (eds), *Architecture in Roman Britain* (CBA Research Report 94), 56–69

Knight, J. K. 2003 *Caerleon Legionary Fortress* (CADW: Welsh Historic Monuments)

Laycock, S. 2008 *Britannia, The Failed State: Ethnic Conflict and the End of Roman Britain* (Stroud: The History Press)

Leahy, K. 2007 'Soldiers and settlers in Britain, fourth to fifth century – revisited', in M. Henig and T. J. Smith (eds), *Collectanea Antiqua: Essays in Memory of Sonia Chadwick Hawkes* (British Archaeological Report, International Series, 1673, Oxford)

Levick, B. 1990 *Claudius* (New Haven: Yale University Press)

Levick, B. 1999 *Vespasian* (London and New York: Routledge)

Lieu S. N. C. and Montserrat, D. (eds) 1996 *From Constantine to Julian* (London and New York: Routledge)

Littlecote Roman Villa – Illustrated Guide (RRM, 1994)

Liversidge, J. 1968 *Britain in the Roman Empire* (London: Routledge & Kegan Paul and New York: Praeger)

Macdonald, W. and Pinto, J. 1995 *Hadrian's Villa and its Legacy* (New Haven: Yale University Press)

Manley, J. and Rudkin, D. 2003 *Facing the Palace* (Sussex Archaeological Society 141)

Mattingly, D. 2006 *An Imperial Possession – Britain in the Roman Empire 54 BC – AD 409* (London and New York: Allen Lane)

Mattingly, H. and Handford, S. 1970 *Tacitus, The Agricola and The Germania* (Harmondsworth: Penguin)

Meates, G. W. 1979 & 1987 *The Lullingstone Roman Villa*, Vols I & II (Maidstone: Kent Archaeological Society)

McCarthy, M. 2002 *Roman Carlisle and the Lands of the Solway* (Stroud and Charleston SC: Tempus)

Miller, M. 1975 'Stilicho's Pictish war', *Britannia* VI, 141–45

Millett, M. 1990 *The Romanization of Britain* (Cambridge and New York: Cambridge University Press)

Milne, G. 1995 *Roman London: Urban Archaeology in the Nation's Capital* (London: Batsford, London

Moffat, A. 1999 *Arthur and the Lost Kingdoms* (London: Weidenfeld & Nicolson)

Moorhead, S. 2001 'Roman coin finds from Wiltshire', in P. Ellis (ed.), *Roman Wiltshire and After* (Devizes: Archaeological and Natural History Society)

Moorhead, S. 2005 'The Hinton St Mary head of Christ and a coin of Magnentius', in N. Crummy (ed.), *Image, Craft and the Classical World – Monographies Instrumentum* 29 (Montagnac)

Moorhead, S. 2009a, 'Three Roman coin hoards from Wiltshire terminating in coins of Probus (AD 276–82)', *Wiltshire Archaeological and Natural History Magazine* 102, 150–59

Moorhead, S. 2009b 'Early Byzantine copper coins found in Britain – A review in light of new finds recorded with the Portable Antiquities Scheme', in Okuz Tekin, *Ancient History, Numismatics and Epigraphy in the Mediterranean World* (Istanbul: Ege), 263–74

Moorhead, S., Booth, A. and Bland, R. 2010 *The Frome Hoard* (London: British Museum Press)

Moorhead S. and Stuttard, D. 2010 *AD 410 – The Year that Shook Rome* (London: British Museum Press and Los Angeles: Getty)

Morris, J. 1973 *The Age of Arthur, Vol. 1: Roman Britain and the Empire of Arthur* (London: Weidenfeld & Nicolson and New York: Scribner)

Mothersole, J. 1927 *Agricola's Road into Scotland* (London: John Lane)

Nash-Williams, V. E. 1950 *The Early Christian Monuments of Wales* (Cardiff: University of Wales)

Niblett, R. 1985 *Roman Hertfordshire* (Wimborne: Dovecote Press)

Niblett, R. 2001 *Verulamium: The Roman City of St Albans* (Stroud: Tempus)

Nixon, C. E. V. and Rodgers, K. B. S. 1994 *In Praise of Later Emperors: The Panegyrici Latini* (Berkeley: University of California Press)

Odahl, C. M. 2004 *Constantine and the Christian Empire* (Routledge, London)

Ogilvie, R. M. and Richmond, I. 1967 *Cornelii Taciti, De Vita Agricolae* (Clarendon Press, Oxford)

Opper, T. 2008 *Hadrian, Empire and Conflict* (London: British Museum Press and Cambridge MA: Harvard University Press)

Ordnance Survey 2009 – OS Explorer Map (1:125000) – Hadrian's Wall

Ottaway, P. 1993 *Roman York* (London: Batsford/English Heritage)

Painter, K. 1977a *The Water Newton Early Christian Silver* (London: British Museum Press)

Painter, K. 1977b *The Mildenhall Treasure: Roman Silver from East Anglia* (London: British Museum Press)

Painter, K. 1999 'The Water Newton silver: votive or liturgical?', *Journal of the British Archaeological Association* 152, 1–23

Parfitt, K. 1995 (ed.), *Iron Age Burials from Mill Hill Deal* (London: British Museum Press)

Parfitt, K. 2011 'Was the Mill Hill Warrior a Druid?', *Kent Archaeological Review*183 (Spring 2011), 68–70

Partridge, C. 1979 'Excavations at Puckeridge and Braughing 1975–9', *Hertfordshire Archaeology* VII, 28–132

Partridge, C. 1981 *Skeleton Green: A Late Iron Age and Romano-British Site* (London: Britannia Monograph 2)

Pearce, J. W. E. 1942 'Siliquae from a find at Mildenhall, Suffolk', *Numismatic Chronicle* 6th Series, Vol. 2, 105–6

Pearce, S. 2008 'The Hinton St Mary mosaic pavement: Christ or emperor', *Britannia* XXXIX, 193–218

Pearson, A. 2002 *The Roman Shore Forts: Coastal Defences of Southern Britain* (Stroud and Charleston SC: Tempus)

Pearson, A. 2006 'Piracy in late Roman Britain: a perspective from the Viking Age', *Britannia* XXXVII, 337–54

Peddie, J. 1987 *Invasion, The Roman Invasion of Britain in the Year AD 43* (Gloucester: Sutton)

Perring, D. 1991 *Roman London* (London: Seaby)

Piggott, S. 1985 *The Druids* (London and New York: Thames & Hudson)

Pitts, L. F. and St. Joseph, J. K. 1985 *Inchtuthil, The Roman Legionary Fortress 1952–65* (Britannia Monograph No. 6, Society for the Promotion of Roman Studies, London)

Pohlsander, H. A. 1996 *The Emperor Constantine* (London and New York: Routledge)

Potter, T. W. 1977 'The Biglands milefortlet, Cumberland', *Britannia* VIII, 149–84

Potter, T. W. and Johns, C. M. 1992 *Roman Britain* (London: British Museum Press and Berkeley CA: University of California Press)

Rahtz, P., Woodward, A. and Burrow, I. 1992 *Cadbury Congresbury 1968–73: A Late/Post-Roman Hilltop Settlement in Somerset* (BAR, British Series 223, Oxford)

Rance, P. 2001 'Attacotti, Déisi and Magnus Maximus: the case for Irish federates in late Roman Britain', *Britannia* XXXII, 243–70

Reece, R. 1988 *My Roman Britain*, Cotswold Studies, Vol. 3 (Cirencester)

Reece, R. 1991 *Roman Coins from 140 Sites in Britain*, Cotswold Studies, Vol. IV (Cirencester)

Reece, R. 1999 *The Later Roman Empire: An Archaeology AD 150–600* (Stroud and Charleston SC: Tempus)

Ridd, S. 1993 *Julius Caesar in Gaul and Britain* (Oxford: Heinemann and Austin TX: Raintree Steck-Vaughan)

Rivet, A. L. F. and Smith, C. 1979 *The Place-Names of Roman Britain* (London: Batsford and Princeton NJ: Princeton University Press)

Robinson B. and Gregory, T. 1987 *Celtic Fire and Roman Rule* (North Walsham: Poppyland Publishing)

Robertson, A. S. 2000 *An Inventory of Romano-British Coin Hoards*, R. Hobbs and T. V. Buttrey, eds (Royal Numismatic Society Special Publication 20)

Ross, A. and Robins, D. 1991 *The Life and Death of a Druid Prince: The Story of Lindow Man* (London: Rider and New York: Summit Books)

Russell, M. and Laycock, S. 2010 *UnRoman Britain: Exposing the Great Myth of Britannia* (Stroud: History Press)

Salway, P. 1981 *Roman Britain* (Oxford: Oxford University Press)

Salway, P. 1993 *The Oxford Illustrated History of Roman Britain* (Oxford and New York: Oxford University Press)

Sauer, E. 2002 'Alchester and the earliest tree-ring dates from Roman Britain', *The Bulletin of the Association for Roman Archaeology* (August 2002), 3–5

Scarre, C. 1995 *Chronicle of the Roman Emperors* (London and New York: Thames & Hudson)

Seager, R. 1997 'Ammianus, Theodosius and Sallust's *Jugurtha*' (www.dur.ac.uk/Classics/histos/1997/seager.html)

Sharples, N. M. 1991 *Maiden Castle* (London: Batsford/English Heritage)

Shepherd, J. 1998 *The Temple of Mithras, London: Excavations by W. F. Grimes and A. Williams at the Walbrook* (London: English Heritage)

Shiel, N. 1977a *The Episode of Carausius and Allectus* (British Archaeological Report 40)

Shiel, N. 1977b 'Carausian and Allectan coin evidence from the Northern Frontier', *Archaeologia Aeliana* 5th Series, 75–79

Shirley, E. A. M. 1996 'The building of the legionary fortress at Inchtuthil', *Britannia* XXVII, 111–28

Shirley, E. 2001 *Building a Roman Legionary Fortress* (Stroud: Tempus)

Shotter, D. 1973 '*Numeri Barcariorum*: A note on *RIB* 691', *Britannia* IV, 206–9

Shotter, D. 2000 'Petillius Cerealis in Northern Britain', *Northern History*, XXXVI, 189–98

Shotter, D. 2002, 'Roman Britain and the "Year of the Four Emperors"', *Transactions of the Cumberland and Westmorland Antiquarian and Archaeological Society* 3(2), 79–86

Shotter, D. 2004 'Vespasian, *Auctoritas* and Britain', *Britannia* XXXV, 1–8

Sills, J. 1996 'The summer of 54 BC', *Spink Numismatic Circular* 104 (September 1996), 334–35

Snyder, C. A. 1998 *An Age of Tyrants: Britain and the Britons AD 400–600* (Pennsylvania State University Press)

Soffe, G. and Henig, M. 2002 'New light on the Roman villa at Thruxton', *The Bulletin for the Association of Roman Archaeology* 13, 6–13

Southern, P. 2001 *Julius Caesar* (Stroud: Tempus)

Speller, E. 2002 *Following Hadrian: A Second-Century Journey through the Roman Empire* (London: Review)

Stead, I. M. 1967 'A la Tène III burial at Welwyn Garden City', *Archaeologia* 101, 1–62.

Stead, I. M. 1995 'The metalwork', in K. Parfitt (ed.), *Iron Age Burials from Mill Hill Deal* (London: British Museum Press), 58–111

Stuttard, D. A. and Moorhead, S. forthcoming 2012 *Antony, Cleopatra and the Year that Shook Egypt* (London: British Museum Press)

Swift, E. 2000 *The End of the Western Roman Empire: An Archaeological Investigation* (Stroud: Tempus)

Taylor, J. 2007 *An Atlas of Roman Rural Settlement in England* (York: Council for British Archaeology Research Report)

Thompson, E. A. 1990 'Ammianus Marcellinus and Britain', *Nottingham Mediaeval Studies* 34, 1–15

Thorpe, C. 2007 *The Earthwork at Restormel Farm, Lostwithiel, Cornwall* (Report no. 2007R031, Historic Environment Service, Cornwall County Council, February 2007)

Tomlin, R. S. O. 1988 *Tabellae Sulis, Roman Inscribed Tablets of Tin and Lead from the Sacred Spring at Bath* (Oxford University Committee for Archaeology, Fascicule 1 of Monograph 16)

Tomlin, R. S. O. 1997 'Reading a 1st century Roman gold signet ring from Fishbourne', *Sussex Archaeological Collections* 135, 127–30

Tomlin R.S.O. & Hassall M.W.C., 2004 'Roman Britain in 2003 inscriptions', *Britannia* XXXV, 344–45

Toynbee, J. M. C. 1962, *Art in Roman Britain* (Phaidon/Society for the Promotion of Roman Studies)

Turner, R. and Scaife, R. 1995 (eds), *Bog Bodies, New Discoveries and New Perspectives* (London: British Museum Press)

van Arsdell, R. D. 1989 *Celtic Coinage of Britain* (London: Spink)

Wacher, J. 1978 *Roman Britain* (London: Dent)

Wacher, J. 1979 *The Coming of Rome* (London: Routledge and Kegan Paul)

Wacher, J. 1989 'Cities from the second to fourth centuries', in M. Todd (ed.), *Research on Roman Britain, 1960–89* (Britannia Monograph Series No. 11), 91–144

Wacher, J. 1995 *The Towns of Roman Britain* (2nd edn, London: Batsford)

Walker, D. R. 1988 'Roman coins from the sacred spring at Bath', in B. Cunliffe (ed.), *The Temple of Sulis Minerva at Bath, II: Finds from the Sacred Spring* (Oxford University Committee for Archaeology), 281–358

Walters, B. and Henig, M. 1988 'Two Busts from Littlecote', *Britannia* 19, 407–10

Walton, P. forthcoming *Rethinking Roman Britain: An Applied Numismatic Analysis of the Roman Coin Data Recorded by the Portable Antiquities Scheme*

Warner, R. 1995 'Tuathal Techtmhar: a myth or ancient literary evidence for a Roman invasion?', *Emania* 13, 23–32.

Warner, R. 1996 'Yes, the Romans did invade Ireland', *British Archaeology* 14

Watts, D. 1991 *Christians and Pagans in Roman Britain* (London and New York: Routledge)

Webster, G. 1983 'The possible effects on Britain of the fall of Magnentius', in B. Hartley and J. Wacher (eds), *Rome and her Northern Provinces* (Gloucestershire: Alan Sutton), 240–54

Webster, G. 1986 *The British Celts and their Gods under Rome* (London: Batsford, London)

Webster, G. 1993a *The Roman Invasion of Britain* (rev. edn, London: Batsford)

Webster, G. 1993b *Rome against Caratacus: The Roman Campaigns in Britain AD 48–58* (London: Batsford and Totowa NJ: Barnes & Noble)

Webster, G. 1993c *Boudica: The British Revolt against Rome* (London: Batsford)

Wedlake, W. J. 1982 *The Excavation of the Shrine at Nettleton, Wiltshire, 1956–71* (London: Society of Antiquaries)

Wheeler, R.E.M. 1943 *Maiden Castle, Dorset: Report of the Research Committee of the Society of Antiquaries of London XII* (Oxford: Oxford University Press)

Wheeler, R. E. M. and Wheeler, V. T. 1932 *Report on the Excavation of the Prehistoric, Roman and Post-Roman Site in Lydney Park, Gloucestershire* (London: Society of Antiquaries)

Wheeler, R. E. M. and Wheeler, V. T. 1936 *Verulamium, A Belgic and Two Roman Cities: Research Report of the Society of Antiquaries London XI* (Oxford: Oxford University Press)

White, R. 2007 *Britannia Prima – Britain's Lost Roman Province* (Stroud: Tempus)

White, R. and Barker, P. 1998 *Wroxeter: Life and Death of a Roman City* (Stroud: Tempus)

Williams, T. 1989 'Allectus's building campaign in London: Implications for the Saxon Shore', in V. A. Maxfield and M. J. Dobson (eds), *Roman Frontier Studies 1989: Proceedings of the XVth International Congress of Roman Frontier Studies* (Exeter: University of Exeter Press, 1991)

Williams, T. 1993 *The Archaeology of Roman London Vol. 3: Public Buildings in the South-West Quarter of Roman London* (London: Museum of London)

Wilmott, T. 2001 *Birdoswald Roman Fort* (Stroud: Tempus)

Wilmott, T. 2008 *The Amphitheatre in Britain* (Stroud: Tempus)

Wilson, R. J. A. 2002 *A Guide to the Roman Remains in Britain* (4th edn, London: Constable)

Wood, I. 2006 'The Crocus Conundrum' in E. Hartley *et al.* 2006, 77–84

Worrell, S. 2004 'Roman Britain in 2003', *Britannia* XXXV, 326

Worrell, S. 2008 'Finds reported under the Portable Antiquities Scheme', *Britannia* XXXIX, 337–67

Acknowledgments

Roman Britain relied for its existence on a mighty team of experts drawn from many walks of life. So does this book, and we are most grateful to the legion of colleagues and friends, whose input into its production has been invaluable.

Many expert scholars contributed wide-ranging knowledge. We are most grateful to Richard Abdy and Ralph Jackson for reading drafts of the text and making such perceptive comments, and to David Shotter, Nick Hodgson, Simon Esmonde Cleary, Richard Hobbs, Anna Tyacke and Ian Leins for their help with various elements of research. Past collaborations with particular colleagues have also had an impact on the tenor of this work, notably John Witherington and Tom King at Ardingly College, Paul Robinson at the Wiltshire Heritage Museum, Catherine Johns and the late Tim Potter at the British Museum, and Leon Geyskens in Antwerp. The Portable Antiquities Scheme has provided much new material, and we are grateful for valuable assistance received from Roger Bland, Philippa Walton, Dan Pett, Sally Worrell, as well as from all other Finds Advisers and Finds Liaison Officers nationally.

Numerous people and organizations have been generous in helping with the provision of images, although sadly not all pictures made it into the final version of the book. We would like to thank Frances McIntosh, Becky Morris, Rob Collins, Laura McLean and Ciorstaidh Hayward Trevarthen of the Portable Antiquities Scheme, Robert Symmons at Fishbourne Palace, Claire Pinder at Dorset County Council, Stephen Clews at Bath & North East Somerset Heritage Services, Jane Laskey at Senhouse Museum (Maryport), Andrew Birley and Adam Stanford at the Vindolanda Trust, James Gerrard at Newcastle University, Vincent Drost at the Bibiothèque nationale de France, Fraser Hunter at the National Museum of Scotland, Steve Minnitt at the Somerset County Museums Service, Bryn Walters and Luigi Thompson of the Association for Roman Archaeology, Juliana Engstrom, a volunteer at the British Museum, and Cathal Galllagher. In addition, we would like to thank all the photographers at the British Museum, Kristin Wenger and Vanessa Minet in the British Museum Company and Richard Kelleher, who designed such excellent maps from complicated originals.

At Thames & Hudson, we are indebted to Colin Ridler, Alice Reid, Sarah Vernon-Hunt and Celia Falconer for their belief in the book and their support and encouragement in seeing it through to publication; to our editor Carolyn Jones, for her grace, wit and wisdom, which made the process both rigorous and enjoyable, and to Karolina Prymaka, for her crisp, clean layout which has contributed so much to the book's appearance. Like Roman captains, navigating their galleys across the stormy English Channel, they have all helped steer our ship unflinchingly on course, cutting their unswerving furrows through the lashing seas of authorial temperament.

As always, we have received unstinting support from our wives, Fiona and EJ. It is thanks mainly to their patience and forbearance that this volume has been able to be written. Without the support and inspiration of our parents in our early years, however, neither of us would have been in a position to write this story in the first place. We dedicate this book to them.

Sam Moorhead and David Stuttard

ILLUSTRATION SOURCES

Maps by Richard Kelleher

p. 1 © The Trustees of the British Museum, London (CM 1977,0903.1)

p. 2 Kunsthistorisches Museum, Vienna

Fig. 2 Vatican Museum, Rome

Fig. 5 Museo Turlonia, Rome

Fig. 6 Capitoline Museum, Rome. Photo © Sam Moorhead

Fig. 8 © The Trustees of the British Museum, London (PE 1852,0806.2)

Fig. 9 © The Trustees of the British Museum, London (GR 1850,0304.35)

Fig. 10 Landesmuseum, Trier

Fig. 12 © The Trustees of the British Museum, London (CM 1935,0404.56; RIC 577)

Fig. 15 © David Stuttard

Fig. 16 National Museum of Scotland, Edinburgh

Fig. 18 © The Portable Antiquities Scheme (PAS ESS-5A2744)

Fig. 19 © Sam Moorhead

Fig. 22 © The Trustees of the British Museum, London (PE 1879,0710.1)

Fig. 23 © The Portable Antiquities Scheme (LEIC-BBD167; RIC 55)

Fig. 24 © Yorkshire Museum Trust

Fig. 25 © The Portable Antiquities Scheme (PAS WILT-D86FB6)

Fig. 26 © Bibliothèque nationale de France, Paris (RIC 338)

Fig. 27 © Musée du Louvre, Paris

Fig. 28 Museum of Somerset, Taunton; photo © Portable Antiquities Scheme (SOM-E6C541)

Fig. 29 © The Trustees of the British Museum, London (CM R 0277)

Fig. 30 © The Trustees of the British Museum, London (CM 1856,1205.58)

Fig. 31 Vatican Museum, Rome

Colour Plates

1 © Richard Abdy

2 © The Trustees of the British Museum, London

3 © The Trustees of the British Museum, London (BMC 724)

4 © The Portable Antiquities Scheme (IOW-D8AA20; ABC 1052)

5 © The Trustees of the British Museum, London (BMC 766)

6 © The Portable Antiquities Scheme (KENT-FF2BC7; RRC 443)

7 © The Trustees of the British Museum, London (BMC 1801)

8 © The Portable Antiquities Scheme (IOW-9CD254; ABC 1193)

9 © The Trustees of the British Museum, London (GR 1911,0901.1)

10 © The Trustees of the British Museum, London (CM 1957,0101.1-34)

11 © The Trustees of the British Museum, London (BMC 32)

12 © The Trustees of the British Museum, London (PE 1951,0402.2)

13 © The Trustees of the British Museum, London (PE 1962,0707.1ff)

14 © The Trustees of the British Museum, London (PE 1965,1201.1)

15 © The Trustees of the British Museum, London (PE 1814,0705.1)

16 © Adam Stanford for the Vindolanda Trust

17 © The Trustees of the British Museum, London (PE 1848,1103.1)

18 © Luigi J. Thompson

19 © The Portable Antiquities Scheme (SF-5A1BE1; RIC 545)

20 © Roger Clegg

21 © The Trustees of the British Museum, London (PE 2005,1204.1; PAS: WMID-3FE965)

22 © The Trustees of the British Museum, London (BMC Sculpture 1463)

23 © The Trustees of the British Museum, London (BMC Sculpture 1916)

24 © The Trustees of the British Museum, London (BMC 379)

25 © The Trustees of the British Museum, London (BMC 204)

26 © The Trustees of the British Museum, London (BMC 103)

27 © The Trustees of the British Museum, London (BMC Sculpture 1917)

28 © David Stuttard

29 © Sam Moorhead

30 Museum of Somerset, Taunton; photo © The Portable Antiquities Scheme

31 Derby Museum and Art Gallery; photo © The Portable Antiquities Scheme (DENO-64DAE1; RIC 624)

32 Museum of Somerset, Taunton; photo © The Portable Antiquities Scheme (RIC 555)

33 Museum of Somerset, Taunton; photo © The Portable Antiquities Scheme (RIC 536)

34 © The Trustees of the British Museum, London (CM B 11477; cf. RIC 34)

35 © The Trustees of the British Museum, London (PE 1946,1007.1)

36 © Somerset County Museums Service

37 © Bryn Walters

38 © The Trustees of the British Museum, London (PE 1975,1002.1ff)

39 © The Trustees of the British Museum, London (PE 1965,0409.1)

40 © The Trustees of the British Museum, London (CM 1951,1115.2713; RIC 34)

41 © The Trustees of the British Museum, London (PE 1967,0407.1.b)

42 © The Trustees of the British Museum, London (PE 1994,0408.33)

Index

Page numbers in *italics* refer to illustrations and captions

Adminius (British prince) 41, 59
Aelia Capitolina 133
Aeneas (mythological character) *219*
Aetius (general) 239, 249–50
Africa (province) 15, 83, 117, 124, 145–46, 149, 152, 164, 199, 228
Agri Decumates 170
Agricola (Pelagian heretic) 244, 246
Agricola, Gaius (governor) 7, 88, 94, 96–99, 101–4, 113–14, 116–17, 119, 127, 130
Agricola, Sextus Calpurnius (governor) 142, 146
Aidan (saint) 248
Alamanni (tribe) 170, 174, 185, 190, 206, 208, 228
Alans (tribe) 230, 236
Alaric (Gothic leader) 235
Alban (British saint) 247
Aldborough 93, 130
Alesia 36
Alexander the Great 22
Algeria 129
Allectus (chancellor and usurper) 7, *156*, 173, 179–81, 184
Alps, 37, 74, 172, 202–3, 232
Ambianum 202
Ambrose (Bishop of Milan) 232
Ambrosius Aurelianus (British general) 250
Amiens 175, 202
Ammianus Marcellinus (historian) 200, 208–9
Anglesey 74–75, 99, 173
Antinous (exotic youth and deity) *108–9*, 131, 132–33
Antioch 61, 150, 169, 186
Antonine Wall 139–41, 143
Antoninus Pius (emperor) *110, 112*, 125, 135, 137–40, *141*, 143
Antony (legionary legate) 36–37
Aphrodisias 49, 61, 124
Apollodorus (architect) 123, 127
Aquileia 199, 232
Arbeia 162
Arles *222*, 231, 237
Armenia 74 91, 132, 142
Arras Medallion *159–60*
Arthur (legendary king) 250
Asclepiodotus (praetorian prefect) 180–81
Asia (province) 15, 67, 96, 117, 137, 150
Athens 132, 147, 207, 210

Atlas Mountains 73–74
Atrebates (tribe) 14, 36, 42, 46, 66, 101
Attacotti (tribe) 209, 212–13, 233
Augustus (emperor) 7, 37–38, 40, 44, *52–53*, 84, 122, 177–178
Augustus (title) 151–52, 166, 177–78, 182–83, 189, 191–93, 197, 209, 211, 213–14, 228–31, 237
Aulus Didius Gallus (governor) 67–68
Aulus Platorius Nepos (governor) 124–25, 129, 133
Aulus Plautius (governor) 44–48, 57–61, 65, 91, 101
Autun 202
Auxerre 244

Bacchus (god) *108–9*, 132, 195, 210
bagaudae 174, 214
Baiae 133
Balkans 37, 170
Bannaven Taburniae 248
Bantham Beach 242
Bar Kokhba (Jewish rebel leader) 133, 142
Barnsley Park 205
Bath 125–26, 243, 251
Bewcastle 200
Bigbury Wood 30–31
Birdoswald 184, 241
Birnie 163
Birrens 141, 200
Bithynia 17
Bitterne 177, 226
Black Mountains 74
Bolanus (governor) 91–96
Bollihope Common 131
Bologna 238
Bosphorus 205
Boudica (British queen) 10, 72–73, 75–76, 77, 78–82, 94, 99, 101, 105, 118, 235
Boulogne 44, 57, 173, 175, 179–80, 182–83, 185, 187, 198, 201, 209–10, 213, 237
Bradwell 173
Brancaster 173
Brecon Beacons 74
Bredgar hoard 45, *54*
Brigantes (tribe) 59–60, 62, 66, 68–69, 92–96, 101, 119, 138–40, 225
Britannia (personification of province) 10, *49*, 61, *124*, 125, 140, *141, 154, 159–60*, 176, 235
Brocchus, Aelius (fort commander) 119
Brough-on-Humber 130
Brough-on-Noe 141

Bruttium 238
Burgh Castle 173
Burgundians (tribe) 171, 236

Cadbury Congresbury 241
Caelius, Roscius (legionary commander and rebel) 90, 97
Caer Gybi 173
Caerleon 96, 117, 146
Caerwent 130, 240
Caesar (title) 149, 151–52, 179, 183–85, 187, 189, 191–92, 195, 206
Caesar, Julius (general and author) 7, 10, 12–17, *17*, 18–28, *28*, 29–40, 46, 52, 59, 61, *85*, 193, 237, 248
Caesaromagus 58, 70, 86
Caistor-by-Norwich 86
Caledonii (tribe) 10, 103–4, 113–17, 135, 139–40, 143–44, 162, 164, 166–67, 187, 194
Calgacus (Caledonian leader) 10, 104, 127, 165
Caligula, Gaius (emperor) 40–44
Camulodunum 39–40, 52, 58–59, 63–66, 68–71, 76–78, 81, 86, 177
Canterbury 46, 66, 69, 197
Cantii (tribe) 34, 45
Caracalla (emperor) 125, 144, 147, 151–52, *154–55*, 161, 163, 165–67, 169
Caratacus (British leader) 10, 42, 44–45, 47, 62–63, 66–67, 73, 82
Carausius (usurper emperor) 7, 125, *159*, 168, 173–80, 184
Cardiff 173
Carinus (emperor) 172
Carmarthen 130
Carpow 148, 187
Carrawburgh 194
Carthage 15, 228
Cartimandua (British queen) 10, 59, 62, 66, 68, 92–93, 95, 101
Cassivellaunus (British king) 30, 32–34
Catuvellauni (tribe) 30, 41–42, 46–48, 57, 73, 79, 225
Cerealis Petilius (general and governor) 77, 94–97
Cerealis, Flavius (prefect) 102, 118–19
Ceres 195
Chalcedon 205
Chamavi (tribe) 206
Chedworth 172, 195
Chelmsford 58, 70, 86
Chester 96, 99, 117, 173
Chesters 162, 225
Christ 6, 192–93, 195, 203, 243–44, 246
Cicero (politician, orator and writer) 18, 35

Cirencester 251
Civilis (governor) 214
Classicianus, Julius (procurator) 84–85, *85*
Claudia Severa (prefect's wife) 119
Claudian (poet) 10, 229, 235
Claudius (emperor) 6–7, 39, 42, 44, 48, 49, *54–56*, 57–63, 65–66, 68, 70–72, 76, 91–92, 101, 119, 124, 137, 162
Cleopatra (Egyptian queen) 82
Clodius Albinus (governor and usurper emperor) 149–51, *154*, 162
Clyro 69
Coddenham 84
Colchester 6, 40, 46, 55, 58, 78, 85, 177, 197
Coleraine hoard 242, *242*
Columella (writer) 89–90, 98
Commius (British king) 14, 23, 25, 27, 34, 36, 38, *50*
Commodus (emperor) 125, 146, 148–49, 151, 162
Constans (emperor) 199–202, 210, 231, 237
Constantine (emperor) 7, 182–83, 185–88, *188*, 189–97, 199–200, 202, *203*, 210
Constantine II (emperor) 199
Constantine III (usurping emperor) 9, 212, 237–38, 241, *242*, 243, 250
Constantinople 197, 205
Constantius Chlorus (emperor) *159–60*, 179–85, 187, 189–91, 195
Constantius II (emperor) 199, 202–6, 209, 211
Corbridge 142, 146, 162, 216, 225
Corbulo (general) 74, 83, 91
Corinth 15
Cornovii (tribe) 57
Council of Arles 197
Coventry 83
Cramond 148, 187
Crassus (plutocrat and general) 18, 20
Crimea 67
Crocus (Alamannic king) 185, 190
Cunetio 227
Cunobelin (British king) 41–42, 45, 52, 58–59, 249
Cyzicus 61

Dacia Ripensis *188*
Dacia 129, 136, 142, 170
Decianus Catus (procurator) 72, 76, 78, 84
Dere Street 102, 162, 216
Dicalydones (tribe) 213
Dido (mythological character) *219*

Dinas Powys 242
Dio Cassius (historian) 10, 45–48, 59, 63, 75–76, 80, 82–83, 133, 150, 163
Diocletian (emperor) 173–74, 178–79, 183, 185–87, 189
Dionysus 132, 195, 210, *217*, *219*
Dobunni (tribe) 47, 59
Domitian (emperor) 99, *108–9*, 116–17
Dour Estuary 178
Dover 14, 23, 46, 129, *157*, 173, 178
Dulcitius (general) 214–15
Dumbarton Rock 242
Dura Europos 147
Durotriges (tribe) 73, 79, 225
Dyrham (battle) 251

Eburacum 187
Edict of Toleration 193
Egypt 132, 152, 186
Eleusis 132
Elne 202
Emesa 147
English Channel 13–14, 20–22, 26, 29, 36–37, 40, 44, 57, 83, 91, 98–99, 102, 151, 171, 173, 175, 180, 198–99, 208–11, 213, 228, 237, 244–45, *245*, 248
Ephesus 68, 130, 210
Erdek 61
Eutherios (eunuch chamberlain) 210
Eutropius (historian) 61–62
Exeter 65, 69, 79, 91, 225

Fens 78, 86, 129, 196, 243
Fishbourne 46, 100
Foclut 248
Fosse Way 65, 69
Franks (tribe) 170, 173–74, 206, 213–14
Fraomarius (Alamannic king) 230
Frilford 211
Frisians (tribe) 173
Frome hoard 6, *158–59*, 177
Frontinus (governor) 96, 98–99
Frugi, Marcus Crassus (general) 60

Gadebridge Villa 205
Galahad (legendary knight) 250
Galerius (emperor) 185–88, 190, 192
Gallia Lugdunensis 147
Gamzigrad *188*
Gaul (Cisalpine) 18–20
Gaul (Comata) 18
Gaul (Transalpine) 18, 22
Germanus (bishop) 9, 233, 243–49

Gesoriacum 57
Geta (emperor) 144, 147, 152, *154*, 163, 166–67, 169
Geta, Gnaeus Hosidius (general) 47–48
Gildas (writer) 234, 236, 240, 249–50
Gloucester 65, 90
Gosbecks 70
Goths (tribe) 170, 229
Gratian (emperor) 228, 230–33
Gratian (governor) 201, 211
Gratian (usurper emperor) 236
Great Casterton 69
Great Persecution 186
Great Walsingham 211
Guinevere (legendary queen) 250

Hadrian (emperor) 7, *108*, 119–34, 136, 138, 161, 164
Hadrian's Wall 7, 93, *105–107*, *110–11*, 127–30, 136–40, *128*, 142–43, 146, 162, 167, 172, 184–85, 194–95, 200, 216, 225, 234, 241, 248
Hadrianople 228, 230
Halton Chesters 162, 225
Hatra 152
Hawkedon 78
Helena (mother of Constantine) 183, 185
Helena (town) 202
Helvetii (tribe) 19
Hengist (Saxon warlord) 249
Hercules (god) 210, *217*, *219*
Hermes (god) 132
Herodian (historian) 16, 164–65
High Rochester 200
Hinton St Mary 195, 203, 205, 222
Hockwold hoard 55, 78
Hockwold-cum-Wilton 78
Holyhead 173, 226
Honorius (emperor) 234, 238, 244
Horsa (Saxon warlord) 249
Housesteads *110–11*, 178, 146, 216, 225
Hoxne hoard 223–24, 242
Hythe 46

Iamcilla (Christian plaque dedicatrix) 243
Iceni (tribe) 10, 55, 59, 66, 71–73, 84, 86, 119
Ilchester 225
Iona 248
Isle of Wight 50, 52, 65, 91, 180
Isurium Brigantum 130
Italica 121
Ixworth 84

Jerome (writer) 215
Jerusalem 133
Jordanes (writer) 215
Jovinus, Flavius (general) 213
Julia (Julius Caesar's daughter) 18, 31
Julia Domna (empress) 147, 154,
    162–63, 167
Julian (emperor) 8, 205–11, 212,
    227, 237
Julianus (emperor) 149
Julius Bassianus (priest) 147
Julius Firmius Maternus (astrologer)
    200

Kelso 216
Kenchester 226
Kingsholm 65
Kinvaston 69

Lancaster 173
Lancelot (legendary knight) 250
Leicester 65, 69
Lepcis Magna 145
Libanius (sophist and writer)
    199, 207
Libya 132
Licinius (emperor) 193, 196–97
Lincoln 65, 69, 184, 197
Lindisfarne 248
Littlecote 108–9, 132, 211, 219
London 46, 64, 66, 69–70, 76–79,
    84–86, 95, 125, 130, 132, 148,
    159–60, 176–77, 180–81, 183–84,
    194, 197, 209, 213–14, 227, 229, 231
Longthorpe 69, 77
Low Ham mosaic 219
Lucca 20
Lullingstone 148, 149, 172, 197, 223
Lunt 83
Lupicinus (general) 208–10, 230
Lupus (bishop) 244, 247
Lupus (governor) 162
Lycia 68
Lydney 211, 226
Lympne 46, 173
Lyons 151, 162, 203, 231, 242

Maeatae (tribe) 144, 162, 166
Maenius (procurator) 130
Magnentius (emperor) 8, 202–6,
    222, 231
Magnus Maximus (usurper emperor)
    229–33
Maiden Castle 65
Marcus (usurper emperor) 236
Marcus Aurelius (emperor) 136,
    142, 145–46

Marius (general and dictator) 15–18,
    151, 193, 226
Marseilles 18, 57
Martin (prefect) 204
Maryport 130, 173, 216, 226
Massilia 57
Mauretania 73, 80, 228
Maximian (emperor) 173–75, 178–79,
    183, 185, 187, 192
Menai Straits 72, 99
Menapia 174
Meonstoke 206
Merlin (legendary sorcerer) 250
Mesopotamia 151, 152, 209, 211, 225
Messalina (empress) 60
Milan 170, 178, 193, 232
Mildenhall Treasure 210, 217, 219
Mildenhall 210, 230
Milvian Bridge (battle) 192, 194
Mithras (god) 194
Moesia 136, 142, 229
Mons Badonicus (battle) 250
Mons Graupius 10, 104, 117, 127, 165
Mons Seleucus (battle) 203
Moray Firth 104, 165
Moridunum Demetarum 130
Mursa (battle) 203
Mytilene 17

Narcissus (freed slave) 44
Narses (Persian king) 185–86
Nene valley 241
Nero (emperor) 55–56, 57, 68, 71–72,
    78, 83, 86–87, 98, 100, 177
Netherby 200
Nettleton 211
Newton-on-Trent 69
Nicomedes IV (Bithynian king) 17
Nicomedia 185–76
Nodens 211, 226

Ocean 20–22, 37, 41–42, 46, 59,
    60–62, 76, 91, 127, 178–79, 184,
    188, 194, 201, 231, 234–35, 238
Ordovices (tribe) 57, 67, 74, 98, 130
Orkneys 103
Orosius (historian) 231, 237
Orpheus (god) 219
Ostia 57, 194
Ostorius Scapula (governor)
    65–67, 71

Palmyra 147
Pamphylia 68
Pan (god) 132
Pannonia 44, 136, 147, 203
Pantarkes (poet) 131

Patrick (missionary) 9, 248
Paul Catena (imperial official) 204–7
Pelagius (heretic) 243–44
Pergamum 15
Pertinax (governor and emperor)
    146–49, 149, 150
Pescennius Niger (general and
    would-be emperor) 149
Petuaria Parisorum 130
Pevensey 156, 173, 180
Picts (tribe) 185, 187, 194, 200,
    208–10, 212–13, 225, 229–30, 234,
    236, 247, 249
Piercebridge 171, 224, 226
Plautianus (consul) 160–61
Plautilla (empress) 152, 163
Pliny the Elder (writer) 73, 94
Pliny the Younger (writer and
    politician) 145
Plotina (empress) 121
Poenius Postumus (legionary camp
    commandant) 79
Pollentia (battle) 235
Pompey (general) 16, 18, 20, 31,
    37, 152
Pontus 72
Portable Antiquities Scheme 6,
    163, 196
Portchester 173, 178, 180
Posides (eunuch freedman) 60
Prasutagus (British king) 10, 71–73,
    75, 78
Probus (emperor) 170–73
Provincia 18–19

Ravenglass 173
Reculver 173
Regini 42, 59, 66, 101
Restormel 69
Ribchester 105, 173
Richborough 45–46, 58, 119, 173,
    209, 213, 249
Risingham 200
River Danube 15, 136, 170, 183,
    186, 229, 236
River Drava 203
River Ger 73
River Kennet 227
River Maas 123
River Medway 47
River Moselle 29
River Nile 132, 152
River Ouse 130, 167, 188, 191
River Rhine 9, 21–22, 43, 90, 94,
    96, 104, 119, 123–24, 136, 170–71,
    173–74, 176, 183, 185, 190, 206–9,
    226, 231, 249
River Seine 180
River Stour 30

River Tay 102, 116, 148, 187
River Thames 33–34, 38, 48, 58, 66, 76, 85, 132, 180–81, 227
River Tyne 127–28, 130, 162, 225
River Yonne 248
Rockbourne 172
Rouen 173, 175, 177
Rudchester 162, 225
Rutupiae 45–46, 58

Sabina (empress) 124–26
Sabinus (general) 47
Sahara 122, 161
Sardinia 146
Sarmatians (tribe) 186
Saturnalia 44, 119
Saxons (tribe) 173, 212–14, 238, 247, 249–51
Seneca (writer and banker) 60, 71–72, 89
Septimius Severus (emperor) 7, 125, 144–47, 149–52, 153–54, 161–67, 169, 187–88
Septimius, Lucius (assassin of Pompey) 160
Septimius, Lucius (grandfather of emperor) 145
Severus, Flavius Valerius (Constantius Chlorus' Caesar) 187, 191–92
Severus, Julius (general) 136–37, 141–42
Seville 121
Shadwell 180
Shapur I (Persian king) 169–70, 185
Shapur II (Persian king) 209, 211
Shapwick 163
Sicily 147
Silchester 36, 66, 100–1, 119, 197
Silures (tribe) 67–68, 74, 96, 98, 130
Siricius (Bishop of Rome) 232
Sittingbourne 45, 54
Snettisham 55
Snowdonia 74
Solway Firth 128
South Cadbury 84, 241
South Shields 163, 167, 216, 225, 241
Staffordshire Moorlands Pan 110–11
Stanegate 117, 128
Stilicho (general) 234–37

Stonea 130
Suebi (tribe) 236
Suetonius (writer) 10, 60, 72, 87, 126
Suetonius Paullinus 64, 73–76, 78–84, 86, 89, 97, 99
Sulis (god) 126
Sulla (general and dictator) 16–18, 151
Sulpicia (prefect's wife) 119
Sulpicianus (would-be emperor) 149
Syria 121, 132, 137, 142, 146–47, 167, 169, 196, 203,

Tacitus (historian) 7, 10, 36, 62, 66, 70–72, 74, 76, 78–79, 81–82, 84–85, 88–91, 93–95, 97–99, 101–104, 113, 116–117, 127, 138
Tanatus 45
Thanet 45
Thanington 30
Theodora (wife of Constantius Chlorus) 183, 185
Theodosius (count) 9, 211, 213–16, 225–29, 236
Theodosius I (emperor) 214, 229, 230, 232, 234–35
Thruxton 207
Thule 103, 187, 229
Tiberius (emperor) 40, 44, 92
Tincomarus (British king) 37–38, 50–51
Tintagel 242
Togidubnus (British king) 10, 59, 66, 71, 100–1, 119
Togodumnus (British king) 42, 44–45, 47, 57
Trajan (emperor) 8, 121–22, 124–25
Trebellius (governor) 89–91, 97–98, 137
Trier 100, 170, 172, 231, 232
Trinovantes (tribe) 34, 46, 58, 66, 70–71, 73, 86, 119
Troyes 244
Trucculensis Portus 116

Ulpius Marcellus (governor) 148, 162
Usk 69, 90
Uther Pendragon (legendary general) 250

Valens (emperor) 213, 228, 230
Valentinian (emperor) 211, 213, 216, 228, 232
Valentinus (exile and rebel) 214–15, 225–27
Valerian (emperor) 169–70, 185
Vandals (tribe) 171, 236
Veneti (tribe) 20–22, 28, 38
Venta Silurum 130
Venutius (British king) 68, 92–95, 101
Verica (British king) 41–42, 46, 52, 59, 66, 101
Verturiones (tribe) 213
Verulamium 33, 40, 69, 78–79, 86, 100, 205, 246–47
Vespasian (emperor) 47, 57, 65, 83, 87, 91–92, 92, 94–96, 101–2, 117–18, 142
Vindolanda Tablets 10, 117–19
Vindolanda 105–7, 118, 124, 173, 225, 241
Virgil (poet) 10, 36, 119, 121, 159, 176–77
Visigoths (tribe) 228, 235
Volusenus (officer) 14, 23, 36
Vortigern (British king) 233, 249

Wall 69
Walmer 6, 23, 26, 29, 34, 193
Walton 173
Wansdyke 243
Water Newton hoard 196, 243, 219–21
Watling Street 65, 213
Welwyn Garden City 50
Wheathamstead 33
Woodchester 172, 195
Worthing 196
Wroxeter 69, 130, 240, 249

York 8, 93, 101, 117, 127, 143, 146, 163, 166–67, 169, 177, 185, 187–90, 197, 216

Zosimus (historian) 201, 207, 215, 230–32, 238